The Lion and the
Journalist

Theodore Roosevelt, Edith Roosevelt, and Joseph Bucklin Bishop aboard the *Balboa* in Cristóbal Harbor, Panama, November 17, 1906.

The Lion and the
Journalist

The Unlikely Friendship of Theodore Roosevelt
and Joseph Bucklin Bishop

Chip Bishop

FOREWORD BY DOUGLAS BRINKLEY

LYONS PRESS
Guilford, Connecticut
An imprint of Globe Pequot Press

For Jane Louise,
beloved and friend

———

To buy books in quantity for corporate use
or incentives, call **(800) 962–0973**
or e-mail **premiums@GlobePequot.com**.

Lyons Press is an imprint of Globe Pequot Press.

Frontispiece courtesy of Anita and Miriam Bishop collection

Text design: Sheryl Kober
Layout artist: Melissa Evarts
Project Editor: Ellen Urban

Library of Congress Cataloging-in-Publication Data is available on file.

ISBN 978-0-7627-7754-9

Printed in the United States of America

10 9 8 7 6 5 4 3 2 1

Contents

Part III: Boldness and Courage

Part IV: Aftermath

Foreword

EVERYTHING THEODORE ROOSEVELT DID THROUGHOUT HIS LIFE WAS DUTY-bound, including the wise self-selection of Joseph Bucklin Bishop as his official biographer. While Bishop wrote numerous books and scores of magazine articles unrelated to our twenty-sixth president, he is best remembered in history for editing *Theodore Roosevelt's Letters to His Children*. A newspaper editor from 1870 to 1905, Bishop was always defending Roosevelt against bad operators in the private sector and government. He was a combination press agent, defense counselor, and let-your-guard-down loyalist. At Roosevelt's request, Bishop left the newspaper world in 1905 to become executive secretary of the Isthmian Canal Commission in Washington, D.C., and Panama. The important post came about because of Bishop's unflinching editorial support of the 1903 Panamanian Revolution, followed by the construction of the Panama Canal, linking the Atlantic to the Pacific. His book, *The Panama Gateway*, remains mandatory reading for anybody even vaguely interested in Latin American history.

It wasn't just political compatibility that led Roosevelt to choose Bishop as his Boswell, though. As is clearly evident from the hundreds of letters T. R. sent to Bishop between 1897 and 1918, their friendship, that mysterious cement of the soul, came naturally to the two Atlantic seaboard intellectuals. No matter what the societal circumstances, Roosevelt and Bishop pulled for each other's daily action. They had a symbiotic friendship, one that developed at the end of the nineteenth century in New York. Roosevelt was New York City police commissioner when they first met, and Bishop was an editor of the New York *Evening Post*. Both reformers fearlessly waged war on Tammany Hall.

Every good statesman needs a top-tier journalist he can trust, and Bishop played that role with Roosevelt. There were times when T. R. didn't correspond with Bishop—the hard-charging weeks in Spanish-ruled Cuba, his yearlong naturalist collection trip for the Smithsonian Institute in British East Africa, his near-death encounter traversing Brazil's Rio da Dúvida. But for the most part, Roosevelt used Bishop as his sounding board on issues ranging from the 1902 Anthracite Coal Strike to the political strategy for the 1908 presidential election to the launching of the Bull Moose Party in 1912.

But it was in the drama surrounding the Panama Canal intrigue that made Bishop one of the indispensable figures in Roosevelt's White House. Dispatched to Panama, traveling around the countryside in the tropical heat of the teeming jungle, Bishop took prodigious notes for Roosevelt's perusal back in Washington, D.C. In a very real sense, Bishop served as Roosevelt's probing eyes and ears in Panama for seven full years, well after T. R. had left the presidency. Because the Panama Canal was Roosevelt's pet project, he regarded Bishop's memos as crucial dispatches, always anxiously awaiting their arrival by mail.

Loyalty, it's been said, is the most treasured quality any U.S. president can have; it's always in short supply. As Chip Bishop makes clear in *The Lion and the Journalist*—a pioneering, smartly rendered biography—the friendship between the president and the reporter was reciprocal in nature. Each man was a confidant of the other. Bishop served as a kind of media watchdog for T. R. throughout his public career, making sure he didn't get blindsided by some print assassin. Bishop, for his part, truly enjoyed the privileges accorded to a trusted counselor. Together they helped stabilize the progressive movement with their sober-minded critiques of modern America. "Your editorials," Roosevelt once wrote Bishop, "are a real comfort to me."

Not that the friendship was on an entirely equal footing. Sometimes Roosevelt's impetuousness ventured into the dictatorial. "Take the 4:25 train," T. R. ordered Bishop in one missive. But Roosevelt so entirely valued Bishop's companionship that he would frequently invite him and his wife, Harriet, to dinner at the White House and at his Oyster Bay home, Sagamore Hill. Although Roosevelt was an optimist, he genuinely enjoyed listening to Bishop's skinny about various scoundrels of the day. Of Bishop's counsel, Roosevelt wrote, "I am always wishing I could see you."

Late in life, plagued by a series of health maladies, Roosevelt entrusted Bishop with the publication of private letters to his six children. The book—*Theodore Roosevelt's Letters to His Children*, published in 1919, just after Roosevelt's death, and a runaway hit—humanized the president much more than T. R.'s *An Autobiography*. It was only Bishop—no one else—to whom T. R. would have entrusted the editing of this deeply intimate and emotional correspondence with his beloved brood.

Legacy meant a great deal to Roosevelt, as it does to all US. presidents. Bishop was the man T. R. thought most suited to write his authorized biography. Bishop proved to be an inspired choice. Drawing on thousands of candid and illuminating letters that Roosevelt wrote to friends and associates, many marked PERSONAL, others clearly written to shed new light on his presidential thinking and decision-making in a turbulent era of progressivism and global expansionism, Bishop produced a two-volume masterwork. *Theodore Roosevelt and His Time Shown in His Own Letters,* published in 1920, has become essential biographical reading.

Now Chip Bishop—the great-grandnephew of Joseph Bucklin Bishop— has seized the historical reins himself. Using the T. R.–Bishop correspondence and an array of wonderful anecdotal events as his literary foundation, our Bishop has written a groundbreaking study of the great symbiotic friendship between the colonel and his editor. It will be impossible to write on T. R. again without first reading this marvelous book.

—Douglas Brinkley

Introduction

Wheels on the Earth

"THE OLD LION IS DEAD," ARCHIE ROOSEVELT WIRED HIS SIBLINGS FROM Sagamore Hill on January 6, 1919.[1] His father, the redoubtable Rough Rider and twenty-sixth president of the United States, had died gently in the middle of the night. In his bedroom at the family estate on a great hill in Oyster Bay, New York, Theodore Roosevelt went quietly to the ages, an act uncharacteristic of someone who otherwise had yielded to few men or forces in his sixty tumultuous years.

"Death had to take Roosevelt sleeping," observed Vice President Marshall, "for if he had been awake, there would have been a fight."[2]

Colonel Roosevelt had spent a typical Sunday, resting and writing letters. He retired at 11 p.m. "Please put out that light, James," he had asked the servant who occupied an adjoining room.[3] At 4:00 a.m., James Amos, a holdover from the White House years, heard shallow breathing next door. Looking in, he was alarmed and summoned a nurse. Moments later, Roosevelt died without waking.[4]

He had been hospitalized in recent weeks for a pulmonary embolism and other illnesses, but had rebounded.[5] Doctors said that a blood clot had traveled from a vein elsewhere in his body—perhaps aggravated by inflammatory rheumatism—to his lungs.

In Oyster Bay, news of the death of its most celebrated resident staggered the populace. Townspeople lowered the flag and hung black crepe on the firehouse. Grief darkened that cold Sunday. "I have lost the best friend I ever had," said Roosevelt's coachman, Charles Lee, "and the best friend any man ever had."[6]

In the memory of millions, there had rarely been anyone quite like T. R. Born in 1858 to a wealthy New York City family, he watched Abraham Lincoln's funeral procession pass beneath an upstairs window of his grandfather's house on Union Square. Roosevelt lived a privileged child's life, developing an intense interest in natural science and all manner of creatures, living and dead. After graduating from Harvard in 1880, he wed Alice Hathaway Lee, his college sweetheart, on his twenty-second birthday. Their daughter, Alice Lee, was born four years later.

Roosevelt chose a career of progressive Republican public service, a path charted by the father whom he hero-worshipped. Elected to the New York State Assembly in 1881 at just twenty-three, T. R. was the youngest ever to serve in that body. To the surprise of few who knew his ambitious old-line commerce-class family, he rose rapidly to become minority leader, and authored more bills than any other New York legislator at the time. "I worked on a very simple philosophy of government," he remembered. "It was that personal character and initiative are the prime requisites in political and social life."[7]

To cope with his wife's death from kidney disease, just two days after the birth of their child, the death of his mother on the same day, and to satisfy his yearning for wide spaces, Roosevelt headed west to build cattle ranches on the banks of the Little Missouri River in Dakota Territory, which was "still the Wild West in those days."[8] He hunted buffalo and brought to his love of nature an advocacy for conservation, later one of the greatest of his legacies.

He finished third in the 1886 New York City mayoral race—"But anyway, I had a bully time"[9]—and turned enthusiastically to writing. He began a naval history of the War of 1812, historical biographies of Thomas Hart Benton and Gouverneur Morris, as well as other well-received volumes on ranch life and the wilderness.

He married childhood friend Edith Kermit Carow in 1886. They moved to Sagamore Hill, a turreted home he had built on Oyster Bay, where they raised six children.

In 1889, T. R. won appointment as civil service commissioner in Washington, D.C., battling office-mongering, rife in government at the time. As he explained, "The opposition to reform is generally led by skilled parliamentarians, and they fight with the vindictiveness natural to men who see a chance of striking at the institution which has baffled their greed."[10]

Eager to escape Washington and return home, though, Roosevelt took an appointment in 1895 as police commissioner of New York City. The first day on the job, he was elected president of the board. Describing his task as "inconceivably arduous, disheartening and irritating,"[11] Roosevelt made bold reforms and midnight street rambles in pursuit of duty-shirking policemen that attracted national attention.

With the election of Republican William McKinley to the presidency in 1896, T. R. captured the coveted post of assistant secretary of the navy. He set about to prepare the service for an expansionist role and, as he saw it, the inevitability of war with Spain over Cuba and the Philippines. "Better a thousand times to err on the side of over-readiness to fight than to err on the side of tame submission to injury or cold-blooded indifference to the misery of the oppressed."[12]

But within a year, Roosevelt answered the call to duty, resigning the navy post to take a New York National Guard commission as lieutenant colonel of the 1st U.S. Volunteer Cavalry Regiment, known as the Rough Riders. Following the destruction of the *Maine* in Havana Harbor, he fought in the Spanish-American War, where he earned legendary status in the battle charge at San Juan Heights. "I would rather have led that charge . . . than served three terms in the U.S. Senate," he later said.[13]

His fame secured, Roosevelt was drafted by the Republicans to run for governor of New York. Elected in 1898 by a slim margin, he challenged entrenched party bosses to accomplish a respectable reform record in just two years. It was in the latter months of his term that national Republican leaders tapped him to run for the vice presidency on McKinley's 1900 reelection ticket. New York political power brokers had arranged Roosevelt's selection, wanting the "meddling" executive out of their way. From a caboose platform, he campaigned vigorously in 567 cities and towns in 24 states while the president, at the top of the ticket, calmly received well-wishers on his front porch in Canton, Ohio. "I feel sorry for McKinley," said one campaigner. "He has a man of destiny behind him."[14]

Destiny indeed intervened. On September 6, 1901, anarchist Leon Czolgosz shot McKinley at the Pan-American Exposition in Buffalo. Roosevelt received the startling news while on vacation with Edith and their children in the Adirondacks. McKinley died of his wounds six days later, and Roosevelt, at forty-two, became president of the United States—the youngest in history.

Roosevelt's presidency shook the world and earned him veneration, along with Washington, Jefferson, and Lincoln, on Mount Rushmore in the Black Hills of South Dakota. His enduring legacy includes successful antitrust battles with railroads, a network of national parks, the National Forest System, construction of the Panama Canal, establishment of the Commerce and Labor Departments, and the Nobel Peace Prize for negotiating an end to the Russo-Japanese War. His premature death in 1919 stunned the world and brought a flood of condolences to Sagamore Hill. So many messages overwhelmed the telegraph office that two additional operators had to be called in. In the end the workload surpassed even their added capacity to manage.

Edith Roosevelt held up better than expected. Her children, grown and scattered, commenced their sad journeys home. Eleanor, the wife of Theodore Jr., the oldest son, arrived first to comfort Edith and make plans for all that followed. The few early callers from outside the family included the late president's private secretary, party leaders, and a diminutive, seventy-two-year-old former New York newspaperman, who had enjoyed a quarter-century of friendship with T. R. His presence at Sagamore Hill in the hours immediately following Roosevelt's death and his closeness to the family were well noted by others; he was, after all, the president's authorized biographer, chosen by the man himself.

Joseph Bucklin Bishop had last seen T. R. on the day before Christmas, a couple of weeks earlier. The former president, then hospitalized, was going over the typewritten manuscript of *Theodore Roosevelt's Letters to his Children*, a book that Bishop had edited for publication. As Roosevelt finished reading the letters, Bishop recalled him saying, "I would rather have that book published than anything that has ever been written about me."[15]

That comment was not self-serving, Bishop understood. He later observed that Roosevelt "had hitched his wagon to a star but was careful to have the rope long enough to keep its wheels on the earth. . . . He was the eager, unresting, unswerving champion of things that ought to be, with a devotion that was a religion, a sincerity that neither yielded nor faulted, a love for the welfare of his fellow men, and a human sympathy with them which was boundless and inexhaustible."[16]

Bishop had been a steady object of Roosevelt's attention from his days as a writer and editor for the *New York Tribune*, *Evening Post*, and *Globe and Commercial Advertiser* in the 1870s, '80s, and '90s, through his tenure in the new century as the president's designated secretary of the Isthmian Canal Commission in Panama.

Beyond the twelve years' difference in their ages, the contrast between the two men could not have been starker. Roosevelt commanded any room, self-certain and gregarious, a nineteenth-century action figure in spectacles, ruggedly built from a lifetime of strenuous physical challenge. Bishop, by contrast, was prim by nature, "undersized and grouchy-looking with a little pointed gray beard and a shiny bald head."[17]

Roosevelt was well-bred, moneyed, Harvard-educated, and from uptown New York. Bishop was a Massachusetts farmer's son, old-line Yankee, and an inveterate schmoozer with typing calluses on his fingertips. John Hay, once an assistant private secretary to Lincoln and an editorial colleague of Bishop's at the *Tribune*, described his personality as rooted in "a Puritan conscience."[18] Yet despite their differences, Bishop maintained an idealized view of Roosevelt: "Nature has made many millions of men, but she has made only one Theodore Roosevelt."[19]

Bishop understood Roosevelt's mind and mood and expressed the president's thoughts with uncanny precision. "I am grateful for the editorial you have just written and for many editorials in the past," Roosevelt wrote Bishop in 1902. "You make exactly the points I should like to have made. You said exactly the things I should like to have said. You help me more than I can express in driving home the points I am trying to make, the lessons I am trying to teach."[20]

Roosevelt rewarded Bishop with enduring friendship, confidence, and insider access to the family. T. R. once wrote to his great friend, "I am always wishing I could see you."[21]

PART I

BEGINNINGS

One

Vegetables and Cobblestones

THE WAMPANOAG TRIBE—LITERALLY THE PEOPLE OF THE MORNING LIGHT because of their easterly location—inhabited eastern Massachusetts when English settlers arrived, hunting the woodlands and fishing rivers and the long and narrow Narragansett Bay. Seekonk—an Indian name derived from *sucki* and hon*ck*, meaning black goose—was one of their settlements.

Chief Massasoit signed a treaty with the newcomers, believing an alliance would protect his people from the neighboring Narragansetts. For £35, the Wampanoags deeded hunting and fishing rights in what is now Seekonk and surrounding communities to Myles Standish and other Puritan settlers. After the violence of King Philip's War, in which hostile settlers beheaded Chief Metacomet, Massasoit's son, colonists in the area prospered as a community of farmers.

But land-hungry Massachusetts and Rhode Island officials laid competing claims to parts of what was called Rehoboth, spawning incessant boundary disputes. In 1812, the Town of Seekonk incorporated from the western half of Rehoboth. In 1862, by U.S. Supreme Court decision, Rhode Island annexed western Seekonk, which became the town of East Providence. The new community assumed half of Seekonk's territory, and two-thirds of its people and valuation, leaving Seekonk to a rural destiny.

All of which confuses the question of where Joseph Bucklin Bishop was born. He arrived September 5, 1847, then in Seekonk, now the village of Rumford in East Providence. His mother, Elzada, was thirty-nine; James Madison Bishop, his father, was thirty-five. Already, they were the parents of three daughters and two sons, and a fourth daughter followed in 1849. The middle name, Bucklin—which he used professionally throughout his life—likely came from the legendary revolutionary figure Joseph Bucklin, who led a 1772 attack on the English ship *Gaspee* in Narragansett Bay.

James Madison Bishop had wed Elzada Balcom of Seekonk in the Newman Church in 1835. The church had been settled in 1643 at the vortex of Rehoboth's original sixty-four-acre common, called the Ring of the Green. It was on the edge of the Ring that James Madison Bishop established his farm in 1837 on what is now Pleasant Street in Rumford. Their first child, Eliza, was delivered a year earlier. Then, in consistent two-year intervals, Julia Almira, Thomas Benton, and Ann Francis joined the family, followed in time by James Madison II, Joseph Bucklin, and lastly, Amey Whipple.

By all accounts, James Madison Bishop was a successful farmer. Records show that in the fall of 1853, he received 50 cents for the best lot of cabbages in a show at a cattle fair in nearby Taunton.[22] Between 1844 and 1853, James served as the town's pound keeper and, for a year, as its sealer of weights and measures.[23] As keeper of the public pound—a large square enclosure protected with a high stone wall—he received wayward livestock and other animals committed to his custody. His farm, a fruitful forty acres of rye, wheat, and vegetables, also contained cows, hogs, and fowl alongside rugged workhorses and faithful carriage mares. A sell-off inventory, completed shortly after James's death in 1864, recorded five tons of hay in the upper barn and thirty bushels of corn on ears, along with large stores of onions, carrots, apples, turnips, and beets. The catalog counted an amazing 1,300 cabbages estimated to be worth $70. The farmer's bounty also included cider, porks, hams, and "1½ barrels of catsup."[24]

An estate inventory listed the expected cane chairs, a farm table, a few kerosene lamps, a good feather bed,[25] and a white stone tea set, perhaps Elzada's. Although the family's belongings included a bookcase, there was no mention of books that it may once have held. Ultimately, the Bishop estate was valued at $3,022.29 (worth $41,640 in 2010), including payments due from borrowers and other receivables. Everything was sold to pay outstanding debts.

By the 1860s, the family already stretched back seven generations in America. There was Phanuel Bishop, innkeeper, Massachusetts senator, and U.S. congressman, whose homestead stood on the other side of Rehoboth's Ring of the Green. And of course there was the infamous Bridget Bishop, whose red bodice and bawdy games of "shove board" had ignited a firestorm of Puritan recrimination in 1690s Salem and led to her execution for witchcraft.

Some 200 miles southwest of where young Joseph Bucklin Bishop was growing up, another mid-century child inhabited a different world in gilded Manhattan. Just three years old, Theodore Roosevelt—affectionately called

"Teedie"—enjoyed the comfort and security of urban privilege. As historian Edmund Morris writes,

> *Through the front window of [his father's] house, he could look down on carriages and cobblestones and hear, coming from Broadway and Fifth Avenue, the rumble and throb of a great city. Through the rear windows, he gazed out into another world, an enormous block-wide garden full of trees and flowers and roamed by ornamental peacocks. Were it not for the weight of asthma, Teedie might consider himself a child of Paradise.*[26]

The affliction frightened Teedie and his family throughout the boy's youth. The asthma disabled him continually, spelling panicked flights to doctors at odd hours of the night and experiments with bizarre remedies. It wasn't unusual, for example, to see Teedie smoking a cigar at his father's urging in the hope that it would restore normal breathing. Worse still, his bouts often were accompanied by periods of melancholy and, while traveling, homesickness. In part, it was the asthma that occasioned Teedie's home tutoring, but it was T. R.'s determination to conquer this chronic malady that drove him to intense physical exertion and extreme outdoor challenges later in life.

The family's wealth had compounded steadily through generations of merchants and most recently from Roosevelt and Son, his grandfather's import firm. Cornelius Van Schaack Roosevelt was making a fortune supplying plate glass to builders across the continent. He was said to be worth a half million dollars, equivalent to $5 million or more today.

Teedie's father, Theodore Roosevelt Sr., was a partner in the import business, managing it efficiently with everyday attentiveness. But beyond his business responsibilities and a constant worry about Teedie's health, the elder Roosevelt nurtured a sweeping charitable passion, a mission to share his wealth and know-how with causes that served the city's underclass. One notable undertaking brought consolation to many of the city's homeless youth in the form of the Newsboys' Lodging House on West 18th Street, where "several hundred stray boys were given a clean bed in a warm room for five cents, a fraction of that charged by the lowest kind of commercial flophouse."[27]

It wasn't the first time that Roosevelt Sr. had gone out of his way to help those less fortunate. The Civil War had presented him with a gut-wrenching quandary. Although his sympathies lay with the North, his wife's family, the

Bullochs—plantation owners and slave holders—supported the rebel cause with fervor. Not yet thirty and in first-rate physical condition, Roosevelt Sr. was a prime candidate for enlistment, but he opted out of service, recruiting, as was permitted, a substitute. In time, perhaps regretting his decision, he found a way to aid soldiers of both sides. At the time, opportunist scoundrels plied the camps, offering liquor and other temptations to weary troops at overblown prices. Roosevelt Sr. lobbied Congress to create, and later served on, a volunteer allotment commission, visiting battlefield encampments to encourage men in uniform to reserve a portion of their pay for their families back home.

Teedie's mother, Martha—known as Mittie—suggested in late 1868 that the family would benefit greatly from a grand tour of Europe. Parents, four children, and attendants sailed in May of the following year for Liverpool and the Continent, following a wide-ranging and lavish itinerary. The precocious Teedie, who turned eleven that October, often complained of being separated from the comforts of home and his friends, especially Edith Carow, with whom he was developing a special friendship. But he found an expressive outlet by making daily travelogue entries in his modest journal.

The Tower of London; a journey up the Rhine; a climb up a Swiss mountainside; castles everywhere; a gondola in Venice; the Viennese opera; evenings in Paris and Berlin; Christmas with the pope at the Vatican—to Teedie they were all wondrous, if not always fully comprehensible, experiences that enthralled him before the family circled back to the Manhattan skyline and home.

Two

Passages

THE THIRD-OLDEST NEW ENGLAND COLLEGE, BROWN UNIVERSITY WAS "THE Baptist answer to Congregationalist Yale and Harvard."[28] From its beginnings in Warren, Rhode Island, in 1764, the school welcomed students of all religions, steadfastly honoring the principles of Roger Williams, the Puritan founder of the state. Having relocated to Providence, Brown was still an all-male school in the 1860s. (Women weren't admitted until 1891.) Fewer than two hundred students attended then, many of them the scions of well-to-do southern New England families. Joseph and his classmates did battle with Homer, quadratic equations, and plane geometry and relaxed with a drama guild, a glee club, and competitive boating, among other pastimes.

Dormitory conditions were hardly homelike, though. Brown historian Walter Cochran Bronson describes "old and worn out floors, ruinous to decent carpets, tumble down ceilings and broken plaster, and ill-fitted window sashes through which the winter wind whistles hoarsely."[29] Students also complained about "the slovenly services of the male chambermaids."

On campus, Joseph Bucklin Bishop was a "genial, companionable fellow," according to an admiring *Providence Journal* profile published during the early years of his service to Theodore Roosevelt. Bishop's brothers at Delta Kappa Epsilon allowed that he was "always liked but not especially popular."[30] At DKE, there were, of course, pins and secret handshakes, and over time its membership included Whitelaw Reid, Bishop's future editor at the *New York Tribune*, and Theodore Roosevelt. Their motto, "Friends from the Heart Forever," bespoke much of the future Roosevelt-Bishop relationship.

Young Bishop was gentlemanly in habit and appearance, it was remembered, but he came up somewhat short in competitive scholarship. The *Journal* reported that his academic achievements were "above the average but not high." He was a "plodding, thinking and self-developing student rather than a mature-minded one—in the sense that some of his classmates were ripe for this world.[31] Nonetheless, Bishop later received the gold key of Phi Beta Kappa, the renowned honor society founded in Virginia during the Revolutionary War.

Dexter Training Ground in Providence hosted an immense crowd of Brown University students on a fine-looking June day in 1863, the end of Bishop's sophomore year. The celebrated Lowell, Massachusetts, baseball club had trekked down to engage the Brown sophomore nine in what would be remembered as a contest for the ages. Bishop—whose abilities lay with the pen, not the bat and ball of this newfangled game—may have stood with his many schoolmates in a ring around the yard alongside Dan Beckwith, his closest friend. When the match concluded, the Brown men stomped and hooted for their team, which had defeated the superior Lowell club with a surprise 22-to-19 win. It was a day that Brown students long remembered with understandable delight.

Among his "large, rather brilliant and decidedly demonstrative, if not famous"[32] class of fifty-three men were notables who left their mark on Rhode Island history. They included a future bishop and Brown president, a number of professors, and Mortimer Hartwell, who later became a respected wholesale merchant in Providence and a member of its Common Council. It probably was Mortimer who introduced Bishop to a cousin, Harriet Hartwell of Providence, the future Mrs. Joseph Bucklin Bishop. Evidence is sparse, but Joseph and Harriet likely courted during Bishop's college years, since they wed after Bishop's graduation, once he was secure in his New York newspaper career.

The class of 1870, the largest in school history to date, celebrated its commencement on the last Wednesday of June. Bishop was not present, however, having been excused. He may have been required to work, or more probably had asked to skip the ceremonies. In commenting on Bishop's nonattendance, the *Journal* noted "he did not rank high in his class . . . he was not a brilliant scholar."[33] Though he earned his degree, Bishop's deficiencies in class may have had something to do with the "enforced labors" he faced as an undergraduate. He taught night school for a while, and, the *Journal* noted, because Bishop was "compelled to help himself in a financial way, he secured a place on the staff of the *Providence Morning Herald*."[34]

His tenure there may have been brief, but it was long enough to give a needy undergraduate his start as a paid writer. Little is known about Bishop's accomplishments at the paper, but, if the assignment pattern for rookie journalists held to later form, he was probably tasked with covering college events, stalking the Providence minor crime beat, and penning obituaries. Like many less-than-privileged undergrads of that era, Bishop had to juggle the demands of school with compulsory work and a respectable modicum of social life. It was a balancing act that set the pattern for his later life in New York, Washington, and Panama.

In the mid-1870s, Harvard was undergoing a scholastic renaissance at the hands of university president Charles Eliot, who was reforming what had been derided as a snooty finishing school into a first-rate institution of research and learning. Unlike Bishop, Roosevelt lived a pampered life at school, his ample family means allowing a "splendidly good" four years. Throughout his time at Harvard, Roosevelt lived in a Winthrop Street apartment that his older sister Anna, known to all as Bamie, had furnished—well apart from the commotion of the Yard. He took his meals at a dining club rather than at the central cafeteria. And the privacy of his lodgings permitted the young naturalist to keep a menagerie of claw-footed and four-legged roommates—specimens all—to advance his knowledge of science and a promising career.

From school, Ted—as he was now known—monitored his father's health, though he was not fully aware of its seriousness. Roosevelt Sr., called "Greatheart" by his worshipping family, had developed bowel cancer, which manifested itself during a torturous U.S. Senate confirmation process following his appointment as collector of customs for the Port of New York by President Rutherford B. Hayes. The senior Roosevelt found himself caught between the president's civil service reform agenda and the old guard's spoils system. It wore on his mind and gnawed at his health. In February 1878, Theodore Roosevelt Sr. died a painful death, shattering his son's bucolic world. The nineteen-year-old student grieved deeply for his father after journeying from Cambridge to New York, reaching his father's deathbed a few hours after the elder's midnight death. "He was everything to me," Roosevelt confessed to his diary.

In time, Ted regained his emotional footing, buttressed by an inheritance of more than $8,000 a year—a goodly stipend then—and improving academic success that placed him high in his class. He was tapped to join the Porcellian Club, Harvard's top social honor. Roosevelt proclaimed himself a "Porc-man," a standing of note not only in the eyes of his classmates but, more crucially, in the view of the fairer sex.

The next year, Ted reluctantly laid down his spectacles to prepare for a boxing match, long remembered. The skinny, twenty-year-old junior could barely make out the features of his opponent. At 5 feet 8 inches and 135 pounds, his asthma diminished, he had qualified in the lightweight boxing class for the final spring bout at the athletic association gym. In the other corner waited C. S. Hanks, known for quickness with his hands and feet, fit enough to endure a long match if necessary. Students crowded the edges of the ring, punching the air with bare fists and shouting their allegiances.

T. R. biographer Owen Wister recalled the moment: "Time was called on a round, Roosevelt dropped his guard, and Hanks landed a heavy blow on his nose, which spurted blood . . . whereat Roosevelt's arm was instantly flung out to commend silence, while his alert and slender figure stood quiet."[35] He explained to the crowd that Hanks hadn't heard the timekeeper, and, in a show of sportsmanship, Roosevelt shook the winner's hand. In conceding the bout, young T. R. won the respect and admiration not only of spectators but most of the other students on campus. Word got around that he was someone special—a fair and tough competitor.

From time to time at school, Roosevelt saw his best female friend, Edith Carow, with whom he had shared a unique attachment since childhood. Teedie and Edie had grown up in Manhattan, just blocks apart. Shy and introspective, she was his sister Corinne's best friend and often visited the Roosevelt mansion. Yet, since the day the seven-year-old neighbor had entered his life, Roosevelt had been drawn to her in ways that would not reveal themselves until years later. During the Harvard days, they cherished the times they could socialize together.

The bond of friendship with Edith notwithstanding, it was seventeen-year-old Alice Lee who turned Roosevelt's head. Her family lived in Chestnut Hill, a brief carriage ride from Cambridge, next door to the family of his best college pal, Richard Saltonstall. She was, in Theodore's eyes, intelligent, utterly enchanting, a cultured beauty beyond words. On the day they met—when he was a Thanksgiving Day houseguest of the Saltonstalls—he prophesied to his diary that one day they would marry. Theodore and Alice courted on and off for eighteen months until the spring of 1879, when he proposed. She rejected him. Crushed, he fled to the Maine woods to air his mind and contemplate his options. Escape was a pattern he followed for a lifetime when emotional pain overcame him.

In 1880, after Roosevelt had promised to forsake the creatures that occupied his naturalist's curiosity and to consider a future in politics, Alice extended her hand. They were wed in October of that year near Chestnut Hill on his twenty-second birthday. By then Roosevelt had graduated Harvard, Phi Beta

Kappa and 21st in a class of 177, and a series of key events had stirred his interest in public affairs: a stint as a Harvard newspaper editor, his ongoing work on a naval history of the War of 1812, and a senior thesis on equal rights for women.

He decided to pursue the law as a prelude to public service. He enrolled at Columbia, but inside of two years he dropped out, dispirited and disenchanted. According to historian Aida Donald, "only later did he explain, more than once in letters and writings, that he found the law lacking in social justice and only a cover to protect wealth and business."[36] Nonetheless, Roosevelt wondered if the decision to end his legal studies would alter the course of the years that lay ahead.

Three

The Very Heaven of Their Aspirations

By his own description, Joseph Bucklin Bishop was enthusiastic and very impressionable in December 1870 when he joined the city staff of the *New York Tribune*, arguably the nation's leading newspaper at the time, and in a metropolis otherwise infamous for the sensationalist journalism of its competitors. How Bishop leapt from the obscurity of the *Providence Morning Herald* to the *Tribune* is not apparent from the surviving record. However, two of his college classmates—Isaac Ford and Walter Hamm—later joined the *Tribune* staff in prominent editorial positions. There were no doubt helpful connections between Brown faculty and *Tribune* editors that smoothed the way for eager young journalists.

As the former farm boy adapted to the great city, Roosevelt was emerging from childhood uptown on the East Side of Manhattan. Now twelve, Teedie was still struggling against the asthma that had constrained him, "embarrassingly undersized and underweight, [having] a scrawny frame with stick arms and stick legs."[37] Then the elder Roosevelt issued a challenge: elevate your body to the quality of your mind. Never one to question a direct command from Greatheart, Teedie responded at once. He increased his activity out of doors, exercised publicly on the family piazza (the broad front porch of their home), and even trained at a neighborhood gym. A commitment to physical self-improvement transformed the "bookish and bug-keeping boy" into a brawny, self-confident youth.[38]

Although each took up his challenge in New York City, only a streetcar's ride apart, a quarter-century still separated the two men from meeting each other.

Bishop described the *Tribune's* "ill-furnished and ill-kept" city room on the fourth floor of "an old, ramshackle, five-story building" fronting Printing House Square in lower Manhattan. "There was scarcely a desk . . . that had not been

11

for many years, in a state of well-nigh hopeless decrepitude, and scarcely a chair with a full complement of its original legs."[39]

A half partition of wood and glass—the latter never washed and very dirty—separated the reporters' room in the "rookery" from the editors' space. Naturally the stable of young writers regarded the editors' front room as "the very heaven of their aspirations." Notwithstanding the shabby environment, Bishop recognized that the *Tribune* offices "harbored a moral and intellectual spirit that I met nowhere else in my 35 years of journalistic experience."[40]

The son of poor New Hampshire farmers, Horace Greeley had founded the *Tribune* in 1841, and by the early 1870s he was recognized nationally as the greatest editor of his day. Bishop recalled that Greeley had the "rosy face of a child and a cherubic expression of simplicity and gentleness." But the editor was also as "careless and disheveled in dress, as if he had put on his clothes in the dark." Despite having this peculiar-looking man at its helm, "[t]he *Tribune* set a new standard in American journalism by its combination of energy in news gathering with good taste, high moral standards, and intellectual appeal."[41]

On his editorial pages over the decades, Greeley consistently championed reform, the daily needs of the working man, and the politics of the Whig Party, which had flourished mid-century—in the presidencies of William Henry Harrison and Zachary Taylor—in opposition to Democrats and protective tariffs. Greeley also used his paper to promote radical and offbeat causes. His famous charge, "Go west, young man, go west," advanced settlement in the Great Plains and beyond and promoted national expansion. In the Civil War era, Greeley vigorously opposed slavery, the rebellious Confederacy, and what he viewed as Lincoln's go-slow attitude toward the prosecution of the war and the secessionists.

From a large, rolltop desk in his cramped and cluttered second-floor office, Greeley churned out editorials in an inscrutable hand, mindless of all else that swirled around him. To deal with his legendary nearsightedness, Greeley wrote with his nose almost touching the paper. His unconventional look and mannerisms led not surprisingly to endless newsroom chuckles and anecdotes. Greeley considered the word *news* to be plural, for example, and corrected anyone who used it otherwise. He once asked a reporter, "Are there any news?" The writer responded, tongue in cheek, "Not a new."[42]

Bishop was not immune to the consequences of his editor's idiosyncrasies. It was understood that Greeley would threaten to fire any writer who reported an inaccuracy. Bishop remembered committing one such gaffe:

*I wrote that the Republican majority in an election in a county of a west-
ern state had been 12,000, that being the figure given in a newspaper of
the locality. On the afternoon of the day in which the item was published,
the managing editor handed me a three-page note written to him by Mr.
Greeley in which my instant dismissal was ordered, on the ground that a
man who was so hopeless a fool as not to know that there were not 12,000
voters in the whole county was of no use in a newspaper office.*

*It took me an hour or more to decipher the note . . . and, when I dis-
covered its verdict on my capacity, I went to the managing editor in great
alarm asking if I was to go. He smiled at my fright, saying that Mr. Greeley
was impulsive and did not quite mean all that he said, that I need not go
this time but that I should be especially careful about election figures since
Mr. Greeley knew the voting strength of nearly every town, city and county
of the United States, and was intolerant of any inaccuracy in stating election returns.* [43]

Bishop survived the incident, realizing in time that in his passion for
accuracy Greeley had a practice of impulsively firing the same individual at
regular intervals. In spite of his brush with unemployment, Bishop remained
a Greeley admirer. "A more whimsical, impracticable, lovable man never lived,
and American journalism has produced few superiors to him as a clear and forc-
ible editorial writer," he wrote.[44]

After just six months as a reporter and assistant city editor, Bishop was
assigned to a "subordinate position" on the paper's editorial staff, and he
promptly took his place in the hallowed editors' room. "It was there that some
of the best talk that it has ever been my privilege to listen to was to be heard
almost daily,"[45] he recalled. At the center of most conversation was John Milton
Hay, a recent *Tribune* hire who had had the honor of serving as a private secretary to President Lincoln.

Roosevelt first met his future secretary of state around this time when the
president-to-be was twelve, formally introduced to the young Hay by his father
in the parlor of their Manhattan home. But for now, it was Bishop's turn to get
to know the great man and begin what would become "one of the longest, most
stimulating and helpful friendships"[46] of his life.

Whitelaw Reid, the paper's managing editor lured Hay to the paper to
enhance the editorial pages with grace and wit. Hay was an instant hit with
readers and, not the least, with young Bishop. "He welcomed me with cordiality

so genuine and hearty as to win my heart for all time," Bishop said.[47] Greeley, for his part, acknowledged that Hay was indeed the most brilliant man who had ever entered his office. Still, on returning to New York from an out-of-state tour in the late fall of 1870, the editor was surprised to find Hay comfortably settled into the editorial room.

Hay already had lived a life of uncommon experience when he strayed off the diplomatic circuit into journalism. He needed work. As biographer William Roscoe Thayer put it, "When John Hay landed at the New York dock on a September morning in 1870 he was already 32 years old, carrying in his memory a treasure of experiences which few could match but counting little, very little money in his purse or in the bank."[48] Born and raised in the Midwest, and admired as a "shy, dreamy, poetic youth"[49] when he graduated from Brown University in 1858, Hay went into the president's service a decade earlier, at just twenty-two. He had become Lincoln's trusted companion, confidant, and sometime surrogate son. Following the 1865 assassination, Hay held important diplomatic postings in Madrid, Paris, and Vienna.

But here in 1871, Bishop had the benefit of getting to know Hay in the close quarters of the *Tribune* newsroom. "He would do nothing but the best," Bishop noted in characterizing Hay's writings on foreign affairs, politics, and literature. "A more conscientious man never lived, but his saving sense of humor forbade that his conscientiousness should ever become a disease." All the while, Bishop conceded, Hay "had a small liking for journalism, great as were his talents for it, and was inflexibly determined to get out of it as soon as possible."[50]

Early one morning at the paper, between one and two o'clock, Hay invited Bishop to go to supper, according to a story that Bishop would recall in his casual memoir, *Notes and Anecdotes of Many Years*. When Bishop declined the invitation because of deadline work, Hay observed, "Bishop. I am sorry for you. You are a son of the Puritans, and a victim of that curious disease called conscientiousness."[51] Indeed, the assiduousness that would drive Bishop's thirty-five-year journalistic career was undoubtedly bred on the Massachusetts farm in the 1860s in the face of demanding chores and paternal expectations.

Hay did, in fact, depart after four years, but that was far from the end of their working lives together. In 1881 Hay returned to the *Tribune* for a temporary stint as editor in Reid's absence and oversaw the Panama Canal treaties for Roosevelt. "It was a liberal education in the delights of the intellectual life . . . to sit in intimate companionship with John and watch the play of that well-stored and brilliant mind,"[52] Bishop said. Notwithstanding their camaraderie at the *Tribune,* Bishop could not, at the time, foresee the pivotal role that Hay would play in his life in the years that lay ahead.

At the time, though, the young Bishop, Hay, and the other editors would have gathered around a rickety conference table, formulating their commentary on the day's events, which included the top local story of the time: the shenanigans of Boss Tweed. New York was choking in the grip of William Tweed, boss of the Tammany Hall political machine. Reform newspapers such as the *Tribune* denounced the kickbacks, phony contracts, and other trouble that routinely corrupted the people's business.

As head of the city's Public Works department, Tweed daily handed out small favors to people in return for votes on behalf of machine politicians. Nothing was out of bounds, not even the sale of land for Central Park or the construction of the Brooklyn Bridge. "For a vote, the machine could offer them food when they were hungry, rent and clothing when they were down and out, legal help when they were in trouble, hot jazz to cheer them up, cold beer to help them forget, and now and then a good job to get them on their feet."[53]

German-born cartoonist Thomas Nast was Boss Tweed's unrelenting journalistic antagonist. In *Harper's Weekly,* he regularly lampooned Tammany Hall with scathing drawings. Reeling under the sharp quill of Nast's pen the Tweed organization offered Nast a half-million-dollar bribe to back off and depart on a long, overseas vacation. Nast declined and intensified the attack. By the early 1870s the Boss was in jail, arrested for financial irregularities associated, ironically, with the Tweed Courthouse. He was later convicted of fraud, and the influence of his infamous machine declined.

Although Bishop felt that Greeley was at the summit of his fame and influence in 1870, evidence indicates otherwise. The editor was growing old, drifting past his prime, and losing his grip on the paper. Reid was now in charge day-to-day while Greeley was writing fewer editorials, preferring to travel about the country on one or another of his eccentric crusades. The ramshackle headquarters continued to deteriorate, and "the aging could be seen, too, in the newspaper itself," according to William Harlan Hale. "The *Tribune* and its staff showed distinct signs of weariness. Uncle Horace had let many sides of the management slip."[54]

Greeley's ultimate distraction was his determination to be elected president of the United States. He had soured on radical Republican Ulysses S. Grant, whose election he had supported editorially in 1868. Disheartened by continuing reports of administrative corruption and upset that the goals of Reconstruction had not been achieved, Greeley was egged on by liberal Republican reformers to challenge Grant within the Republican Party. Meeting in Cincinnati in 1872, a splinter group nominated Greeley for president on a platform of equal rights for blacks, amnesty for the South, and civil service reform. The nominee boldly asked for support from the same Democratic Party he had often criticized. Astonishingly, he received it.

"How anyone who had been associated with Mr. Greeley, or was familiar with his personality, could think of him as fit to be president of the United States, is incomprehensible," Bishop later wrote. "His nomination was simply the incredible first step in a pitiful tragedy." Yet Bishop showed compassion for his editor. "If he had not been the most simple-minded of men, he would have realized it himself. But not only did he not realize it, he believed in his innermost soul that he was the best man in the country for the nomination at the time."[55]

Greeley enthusiastically stumped the country in search of votes, often clad in black swallow-tail coat and trousers, a black velveteen waistcoat, and a white muslin string necktie. While Bishop judged his campaign "artificial" and "hopeless," he gave Greeley credit for a series of speeches notable for their intellectual force and eloquence. Grant's followers, however, showed the Democratic candidate little mercy, ridiculing Greeley as a fool and an extremist. With withering drawings in *Harper's Weekly*, Nash ridiculed him and administered the political coup de grâce that sealed Greeley's fate.

A few days before Election Day, Greeley came off the stump in New York to be with his ailing wife. On October 30, at four in the morning, Mary Cheney Greeley died. In a letter to his *Tribune* business manager a few days later Greeley confessed, "I am not dead but I wish I were. My house is desolate, my future dark, my heart a stone."[56] In the end, he won electoral majorities in only six states and just 43 percent of the vote against the victorious Grant.

Burdened by the loss of his wife and the humiliation of presidential defeat, the "greatest editor of his day" rapidly fell into despondency and delirium, checking himself into Dr. George Choate's private sanitarium in Westchester County. There, on November 29, 1872, Horace Greeley died, well before the electoral votes were cast. By the time of the official count, he had lost even the sentimental support of his backers, and he received none of the few votes he had earned.

Joseph Bucklin Bishop, following his graduation from
Brown University and about the time of his marriage to
Harriet Hartwell (ca. 1872). *Author collection*

Bishop observed that Greeley went to his grave with the sad belief that
many of his old friends had come to hate him. "This could not have been true,"
Bishop wrote. "For no man, friend or foe, could hate that simple, honest soul."[57]

A few weeks later, as the steam train shuddered along the Connecticut shoreline toward Providence, Bishop stared out at the passing chop of Long Island
Sound. The grandiose Greeley funeral—staged by his daughters despite their
father's wishes for something simpler—no doubt played in his mind, but his
thoughts soon turned to Harriet Hartwell, the young woman from Providence
whom he had known at Brown and was to wed that Saturday.

They had probably planned the wedding by exchange of letters since
Bishop was stuck in New York, preoccupied with the fallout of the implausible
Greeley campaign and the deaths of the editor and his wife. Harriet and the

Harriet Hartwell Bishop, about the time of her marriage to Joseph
Bucklin Bishop (ca. 1872). *Author collection*

Hartwell family had arranged for a ceremony in the Newman Congregational
Church, a historic, white-steepled edifice in the Rumford neighborhood of East
Providence, a short distance from the farm where Bishop grew up. Bishop knew
the old church well; he had often attended services there as a boy.

On December 14, 1872, the usually unadorned church interior would have
blushed with Christmas ornamentation, handmade grapevine wreaths, and rows
of shimmering beeswax candles. Friends and neighbors ringed the old church
in silent salute as the simple ceremony took place. Reverend James Barney performed the marriage rites for Bishop and Hartwell just as the ceremony had
been performed for countless others since the 1640s, when Reverend Samuel
Newman built the original church in the Seekonk wilderness.

In all probability it was her uncle John Bryant Hartwell who offered Harriet's hand to Bishop. Her parents, Samuel and Lucy Hartwell, worked the land in scattered tiny villages near the Connecticut River in New Hampshire, raising five children, Harriet being the fourth. But Lucy had died in the spring of 1859, and Samuel followed a year and a half later.[58] Harriet and her younger brother, Frederick, were eleven and ten respectively, and, within a year, they went to Providence to enter the care of her uncle John and his wife also named Harriet.

Shortly after their wedding, Joseph and Harriet Bishop bid farewell to their families and set out for New York City. Their union in time produced three children and endured for nearly half a century in New York City, Washington, D.C., and Panama. As the farmer's daughter anxiously set up house in the bustling metropolis, Bishop returned to his editor's desk at the *Tribune*. But it wasn't long before he faced a crisis of confidence that would send him on a cross-country journey in a worried bid to salvage his career.

Four

Awakenings

"I SHALL START TONIGHT FOR THE WEST," BISHOP WROTE TO HAY, "STOPPING to rest as my strength requires on the way." At twenty-nine, after more than six years as a *New York Tribune* editor, he was in a funk. Feeling underappreciated, he was growing disenchanted with newspaper work. "If I were never to write another line for one of them, I should most fully satisfy my present disposition toward them," he admitted. Hay, who had departed the *Tribune* a few years earlier, had urged Bishop to do the same, but the young editor was not yet inclined to follow his friend's advice. "I am not disposed to let this setback break me. Its chief lesson to me will be to give up taking the field of human knowledge with so much 'by-storm' as I have been hitherto attempting."[59]

Bishop planned to rest and sort things out during a cross-country train trip and a visit of a few weeks with his older brother, Thomas Benton Bishop, a prosperous San Francisco land attorney. The first leg of the journey took him from New York City to Buffalo where he rode the Lakeshore Road steam train around the Great Lakes to Chicago. Hay was unable to meet Bishop's request for a rail pass and instead sent him a $20 check (about $400 in 2010) to cover the fare, along with a note of encouragement.

"Few things have ever touched me more deeply," Bishop replied. "The tears in my wife's eyes, when I read her your letter, frightened the baby, but they spoke the feelings of both our hearts."[60] The Bishops' first child, Alice, was just over a year old, but Bishop was leaving them behind for eight self-searching weeks.

Cross-country train travel in the 1870s was tolerable if not comfortable. Bishop's steam-belching locomotive, outfitted with a giant snowplow, hauled a handful of passenger coaches and a coal car in its set. Since the golden spike had joined the Central Pacific and the Union Pacific railroads at Promontory Point, Utah, in the spring of 1869, railroads had largely replaced wagon trains and round-the-Horn sea travel as the preferred way to span the continent. West of

Chicago, it was a six-day rail journey across endless miles of prairie and through treacherous mountain passes. Pullman sleepers and dining cars were rare at that time; travelers usually fed themselves at dining stops every hundred miles or so, usually at stations or nearby restaurants. The process was hardly leisurely: You had to order, wait, eat, pay, and get back to the train before its scheduled departure, or it left without you.

Traveling alone in winter on a long journey, Bishop had abundant opportunity to reflect on his circumstances back in New York and also to engage fellow travelers in discussions of current events, some of which he had written about for the *Tribune*. There was, for example, the prior year's triumphant Centennial Exposition in Philadelphia, the first world's fair held in the U.S. It had marked not only the hundredth anniversary of the Declaration of Independence (signed in Philadelphia), but also the emergence of America as a world industrial power. Most of the ten million visitors to the fair gawked at the largest steam engine ever built, Alexander Graham Bell's newfangled telephone, and three hundred Native American tribesmen—imported from their homelands—who camped out on the expo grounds for all to see.

The disputed presidential election of 1876 was also a hot topic of the day. As the train plied west in February 1877—more than three months after Election Day—the contest remained unresolved. Democratic governor Samuel Tilden of New York had beaten Ohio's Republican governor Rutherford B. Hayes in the popular vote and led in electoral votes, 184 to 165. Yet 19 of 20 untallied electoral votes were in dispute in three southern states, and leaders of both parties in Florida, Louisiana, and South Carolina claimed victory for their candidate amid charges of fraud and threats of violence. In Oregon, the vote of an elector was under challenge as well. To resolve the dispute and pick a president, Congress formed a special electoral commission. In the end—which came just days before the March 4 inauguration date—and after a series of party-line votes, the commission sided narrowly for Hayes, awarding him all 19 electoral votes in question. Together with Hayes's capture of the Oregon elector's vote, these gave the Ohio governor a one-vote edge in the Electoral College and possession of the White House.

Four decades later, in a California newspaper interview, Bishop claimed that he had been politically active in New York in 1876 and had personally conducted Hayes's campaign while working for the *Tribune*. In that same interview, he conceded that Tilden—a Tammany Hall foe—had been cheated out of the presidency.

No surviving evidence can be found to support Bishop's claim of involvement in the Hayes campaign. If he were connected with it, it would have been his first foray into politics on the presidential level. In 1872, he had sat on the sidelines while Horace Greeley made an ill-fated run. But in 1876, New York was a battleground state, drawing volunteer campaign workers from all over the nation. The race was particularly intense among partisans, but the candidates stayed at their respective statehouse desks while surrogates took to the stump.

It was the same 1876 presidential campaign that stirred political awakenings in T. R. Just eighteen and at Harvard for a month, he took a discernible role in a torchlight parade through the streets of Cambridge in support of Hayes, who was, after all, the aspirant of the party long supported by the Roosevelt family.

All at once, from a second-story window, came the jeering voice of a Democratic senior: "Hush up, you blooming freshmen!" Albert Bushnell Hart, who was in the crowd, noted the effect of this insult upon his classmates and upon one of them in particular: "Every student there was profoundly indignant. I noticed one little man, small but firmly knit. He had slammed his torch to the street. His fists quivered like steel springs and swished through the air as if plunging a hole through a mattress. I had never seen a man so angry before. 'It's Roosevelt from New York,' someone said."[61]

Bishop arrived, grimy and weary, at the San Francisco railway station in late February 1877. He planned to stay for a while to repair his mind and receive his brother's counsel on the uncertainty he was feeling about his situation in New York. The dampness of the fog that rolled off San Francisco Bay each morning and the city's temperate climate offered Bishop a revitalizing change from the drafty rough-and-tumble of the long, cross-country journey.

At thirty-six, Thomas was seven years Joseph's senior and already wealthy. He was born to be a lawyer, his contemporaries said. Dark, sunken eyes set off a handsomely long and narrow face, accented with a full mustache and beard and an ample forehead. Thomas had for three years attended Brown University but failed to return for his senior year. Instead, he took up law at Albany Law School before heading west to San Francisco following the Civil War. There he found his fortune in courtrooms consumed by complex and lengthy land battles.

The 1848 discovery of gold at Sutter's Mill in Coloma, California—halfway between Sacramento and Lake Tahoe—lured thousands of prospectors to California inside five years. At the end of the Mexican-American War, Mexico ceded California to the U.S., and land ownership became a major flashpoint of hostility between native Californians and the new settlers.[62] The Treaty of Guadalupe Hidalgo, which governed the land transfer, sought to protect Mexican citizens' property rights, but uncertainties about land titles and differences in Mexican and American mapping systems led to widespread legal entanglements. Thomas saw opportunity both in the turmoil and in the California Land Commission's attempts to resolve the disputes.

He and his law partners at Porter & Holliday swiftly earned notoriety as the most influential land attorneys in San Francisco, often representing California's largest estates. Thomas was "feared and respected for ingenuity in both attack and defense," and was viewed as "an accomplished analyst who could tear an argument or a sophistry into fragments, as deftly and thoroughly as one destroys a bit of paper."[63] His fees were often paid in land, so by the time Joseph arrived Thomas was a land magnate. "He lived in grand style," said his great-grandson and namesake, Thomas Benton Bishop of Charlottesville, Virginia. "In time, the elder Bishop's wife, Josephine, became a collector of esoteric Buddhist palm-leaf manuscripts and a world traveler; their four sons were ribald spenders."[64]

Northern California mesmerized Joseph. "The climate is simply perfect, and the state is crowded with beautiful scenery," he wrote to John Hay. "I was charmed with the state, and, were it not so far from home, I would take up my abode there." Joseph observed an appealing contrast: "San Francisco has all of the generous cordiality one finds in other cities not so far west, but it is more cosmopolitan, more intellectual and more refined."[65]

Perhaps Thomas tried to dissuade Joseph from continuing in journalism, or maybe he offered to connect him with associates in the San Francisco press to enable a fresh start. More likely, the elder brother advised the younger to steer a course through the shoals of bloodthirsty New York newspaper wars and stay clear of office intrigues. In all likelihood Thomas also offered money—at least enough to cover Joseph's return trip and to comfort his family back in Manhattan. Whatever the nature of their conversations, Thomas had a substantial and long-remembered effect on his brother's career at a moment of personal crisis.

"I am back at my desk again, greatly improved in health," Bishop wrote Hay in late April 1877. In California, "There was so much that was new and interesting that I was enabled to forget my work completely, and, of course, that was the first step toward recovery."[66] Hay had instructed Bishop, not yet thirty, in the lesson of limits, to temper his ambition to a disciplined pace, and to profit from events he could not control. A lesson from Lincoln perhaps, it taught a fundamental survival skill to a young man challenged daily by commanding elders in a combative arena.

Bishop indicated that he was going to follow Hay's advice and "learn the lesson of indolence." But bitterness still seethed. On *Tribune* stationery he wrote to Hay: "New York journalism, looked back at across the continent, seemed to me a most ingeniously contrived machine for the slaughter of ambitious young men. It lost all of its glittering charm and stood horribly naked before my eyes."[67] It was strong stuff but not cruel enough to dishearten him fatally.

More than a year after returning from San Francisco, he told Hay, "There is no tendency in this office to proclaim at the house tops whenever a man does a good thing."[68] Joseph prospered fruitfully, if restlessly, at the *Tribune* for six more years.

Five

Sweet and Pleasing

IN THE LATE FALL OF 1880, THEODORE ROOSEVELT, NEWLY WED, WANDERED into a dingy hall atop a boisterous saloon—the home of the New York 21st District Republican Association. Motivated by curiosity and a sense of obligation to his father's reformist legacy, T. R. liked what he saw: dozens of working-class men, mostly German and Irish immigrants, drinking and socializing to the rhythm of city and state politics. It was an oddly uncomfortable fit for the scion of an upper-crust family whose politics were usually limited to an occasional donation and a vote on Election Day.

The Morton Hall clubhouse was a machine nest, though. Precinct boss Jake Hess saw to it that voters in his safe Republican district sent predictably loyal soldiers to Albany to do the bidding of the state's party boss, U.S. Senator Roscoe Conkling. T. R. hadn't fully immersed himself in politics, however. Besides spending time with his bride, he was dabbling uncomfortably in law at Columbia and finishing the first of his thirty-eight books, *The Naval War of 1812*. The hall offered a taste of something refreshing and enticing.

A year later, Roosevelt found himself at the fulcrum of an intraparty squabble over whether the district's assemblyman should be returned to office. Some in the party found T. R. an appealing if peculiar alternative to candidate William Trimble. With the support of Hess's rivals, Roosevelt upset the incumbent at the district convention and won the endorsement of the *New York Tribune*. Citing him as "a gentleman every way worthy of his parentage" and a person "with very definite ideas of honorable and useful politics," the paper counseled that "the City of New York cannot afford to have him defeated."[69]

Just eight days after the convention, Roosevelt easily outpolled his Democratic rival—a recently fired director of an insane asylum—to win the seat in the state legislature. At the tender age of twenty-three, T. R.'s political career had begun.

While Roosevelt was touring abroad and immersing himself in politics at home, Joseph Bucklin Bishop had been helping *Tribune* readers fathom the horror of the nation's second presidential assassination in sixteen years. On July 2, 1881, a deranged office-seeker in Washington, D.C., had shot President James Garfield, in office for less than four months. As was the practice of the day, the president had no bodyguards. The assailant, Charles Guiteau, had demanded a European ambassadorship as payback for a campaign speech he had written for the president. When officials rebuffed his constant pestering, Guiteau bought an ivory-handled pistol and began stalking his victim. On the day Garfield was leaving the D.C. railway station on a trip, Guiteau approached from behind and fired point-blank. A bullet lodged near the president's spine. He lingered all summer as doctors sought to extract the bullet without the benefit of antiseptic treatment.

Bishop recalled "the most moving and impressive scene I have ever beheld" outside the *Tribune* offices in Printing House Square on the night Garfield was shot. "What I saw on that evening was a great sea of faces, deadly pale under the glaring electric light, all lifted toward the high-hung bulletin board, and all stern and tense in a silence that no voice disturbed. Far into the night this silent mass remained."[70]

In the editors' room, Bishop and Hay patiently listened to the wails of Garfield partisans, demanding that the paper assign editorial blame for the attack. Surely it was the fault of a Republican splinter group or the consequence of Democratic machine politics, they insisted. Dismissing their demands, the senior editor kept a cool head in the crisis, Bishop recalled, "much as Lincoln would have done."[71] Hay had demonstrated steadiness under pressure, an essential attribute of a great editor and an example that Bishop absorbed.

In "The Day's Lesson," an unsigned July 6, 1881, editorial that rings with the tones of Hay's gracious prose, the *Tribune* congratulated the people "for their loyalty to law and justice" rather than assigning blame for the shooting. A challenge followed. "Great events educate," the editorial read. "This people ought to go from the bedside of a wounded president with some of his own lofty and heroic spirit. With him to lead them, or only with his precious memory to cherish, people ought to prove themselves hereafter more worthy of their freedom for the trial through which they are passing."

Ten weeks after the shooting, President Garfield died of a massive heart attack, a ruptured aneurysm, and blood poisoning. A *Tribune* editor—perhaps Hay—voiced mournful optimism: "There can be no ironical whispering

Secretary of State Blaine aids President Garfield following the shooting in Washington, D.C. Assassin Charles Guiteau is restrained at left. From a July 1881 English engraving. *Images of American Political History and Wikimedia Commons*

of the trees as they bend lovingly over his grave. Rather will the flowers that are planted there look up with hopeful eyes to tell the secret of immortality."[72] Vice President Chester A. Arthur—who had been collector of customs for the Port of New York prior to Greatheart Roosevelt's nomination—assumed the presidency.

The grand capitol in Albany received the upstart assemblyman on the second day of 1882. Dressed formally in coattails, silk top hat, pince-nez, and English sideburns, T. R. strode into the chamber with more confidence than the youngest member of the assembly had a right to feel. He drew immediate guffaws from some of the old-line Republicans and Democrats. T. R. deferred to no elder or equal, determined to bring his own sense of integrity and decency to the legislature even if he had to accomplish his goals single-handedly. His was a mission to do the people's business honorably and to break up the cabal of businessmen and politicians who he believed were benefiting from graft.

The assembly met for only a few months of its members' one-year terms, and Roosevelt determined to make the most of his time there. He would work hard for his city, he promised, while digesting the unfamiliar methods of New York state politics. From the perspective of this well-mannered

Theodore Roosevelt as a New York State assemblyman (1881–84).

Theodore Roosevelt Collection, Harvard College Library (520.13.-002)

Manhattan Republican from the "silk stocking" district, opposition Democrats and their Tammany Hall chieftains were "vicious, stupid-looking scoundrels."[73] T. R. observed later, "My first days in the legislature were much like those of a boy in a strange school. My fellow legislators and I eyed each other with mutual distrust."[74]

He soon took advantage of an opportunity, though, after observing that T. R. Westbrook, a state supreme court judge, had developed a too-cozy connection with financial mogul Jay Gould, who owned a major chunk of the nation's railroads, the Western Union Telegraph Company, and the influential *New York World*. Gould now wanted control of the Manhattan Elevated Railroad and was making headway, thanks to Westbrook's friendly rulings. "I am willing to go to the very verge of judicial discretion to serve your vast interests," the judge wrote his pals.[75] Roosevelt demanded an investigation.

Assembly graybeards warned T. R. to ease up, but he persisted in detailing what he felt was an outrageous display of cronyism. New York City editorial pages, save the *World*, lauded the freshman legislator's courage. Following several failed attempts to win assembly votes for the Westbrook probe, Roosevelt finally succeeded. His preliminary victory, however, brought out industry lobbyists and bribe-makers. They convinced the legislature to adjourn before taking action. In the end, Westbrook died mysteriously in his hotel room, but not before T. R. had achieved statewide notoriety as an ambitious and principled young man of whom great things could be expected.

Roosevelt was reelected twice, in 1883 and 1884, by impressive margins. At the start of his second term, Republicans nominated the twenty-four-year-old for assembly speaker and de facto party leader. It was a sincere but empty gesture, since Democrats controlled the chamber and elected one of their own. Nonetheless, as David McCullough observes, "It was almost unconceivable prominence for one so young and inexperienced, let alone so unconventional."[76]

Although he fell short, Roosevelt did catch the attention of Grover Cleveland, New York's Democratic governor. Cleveland shared Roosevelt's passion for reform and enlisted the new minority leader in the cause. Cleveland and others wanted to do away with the deep-rooted system that rewarded machine loyalists with government jobs to the exclusion of others. Reform would not happen all at once, advocates agreed, but legislation that proposed to reserve one in ten state jobs for those who passed objective examinations was a meaningful change. Working in tandem, the Democratic governor and the assembly's Republican leader mustered the votes to beat back Tammany and enact reform. It was another impressive achievement for T. R. that raised his profile among the growing legion of voters who had had their fill of the spoils system.

While Roosevelt was in Albany cutting his political teeth, Joseph Bucklin Bishop continued to slog away in the editorial trenches at the *Tribune*. Feeling as professionally insecure as ever, he sent John Hay writing samples to be set aside and shared later with prospective employers, "to protect myself against future emergencies."[77] Bishop's family had grown to include a son, Hartwell, named to honor his mother's family. Harriet, now known as Hattie, was fully occupied at home with the baby and daughter Alice, now four and a half.

To augment his *Tribune* salary and extend his journalistic reach, Bishop signed on as an American correspondent for the London *Daily News*, a preeminent liberal newspaper in Great Britain. Founded by Charles Dickens in 1846, the paper faltered commercially after just seventeen issues. By 1881, with Frank Harrison Hill in charge, the *Daily News* was thriving, "consistently combining clarity of political statement with journalistic excellence in the service of the principles of advanced liberalism."[78]

London in the 1880s was the world's largest city. There was much poverty; disease was rife, and sanitation poor. But there was also wealth and luxury in the city's West End, and a growing sense of social obligation among the middle class. Against that backdrop, Bishop would have filed stories there about the Garfield assassination, the opening of the magnificent Brooklyn Bridge, and the final, tragic surrender of Native Americans to white settlers in the West. Literate Londoners had an insatiable urge to understand the contradictions of America, the land of the Great Experiment, and *Daily News* readers at least were seeing the century-old nation through Bishop's lens. Still, despite his accomplishments, he was restive.

However, he had news that he would have discussed with Hattie in July 1883. Edwin Godkin, famed editor of the *New York Evening Post*, had approached him discreetly a week earlier. Godkin had read Bishop's work at the *Tribune* and wanted him to join the editorial staff of the *Post*. According to Bishop, Godkin "detest[ed] dishonesty and trickery in political and public life." Bishop believed this was an opportunity to escape the suffocation of the *Tribune*. "The *Post* is the home of absolute intellectual freedom, intellectual courage, and intellectual honesty," he wrote. "Without those, there can be no great newspaper."[79]

Bishop had already made up his mind that he needed a change.

Six

Mules in the Pasture

IN THE SWELTERING SUMMER OF 1883, ON THE NINTH-FLOOR EDITORIAL OFFICES of the *Evening Post*, Bishop began a time of his life that he would remember as "the most enjoyable and profitable of my journalistic career of 35 years."[80] From the waning days of Reconstruction through the close of the Industrial Revolution, Bishop thrived under Edwin Godkin's tutelage. "As a purely intellectual man, he ranked above Greeley and others," Bishop said.[81]

The ten-story *Evening Post* building, erected in 1875, sat strategically in lower Manhattan at Fulton and Broadway—between City Hall to the north and the New York Stock Exchange on Broad Street to the south. Energetic copy boys snapped up the day's closing quotes and sprinted back to the newsroom in time for the presses to roll. From that vantage point, reporters and editors could also keep a close eye on the mischief of Tammany Hall, whose bosses still ruled city government.

The *Evening Post* began under Federalists Alexander Hamilton and John Jay, who founded it in 1801 in opposition to President Thomas Jefferson and the emerging Democrat-Republican Party. Under William Cullen Bryant, its legendary editor for fifty years, the broadsheet earned a first-rate reputation as a vigorous opponent of slavery and backer of trade unions. Linking conditions in the South with the plight of striking New York garment tailors in 1836, Bryant observed that the tailors were "condemned because they are determined not to work for the wages offered them. If this is not slavery, we have forgotten its definition."[82]

To advance his progressive political views, German émigré Henry Villard bought control of the *Evening Post* in 1881 and installed Carl Schurz as editor and Godkin as associate editor. Schurz, a liberal zealot, was the first native of Germany to have been elected a U.S. senator and later served Rutherford B. Hayes as secretary of the Interior. Born in Ireland to English parents, Godkin served as a Crimean War correspondent for the London *Daily News*, immigrated to New York, and founded the respected leftist weekly, *The Nation,* at the end of the Civil War. The narrow number of *Nation* subscribers relished Godkin's progressive Republican views, advocacy of civil service reform, and campaigns against corruption in government. By 1881, he had merged *The Nation* with the *Evening Post,* but within two years he realized that the paper's editorial room had "too many mules in the same pasture."[83]

In fact, Schurz and Godkin were at odds over the tenor of the paper's opinions. "Schurz employed argument and calm exposition while Godkin varied his argument with ridicule, cutting irony, and even denunciation."[84] Schurz's opinions were "too narrow in range and too arid," Godkin believed, and drastic measures were needed to raise the editorial bar. By mutual agreement, Godkin had two years to whip the editorial pages into shape. But within days of Schurz's departure on vacation in August 1883, Godkin fired writer Robert Burch and brought in "a brilliant young editorial writer" from the *Tribune,* Joseph Bucklin Bishop.

Bishop thus began what he described as his "liberal education in thinking" and "intimate companionship" with Godkin. It endured throughout their mutual tenure at the paper. At the daily morning conference of editors, "all he asked of you was perfect frankness and sincerity," Bishop recalled, "and the possession of a real thought."[85] Bishop's admiration for his editor deepened over the years. Even taking into account the New Englander's propensity for hyperbole, Bishop thought Godkin "the best and most widely-educated man who has entered journalism in this country."[86]

More than any other trait, Godkin's assurance of his own rightness struck Bishop. "He not only assumed to be always right; in most cases he was right," Bishop said.[87] Nonetheless, Godkin remained open to opposing views when they were well reasoned and skillfully presented. Godkin allowed Bishop wide latitude in writing editorials. Usually he wrote as Godkin saw it, no matter the subject. But over time, Bishop's pen found a voice of its own in politics. His observations and opinions in the *Evening Post* assaulted Tammany in city and state government and promoted civil service reform along with those who advocated good government.

In 1884, Bishop inaugurated the paper's popular "Voter's Guide" that, over several decades, became an election-time staple for readers. He unearthed incriminating letters from James G. Blaine, the 1884 Republican presidential nominee, which played a critical role in Blaine's defeat. And the rival *New York Sun* acknowledged Bishop for championing the novel Australian paper ballot by which voters selected candidates on unbiased state forms—in private—for the first time.

From today's perspective it is hard to imagine that most states did not use secret ballots for presidential voting before 1880. Prior to that year, voters orally announced their choices to election officials at their polling places, or used party-printed forms to make their selections. Boss Tweed's admission that his henchmen routinely had falsified the ballots of New York voters and the Tilden-Hayes electoral fiasco of 1876 led to calls for reform.

Henry George, a candidate for mayor of New York, called attention to an innovation from Australia. There voters used standardized paper ballots, printed at government expense, that listed all candidates for office, regardless of party affiliation. Taking up the call for reform, Bishop wrote about the ballot's popularity with Australian election officials and voters and encouraged New York to follow Australia's example. Massachusetts adopted the Australian ballot in 1888; New York followed two years later, but only after the governor vetoed authorizing legislation three times.

On the upside, the Australian ballot reduced fraud and increased cross-party voting. But it also stood as a barrier to voters who were unable to read, or read well enough to understand it. By 1896, however, 39 of the 45 states had adopted the secret ballot. As Jill Lepore notes, the Australian ballot provided "an elegant solution to problems created by the sudden and dramatic expansion of the electorate in a time of vast economic inequality. . . . It brought voting indoors, contained it in compartments and made it safer, quieter and more orderly, more like an assembly line."[88]

In 1883, the Badlands of western Dakota Territory witnessed a horrendous government-sanctioned massacre. Commercial hunters slew an estimated 10,000 buffalo on the plains in late summer, leaving few of the species for the arriving Theodore Roosevelt to stalk. Not yet twenty-five, and having just completed his second term in the New York Assembly, T. R. had endured five days on a train, alone, in eager anticipation of two weeks' rest and recreation. Unaware of the slaughter that had occurred days before his arrival, Roosevelt planned a routine hunt amid the glorious solitude of endless grasslands and copper-hued buttes.

Beyond escaping the unpleasantness of New York politics, Roosevelt was also thinking of going into the cattle business. In his vision, he would populate a ranch with steer that would fatten on the rich prairie and be slaughtered and shipped east in refrigerated railcars to the Chicago meat-packing plants.

Eventually, he imagined, his product would be served at white-tablecloth-clad tables in restaurants back east.

It wasn't simply a pipe dream. At the time, "ranching was in the aristocratic tradition." It required owning and managing a great deal of land, and, as David McCullough observed, it also demanded "courage, horsemanship, offering deliverance from the tedium and pettiness of trade. It was adventurous. It was romantic."[89]

Arriving in the Little Missouri settlement along the river of the same name, T. R. discovered "a land of vast silent spaces, of lonely rivers and of plains where the wild game stared at the passing horseman."[90] The improbable would-be entrepreneur from New York City connected with young Canadian cowboys Sylvane Ferris and Bill Merrifield and, in a spontaneous partnership, handed them $14,000 for a herd of cattle. Ferris and Merrifield agreed to winter with the herd and plow Roosevelt's investment into an expansion of their Maltese Cross Ranch.

Business accomplished, Roosevelt and a guide embarked on a days-long pony ride into eastern Montana in search of the elusive Lonesome Stranger buffalo. T. R. bagged a bull, and the men celebrated by chopping the animal to pieces, feasting on it, and hauling the prized remains back to ranch. One can envision the satisfied grin on the face of the bespectacled horseman as he rode east. Not only had he enjoyed a bountiful hunt, but he had also staked a claim to life as a Dakota rancher. From that point on, he would always have his own refuge. T. R. had gone to the Badlands and conquered them.

Years later, Roosevelt fondly remembered his early time in the West: "I do not believe there was any life more attractive to a vigorous young fellow than life on a cattle ranch in those days. It was a fine, healthy life too; it taught a man self reliance, hardihood and the value of instant decision . . . I enjoyed the life to the full."[91] But harsh weather was looming, and T. R. knew he had to head home to campaign for reelection. More importantly, his wife, Alice, was pregnant.

On February 5, 1884, in Albany, Roosevelt delivered one of the best speeches of his young political life. It helped to advance his Reform Charter Bill—known as the Roosevelt Bill—through the Assembly, and put New York City aldermen on notice that their sometimes-corrupt powers of appointment were waning. The *Evening Post* hailed T. R.'s remarks as "admirable both in clearness and force."

Returning to Manhattan from the capital on February 8, Roosevelt learned that his mother, Mittie, was ill with what everyone assumed to be a midwinter cold. Mittie and Roosevelt's sisters, Bamie and Corinne, had been caring for Alice, who was just twenty-two and nine months pregnant. She was resigned to T R.'s frequent absences in Albany and tolerant of his recent escape to the West. The following Tuesday, Roosevelt looked in on his mother, kissed Alice good-bye, and took the train back to Albany, fully expecting that the birth was still days away.

The next morning, Roosevelt was happily accepting the congratulations of his Assembly colleagues on the birth of a daughter, announced earlier to him in a telegram from home—but the joy of his child's arrival was painfully short-lived. A few hours later, Roosevelt opened a second telegram that sent him rushing home. The baby was fine, but Alice was suddenly and desperately ill, and his mother, Mittie, had taken a turn for the worse.

One can imagine the agony of Roosevelt's hours alone on the train as it made its way alongside the Hudson that cold, dark February. Only hours earlier T. R. had stood at life's pinnacle—wealthy, powerful, famous, and gifted with a large and loving extended family. As the train plied its way south, his world had turned uncertain and terrifying. Edmund Morris expertly portrayed the scene after T. R.'s late-night arrival at his family's dimly lighted Manhattan home.

Alice, dying of Bright's disease, was already semi-comatose as Roosevelt took her into his arms. She could scarcely recognize him, and for hours he sat holding her in a vain effort to impart some of his own superabundant vitality. Meanwhile, on the floor below, Mittie was expiring with acute typhoid fever. The two women had become very close in recent years; now they were engaged in a grotesque race for death.[92]

In his diary, Roosevelt marked Valentine's Day 1884, the fourth anniversary of his engagement to Alice Lee, with a bold *X* and a crushing entry "The light has gone out of my life." Alice had died at 2 p.m. that day of acute kidney failure. Eleven hours earlier, Mittie had succumbed to typhoid fever. That night, he felt desperately alone, unsure of his future or the fate of two-day-old Alice.

For the rest of his life, Roosevelt would avoid mention of his wife's name, and failed even to note her existence in his 500-page autobiography. There was, however, a single exception to his self-imposed rule. Later in 1884, while working alone in his cabin in the Dakota Territory, he wrote a private memorial to his late wife.

She was beautiful in face and form, and lovelier still in spirit; as a flower she grew, and as a fair young flower she died. Her life had always been in the sunshine; and there never came to her a single great sorrow. Fair, pure and joyous as a maiden; loving, tender and happy as a young wife; when she had just become a mother, when her life seemed to be but just begun, and when the years seemed so bright before her—then by a strange and terrible fate, death came to her.[93]

Bamie raised Alice well outside of her father's vigorous orbit. She told Alice of her mother's charm and beauty and showed her photographs. As an adult, Alice openly criticized her father's inability to bring forth his late wife's memory. "My father never told me anything about this. In fact, he never even mentioned my mother to me, which was absolutely wrong. He never even said her name."[94] We can only imagine the depths of grief that committed him to this silence.

Not long after Alice Lee's death, Roosevelt turned his back on the Manhattan brownstone he and his wife had shared, focusing his attention on Leeholm, a Long Island manor house he was planning at Cove Neck, adjoining Oyster Bay. In years past, T. R.'s family had passed idyllic summers in the area, frolicking in the waters and prowling woodlands for specimens to fill his naturalist's collection. In 1880, shortly after his wedding, Roosevelt had purchased sixty acres of farmland which included a great hill standing sentry over the bay. Architects designed and sited a manly home on that rise, with three floors of gables, dark oak paneling, numerous bedrooms, giant fireplaces, and a veranda on which to rest and take in the view.

But was there now a purpose for such a dwelling, especially one named Leeholm? Bamie had convinced T. R. that little Alice needed a fine home in which to grow up. So he began construction on the freshly named Sagamore Hill later in 1884, in tribute to Mohannis, an Algonquin chief, or sagamore, who presided over the Oyster Bay area generations earlier. T. R. took great satisfaction in knowing that he would have a splendid home there, not only for his daughter, but as a showcase for the trophies he planned to bring back from the Dakotas.

Seven

The Lost Cause

SOME 2,000 MILES SOUTHWEST OF NEW YORK, AND SEVERAL YEARS EARLIER, the steam tender *Taboguilla* pitched toward the mouth of the Río Grande in the Bay of Panama. On board with her father and a collection of distinguished guests, Ferdinande de Lesseps, age seven, gleefully anticipated the start of the groundbreaking ceremony for the Panama Canal. Her father, Count Ferdinand de Lesseps, a seventy-five-year-old career diplomat from Paris, had arrived on the Isthmus of Panama with his family at the end of December to keep a promise to turn the first shovel of earth by January 1, 1880. Little Ferdinande would do the honor, the count insisted.

The bishop of Panama was on board the *Taboguilla,* as were government officials from Colombia, of which Panama was still a province. As guests feasted on an elegant meal in the tropical humidity and shared repeated toasts of chilled French champagne, no one paid much notice to the rapidly ebbing tide. When the boat could get no closer than two miles from the intended ceremonial spot, de Lesseps rallied his dispirited guests and his tearful daughter with an emergency plan. Armed with a special shovel and pickax brought from Paris, de Lesseps dismissed the tide and the position of the boat, saying that the ceremony could just as well be conducted on the ship.

A champagne box, filled with damp soil, was brought forward, and Ferdinande administered the first blow of the pick to its contents, amid enthusiastic applause. It was good theater and not untypical for the white-haired, mustachioed count, known affectionately to his countrymen as *Le Grand Français.* But the uncooperative tide foretold the bleak fate of the French undertaking in Panama.[95]

The vision of a waterway across the narrow, Latin American isthmus—connecting the Atlantic and Pacific oceans—had occupied the dreams of Spanish kings and explorers since the sixteenth century. Columbus himself had sought a hidden strait out of an abiding faith that God had already created a sea path from the Atlantic to the Indies. Later, in the 1690s, the Scots failed miserably—in what is now known as the Darien Scheme—to establish a trading colony on the isthmus that would have united the riches of the Far East with the markets of Western Europe. But starvation, the elements, and disease put an end to their ambitions within two years.

The discovery of gold in California in 1848 again sparked the need for a passageway between the coasts of the expanding nation, one that circumvented the dangerous journey across the savage heartland and the forbidding Rocky Mountains. Early in 1849, New Yorkers William Aspinwall, John Lloyd Stephens, and Henry Chauncey received a concession from Colombia to survey the right-of-way for a railroad linking the coasts and organized the Panama Railway Company. By the fall of 1851 they had spent a million dollars to lay just eight miles of track, their efforts hampered by swamp and jungle. Work crews battled intense heat and humidity and constant deluges of soaking rain. As the company later described,

> *Early in the morning of January 27, 1855, two construction gangs, working toward the other, realized they could see each other. Lanterns with rancid whale oil in their fonts were lighted. The work gangs met and mingled, as an air of anticipation and excitement surrounded the area. The last rail was set in place on pine crossties. The final spike was held in position. Builder George Totten stood in the pouring rain with a nine-pound maul ready. He swung the hammer, and the spike sank into the tie with a thud.*[96]

The next day, a train rumbled south toward the Pacific, and the oceans were linked. The cost was shocking: Not only had $6.6 million been spent on construction, but thousands of workers had succumbed to malaria, yellow fever, and cholera. Financially, it was worth every penny. By 1857, the railroad had transported thousands of passengers and $700 million in prospector gold across Panama.

Bishop later described the region outside the port cities as little more than a wilderness. "Along the line of the railroad there were a few scattered villages composed of rude buildings and shacks whose population was mainly native. . . . [I]t was for the most part an impenetrable jungle."[97]

The inhospitality of the landscape was but one of the grave obstacles to de Lesseps's plan for a unifying waterway. Millions of francs had to be raised privately in France and through public subscription. Managers and engineers had to be convinced to leave their families for the duration of the project at high risk to their own lives. Large construction equipment had to be imported. Thousands of laborers to dig and blast through the Continental Divide had to be recruited from Jamaica and other Caribbean islands, and housed, fed, and cared for medically. Throughout, de Lesseps had to defend his controversial vision of a canal dug at sea level, without locks, against skeptics—mainly experienced engineers, unlike himself—who doubted the feasibility of his plan. Bishop later wondered whether de Lesseps was "an enthusiast so blind as to be irresponsible or was he so bent upon success that he was willing to adopt any means to secure it, or was he the foremost imposter of his time?"[98]

The canal was meant to be a bold second act for de Lesseps, who had planned and directed the construction of the Suez Canal in Egypt in 1869. The Suez project brought de Lesseps worldwide fame, but "his success with the Suez Canal seemed to have turned his head so completely that all obstacles were virtually invisible to him," Bishop observed.[99]

From a distance, Americans were watching events in Panama with a careful eye. The Monroe Doctrine, after all, had warned the rest of the world in 1823 not to interfere with or colonize the Americas, lest their actions be viewed as aggression and cause for intervention. De Lesseps tried to charm America during high-profile visits to New York and Washington, D.C., but not one American stepped forward to help finance the venture. President Hayes received the count cordially at the White House, but upon his departure Hayes sent the Senate a special message in which he asserted that the "policy of this country is a canal under American control."[100]

"*Travail commence*,"[101] de Lesseps declared on February 1, 1881, but it took almost another year for the first French crews to cut into Panamanian soil. To transport the excavated dirt and rock away from the excavation sites de Lesseps realized that he had to acquire a controlling interest in the Panama Railway. The price tag was a staggering $25 million including, of course, cash bonuses to the owners-directors.

Work on the canal began on a large scale in 1883 and steadily expanded through 1884 under the capable director-general Jules Dingler. By early 1885, however, the project was falling into serious financial trouble. Cost overruns had drained the available capital, and malaria and yellow fever had decimated the workforce, along with an elite corps of young engineers, dubbed "the flower of France." In the ocean cities of Aspinwall (later Colón) and Panama City, disease flourished. "They were without even the most elementary provisions for health protection," Bishop recalled. "They had no sewers, no water supply, and no sanitary appliances whatever. Their only scavengers were the huge flocks of buzzards that circled constantly above them."[102]

Yellow fever was especially rampant. The fear in Bishop's words resounds across the years: "The most vigorous among the living today might be among the dead and buried tomorrow, smitten without warning by the swift and mysterious scourge."[103] Unknown to all, the acute viral disease traveled from engineer to supervisor and from rail hand to laborer by the saliva of the omnipresent mosquito. Within a few days of being bitten, fever and headache developed, followed by chills, a slowed heart rate, and then nausea and vomiting. The vomitus was all-telling: dark, and like coffee grounds from the deadly internal bleeding. Finally came delirium, coma, and death. Bishop estimated that two of every four—and possibly three-quarters of those who came from France—fell to yellow fever during the French canal construction period. "Men saw companions fall dead beside them, one after another," he wrote.[104]

Well-meaning doctors and nurses at hospitals built to treat the sick and dying unintentionally promoted the spread of the disease. To keep hordes of ants from infesting hospital beds and their helpless occupants, the caretakers set bed legs in pans of water, unknowingly creating the perfect habitat for breeding mosquitoes.

The fate of Director-General Dingler is a tragic case-in-point of the suffering so many endured there. Before he could move his family into a plush residence built for them on Ancon Hill near Panama City, Dingler's wife, son, and daughter all died of the fever within a few months of each other. Devastated, Dingler returned to France brokenhearted, dying soon after in an insane asylum. U.S. Army surgeon, Colonel William Gorgas, who later won acclaim for discovering the primary role of mosquitoes in transmitting yellow fever, told of a French engineer who said he had come to Panama with a party of seventeen young Frenchmen. Within a month, all but the engineer had died of yellow fever.

In his narrative about the French era in Panama, Bishop also criticized the inhabitants of Colón and Panama City for behavior he found offensive—not unexpected for someone with a "Puritan conscience." The cities, Bishop wrote, had "all the debasing qualities of a mining camp or rude frontier town, with the usual facilities for gambling, drinking, vice and general debauchery, supplemented by tropical laxity in morals and conduct."[105]

Historian and diplomat J. A. Froude summed up the environment and undertaking thus:

In all the world there is not, perhaps, now concentrated in any single spot, so much swindling and villainy, so much foul disease, such a hideous dung heap of moral and physical abomination as in the scene of this far-famed undertaking of 19th Century engineering. . . . The scene of operations is a damp, tropical jungle, intensely hot, swarming with mosquitoes, snakes, alligators, scorpions and centipedes, the home, even as nature made it, of yellow fever, typhus and dysentery, and now made immeasurably more deadly by the multitudes of people who crowd hither.[106]

In a desperate bid to keep his project from faltering, de Lesseps returned to France in 1886 to seek further underwriting from company's stockholders. As he accepted the funds, de Lesseps finally yielded to demands that the canal be designed with locks to raise and lower ships between the oceans of differing heights. Later, when he sought and failed to get enough takers for lottery bonds issued by the French government, de Lesseps acknowledged that the end was at hand. His company went into receivership in January 1889, having spent $287 million—equivalent to $6.9 billion in 2010—on a failed enterprise. An estimated 20,000 people died in the decade long endeavor. Ultimately, de Lesseps's venture failed not only because of his stubborn resistance to a cheaper, more practical lock canal, but also because of fiscal mismanagement, insufficient capital, inadequate equipment, and the horrific loss of human life.

A subsequent investigation revealed evidence that French government officials and even Paris newspaper editors had taken bribes for their support. A French court found de Lesseps guilty of fraud and mismanagement, fined him, and sentenced him to prison. Because of his age and infirmity and, according to Bishop, his condition as a physical and mental wreck, de Lesseps never went to jail. He died in 1894 at age eighty-nine, an invalid at home. *Le Grand Français* was buried in Paris's Père Lachaise Cemetery without great ceremony or large crowds in attendance. The Suez Canal Company paid the funeral expenses, and in the eulogies the word "Panama" was never mentioned.[107]

When Bishop later surveyed the Panamanian landscape after Roosevelt took up the challenge to finish the canal, he noted the old French machinery and "toy-like locomotives" still visible to passengers on the Panama Railroad.

Time had retired them from active service as completely as if they had never existed, leaving them stranded as mere junk among the ways de of progress. Covered with the softening mantle of vine and leaf and flower, and overshadowed by waving palms, they stood in silent dignity as the fitting monuments of a lost cause, making a spectacle so eloquent with the sadness of failure, the pathos of defeat, that few beholders could contemplate it unmoved, and no Frenchman could look upon it with eyes undimmed.[108]

Eight

The Mulligan Letters

THEODORE ROOSEVELT AND JOSEPH BUCKLIN BISHOP SHARED AN AVERSION TO James G. Blaine. With all their might, but without collaboration, they tried to stop him from becoming president of the United States.

Despite a "warm, captivating, and magnetic personality" and a successful career as Speaker of the U.S. House of Representatives, U.S. senator, and secretary of state for two presidents, fifty-three-year-old James Gillespie Blaine aroused lingering suspicion among the political cognoscenti.[109] Their distrust traced to the infamous Mulligan Letters, revealed eight years earlier by a disgruntled railroad company bookkeeper. The letters revealed that Blaine had secretly profited from his position as speaker in the sale of Texas and Pacific Railway bonds. Even though Blaine had vigorously denied the allegation from the floor of the House of Representatives, it was damaging enough to deny him the 1876 Republican presidential nomination—which went to Governor Rutherford B. Hayes of Ohio—and the 1880 nomination, which went to U.S Representative James A. Garfield, also of Ohio. At one point, Blaine had conceded to Bishop, "I am the Henry Clay of the Republican Party; I can never be president."[110]

By 1884, however, there was a sense among party regulars that all was forgiven, and that "The Plumed Knight" would earn his presidential reward for being the foremost Republican leader of the post–Civil War period. Beyond his years of public service, Blaine was also "adored for being Blaine, for his very real human warmth and a love of people, for his brains and loyalty and that gorgeous surplus of personal grace called magnetism."[111]

Indeed, Blaine was the clear favorite for the nomination as delegates arrived at the creaky old Exposition Hall in Chicago in early June. Republican Chester A. Arthur was in the White House, having succeeded the slain Garfield. Yet Arthur's ambition to be elected in his own right was tempered by the well-kept

James G. Blaine's bid to become president in 1884 was stymied
by Republican reformers and corruption charges published in
the *Evening Post* by Edwin Godkin and Joseph Bucklin Bishop.

Library of Congress Prints and Photographs Division

secret that he was suffering from Bright's disease, the same kidney ailment that
had killed Roosevelt's wife.

Roosevelt had arranged for four independent Republicans, including himself, to go to Chicago as at-large New York State delegates pledged to Blaine's
dark-horse opponent, Senator George Edmunds of Vermont. T. R. had never
met Edmunds, but the latter's reputation as incorruptible swayed the assemblyman, who believed the candidate could restore the party to its Lincolnian
ideals.

T. R. believed that Blaine, with his "long, pale face, luminous dark eyes, and silvery beard," was the most politically dangerous man in America, a view shared by *Evening Post* editor Godkin and Bishop.[112] Godkin saw Blaine as morally deficient, someone who found the spoils system convenient and acceptable. Bishop recalled that Godkin "threw himself into the task of preventing Blaine's election with all his force and with an unshakable conviction of ultimate success."[113] Like T. R., the newspaper favored Edmunds.

As the convention opened, Roosevelt and Henry Cabot Lodge—Massachusetts party chairman, T. R.'s political mentor, and lifelong friend—mounted a floor challenge to Blaine's handpicked candidate for temporary chairman, Powell Clayton. The post was essentially meaningless, but T. R. and Lodge believed that a rebuke to Blaine in the opening round of convention balloting would expose the frontrunner's vulnerability and send a signal to delegates that the nomination would not serve as a coronation. Instead, the insurgents proposed former U.S. representative John Lynch, a black man from Mississippi, who supported President Arthur. Demanding a convention roll-call vote for temporary chairman, Roosevelt thundered from the floor, "It is a fitting thing for us to choose to preside over this convention one of that race whose right to sit within these walls is due to the blood and treasure so lavishly spent by the founders of the Republican Party."[114] When the all-night arm-twisting wound to a close and the votes were tallied, Lynch edged out Clayton by a slim 40 votes.

More significantly, Roosevelt had played his first part on the national political stage. He had caught the notice of politicians across the land, and the editorial applause of influential newspapers in Chicago, New York, and other major cities. Godkin's pages saluted Lodge and T. R. for teaming up to outmaneuver the party bosses and advance Edmunds's candidacy.

In the glow of the national spotlight, Roosevelt also enhanced his already-considerable skills of playing reporters and editors to his advantage. He stayed accessible, befriended them, and consistently offered the irresistible quotes that readers enjoyed. It was an art that he perfected in the ensuing years with many influential journalists, including Bishop.

Blaine eventually secured the nomination on the fourth ballot, in spite of Roosevelt's and Lodge's efforts to unite the opposition candidates against him. Blaine's final delegate count was 541 against 207 for President Arthur, and 41 for Senator Edmunds. Although disappointed, Roosevelt reveled in the experience. When asked by a convention reporter whether he would support the Blaine ticket in the fall over the expected Democratic nominee, Governor Grover Cleveland of New York, T. R. at first demurred, explaining that he was preoccupied with planning a stay on his cattle ranch in the Dakotas. One *Evening Post* reporter even quoted him as favoring Cleveland in the matchup. But by the time T. R. had reached St. Paul, Minnesota, on his journey west, he had softened his stand. "I have no personal objection to Blaine," he told reporters. "I think you will find there will be no fatal disaffection. I believe Blaine will be elected."[115]

That summer of 1884, Roosevelt built a second, larger ranch house in the wilderness, about thirty-five miles north of Medora, with the help of his Maine hunting pals Bill Sewall and Wilmot Dow. It was called Elkhorn, and its seclusion in the cottonwoods perfectly suited Roosevelt's need for solitude. He spent most of his time in the Badlands, and from there headed, on occasion, to Montana in search of the big game that populated the Bighorn Range.

Meanwhile, Republican Party reformers were fretting over Blaine's nomination, convinced that his election would set back their efforts to curb political patronage and extend civil service reform to state and local government. The 1883 Pendleton Act had, in theory, put an end to the spoils system in Washington by ensuring that federal employees were chosen through a competitive merit program. Along with their supporters in the press, Republican reformers were labeled Mugwumps, derided by Blaine loyalists for sitting on the fence with their "mugs" on one side and their "wumps" on the other.

During the fall campaign, the *New York Times, Harper's Weekly* editor George Curtis, and Edwin Godkin led the anti-Blaine and pro-Cleveland movements in the media. Godkin had settled on a strategy to revive the corruption charges of the Mulligan Letters and bring them to the attention of his readers.

The letters appeared to show that Blaine used his influence as speaker in 1869 to ensure passage of a land grant for the Little Rock and Fort Smith Railroad. An illegal quid pro quo followed.

In gratitude, Warren Fisher, one of the firm's contractors, allowed Blaine to sell securities in the railroad company and, at the speaker's insistence, pocket a suspiciously large commission on bonds. When the railroad had financial difficulties—that resulted in the bonds becoming nearly worthless—one of the firm's wealthy backers, Tom Scott, bought the almost-worthless bonds back from Blaine and his friends at a price well above their market value.[116]

In return, it was alleged that Blaine advanced legislation to benefit Scott's railroad, the Texas and Pacific.

Believing that the Republican's bid for the White House "presented a moral question of the first magnitude," Godkin, Bishop, and the rest of the *Evening Post* editorial team set out to indict Blaine for "never performing a single service for good government," and most of all for selling his influence. "No American newspaper has conducted a more effective campaign fight than that which the *Evening Post* waged in 1884," historian Allan Nevins wrote.[117] It was a solemn but invigorating undertaking for Bishop, a determined moralist who never hesitated to engage his rigid New England disposition.

The editors hanged Blaine in newsprint, using his own words from speeches eight years earlier when he had tried to rebut the Mulligan Letters. They believed that Blaine had contradicted himself and consequently admitted to wrongdoing. In the middle of the 1884 general election campaign, another set of Mulligan Letters surfaced. By September, the editors had uncovered six more, and by election eve the number of freshly incriminating letters had grown to ten.[118]

The *Evening Post* drew the contrast between the allegations in the Mulligan Letters and Blaine's denials by employing parallel columns in the paper day after day:

Blaine Lie No. 5

I want you to send me a letter such as the enclosed draft. Regard this letter as strictly confidential. Do not show it to anyone. If you can't get the letter written in season for the nine o'clock mail to New York, please be sure to mail it during the night.	*My whole connection with the road has been open as the day. If there had been anything to conceal about it, I should never have touched it. Wherever concealment is advisable avoidance is advisable, and I do not know any better test to apply to the honesty and fairness of a business transaction.*
Sincerely, J.G.B. *(Burn this letter.)* *—Blaine to Fisher, April 16, 1876*	*—Blaine's speech in Congress, April 24, 1876*

Blaine Lie No. 9

Third—I did not own and never did own an acre of coal land or any other kind of land in the Hocking Valley or in any other part of Ohio. My letter to the Hon. Hezekiah Bundy in July last on this same subject was accurately true.

Very truly yours,
J. G. Blaine
—Letter to William McKinley,
October 4, 1884

Received of James G. Blaine $25,108.50, being payment in full for one share in the association formed for the purchase of lands known as the Hope Furnace Tract situated in Vinton and Athens counties in Ohio. This receipt to be exchanged for a certificate when prepared.

—J. N. Denison, Agent
December 15, 1880[119]

The parallel columns predictably won wide praise from Republican reformers and Cleveland Democrats and searing criticism from Blaine supporters, including other influential newspapers. Some of the *Evening Post*'s editorials were even reprinted in pamphlets circulated throughout New York by Cleveland supporters.

In response, Blaine took to the stump. Over six grueling weeks in the fall, he delivered more than 400 speeches, mostly in New York and the Midwest. New York's prized 36 electoral votes—more than any other state—were crucial for a national victory. When the sun rose on November 5, 1884, the day after Election Day, the New York outcome was still hanging in midair. It wasn't until several days later that Cleveland, the favorite son, was declared winner of the New York popular vote by a narrow margin of 1,047 votes out of more than 1.1 million cast. In the Electoral College, New York gave Cleveland almost his entire electoral margin, 219 to 182.[120]

Other factors of course influenced the outcome of the election, but none was more decisive than the *Evening Post*'s fiery anti-Blaine crusade. Godkin, Bishop, and the editorial team knew that they had played a significant role in influencing the voters who seated Cleveland as the first Democrat in the White House since before the Civil War.

Roosevelt had kept his promise to the party and campaigned for James Blaine, but soon after Blaine's loss, T. R. returned to Elkhorn. Over the next several years, he shuttled west and east as the seasons allowed, spending down his inheritance. During one spring roundup near Medora, he worked the herd for days notwithstanding a painful broken rib suffered when he was thrown from his horse. The rigors of ranch life had transformed him physically; Roosevelt now looked "rugged, bronzed, and in the prime of health."[121] Yet success as a rancher was ultimately not to be. Severe drought and the harsh winter of 1886–87 doomed much of his herd and drove market prices to the bottom. His four-year ranching venture had cost him $70,000, equivalent to more than $1.7 million in 2010.

Nonetheless, the experience molded and toughened Roosevelt. The eastern dandy now had a wider view of his nation and a deep appreciation for the land and people who would become his constituency. "We knew toil and hardship and hunger and thirst," he wrote years later. "And we saw men die violent deaths as they worked among the horses and cattle, or fought in evil feuds with one another; but we felt the beat of hardy life in our veins, and ours was the glory of work and the joy of living."[122]

Nine

Snapshots

THOUSANDS GATHERED ON BEDLOE'S ISLAND IN NEW YORK HARBOR TO WITness the long-anticipated event on the gloomy morning, made worse by heavy mist and cold rain. *La Statue de la Liberté*, a gift from France to the United States that was once criticized and even shunned by many Americans—was to be welcomed officially. Celebrating the friendship of the two nations since the pivotal days of the American Revolution, President Cleveland warmly accepted Auguste Bartholdi's 151-foot copper-clad sculpture. "She holds aloft the light which illuminates the way to man's enfranchisement," the president said. "A stream of light shall pierce the darkness of ignorance and man's oppression until liberty enlightens the world."[123]

Cleveland was not, however, the sole celebrity on the dais that day. Aged and bareheaded, *Le Grand Français* swelled with the pride of his nation, even if many in the crowd couldn't understand his remarks. Ferdinand de Lesseps, architect of France's ongoing attempt to dig a canal across Panama, shared his grandiose observations of the day beneath the wind-whipped *Tricolore*.

Ordinarily, Theodore Roosevelt would not have missed an event of this significance in his home city—especially since he had been a member of one of the committees raising funds for the statue's foundation and pedestal—but on that Thursday, October 28, 1886, he was absorbed in the closing days of a vigorous campaign for mayor of New York City. "Working with all the strength of his blizzard-like constitution," T. R. was cramming eighteen-hour campaign days with party rallies and lectern-thumping orations.[124] Despite widespread popularity, the just-turned-twenty-eight-year-old candidate was no shoo-in for election. He faced formidable opposition from two noteworthy candidates: Democrat Abram Hewitt, a seasoned, benevolent industrialist, and Henry George, a fiery Labor Party radical.

A few months earlier, Republican Party bosses had unexpectedly approached Roosevelt to make the run. Hesitant and uncertain, he had reluctantly agreed—believing it his civic duty to run and an opportunity to strengthen his long-term standing with the party. What the bosses and the voters did not know was that T. R. had previously reserved two tickets for a transatlantic crossing on November 6, just four days after the election. He was planning another escape.

The bespectacled young man with the Dakota cowboy image gave the campaign all he had, believing from one day to another that he would win or that he couldn't possibly survive a splintered, three-way race. Influential newspapers and magazines divided their support. Godkin's editorials in *The Nation,* now a weekly supplement to the *Evening Post,* backed Hewitt, advising that he was "just the kind of man New York should always have for mayor."[25] The *Evening Post* itself said coolly that "if T. R. is elected, we would not have a word to say against him."[126]

It was "a splendid contest" in T. R.'s view, an opportunity to exercise his political skills. More important, he believed that he could advance municipal reform and draw attention to the needs of the city's underclass. Voter turnout on Election Day was huge by recent measure but ominously, the number of voting Republicans appeared to be short of expectations. In the days before and after the Statue of Liberty's dedication, without T. R.'s knowledge, party chieftains had quietly put out the word to rank-and-file Republicans that they should vote for Hewitt, not Roosevelt, to block the surging radical, George. The final count gave Hewitt 41 percent, George 31 percent, and, in last place, Roosevelt, 28 percent.

T. R. was not accustomed to losing at the polls, but he insisted that he was not disappointed, and that he had benefited from the experience. His recognition had soared among New Yorkers and those across the nation who followed politics closely. He could not dwell on the loss, he concluded, because he and his sister Bamie had to prepare for a voyage to England where he would marry the waiting Edith. Lest others prematurely discover his plans, he had made reservations aboard the steamship *Etruria* under the pseudonym of "Mr. and Miss Merrifield."

Alice Lee had been dead for more than a year when Roosevelt began to court Edith Carow, his sister Corinne's favorite childhood playmate and a frequent guest at the Roosevelt home. A headstrong child who had matured into a strong-willed adult, Edith was wise and worldly, content to wait patiently for what she wanted. She had grown up comfortably on Manhattan's Union Square and received the finishing proper for a young lady of the era. She had attended the first Roosevelt wedding, where she was said to have "danced the soles off her shoes" at the reception, returning to New York "still in love with the groom."[127] Now, he was available and interested.

Edith Kermit Roosevelt, second wife of Theodore Roosevelt, in a 1902
painting by Theobald Chartran. *Theodore Roosevelt Collection, Harvard College Library*

They began a private courtship, allowing their fondness for each other to
grow into something more. During T. R.'s expeditions to Elkhorn Ranch in the
Dakotas, they communicated in a stream of letters—all but two later burned
by Edith as was the custom in an age that lived fiercely by the tenets of privacy.

Theodore had proposed to Edith in November 1885, and she had accepted.
They agreed to delay a formal announcement until some Carow family matters were settled and after T. R.'s cattle business had stabilized. Just over a year
later, on a foggy day in London, they exchanged wedding vows in St. George's
church at Hanover Square. Roosevelt memorably wore bright orange gloves
at the ceremony, according to legend, to reveal himself in the fog. Edith was
"lovely-looking . . . with a quiet kind of dignity."[128] Following a fifteen-week

honeymoon in Europe, the couple settled down at Sagamore Hill to begin an eventful life together.

Set on a vast expanse overlooking Oyster Bay, the house stood bold as a martinet, a proud Victorian with twenty-three rooms on three floors. Heavily lidded with massive green awnings, a parade of windows encircled and embraced it. Sagamore Hill was classic Theodore Roosevelt—or, as Edmund Morris described, it was "Huge, angular, and squat . . . on a grassy hilltop with all the grace of a fort."[129] Roosevelt prized his new home, in which shelves of his favorite books and a menagerie of big-game trophies surrounded him. The house served as his only home from 1885 until his death. In latter years it served as a summer White House.

Allan McLane Hamilton, grandson of Alexander Hamilton, observed that Joseph Bucklin Bishop, "who has much caustic wit, became Mr. Godkin's able assistant [at the *Evening Post*] and wrote many of his most brilliant editorials."[130] Bishop's influence had never been stronger than in 1885–86, when the Blair Educational Bill was before the U.S. Senate. A vestige of well-intentioned Reconstruction programs, it proposed to spend $100 million to improve education in the South. It was the kind of federal initiative that readers would expect the paper to stand behind, if not aggressively promote.

The next day, the *Evening Post* acknowledged that

> *we are ready to admit that more Southern voters might be able to read ten years hence if the $100,000,000 should be appropriated by Congress, for use chiefly in Southern schools, than if the states were left to their own resources; but we insist that this temporary gain in intelligence would be purchased at the cost of a permanent loss in character vastly more important—the loss of self reliance and self respect.*[131]

Over the next four years, the Blair Educational Bill repeatedly passed the U.S. Senate by significant margins, but it never came before the House of Representatives or reached the desk of President Cleveland or his successor. In March 1890, weakened by constant opposition from the *Evening Post*, the Senate finally defeated the bill 43 to 39, with, remarkably, most southern senators voting against it. As Horace White, a subsequent editor of the *Evening Post*, observed, "It was the general belief at the time that the arguments advanced by the *Evening Post* were chiefly instrumental in defeating the measure."[132]

Six months before the Statue of Liberty dedication and Roosevelt's mayoral loss, President Cleveland drew the attention of the nation to the White House when he married twenty-one-year-old Frances Folsom, a college student and his ward. In the ceremonial Blue Room, the rotund, middle-aged president made Folsom, a woman of acknowledged beauty and charm, the youngest first lady in history. As they exchanged vows before a small circle of invited guests, "the bells of the city churches rang out a glad greeting [and] a salute of cannon announced the union of the happy pair."[133] Over the next seventeen years, Grover and Frances Cleveland raised a family of five children.

Cleveland's love life had raised eyebrows before. In September 1874, a son was born in Buffalo to Maria Halpin, the tall and pretty thirty-six-year-old widowed companion of then-Buffalo attorney Grover Cleveland. Halpin named the child Oscar Cleveland. While never admitting paternity, Cleveland assumed responsibility for the child, supporting him in an orphans' home while Maria struggled with alcoholism. The scandal simmered below the surface until 1884 when Cleveland ran for president on the Democratic ticket. In July the *Buffalo Evening Telegraph*, a newspaper described as a "despised rag," covered its front page with the story, dubbed "A Terrible Tale."[134] In response, the candidate urged his handlers to tell the truth, and his supporters obediently argued that Cleveland had been responsible and honorable.

Republicans exploited the issue for its political value, of course. Across the country, they staged mocking parades of cross-dressing men pushing baby carriages who chanted, "Ma, Ma, where's my Pa?" Cleveland Democrats yelled back, "Gone to the White House, ha, ha, ha!"

Now, of his wedding to Folsom, the president complained publicly about "the colossal impertinence" of "those ghouls of the press."[135] Barred from covering the event from inside the White House, reporters had camped out on the grounds and then trailed the couple on horseback as the presidential carriage made its way to a train station and then to a secluded honeymoon cottage in the resort of Deer Park, miles from Washington.

Bishop responded to the coverage controversy in an article in *Forum* magazine. Citing "the intolerable lengths to which the modern system of personal espionage has been carried," he scolded his colleagues for being "possessed with the idea that anybody's business is everybody's business. Nothing is sacred," he fumed. He scoffed at the journalists' mission outside the presidential honeymoon cottage:

It was to stand in the trees and shrubbery, at a distance of 300 yards, and watch the president and his bride. . . . They recorded the hour when the president first appeared at the window; examined the dishes when meals were sent from the hotel to the cottage. . . . They distended their ears to catch every scrap of conversation which floated from the piazza when the beleaguered pair ventured out of doors; took notes of the garments worn by both, and recorded every nod and look and smile of both throughout the day. They stood in the bushes until the lights in the cottage were out, when they carefully noted the hour; then they wrote out the results of their day's watch in jubilant accounts, many columns in length, and sent them to the leading newspapers of the land, and those newspapers published them in their most conspicuous columns.

Bishop wagged his editor's finger: "No other kind of people, in private life, pry about their neighbors' houses, peep into their windows, listen at their keyholes, and try in other ways to penetrate the sanctities of their homes." He also warned of the consequences he foresaw. "The newspapers will soon discover the mistake they are making. They will perceive it first in the weakening of their own editorial influence. The paper which does it must inevitably be denied admission [to its readers' households] sooner or later." He concluded, "It is not true that indecency 'pays' better than decency but that in journalism, as in every other reputable calling, the honorable, self-respecting course is the only one that 'pays' in the long run."[136]

Bishop, of course, never worked for one of the era's scandal sheets and so was never asked to hide in the bushes—despite the popularity of that type of journalism during his time in the industry. By the mid-1880s his moralism had become something of a Victorian prudishness, a schoolmarm's chastisement of those who he felt violated his standards. But Bishop wasn't afraid to dig deep into a person's life when morality was on his side.

Of the Tammany Hall crowd, the *Evening Post* wrote in 1890, "Its sole object is to plunder in any form which will not attract the immediate notice of the police." And so began the newspaper's campaign to expose government leaders, including the city's new mayor, Hughie Grant, successor to Abram Hewitt. "He is an ignorant and unprincipled son of a saloonkeeper," Godkin told his readers, noting that the mayor's previous stint as sheriff had been "loose and corrupt," and that the men he appointed were "the worst of Tammany."

Joseph Bucklin Bishop and Horace White helped Godkin fashion a simple but brilliant strategy to expose the corrupt leaders who had grabbed control of City Hall again. The editors planned to publish their "biographies," digging deep into the officials' seamy backgrounds and revealing their offenses. Godkin and company believed that voters generally knew their leaders were a bad lot, but they didn't have the full story. The editors "determined to probe that gulf, to give the city a whiff of its fumes and to show how the Tammany organizers reeked with slime," *Post* historian Allan Nevins observed.[137]

Readers of the April 3, 1890, issue devoured nine dense columns of Tammany life sketches that covered twenty-seven of the organization's executive committee members, including Mayor Grant and his closest henchmen. Grant was accused of pocketing illegal auction fees while sheriff and taking "extra compensation fees" for his trouble. Others were tagged for dealing in scandalous contracts, thievery, brutal assault—even conspiracy to commit murder. One amusing sketch recounted Sheriff Grant's reaction to a challenge from his Tammany inner circle: "What do youse fellows want? Do youse want to break up the organization?"[138]

A sensation, the biographies drew widespread public comment and support from applauding newspapers in Boston, Philadelphia, and the West. The sketches appeared later in a best-selling pamphlet. Not surprisingly, the biographies also drew criminal libel suits from some of the accused, which caused Godkin to be summonsed and arrested multiple times. In the end, however, the charges against the *Evening Post* were dismissed, and the paper continued printing exposés of people among Tammany's thousand-member Committee on Organization and its 4,500-member General Committee.

The Grant administration sailed to reelection in 1892, nevertheless, on the strength of Tammany's skilled politics and its resulting popularity among the working class, but the damage festered. Joseph Pulitzer's sensationalist *New York World* joined the anti-Tammany crusade, and by early 1895 reformist William Lafayette Strong had taken office as mayor. Nevins wrote that Strong's administration was one of the best ever for New York. Especially noteworthy, he felt, was his appointment of a transforming figure to the city's Board of Police Commissioners, a native son, brazenly outspoken in his determination to end the patronage appointments of police officers and licentiousness in the city's saloons, especially on Sundays. His name was Theodore Roosevelt, and from the editors' room of the *Evening Post*, Joseph Bucklin Bishop was watching and taking notes.

PART II

CHANGES

Ten

A Close Personal Friendship

THE LIVES OF THEODORE ROOSEVELT AND JOSEPH BUCKLIN BISHOP DID NOT collide in a cataclysmic moment; rather, the two disparate men from urban Manhattan and rural Massachusetts happened upon each other uneventfully as each pursued his daily work. Each had an Ivy League education. Both were family men whom morality guided, and they shared an interest in, if not a preoccupation with, good government and the dissolution of corruption and vice in public service.

"With the entrance of Roosevelt upon his service as police commissioner in New York City, in the spring of 1895, there began between him and myself a close personal friendship," Bishop remembered, "which continued unbroken throughout his career, growing steadily in mutual confidence and affection with time. I was closely associated with Roosevelt during the entire period of his police service."[139]

Bishop claimed to be "in almost daily, confidential contact" with Roosevelt as the new commissioner reformed crooked police practices and instituted the merit system for jobs and promotions. Little evidence of their earliest communication has survived, but they would have begun to exchange regular letters—a practice that became their routine for nearly a quarter-century. They probably met in 1895 to talk reform and share information. The *Evening Post*, according to Bishop, was "cordially supporting" Roosevelt's intentions at the time. In fact, the paper stood tall for him. "Commissioner Roosevelt's acts and words since entering his duties give gratifying assurance that the high expectations formed of his usefulness in the Police Department will be realized," an early editorial enthused.[140]

Among public officials, Roosevelt had learned in Albany and perfected in Washington, D.C., a promotional strategy that produced results. He surreptitiously but methodically furnished valuable and oftentimes insider information to favored journalists, ensuring good coverage and frequent editorial support.

Theodore Roosevelt as president of the New York City Board of Police Commissioners (ca. 1895–97).

Theodore Roosevelt Collection, Harvard College Library (Roosevelt R500.F69a-018)

While police commissioner, he asked reporters to join him when he covertly prowled the nighttime streets in search of sleeping patrolmen and other scofflaws. "He began the fight at once, using in it the weapons he had employed in its predecessors: full publicity, strict enforcement of law and utter disregard of partisan political considerations," Bishop observed.[141] As journalism historian Stephen Ponder put it, "he was developing a rationale for using the press to shape public opinion that drew both from his notion of expanding executive power as a steward of the people, and from the Progressive view that properly informing the public was necessary to create support for reform."[142]

Editions of the city's many other newspapers littered the *Evening Post* city room, and Bishop scanned them daily for clips to forward to Roosevelt. "Thought you would enjoy this," he often wrote. "In case you haven't seen this, you have earned the editors' unfailing admiration." In his cover notes and choice of clips, Bishop flattered Roosevelt and played to his generous ego. Sweet talk often was Bishop's way to enhance associations with the high and mighty whom he encountered, a strategy that led future critics to accuse him of sycophancy.

At police headquarters on the morning of May 6, 1895, Roosevelt's three fellow police commissioners unanimously selected him to preside over the board. "We will lose no time . . . in taking charge of the department," the new leader promised.[143] That role had not been Mayor Strong's first choice for Roosevelt, however. At the beginning, the mayor thought T. R. would make a terrific commissioner of street cleaning. Not surprisingly, T. R. turned him down.

Influential newspapers across the country applauded Roosevelt's appointment. The *Baltimore American* editorialized that there was "the finest opportunity for reform in [New York] to be found anywhere in the country, and Mr. Roosevelt will attack it with the zest of a man who never gets tired as long as he is on a trail." The *Buffalo Express* remarked that "cleansing of the Augean stables is Mr. Roosevelt's specialty."[144]

It was a breath of clean air. Before, Republican and Democratic commissioners had rewarded loyalists with jobs—that is, once a party "tariff" had been paid by the appointee. "The entire force was permeated with corruption in every department of activity," Bishop recalled. "A very large revenue was collected by the force from vice and crime, and the unlawful sale of liquor."[145]

Taking a cue from Mayor Strong's campaign platform, Roosevelt vowed to put an end to patronage appointment of policemen. He warned that "every man on the force will have to stand upon his merits . . . without regard to politics."[146] Roosevelt told the city's Good Government Club a month later, "It has been said that non-partisanship and civil service in the force would be impracticable. We will show all men to the contrary."[147]

Within weeks, Roosevelt took on another untouchable practice. Many city saloons sold spirits on Sundays in violation of state law and the determined opposition of the clergy. The cynics—Bishop included—protested that Tammany had made the law just so it could be broken by those who would pay bribes to the organization to ensure police protection. As the *Evening Post* explained, "Sunday selling was forbidden in order that the privilege of violating the law might be sold for the benefit of politics."[148]

Roosevelt's determination to halt liquor sales on the Sabbath won a nod from Bishop's paper, as he had hoped. "When . . . the Police Board makes a determined effort to enforce the law, not a little but entirely, it is taking the first step toward police reformation and towards the honest enforcement of all laws, and should be upheld by the entire moral sentiment of the community."[149]

That Roosevelt should crusade against bribery and the purchase of appointments came as no surprise to champions of civil service reform who had been watching his career. He had been named federal civil service commissioner in the spring of 1889 after Senator Benjamin Harrison of Indiana beat incumbent Grover Cleveland and reclaimed the presidency for the Republicans. During the campaign, Harrison promised to reform the federal civil service, and early in his term he turned to Roosevelt to make it happen. "To the victor belongs the spoils—the cynical battle-cry of the spoils politician in America—is so nakedly vicious that few right-thinking men of trained mind defend it," T. R. reminisced of his six years as civil service commissioner.[150] Bishop stated grandly that "There was no more peaceful abode of official life in Washington in May 1889 than the serene home of the Civil Service Commission when Theodore Roosevelt, in abounding health and vigor from his six years of ranching and hunting life, walked in and took possession after the retirement of the incumbents."[151] As a New York assemblyman earlier in the decade, Roosevelt had helped to enact the first state civil service law in the nation.

Organizationally, T. R. was one of three civil service commissioners, but the others behaved like the worst of sedentary bureaucrats, caring little about the law they were supposed to oversee. In 1883, Congress had passed the Pendleton Act, covering a fraction of federal workers with the classified merit system, but as Bishop later observed, "Its enforcement had been quite uniformly so gentle that the business of practical politics had not been seriously disturbed." His cynicism about the law ran deep. "It would serve as a stop for a few 'long-haired cranks,' and would amount to nothing in practice."[152]

Intent on enforcing the spirit of the Pendleton Act, Roosevelt probed corrupt hiring practices at the New York City Customs House, then took his hesitant colleagues on a tour of hot spots in the West to look into whether government agencies were obeying the law. On departing the capital for his inspection tour Roosevelt declared, "We have to do two things. One is to make the officials themselves understand that the law is obligatory, not optional; and the other is to get the same idea into the heads of the people."[153]

In his autobiography, Roosevelt served up a heart-wrenching example of the spoils system's real-world consequences. He told of a "pallid and careworn" widow with two children who had been ordered to vacate an $800-a-year federal job that she had worked dutifully for thirteen years. As T. R. told the story, her bureau chief learned that an influential U.S. senator wanted the job for a friend. Her chief pleaded with the woman to quit her job so he would not lose his. "And go she did, and turned out she was," Roosevelt related with period affectation, "to suffer with her children and to starve outright or to live in semi starvation." The senator had his way in the end, but, thanks to the empathy and cooperation of another government official, T. R. got the mother back to work. He acknowledged, however, that it was a "somewhat lower position."[154]

In Baltimore, he addressed his most challenging target yet: hundreds of postal workers who, under the authority of Postmaster General John Wanamaker, owed their jobs to political favoritism. Worse, Roosevelt discovered that the mailmen were buying votes for the reelection of President Harrison. T. R. demanded that the workers take competitive entrance examinations to measure their qualifications, but Wanamaker and his Republican friends resisted, declaring that they had had enough of the determined commissioner. "A tremendous uproar filled the land," Bishop remembered. Vocal party leaders called on Roosevelt to back off or resign. Partisan newspapers echoed the demand. "Go at it, Roosevelt," wrote the *Albany Evening Journal*. "If any man can repeal the Pendleton Law during the coming four years, his name is Teddy. The American idea of party, party power and party responsibility will survive the Mugwump attack made under the guise of civil service reform."[155]

In speeches and newspaper columns, Roosevelt vigorously defended the righteousness of his crusade while restlessly looking over his shoulder for backing from Congress and the president who had appointed him. Partisans demanded that Congress scrutinize the commissioner's work, but an oversight committee, after hearing the critics and the defendant, upheld Roosevelt's actions. Rebuffing calls from top party insiders, Harrison declined to remove his fervent aide. When Cleveland returned to the White House in 1892, Roosevelt opponents saw an opportunity to slow or reverse the reform process. In a Christmas Day editorial, the *New York Times* weighed in with Cleveland to keep Roosevelt. "A party platform is not his god. He does his own thinking, and that thinking is along a high plane. He has made a civil service commissioner for his country, not his party."[156] Cleveland agreed and allowed his political collaborator from the Albany years to continue.

By May 1895 when Roosevelt resigned to become New York's police commissioner, the classified service had been extended to practically the entire executive branch of the federal government: up to 85,000 workers, according to Bishop's count. "The great value in [Roosevelt's] six years of service did not lie in the increased number of places brought within the rules but on the revolution he had accomplished in the minds of both the politicians and the people regarding the law and its merits," Bishop concluded.[157]

In success also lay revelation for Roosevelt. "I was already growing to understand that mere improvement in political condition by itself was not enough. I dimly realized that an even greater fight must be waged to improve the economic conditions and to secure social and industrial justice."[158] The newly emboldened police commissioner's candid observation forecast a hopeful future for the city's vast underclass.

Eleven

The Final Exam

THE "SHY, DREAMY, POETIC YOUTH" OF BROWN UNIVERSITY IN THE 1850S AND the "most brilliant man" who had ever walked into Horace Greeley's office in the 1870s was now, in the spring of 1897, favored to become President McKinley's ambassador to the United Kingdom. John Hay, Lincoln's confidant, had lived yet another lifetime since he and Bishop had shared the editors' room at Greeley's *New York Tribune.* In 1874 Hay had married Clara Stone, daughter of a wealthy Cleveland industrialist, becoming financially secure enough to spend his time writing prose and poetry and roaming the world. When he grew weary of wanderlust, he assented to President Hayes's call to serve as assistant secretary of state. Hay had also, with John Nicolay, written the first part of an exhaustive ten-volume life of Lincoln in 1890.

On stationery embossed with EDITORIAL ROOMS, THE EVENING POST, Bishop wrote to Hay, offering hope that Hay "could have the English mission." But the wish was an afterthought to the prime purpose of the missive to his mentor. Bishop wanted to deal with Hay's twenty-year-old act of goodwill toward him. "Probably you have forgotten all about it," Bishop began, "but when I broke down in health in 1877 and wished to get to California, you sent me $20 to help me on the way." Bishop reminded the great man of what Hay had said to him about the money in an accompanying letter: "If I objected to it, I might use it and later pass it on to some other fellow who was not very well." Bishop advised Hay that he was passing on the twenty dollars (now worth 21 percent less because of a severe recession in the 1890s) to the widow and children of one Philip Welch, "the poor fellow who went on grinding out jobs while a cancer was eating away his life." Admitting that he felt no sense of obligation to Hay, Bishop explained that the gifting gave him great pleasure and that he wanted his friend to know it. "You did for me in the most discouraged hour of my life, more than any other person save my own brother," Bishop wrote, "and I shall never cease to remember it with pleasure and gratitude."[159] But friendship had

John Milton Hay (ca. 1894–1902).

Pach Bros. Theodore Poosevelt Coilection, Harvard College Library (Roosevelt R570.P93p-0C3)

its limitations. Two weeks later Bishop gently scolded Hay for giving a rival journalist "a scoop over me in the matter of your appointment" as ambassador to the UK.

Among the swarm of reporters camped across the street from New York City police headquarters to observe the daily comings and goings of cops and crooks was forty-six-year-old Jacob Riis of the *Evening Sun*. He had emigrated from Denmark twenty-five years earlier, landing in New York to work as a carpenter. The story goes that Riis spent his last krone on a pistol to defend himself against what he had heard about hostile Native Americans and wild animals. Instead, he did battle with the vermin and disease that crowded his home in the immigrant slum. But by the spring of 1895 Riis, "a big, rumpled, noisy, sweet-natured Dane" had risen to become the most influential reporter in the city.[160]

Riis often beat the pack of newsmen to the station steps where, with persistent questions, he often got the scoop on the city's latest robbery or murder. Riis's assertiveness caught the notice of Roosevelt, encamped in his office a few floors above the street. For the police commission president, it was easy to co-opt the veteran reporter, redirecting his attention from cops and robbers to broader public policy issues that Roosevelt felt newspaper readers ought to learn about. Roosevelt knew that some of his officers, who were supposed to be on night patrol, were instead dozing off in secluded hideaways or, worse, abusing the authority of their badges by brutalizing offenders with kicks to the groin and nightsticks to the head. Roosevelt wanted to see all this for himself, but he understood that having Riis's validating eyes along for a tour would draw public attention to the situation and make remedial action politically easier to accomplish.

Five years earlier, Riis's book, *How the Other Half Lives,* had exposed the appalling living conditions in the city's slums, in elegant text and groundbreaking, flash-lit photography. It had shocked Roosevelt, who felt compelled to do something about it. Together, in the small hours of the night, in the spring of 1895, the two men went undercover and prowled the back streets and alleys of the Lower East Side, lit only when rays of dim gaslight refracted on the heavy, rank mist. When they encountered a blatant police transgression, the shadowy figures paused only to record the badge numbers of the offending officers and the identities of those who gave them cover.

Since Roosevelt was also a member of the city's Board of Health, he and Riis also waded through some of lower Manhattan's loathsome tenement houses on summer nights, inspecting the overcrowding and filth brought to the surface by Riis's exposé. To gain access, they often had to step over heat-stricken horses, lying dead in the street where they had fallen. Roosevelt also remembered, "We visited East Side tenements together to speak to families about having their husbands and fathers home instead of in saloons on Sundays." He added, "We did everything to alleviate their suffering. On hot summer nights, much of it was heartbreaking, especially the gasping misery of little children and their worn-out mothers."[161]

Their shared experiences on the streets of New York created a lifelong bond between Roosevelt and Riis, one that transcended their mutually useful relationship of the 1890s. "I loved him from the first day I saw him," Riis admitted. [162]

"He and I looked at life and its problems from substantially the same standpoint," Roosevelt recalled. "Our ideals and principles and purposes, and our beliefs as to the methods necessary to realize them, were alike."[163]

Bishop, still writing for the rival *Evening Post*, observed that Roosevelt had "formed an intimate friendship with Riis which lasted throughout the latter's life, and spoke of him when he died [in 1914] as, next to his father, the best man he had ever known."[164] Although we know little about the Bishop-Riis relationship, hearing T. R.'s supreme praise for Riis couldn't have been easy for Bishop, who sought the coveted designation of being Roosevelt's best journalist friend.

Riis wrote passionately about what he and Roosevelt observed on their tours, and T. R. did what he could to redress the social tragedies he witnessed, pressing city agencies to develop "model tenements" and other curative actions. He was notably proud of his and Riis's abolition of police-run poorhouses, which to T. R. were "simply tramp lodging houses, and a fruitful encouragement to vagrancy."[165]

Roosevelt emerged from his experience not only empathetic with the victims of poverty, but also angry at those he viewed as perpetrators.

Not a few of the worst tenement houses were owned by wealthy individuals who hired the best and most expensive lawyers to persuade the courts that it was "unconstitutional" to insist on the betterment of conditions. . . . After my experience with them, I became more set than ever in my distrust of those men, whether business men or lawyers, judges, legislators or executive officers who seek to make of the Constitution a fetish for the prevention of the work of social reform.[166]

It was a life-altering lesson for T. R., one that evoked his late father's social values and profoundly shaped his later views as governor, president, and statesman.

In vivid contrast to the protective instincts of Edith Roosevelt, Theodore was trusting by nature—until he was crossed. According to Bishop, Roosevelt put his faith in friends and colleagues until they showed themselves to be unworthy; then he turned away from them for all time. There was no second chance.

Midway into T. R.'s tenure as police commissioner, his friendship with Bishop withstood the strain of a severe test. Bishop had warned T. R. to be careful of Andrew Parker, a thirty-five-year-old fellow commissioner who was handsomely bearded, a brilliant, strong-willed lawyer, and a former assistant district attorney. A Democratic appointee, Parker had evaded Tammany's grasp to work his own agenda. But he was becoming openly resentful of Roosevelt's high public profile as commissioner. "He thinks he's the whole board," Parker had told a reporter for the *Evening Post*.[167]

Bishop had cautioned Roosevelt that Parker was a tricky and unscrupulous politician. "He covers his designs with fervid professions of devotion to you, but he wants to thwart your reforms," he warned.[168]

Roosevelt chuckled in disbelief. "He has supported me. He may be, as you say, a tricky politician, but I am sure that he is loyal. Why, only yesterday, I boxed with him, and he boxes like a gentleman."[169]

"Parker is a snake in the grass, and sooner or later he will smite you," Bishop insisted. "The man is a political schemer by nature, possessing a certain order of low cunning. . . . He covers his designs with a plausible profession of virtuous convictions."[170]

Roosevelt said no more about Parker. Unsure of whether he had convinced Roosevelt of the impending threat—and whether he had curried further favor with him—Bishop kept a respectful silence as well.

The next chapter of their trial came after Roosevelt, Bishop, Parker, and a few others had enjoyed a dinner of beef and politics at a Midtown steakhouse. At evening's end, Roosevelt and the others spun off while Parker and Bishop buttoned up against the chilly evening for a walk toward their homes. "At that point, the wily commissioner sought to make trouble between Roosevelt and me," Bishop recalled. As they walked along the shadowy Manhattan sidewalk, Parker asked the editor to dissuade Roosevelt from talking so often to the newspapers because, he said, it harmed the commissioners' work.

"Stop Roosevelt from talking?" Bishop responded in mock disbelief. "He *has* to talk." And then Bishop added the fateful lines: "The peculiarity about him is that he has what is essentially a boy's mind. What he thinks he says at once, [he] thinks aloud. It is his distinguishing characteristic, and I don't know if he will ever outgrow it."[171]

On hearing what could be viewed as a gross personal insult to the commission president, Parker thought he had the ammunition to break the Roosevelt-Bishop bond and perhaps weaken the editorial support of the *Evening Post*. But Bishop uttered a crucial addendum to his evaluation: "He has great qualities that make him an invaluable public servant: inflexible honesty, absolute fearlessness, and devotion to good government which

THE FINAL EXAM

amount to religion." Bishop had no intention of asking Roosevelt to stop talking to the press. "He wants the public to know what the police board is doing so that it will have popular support," Bishop explained. Parker received the explanation in cold silence.[172]

Before the city's church bells rang the Angelus the next day, Roosevelt was on the telephone to Bishop, inviting him to lunch. Bishop coolly recalled the mealtime discourse: "As soon as we were seated at a narrow table, he leaned forward, bringing his face close to mine and, with appalling directness, said, 'Parker came into my office this morning and said, 'You think Bishop is a friend of yours, don't you?'

" 'Yes,' I replied.

" 'Well, you know what he said about you last night? He said [you told him that I] had a boy's mind and it might never be developed.'"

"Roosevelt's eyeglasses were within three inches of my face," Bishop remembered, "and his eyes were looking straight into mine. Knowing my man, I did not flinch.

" 'Roosevelt, I *did* say that. Did he tell you what else I said?'

" 'No, that is what I want to hear.

"When I told him, Roosevelt brought his fist down on the table with a bang, exclaiming, 'By George, I knew it!'

" 'There, Roosevelt,' said I, 'is your snake in the grass of which I warned you—the meanest of mean liars who tells half the truth.'"[173]

Bishop surely pursed his lips with smugness when he later typed this dialogue into the manuscripts of *Theodore Roosevelt and His Time* and *Notes and Anecdotes of Many Years*. His conclusion? "This incident established our friendship so firmly that nothing was able to disturb it."[174] Bishop also committed to print a welcome expression of confidence that he claimed Roosevelt had given him more than once: "What I value in you is that you give me the advice you think I need rather than the advice you think I'd like to have."[175] Hardly the words to describe a sycophant.

Once Parker failed to suppress the publicity Theodore Roosevelt was getting for his police reforms, he "threw off all disguise and became an open opponent of Roosevelt's policies," Bishop noted. The commissioners' mutual antagonism descended into hatred as Parker forced the board into gridlock over police promotions with obstructionist votes and absences from meetings. In May 1896, Mayor Strong asked Parker to resign. When he refused, the mayor brought him to administrative trial, charging negligence, malfeasance, and misfeasance.

69

For nearly another year, Roosevelt pursued his reform campaigns, fighting Sunday liquor sellers and partnering with Jacob Riis to lift some of the burdens of New York's poor through government intervention. By April 1897, when he resigned as commissioner, Roosevelt knew that he had accomplished most of what he had set out to do. The police department had undergone a moral transformation under T. R., and a new standard of excellence had been set for the future. In Bishop's lifetime, "The force never reverted to the disgraceful condition in which he found it. Appointments and promotions were never again made on the basis of boss favor and cash payment alone but mainly on merit, and the levying of blackmail as a general police practice was never resumed."[176]

Despite the achievement, Roosevelt believed that he had paid a price for his zeal, and he shared his fears with Bishop during what the editor described as a long and intimate conversation.

"This is the last office I shall ever hold," Roosevelt confided, assessing that he had simply offended too many powerful politicians and interests. "It was the only course I could honestly pursue, and I am willing to abide by the consequences."[177]

At about the same time, Roosevelt's friend Senator Henry Cabot Lodge began talking to the newly installed administration of President McKinley about a role for Roosevelt, specifically as assistant secretary of the navy. There was, however, an obstacle, Lodge reported to Roosevelt. McKinley knew Roosevelt to be a firecracker and wanted no international crisis—in smoldering Cuba or anywhere else—to get in the way of his goal to restore good times in the country. In a candid letter to T. R., Lodge wrote, "Absolutely the only thing I hear adverse is that there is a fear that you will want to fight somebody at once."[178]

Twelve

Fifty-Four and a Half Weeks

CUBA—FEWER THAN A HUNDRED MILES FROM WHAT WOULD BECOME THE State of Florida—came under European influence in the fall of 1492 when Christopher Columbus explored its northern coast during his first voyage across the Atlantic. He returned two years later, mindful of Pope Alexander VI's command to Spain to colonize the New World and convert its pagan natives to Catholicism. Within fifteen years, Spain had driven its first permanent stake into Cuban soil, and by 1514 had founded a settlement at what would become the capital, Havana.

The native Cubans mollified their conquerors with tobacco, teaching them how to roll its leaves into cigars for smoking. With the introduction of slavery to the island, Cubans prospered at growing sugarcane and exported to the U.S. market more than 80 percent of its crop. By 1825, most of Spain's New World colonies had won their independence, except Cuba and nearby Puerto Rico. By the late nineteenth century, with slavery abolished, Cubans took up arms and launched a fervent bid for independence, inspired by the heroic revolutionary José Martí. Tales of Cuban rebellion and Spanish repression reached New York, where Pulitzer's *World* and Hearst's *Journal* sensationalized events in print, agitating for U.S. intervention and whipping up an empathetic frenzy among their readers. The age of yellow journalism had arrived.

"Is this not too small for him?" wondered Navy Secretary John Long, referring to the prospect of Theodore Roosevelt becoming his assistant secretary. "Roosevelt has the character, standing, ability, and reputation to entitle him to be a cabinet minister."[179]

Long, an aging politician and former Massachusetts governor, could sense Roosevelt's shadow creeping up on him, even before President McKinley made T. R.'s appointment official on April 6, 1897. Just two days later, the Senate confirmed Roosevelt, and he moved confidently into the flamboyant State,

71

War, and Navy Building next to the White House. The *Washington Post,* a harsh opponent of T. R.'s earlier federal civil service reforms, was now having second thoughts. "He is a fighter of indomitable pluck and energy, a potent and forceful factor in any equation into which he may be introduced. A field of immeasurable usefulness awaits him—will he find it?"[180]

Naval warfare had intrigued Roosevelt since he had begun writing his *Naval History of 1812* while still at Harvard. He had further schooled himself with the work of naval historian Alfred Thayer Mahan. At the end of the nineteenth century, the European powers, which had already colonized much of the globe, were dispatching navies to expand their empires in Asia, Africa, and the Pacific. Germany had covetous eyes on South America, and Spain had a centuries-old but increasingly tenuous hold in the Caribbean and the Philippine Islands. In his new post, Roosevelt determined to add new muscle to the navy, not from strictly imperialist intentions—which were rocking Hawaii, for example—but to bolster national defense and prepare for what he believed was an impending confrontation with Spain over Cuba.

Roosevelt took almost immediate charge of the navy despite his subservient rank to Long and, of course, the president. The launch of his naval initiative came on June 2 at opening exercises at the Naval War College in Newport, Rhode Island. There, by a restless sea on a late-spring morning, the assistant secretary articulated policies that grabbed the world's attention and sent shudders through the rest of McKinley's War Department. Bishop later observed that Roosevelt's message was not hastily conceived but rather "clearly the result of several years of serious thought and study of the subject." The speech contained "all the principal ideas which he expounded with such tireless energy during that period."[181]

Attired in a derby, vest, and tails, his spectacles glistening, Roosevelt overlooked a field of blue dress uniforms and declared, "Preparation for war is the surest guarantee for peace. . . . Those who wish to see this country at peace with foreign nations will be wise if they place reliance upon a first-class fleet of first-class battleships rather than on any arbitration treaty which the wit of man can devise."[182]

Speaking of the Kaiser's designs on Venezuela, Roosevelt declared, "If we possess a formidable navy, small is the chance indeed that we should ever be dragged into a war to uphold the Monroe Doctrine." Hopeful that the German emperor would get the message, he later said, "If Germany intended to expand her empire here, she would have to whip us first."[183] The *Washington Post,* now fully won over to Roosevelt, applauded: "Well done, nobly spoken!" Its cheering verdict echoed in editorial pages from coast to coast.

In the days following the Newport speech, Bishop wanted the *Evening Post*—still one of New York's most respected editorial voices—to back Roosevelt to the hilt. To bolster his case, he drew on the best available source. "I have started the Intelligence Office at work to prepare you," Roosevelt advised "I think you will be able to make a more comprehensive and intelligent article on the Navy than anyone outside of the Department." In a revealing aside to his friend he admitted, "I have thoroughly enjoyed this work; but do you know I really miss the police work?"[184]

Two days later, Roosevelt provided the material Bishop wanted. "I made our men gallop, and I have the enclosed for you," he wrote.[185] In a follow-up letter to Bishop—the third in five days—Roosevelt again looked over his shoulder. "I wish you could take part in some of my experiences here in dealing with the politicians . . . but thank Heaven I have no Parker here!"[186]

A thorough review of the *Evening Post* over the following sixty days reveals no article or editorial on the naval buildup. Were the fruits of Roosevelt's staff "gallop" inadequate for a story? Did Godkin kill Bishop's initiative out of concern that a pro-armament piece would undermine the paper's antiwar stance? Bishop's memoirs are silent, and the record remains otherwise blank. Also silent on the issue were two popular literary magazines of the era, *Scribner's Monthly* and the *Century*, for which Bishop often wrote. If Godkin refused to favor Roosevelt's naval initiative in his pages, why wasn't Bishop able to persuade another publication to run an approving story, which the assistant navy secretary was clearly anticipating?

A partial answer may lie in Bishop's preoccupation with the upcoming 1897 New York mayoral campaign. After all, politics were his editorial beat at the *Evening Post*. For the July 1897 issue of *Century*, Bishop did denounce the political process with an article headlined ARE THE BOSSES STRONGER THAN THE PEOPLE? Arguing that "boss government . . . is destructive of popular government," Bishop explained that "it concentrates in one man, as soon as it reaches perfection, all the powers of the State, executive, legislative and judicial, and this man is not chosen by the people for the position." The antidote he proposed was the "resumption of the duties of citizenship." the active participation of voters in the party nomination process and at the ballot box. "If we desire to have our public affairs managed in an honest and intelligent manner, we must take the trouble to bear our part in their management."[187]

The *Evening Post* notwithstanding, T. R. did take additional steps to win over public opinion. He befriended the young but already authoritative editor William Allen White, whose views at the *Emporia Gazette* in Kansas influenced much of the Midwest. As Edmund Morris observed, Roosevelt was determined "to teach him the gospel of expansionism" [188] so that White could advance the concept nationwide.

Secretary Long was not one to sweat out the tropical Washington summers at his desk even if peace were threatened. Satisfied that the Cuban issue was under control and that volatility in the Pacific had quieted with the annexation of the Hawaiian Islands, Long set out on a six-week-long vacation in New England. With the ever-efficient Roosevelt in Washington to keep an eye on Cuba and attend to routine navy business, Long felt comfortable taking a break.

With the secretary temporarily out of the way and his friend, the president, next door, T. R. saw his opening. He dusted off shelved naval readiness plans and, armed with the wisdom of Alfred Thayer Mahan, updated them in anticipation of coming events. His new strategy assumed a war with Spain to free Cuba, a blockade of the island, and a small landing force of army troops. In the Pacific, the Philippines would be assaulted as well.

Roosevelt repeated his justification for armed conflict often. "I abhor unjust war," he declared years later. "I abhor violence and bloodshed. . . . I advocate preparation for war in order to avert war."[189] Bishop offered a succinct rationale for Roosevelt's intervention in the Caribbean. "He was frankly, adamantly in favor of interference in Cuba on the grounds of Humanity."[190]

When the president unexpectedly invited Roosevelt on a carriage ride through Washington's Rock Creek Park, the latter took full advantage of the unfettered access. The imperial-looking president and the energetic assistant secretary talked over Roosevelt's plans to reenergize the navy—six new battleships, the same number of large cruisers, and seventy-five torpedo boats. The president seemed pleased. As their team clip-clopped its way through the city's favored leafy oasis, talked turned to the threat of war with Spain and to Roosevelt's stunning admission that he would go off to fight personally if and when war came.

Long returned to Washington in September rested and carefree, but soon discovered that his disinclination to support a naval buildup didn't matter much anymore. McKinley had embraced Roosevelt's guarantee that "the Department would be in the best possible shape that our means would permit when war began."[191] To ensure that his promise held, Roosevelt continually prodded Long to act. In a letter to the secretary, T. R. warned of the consequences "if we should drift into a war with Spain and suddenly find ourselves obliged to begin it without preparation. Certain things should be done at once."[192]

Roosevelt's maneuvering in Washington interested Bishop, but the campaign to occupy City Hall in New York absorbed the editor's efforts and attentions. The next mayor would preside over a vastly larger city. New York City as we know it today was being formed by uniting the independent cities of Manhattan, Brooklyn, Queens, the Bronx, and outlying areas. Bishop and Gockin viewed consolidation as premature for the city's well-being. According to *Evening Post* historian Allan Nevins, they believed that "if the separate governments of New York and Brooklyn were both corrupt, as they had been with few interruptions for a long generation, their union would simply present a harder problem for reformers, and fatter jobs and more boodle for the bosses."[193]

Tammany Hall had handpicked Robert Van Wyck, the chief justice of the City Court, as its mayoral candidate to run against reformer Seth Low, who had served with distinction as mayor of Brooklyn and president of Columbia University. Van Wyck not surprisingly won easily. Demoralized but never broken, the *Evening Post* declared, "Four years is a long time to wait, undoubtedly, for another attack on Tammany, but in those four years, Tammany will be furnishing us with plenty of ammunition."[194]

With frost threatening the air of Sagamore Hill, Edith Roosevelt journeyed to Washington to be with her husband. Now thirty-six, she was pregnant with their fifth child. The Roosevelts and most of the children settled into a comfortable, rented Georgetown home and made ready for the birth. Historian Kathleen Dalton recalled that "Edith went into labor unexpectedly in the middle of November, and their son Quentin was born on the nineteenth. Complications from childbirth and the flu laid her low, though she rallied briefly in December. During the early days of 1898, Edith's illness worsened."[195]

Her health continued to deteriorate against the backdrop of the Cuban crisis, and by early March she reluctantly underwent surgery to remove a large abscess from her groin. As spring came to the Potomac, though, she began to mend. Roosevelt was forthcoming about Edith's illness with close friends— including Bishop—and about his reluctance to leave his ailing wife if war with Spain demanded his immediate participation.

Early in 1898, rioting Spanish loyalists destroyed the Havana newspaper offices of Cuban sympathizers. President McKinley responded by dispatching the battleship *Maine* to Havana to protect American citizens and interests. But disaster loomed in the February darkness as the ship lay in the harbor, its crew of hundreds restless in their early sleep.

At 9:40 p.m. on February 15, a huge explosion tore through the ship. Detonated gunpowder destroyed the forward third of the vessel where most of the crew lay. The remains of the vessel quickly sank, becoming a graveyard for 268 American sailors. Speculation as to the cause, which has lasted more than a century, centered on the possibilities of a Spanish-laid mine, a Cuban instigation to war, a false-flag act of deliberate destruction by America meant to justify attack, and simply a horrible accident. "The *Maine* was sunk by an act of dirty treachery on the part of the Spaniards, I believe," said Roosevelt, "though we shall never find out definitely the cause, and officially it will go down as an accident."[196]

Reflecting the McKinley administration's reluctance to go to war with Spain, Secretary Long said he believed that the explosion had been an accident. But one New York newspaper agitated for war with a headline screaming REMEMBER THE MAINE—TO HELL WITH SPAIN! Pressure from Congress and queries from a more even-tempered public led to a formal Naval Court of Inquiry. It determined that an underwater mine had caused the explosion, though subsequent investigations found otherwise. Whatever the cause, Roosevelt felt that war was inevitable. "The revolt in Cuba had dragged its weary length until conditions on the island had become so dreadful as to be a standing disgrace to us for permitting them to exist."[197]

As *Evening Post* historian Allan Nevins put it, "[T]he explosion caused a wave of horror and indignation unparalleled since Fort Sumter." Observing that the chances were "enormously in favor of the theory that the blowing up of the *Maine* was due to an accident," the *Evening Post* asked its readers to suppose "if it were shown that she was destroyed by foul play . . . what would that prove—that we should instantly declare war with Spain?" The editors answered their own question, "By no means. It is simply inconceivable that the Spanish authorities in Cuba, high or low, could have countenanced any plot to destroy the *Maine*. Make them out as wicked as you please, they are not lunatics."[198]

The irrational yellow press intensified its war chant with each daily edition. One cartoon ridiculed President McKinley as a weak and vacillating woman in a bonnet and apron. It questioned whether his timidity would lead to public repudiation of the Republican Party in the next election. Godkin used the moment to slam his rivals as "a totally irresponsible force, without the restraint of conscience, science, law, or the police."[199] The president no doubt heard from Roosevelt who wrote to a friend at the time, "The blood of the murdered men of the *Maine* calls not only for indemnity but for the full measure of atonement which can only come by driving the Spaniard from the New World."[200]

As Secretary Long once again slipped out of his office—this time for a half-day of errands—he ordered his assistant secretary not to take "any step affecting the policy of the administration without consulting the president or me." Undeterred, Roosevelt cabled Commodore George Dewey to prepare his Hong Kong–based naval force, the Asiatic Squadron, for war. "Keep full of coal," he ordered. "In the event of declaration of war with Spain, your duty will be to see that the Spanish Squadron does not leave the Asiatic coast and then, offensive operations in the Philippine Islands."[201] Long was outraged when he returned to work to discover what Roosevelt had done—but he didn't rescind T. R.'s order. Of the incident, author Paul Grondahl concluded, "It was Roosevelt who sparked the Navy to war."[202]

McKinley brought the national suspense to a close on April 11 1898, when he sent Congress a call to war. Following a week's debate, Congress consented, declaring the people of Cuba free and independent, demanding Spain's surrender, and authorizing the president to engage the nation's land and naval forces. Spain quickly cut diplomatic ties with America, and the administration ordered a naval blockade of Cuba. On April 24, Spain declared war on the U.S.; a day later, the U.S. responded formally in kind. Once war had been declared, Nevins wrote, the *Evening Post* editorial page "rose with fighting enthusiasm.' Maybe so. But on balance, the paper opposed the war The editors believed that the Cubans' plight could be alleviated without direct conflict. In an illustrated magazine supplement marking the *Post's* centennial in 1901, Horace White—Godkin's successor—recalled that the paper believed "the government of Spain would concede everything that we demanded, even to a complete withdrawal from Cuba, if she were given a little time to reconcile her people to that policy."[203]

In its declaration of war, Congress authorized the raising of three national volunteer regiments to aid the fight. McKinley asked all able-bodied men of age to fight. But on two occasions, the president had asked Roosevelt directly not to sign on, pleading that he needed him next door to help direct the war. Roosevelt had, of course, previously informed McKinley of his desire to fight and was trying to find his way into uniform. Ultimately, Secretary of War Russell Alger offered him command of one of the national volunteer regiments. According to Bishop, Roosevelt declined, admitting that he was not yet ready to equip and lead a force into action. "He recommended for the command his friend Army surgeon Leonard Wood," Bishop wrote, "saying to the War Secretary that if he could appoint Wood colonel, he [Roosevelt] would accept the lieutenant colonelcy. This was done, and the famous regiment of Rough Riders was formed."[204]

Roosevelt was itching to fight. "He could not bear to sit out what might be the only war of his lifetime," Edmund Morris observed. Expressing President McKinley's "very great regret," Long accepted Roosevelt's resignation, concluding his fifty-four and a half tumultuous weeks as assistant secretary. "But now that you have determined to go to the front, I feel bound to say that while I do not approve of the change, I do most heartily appreciate the patriotism and the sincere fidelity to your convictions which actuate you."[205]

Roosevelt later disclosed a personal reason for going to war at age thirty-nine and leaving behind his large and growing family. "I had always felt if there were a serious war, I wished to be in a position to explain to my children why I did take part in it and why I did not take part in it."[206] No doubt Roosevelt still carried the unresolved guilt of his father's refusal to put on a uniform in the Civil War. Edith Roosevelt concluded that her husband's imminent departure "was the only honorable thing for a man with his views to do."[207]

Thirteen

A Hundred Great Days of Fighting

In May, Roosevelt had left Washington with orders to report to San Antonio, Texas, where his band of cowboy brothers had assembled and received hasty training. Few of the 1st U.S. Volunteer Cavalry needed instruction in horsemanship or marksmanship. These men were cowhands, hunters, lawmen, prospectors, and even some Native Americans from the Southwest Oklahoma, and Indian territories. The army had given priority to "young, sound, good shots and good riders," men who could prevail in Cuba's oppressive jungle climate.

The Rough Riders were already famous. The nation had followed their movements in the war-obsessed papers and embraced their colorful uniforms and apt moniker. The name was not new; Buffalo Bill's Wild West and Congress of Rough Riders of the World was hugely popular at the time, and, as Bishop later observed of Roosevelt's men, "under that picturesque title, they passed through the war and into history."[208]

"There never was a regiment better worth bragging about than ours," T. R. declared. "They had a fighting edge, the cool and resolute fighting temper."[209] But Roosevelt had served only three years in the New York National Guard. Bishop's *Evening Post* worried:

> *Organized but four weeks, barely given their full complement of officers and only a week of regular drill, these men have been sent to the front before they have learned the first elements of soldiering and discipline . . . they have been sent with only their carbines and revolvers to meet an enemy armed with long-range rifles . . . there have been few cases of such military cruelty in our military annals.*[210]

Ready or not, the Rough Riders left San Antonio by train for Tampa. "For four sweltering days, seven trains chugged eastward, spewing a trail of cinders, vomit, and manure across the face of the Old Confederacy," Edmund Morris observed.[211] While his troops waited impatiently in Tampa for embarkation to Cuba, Roosevelt received permission to spend his nights with Edith, who had hurried south to join her husband. Colonel Wood gave his deputy permission to stay at the plush, turreted Tampa Bay Hotel with his wife, "as long as he arose at four and got to the camp ten miles away to drill with his men."[212]

Tampa whirled with confusion. The early-June humidity was intense; the flies and gnats seemed to be in charge. Trainloads of uniformed men along with their horses and weapons occupied miles of track, waiting with impatience for the signal to go. The war against Spain had officially begun, but the Rough Riders' departure for Cuba had stalled. Some 1,060 newly-trained recruits and 1,258 of their mounts, all under the command of Colonel Leonard Wood and Lieutenant Colonel Theodore Roosevelt, had to make do with meager supplies and endless boredom. The army regulars who waited beside them eased the monotony by ceaselessly cleaning their weapons around smoky campfires, day and night.

During these seemingly endless days, Roosevelt kept in touch with his children. From Tampa he wrote:

Blessed Bunnies,

It has been a real holiday to have darling mother here. Yesterday, I brought her out to the camp, and she saw it all: the men drilling, the tents in long company streets, the horses being taken to water, my little horse, Texas, the colonel and the majors, and finally the mountain lion and the jolly little dog, Cuba, who had several fights as she looked on. The mountain lion is not much more than a kitten as yet but it is still very cross and treacherous.[213]

That poignant note became the first of hundreds included in *Theodore Roosevelt's Letters to His Children*, which Bishop edited for publication in 1919, the year Roosevelt died. "Whenever he was separated from them . . . he sent them these messages of constant thought and love," Bishop wrote in the book's introduction, "for they were never for a moment out of his mind and heart."[214]

After waiting days for army commanders to organize the troop transport, T. R. had had enough. With help from his bullish men, he seized an empty coal train, loaded his troops, and pushed on the nine miles to the Tampa wharf without most of the regiment's horses. A shortage of vessels for the sail to Cuba meant that only senior officers could take their mounts. Worse still, Roosevelt learned that there was enough room on board for only three quarters of the Rough Riders. The others had to stay behind.

The chaos of the Tampa camp repeated itself waterside as thousands of troops and tons of provisions competed for space on too few transports. Roosevelt, with assistance from Colonel Wood this time, commandeered haulage for his men. Along with thirty other vessels, the steamer *Yucatán* was held in port for another six sweltering days while generals and admirals sorted out a reported enemy threat on the high seas. Finally, on June 14, a twenty-five-mile flotilla of ships full of warriors hell-bent for action left the port. They steamed slowly for Daiquiri, east of Santiago, on Cuba's southeast coast.

Roosevelt faced the wet sea breeze from the bridge of the *Yucatán*, attired in the Rough Rider uniform of blue flannel shirt, brown khaki trousers, leggings, and boots. A damp, blue polka-dot handkerchief drooped casually around his neck, and a slouch hat—with insignia bearing crossed sabers and the numeral "1"—topped his head. Sewn carefully inside his hat were extra pairs of spectacles so he could be sure to see who was shooting at him in the combat that lay ahead, more dangerous by far than boxing C. S. Hanks at Harvard so many years before.

Richard Harding Davis in time became an honored celebrity. In June 1898, the dashing adventurer and popular novelist, on assignment for the *New York Herald,* was covering the Spanish-American War from the front. Harnessing the media as usual, Roosevelt sought out journalists to record the war story and keep his name in print. A personal favorite of the lieutenant colonel, Davis had mixed well with him and the rest of the officers at the Tampa Bay Hotel, and Roosevelt had an acute sense that Davis would popularize the legend of the Rough Riders.

As the American flotilla cautiously approached Daiquiri on June 22, Cuban *insurrectos* emerged to guide the *Yucatán*'s landing. Some men and horses were lost in the chaos, but all in all, it was a straightforward maneuver; not an enemy shot was fired. "It was one of the most weird and remarkable scenes of the war, probably of any war," Davis wrote. "An army was being landed on an enemy's coast at the dead of night, but with the same cheers and shrieks and laughter that rise from the bathers at Coney Island on a hot Sunday."[215]

The next day, the landing force braved a downpour, marching west along the coast to Siboney, where they paused to dry out around sizzling campfires. All the talk was of meeting the Spanish at Santiago. Shortly after dawn, the

Rough Riders climbed a ridge trail that led to the Camino Real—the road to Santiago. "It was a mountainous country, covered with thick jungle, a most confusing country,"[216] Roosevelt remembered. A significant impediment lay ahead. The *insurrectos* had forwarded intelligence that the enemy was entrenched at Las Guasimas, a convergence of two trails in thick jungle three miles up the road. When the American generals ordered an attack, the regulars and cavalry opened fire on the Spanish hidden on ridges and in jungle cover. "Colonel Wood, to the right, and Lieutenant Colonel Roosevelt, to the left, led a charge which turned the tide of battle and sent the enemy flying over the hills toward Santiago," the *Tarrytown Argus* later reported.[217] Roosevelt recalled that bullets flew over his head, "making a sound like the ripping of a silk dress, with sometimes a kind of pop."[218]

In a letter to his sister Corinne from Las Guasimas, Roosevelt summarized the skirmish. "The fire was very hot at one or two points where the men around me went down like ninepins. We struck the Spanish and had a brisk fight for 2½ hours before we drove them out of their position. We lost a dozen men, killed or mortally wounded, and 60 severely or slightly wounded. . . . [I]t was a good fight. I am in good health."[219]

With pencil and pad in hand and weapon at the ready, Davis surveyed the action. After spotting the enemy with his field glasses and advising Wood and Roosevelt of its position, Davis found himself at the center of a heartbreaking episode.

Fifty yards farther on, around a turn in the trail, behind a rock, a boy was lying with a bullet wound between his eyes. His chest was heaving with short, hoarse noises which I guessed were due to some muscular action entirely, and that he was virtually dead. I lifted him and gave him some water, but it would not pass through his fixed teeth. In the pocket of his blouse was a New Testament with the name "Fielder Dawson, Mo." scribbled in it in pencil. While I was writing it down for identification, a boy as young as himself came from behind me down the trail.

"It is no use," he said; "the surgeon has seen him; he says he is just the same as dead. He is my bunkie; we only met two weeks ago at San Antonio; but he and me had got to be such good friends—but there's nothing I can do now."

He threw himself down on the rock beside his bunkie, who was still breathing with that hoarse, inhuman rattle, and I left them, the one who had been spared looking down helplessly with the tears creeping across his cheeks.[220]

Accounts that maintained vital congressional support for the war. President McKinley also understood that the press was an ideal tool with which to mold public opinion, and his subsequent management of war news laid the foundation for Roosevelt's symphonic play of the press in the years that followed. Stephen Ponder has observed that McKinley was the first president to centralize the flow of press information from the Executive Mansion. "A 'war room' with maps and 20 telegraph lines was installed adjacent to the president's office," Ponder noted. "Relocated and expanded press facilities made it more convenient for reporters to talk with the president or his secretaries."[221] Fleet headquarters at Key West, Florida, tried to impose military censorship on war news, but aggressive reporters on assignment in Cuba were not to be denied their story.

The sensationalist *New York World* and the *New York Journal* dispatched war reporters to Cuba, as did the *New York Sun* and Davis's *Herald*. Before hostilities broke out, William Randolph Hearst's *Journal* sent artist Frederic Remington to Havana to add a visual dimension to the story. According to legend, Remington telegraphed his chief, "Everything is quiet. There is no trouble here. There will be no war. I wish to return." Hearst is said to have wired back immediately: "Please remain. You furnish the pictures, and I'll furnish the war."[222]

Ever cautious about being misrepresented or misquoted, Roosevelt carefully managed his reputation through favorable press coverage of his heroism in Cuba. When he was assistant secretary of the navy, Roosevelt was falsely quoted by the *Journal* in a front-page story: "It is cheering to find a newspaper of the great influence and circulation of the *Journal* tell the facts as they exist, and ignore the suggestions of various kinds that emanate from sources that cannot be described as patriotic or loyal to the flag of this country," the paper quoted him as saying. Roosevelt was furious. The next day, he denounced the report as "false, fictitious, and fraudulent from the first word to the last," adding, "I have never given a certificate of character to the *Journal*."[223]

Godkin's *Evening Post* got a team of reporters into Cuba, mainly to burrow in with the *insurrectos*. The best remembered of the lot was E. G. Bellairs, who penetrated the island on a blockade runner from the Bahamas. His adventures among the Cuban freedom fighters won acclaim from editors and readers, but his career soon fizzled when it surfaced that he had used an alias to disguise a criminal past, and he was fired. The paper maintained its editorial opposition to the war, believing that differences with Spain and the plight of the Cubans could be resolved without military confrontation. But it was too late for pacifist pleading. The U.S. war machine was rolling. As June turned into July, the Battle of San Juan Heights lay just ahead for Roosevelt and the Rough Riders.

Control of the outpost at Las Guasimas was the first step in taking Santiago, where more than 5,000 Spanish regulars stood guard. After the fighting had cooled there, the Americans lingered at Las Guasimas for eight frightful days, fending off the debilitating effects of fever and burying their dead. Only when the men were partially resupplied did the order come to go forward. Rough Riders and regulars trooped the eight miles along the Santiago road toward the next obstacle: San Juan Heights. There, two steep and grassy hills divided by a river valley overlooked the city. On the left was Kettle Hill, so named by the men of the forward units because of the abandoned cauldrons, used in the sugar-making process, that dotted the landscape. In all, about a thousand Spaniards held positions in the Heights. The Americans wondered whether the Spanish would stand and fight for territory that was not their homeland.

Because of the losses incurred at Las Guasimas, Colonel Wood took command of a cavalry brigade of regulars, leaving Roosevelt in sole charge of the Rough Riders with the new rank of colonel. The battle plan called for the regulars to lead the fight for Kettle Hill; the Rough Riders would join midbattle. As artillery teams softened the Spanish, the Rough Riders and regulars made their way stealthily along the San Juan River, ducking into the tall grass along the riverbanks to avoid sniper fire and returning shots when they could. "I had not enjoyed the Guasimas fight at all," T. R. later wrote, "because I had been so uncertain as to what I ought to do. But the San Juan fight was entirely different."[224]

Richard Harding Davis told his readers of the events that propelled Roosevelt into glory. "Colonel Roosevelt, on horseback, broke from the woods behind the line of the Ninth [Regiment] and finding its men lying in the way, shouted, 'If you don't wish to go forward, let my men pass.'"[225] Responding to an order to rush the hill, the regulars jumped into line with the Rough Riders and charged. "I waved my hat, and we went up the hill with a rush," Roosevelt recalled.[226] Against a retreating enemy—stunningly incapable of an effective counterattack—Kettle Hill fell in twenty minutes.

Later, on neighboring San Juan Hill, "the wolf rose again in Roosevelt's heart,"[227] Edmund Morris wrote. The troops sprang into battle. "Again, Roosevelt pounded over lower ground under heavy fire," Morris wrote, "again he surged up grassy slopes, and again he saw the Spaniards deserting their high fortifications."[228] Roosevelt's audacity and courage moved the forces on San Juan Hill. Had it been another leader with less charisma and spunk, the order to charge may not have been given, and the cavalry may not have had the same enthusiasm in their charge uphill.[229]

San Juan Hill fell in about an hour at the cost of eighty-nine Rough Rider lives and hundreds of casualties among the regulars. "There was some close fighting, and we took a few prisoners," Roosevelt allowed. "We also captured the Spanish provisions and ate them that night with great relish."[230]

The struggle for Santiago de Cuba contrasted dramatically with the events on San Juan Heights. Attention turned to the city's harbor, where a fleet of Spanish cruisers lay in waiting, their men alarmed by events taking place in the hills above. When the ships tried to run an American blockade, the navy opened fire and within hours routed the Spanish. A dignified surrender was arranged days later, and on July 17 the curtain began to descend on Spain's centuries-old colonial domination of Cuba. By mid-August, the victor and the conquered had signed an armistice, and America assumed control not only of Cuba but also of the Philippines in the Pacific.

John Hay had observed T. R.'s warring days from the splendor and comfort of his ambassador's residence in London. "Dear Roosevelt," he began. "I am afraid I am the last of your friends to congratulate you on a brilliant campaign . . . you obeyed your own daemon. You have written your name on several pages of your country's history . . it has been a splendid little war."[231]

For his part, Roosevelt measured his battlefront experience through the prism he knew best: public service. "I would rather have led that charge . . . than served three terms in the Senate," he proclaimed.[232] "In the Cuban fighting . . . my business was to be where I could keep utmost command over the regiment and, in a rough-and-tumble, scrambling fight in the thick jungle . . . it usually meant I had to be at the front."[233] Despite dreadful losses and suffering that his men had endured, he had moved further into the vanguard of the nation's consciousness because of the press's worshipful coverage of his deeds. When Davis died in 1916, Roosevelt wrote a selfless tribute in appreciation of his friend. "He was as good an American as ever lived. He so won the esteem and regard of the regiment . . . we gave him the same medal as worn by our own members."[234] Richard Harding Davis had become an honorary Rough Rider.

Despite the peace, the Rough Riders languished in Cuba, short of food and reeling from "Cuban fever." The disorganization that had frustrated them on arrival in Tampa was now stifling their return home. The mismanagement of men and supplies so angered Roosevelt that he wrote public letters of protest that newspapers gleefully published. Of his fate in battle, he wrote that he was sorry he had not been severely wounded in Cuba, but nonetheless acknowledged to Henry Cabot Lodge: "I feel that I have done something which enables me to leave a name to the children of which they can be rightly proud."[235]

Sensing an immediate political opening for Roosevelt, Senator Lodge was making the rounds of New York Republican leaders, pitching the war hero as the evident choice for governor. The convention and election, he reminded them, was just weeks away, and there was little appetite for more time under the leadership of Republican incumbent Frank Black. On such matters, the only opinion in New York that mattered was that of U.S. Senator Thomas Platt, party boss. Platt understood, despite deep reservations about the independent-minded Roosevelt, how effortless it would be to turn Roosevelt headlines into Republican votes. But first the Rough Rider had to get home.

Colonel Roosevelt's public reprimand of the army's disorganization certainly angered the brass in Washington, but it achieved the intended result. On August 8, the Rough Riders steamed out of Santiago, bound for a month of quarantine and rest at Montauk Point, New York, the easternmost point of Long Island, a hundred miles from Oyster Bay. There, cooled by breezes off Long Island Sound and the Atlantic, Roosevelt's men not only regained their health, but they also enjoyed an unexpected reunion with the four companies of Rough Riders left behind in Tampa.

In the days before the regiment disbanded, Roosevelt offered his men "a short sermon" about the future, perhaps with himself in mind. Standing before them, ramrod straight but tempered by his trademark neck scarf and slouch hat, T. R. noted "how proud [he] was of them, but warned them not to think that they could go back and rest on their laurels, bidding them to remember that for ten days or so, the world would be willing to treat them as heroes, yet after that time they would find that they had to get down to hard work just like everyone else."[236]

To reward their colonel for his bravery and leadership, the Rough Riders pooled their funds and presented Roosevelt with a bronze of Remington's stirring *Bronco Buster,* which today occupies an honored space at Sagamore Hill.

Colonel Theodore Roosevelt at Camp Wikoff, New York, following his return from the Spanish-American War. *Theodore Roosevelt Collection, Harvard College Library (Roosevelt R 6C.3.EL61-132)*

"Afterward, they all filed past, and I shook the hand of each to say good-bye," Roosevelt remembered.[237]

By September 15, 1898, the Rough Riders had relinquished their weapons and horses and bid their colleagues a reluctant farewell. They had shared a lifetime of noble achievements in a hundred momentous days. Their camaraderie in battle and sterling victory had placed the nation, intentionally or not, on the world stage. The regiment disbanded, its work done and legacy secured.

The transition to civilian life for many of the Western cowboys proved difficult, as their colonel had foreseen. For many, physical and mental wounds precluded a quick return to profitable work, and private funds had to be raised for their welfare. Many celebratory reunions followed down through the years, some with Roosevelt in attendance. Jesse Langdon of North Dakota—who had enlisted in San Antonio at age sixteen and attended the final reunion—died in 1975, at the age of ninety-four. The last of the Rough Riders, he had outlived the colonel by more than half a century.

Fourteen

Of Party and State

U.S. Senator Thomas Collier Platt, the "Easy Boss" of New York Republicans, waited impatiently in his Fifth Avenue Hotel suite. With a scruffy white beard, side whiskers, and a glossy scalp, he was still, at sixty-five, the undisputed master of party politics and kingmaker of New York State. Platt was eager to crown Colonel Roosevelt—if only he would show up for their appointment.

The offer had materialized a few days earlier on Montauk Point when a Platt lieutenant, Congressman Lemuel Quigg, arrived among the disassembling troops to ask Roosevelt whether he would accept the governorship if the party nomination could be arranged. Quigg's report: "Like a crack from a rifle, the gallant colonel came back with, 'Would I? I would be delighted!'"[238]

The deal was sealed when Platt and Roosevelt eventually sized up each other, face-to-face, at Platt's hotel. "He made no pretense that he liked me personally," Roosevelt later wrote. "But he deferred to the judgment of those who insisted that I was the only man who could be elected."[239] In fact, Platt took caution not only because he disapproved of the recent war and Roosevelt's starring role in it, but also because he wasn't certain Roosevelt as governor would defer to him. T. R. assured Platt that he would consult with him and other party titans on legislation and appointments, but repeated what he had said to Quigg: "I should have to act finally as my own conscience and judgment dictated."[240]

A streetcar's ride downtown at the *Evening Post,* Joseph Bucklin Bishop was feeling professionally stale. Now fifty-one, he had worked for Edwin Godkin for a decade and a half. His years there had had an ineradicable influence on the politics of the city and state, true. His marriage to Harriet had passed the quarter-century mark; daughter Alice was twenty-two, and showing every sign of becoming a spinster; son Hartwell was off to Harvard with a law career in mind; and twelve-year-old Farnham was demonstrating a family talent for writing.

Thomas Collier Platt (ca. 1865-1880) before he became Republican Party boss of New York State and nemesis of Governor Theodore Roosevelt. Photo by Mathew Brady and Levin Corbin Handy.

Library of Congress Prints and Photographs Division

Bishop's contact with Roosevelt, forged in the police commission era, had waned during the colonel's adventuresome days in Cuba, yet his admiration for T. R.'s character and heroics made him long to resume their regular talks and letters. Adding to Bishop's restlessness was Godkin's decline in health; the great editor was often absent from the paper's once-stimulating daily editorial conferences. New and abrasive figures were gaining influence in the newsroom and in editorial columns. But the paper's increasingly hands-off international stance, in contradiction to what Roosevelt was saying and doing, made Bishop's days restless and uncertain.

The *Post* had consistently opposed the war and its cost to the American treasury, and the paper disdained the rabble-rousing yellow journalists for generating public passion for the fight. Now, late in the summer of 1898, it concluded that the whole enterprise was "criminally unnecessary." *Evening Post* editorials, some of which Bishop wrote with pursed lips against his instincts and beliefs, opposed the annexation of Cuba and the Philippines. Others alleged "indisputable evidence that the European virus of imperialism, economic and political, had entered America's veins."[241] Eventually the paper refused to support Roosevelt for governor, reasoning that the national fallout from his bold, imperialist bent would be worse than short-term Tammany-led activities under the Democrats.

Within a week of his overwhelming nomination for governor on September 27, 1898, Roosevelt dived back into the high-energy campaign mode he had honed in races for the state assembly and the New York mayoralty. He spared his Democratic opponent, New York Supreme Court judge Augustus Van Wyck, much of his attention and chose instead to condemn his opponent's Tammany bosses. Roosevelt played on his status as a worshipped cult hero, usually appearing alongside one or more of his colorful Rough Rider pals. Stumping tirelessly from the backs of steam trains up and down the Hudson and across the Adirondacks, the perpetually hat-waving candidate seized the raw patriotic fervor of voters and gave voice to progressive causes supported by unionized working men. "By the sheer force of personality, he drew crowds of 20,000 and more. Voters saw him as sincerity six feet high"—even though he was, in fact, just five feet eight inches tall," historian Kathleen Dalton observed.[242]

On Election Day, the well-greased New York Democratic machine turned out a surprisingly strong vote for Van Wyck. But Roosevelt prevailed, edging his way to the statehouse by 49 to 48 percent on a plurality of about 8,000 votes out of 1.35 million cast. "I have always maintained that no man besides Roosevelt could have accomplished that feat in 1898," Senator Platt wrote in his memoirs.[243] Back at Sagamore Hill, Edith and the children had a reserved celebration; they were apprehensive about their future and the dreaded move to the "dismal old" governor's mansion in Albany.

Roosevelt had been governor of New York barely seventy-two hours when he resumed an exchange of letters with Bishop, the keen analyst of New York politics. T. R. recognized at the outset of his term that he should rely on the wily editorial writer for counsel. But beyond the written word, a wondrous new means of communication was now available in the governor's mansion, and Bishop was

Roosevelt and family at Sagamore Hill (1903). Back L-R: Ted, Alice, Kermit, and Ethel. Front L-R: Quentin, the colonel, Archie, and Edith Kermit Roosevelt.

Pach Bros. Theodore Roosevelt Collection, Harvard College Library (Roosevelt R500.P69a-086)

quick to recognize its benefit: "That is a good idea about talking over the telephone," Roosevelt wrote to Bishop, "and I will take advantage of it."[244]

Inauguration Day in Albany, or January 2, 1899, would be recalled for years as the bitterest of frigid days. But not even below-zero temperatures dissuaded crowds from clogging the sidewalks to welcome Roosevelt to the hulking new state capitol building on the city's great hill. Doffing his silk topper, the forty-year-old governor marched with a wide smile and flashing teeth among the parade of war veterans, whipping flags, and brass bands whose instruments the cold had silenced.

Edith and the children made an amazingly swift adjustment from the comforts of Sagamore Hill, buoyed by an end to the long New York–Washington commutes. Edith did wince, however, when T. R. had wrestling mats laid down at the mansion so he could resume a bit of the strenuous life he had enjoyed while in uniform. The mansion also "made a good home for the raccoon, possum, guinea pigs, rabbits and squirrels they [the children] kept as pets, a fine arrangement until the stench wafted up to disturb Edith's guests in the parlor above."[245]

Roosevelt came to office when the tyrannical boss system of party politics was at its pinnacle in America's big cities—despite all the reforms enacted over the preceding decades. Bishop knew that Senator Platt ruled New York. "He dictated all appointments, including those for the bench, and exercised all the powers of the Legislature. Under the guise of campaign contributions he collected vast sums from the corporations, and these he used to defray the election expenses of candidates for the Legislature."[246] But in his inaugural address Roosevelt took another view, observing that "[t]he usefulness of a party is strictly limited by its usefulness to the state, and, in the long run, he serves his party best who helps to make it instantly responsive to every need of the people."[247]

The inevitable clash between Governor Roosevelt and Senator Platt came over the appointment of a state director of public works. The previous office holder had been caught up in scandal over construction of the Erie Canal, and Roosevelt saw an immediate opportunity to reverse the state's culture of corruption with a choice nominee. But Platt preempted the governor by presenting his candidate, Francis Hendricks of Syracuse, along with a presumptuous telegram from Hendricks saying that he was very pleased to accept the job. Roosevelt fumed, and the predictable explosion followed. "I am at my wits' end in my endeavor to get the best men to serve with me," Roosevelt said gloomily in a letter to Bishop. "It will be a sheer impossibility for me to get the best results if I cannot get really first-class men to take the biggest places."[248]

Roosevelt confronted Platt directly but respectfully, saying that he was sorry but he could not give the appointment to Hendricks. "I declined to lose my temper, merely repeating that I must decline to accept any man chosen for me, and that I must choose the man myself."[249] Stung by the governor's blunt determination, Platt unexpectedly withdrew the nomination. Roosevelt understood that he had to work with Platt over the long term, however, so he devised a way for both of them to save face. He offered Platt a short list of four acceptable substitutes and urged him to select one. The compromise candidate was Colonel John Nelson Partridge, an eminent engineer and Civil War veteran. In the same letter to Bishop, Roosevelt declared that he and Senator Platt had found the right nominee. Partridge struck him "as a thoroughly upright man, who cannot be swayed by any improper consideration whatever, no matter whether it be fear or self-interest."[250]

The governor chose a low-key approach when it came to keeping his pledge to Platt. The two met frequently for breakfast, usually on Sundays in New York City, a neutral site between Albany and Washington. There was nothing secret about their summits; on the contrary, Roosevelt wanted the public to know that he was trying to get Platt to come around on important matters. "No impartial person can examine the records of the Roosevelt Administration at Albany and not reach the conclusion that in all matters of serious controversy with Platt— at these breakfasts and elsewhere—Roosevelt came out the victor," Bishop observed.[251] Taking the long view in his later years, Platt concurred: "Roosevelt from the first agreed that he would consult me on all questions of appointments, legislative or party policy. He religiously fulfilled this pledge, although he frequently did what he pleased."[252]

Owen Wister, the Western fiction writer and close friend of Roosevelt, observed with tongue in cheek that "[t]hose Sunday morning breakfasts . . . have disturbed Mr. Platt's digestion even more seriously than they have scandalized the parlor pets of Virtue."[253] Chief among those pets, in Wister's view, was Godkin's editorial page, which condemned the governor's get-togethers as "breaking bread with the Devil."

Whether Bishop ever found himself pressured into writing anti-Roosevelt opinions for the *Evening Post*, he certainly never volunteered for the assignment. It is likely, however, that he stepped up to excoriate Platt whenever the chance presented itself. On the Boss's election to the U.S. Senate in 1897, the paper called him "probably the most despised in the community . . . who has neither character nor intelligence fit for legislative purposes." It went even further, denouncing the legislature for choosing a man "popularly believed to be most of his time engaged in bribery and corruption."[254]

Although he learned to work with Platt, Roosevelt was troubled by the public's perception of his association with someone of dastardly repute. Writing confidentially to Bishop about six weeks into his term, Roosevelt admitted, "I really very much want to see you, just to tell you a little how things are going."[255] We can never know whether the rookie governor wanted to influence the *Evening Post*'s disapproving view of his administration or whether he just needed a friend with whom to talk.

Despite their deepening friendship, Roosevelt and Bishop clashed over another of the governor's early priorities: statewide police reform. While commissioner, T. R. had put an end to police patronage in New York City; now he wanted to effect the same change in the state's other large cities. The plan was deceptively straightforward. The Republican governor angled for legislative authority to appoint a statewide police czar and other officials for New York, Albany, Troy,

Syracuse, Rochester, and Buffalo. He would dissolve local police boards and make police appointments under civil service rules without political interference.

An *Evening Post* statehouse correspondent predicted early on that the scheme would not "go down," and that it would result in little more than a fight for party advantage. All the affected cities had Democratic administrations, and they stood to lose massive patronage plums. Roosevelt took a more high-minded view, arguing that the bill's intent was to produce a first-class administration of police affairs. It would "also prevent politicians and political associations from exercising influence directly or indirectly on the career of a policeman, either to his damage or benefit," he argued.[256]

In a surprising editorial rebuke, Bishop rejected the idea as "undesirable" and characterized the governor's approval of it as "incomprehensible." He explained to *Evening Post* readers that the bill "takes away from every large city in the state the right to control its own affairs and lodges them in the hands of a state official appointed by the Governor." Bishop asked, "Why maintain a pretense of self-government in our cities? Why not turn them entirely over to the state to be ruled?"[257]

The day the editorial appeared, Roosevelt hurriedly dictated a three-page letter. "My dear Bishop . . . I am exceedingly sorry that you feel as you do about it. I do not believe that the bill will pass because Tammany will fight it with every resource of corruption at its disposal." He clarified that he did not want the new police commissioners to be "tools of the Republican Party," and that he was only making "a genuine and honest effort to get them [the police] absolutely out of politics." Later in the letter, Roosevelt addressed his friend's integrity. "I shall not try to convert you to my way of looking at this, for I know you won't be converted *except by your own judgment* [emphasis original]; but I do most earnestly ask you to exercise that judgment, to look at the bill with the utmost care."[258]

Bishop remained unmoved. In a follow-up editorial three days later, he argued that it was "preposterous" to jam the bill through the legislature without hearings and with only two weeks left in the session. It looked to him, he said, like "the usual Platt method." Moreover, Bishop contended, "An enormous state force would be created, directed absolutely from Albany and capable, in the hands of a partisan governor, of being converted into a tremendous political machine." But in a bow to his friend in Albany, Bishop added, "Nobody doubts that Governor Roosevelt would use this power to make this force nonpartisan and efficient, but we shall not have him for Governor always."[259]

Again Roosevelt swiftly responded: "I value you too much to go into recrimination. . . . [T]he police force is a semi-military organization. There is no more reason in abstract right for putting it under the City than for putting the National Guard under the City." He added a scold: "It is characteristic of the Goo Goos"—a derogatory term for government reformers—"but it is not worthy of you to make such a question one of morals."[260]

The next day, Roosevelt tried the Platt approach on Bishop, allowing that letters were inadequate to make his case. "Yes, writing is unsatisfactory, and if you cannot come here [to Albany], I will get you to dine or lunch with me the first time I get down [to New York] after the legislature adjourns," T. R. resolved. "Then I will explain to you the merits of the police bill if it passes, and you shall explain to me its demerits if it fails."[261]

The newspaper did not relax its opposition to the police bill, repeating a few days later that Roosevelt's term was only two years. "This bill puts it in the power of every Governor to change the politics of the proposed Police Department to suit himself. A Democratic Governor would give us a Democratic State police, and a Republican Governor would give us a Republican State police."[262]

The following day, Republican support for the bill rapidly eroded as T. R. signaled his opposition to proposed exemptions for certain of the big cities. With Tammany-led Democrats united in opposition and the affected cities crying foul, the idea sank. "Governor Roosevelt does not seem to mourn the death of the scheme," an *Evening Post* reporter observed in a dispatch from Albany. "In fact, he appears to be relieved. The general opinion in Albany is that there will be no more police legislation at this session of the Legislature."[263]

Bishop's editorials in the *Evening Post* didn't kill the police bill, although they may have accelerated its demise. What the exchange of resolute opinions and hurried letters of mid-April 1899 does suggest, however, is that Joseph Bucklin Bishop did not always do Theodore Roosevelt's bidding reflexively as some historians have suggested. Roosevelt had conceded that Bishop's judgment would rule in matters of disagreement, and in this case it clearly did. Tellingly, perhaps, the letter archives of the Library of Congress contain no further Roosevelt-Bishop correspondence for the rest of 1899.

From his earliest days as a state assemblyman, Roosevelt astutely recognized the power of newspapers and magazines. He understood fully how their stories and opinions swayed public attitudes and made or broke political careers. By making real news in whatever office he held, he captured press and public attention, and, by cozying up to reporters and editors such as Bishop, he further advanced his public record and tapped into sources of political intelligence.

While governor, he called correspondents into his office twice daily and gave them the Roosevelt spin on policies and proposals. Journalists welcomed the frequent audiences; they marveled at his astonishing intelligence, outsized personality, and unquestioned integrity. He made great copy no matter what he did or said. If he felt a reporter was not treating him fairly, Roosevelt unhesitatingly called or wrote to the man's editor. Once, he complained to the *New York Times* that its statehouse reporter was a Tammany Hall tool and had been "persistently, consistently, throughout the winter, perverting the news to discredit me."[264] Around the same time, through Bishop, Roosevelt also advised the *Evening Post*: "I was told you might employ Murlin of the *Tribune* as a correspondent up here. My experience with him has been that he is a tricky and unsafe man."[265]

Roosevelt's term as governor both instigated and characterized the Progressive Era, a time when various bodies began identifying and addressing domestic economic and social ills. Much of the push for this age of reform came from disparate groups such as labor unions and individual crusaders like journalist Jacob Riis. The Progressive Party had not yet taken shape, but the movement was forming, and T. R. had been agitating for those principles for years. The man whose father had protected vagrant New York City newsboys, the assemblyman who had pushed for civil service reform, and the commissioner who had fought corruption in city police ranks was determined to bring meaningful change to life in New York on multiple fronts.

During the first eighteen months of his gubernatorial term—before the vice presidential prospect diverted his attention—Roosevelt pushed for a unified, statewide code of civil service laws to rid public service of most of its patronage. He extended the eight-hour workday and minimum wage to all state employees. He cleaned up oppressive sweatshops and regulated the use of tenement housing for garment assembly. He took the first tentative steps toward enacting women's suffrage, supporting the election of women to school boards—although not yet to statewide office.

It was, however, in the preservationist movement that Roosevelt left his most significant mark on New York State. At the urging of a friend, forester Gifford Pinchot, Governor Roosevelt brought conservation ethics to state policy. The protection and preservation of natural resources came organically to the child naturalist and Badlands cattle rancher. "Unrestrained greed means the ruin of the great woods and the drying up of the sources of the rivers," Roosevelt explained to the state's conservation commission.[266] By the time he left the governor's office in late 1900, the Roosevelt administration had conserved vast forests in the Adirondacks, established state parks in the Catskills and elsewhere, and helped protect Palisades Park along the Hudson

It must have been difficult for the lifelong gamesman in him to admit, but Roosevelt wrote at the time, "The people of the forest regions are themselves growing more and more to realize the necessity of preserving both the trees and the game.... A live deer in the woods will attract to the neighborhood ten times what could be obtained from the deer's dead carcass." He clearly understood the delicate balance of competing ecosystems.

The boldest achievement of Roosevelt's inaugural year as governor was tax reform: an initiative to tax the licenses—or franchises—of corporations that provided state-sanctioned public services. New York City's hugely profitable street railways, bridge, and tunnel companies returned no revenue to the state; rather, the grateful organizations kicked back bribes and other cash gifts to legislators and their political parties. It was a rich source of largesse for Tammany and Platt's organization. Governor Roosevelt felt that "it was a matter of plain decency and honesty that these companies should pay a tax on their franchises,"[267] and he backed legislation to accomplish just that. Predictably, Platt was outraged. He implored the governor to kill the bill by detouring it to a study committee. Roosevelt, Platt remembered, "clenched his fists and gritted his teeth."[268]

Bishop observed afterward that "the bill aimed a deadly blow at the very center of the Big Boss and Big Business combination." If it were to become law, he said, "no corporation would buy protection in [the] future because of uncertainty that the goods would be delivered."[269]

The state Senate went along with the franchise tax, knowing that Platt and Tammany would defeat it later in the Assembly. Roosevelt met the challenge by sending the lower chamber an emergency message, thereby advancing it to immediate consideration. Fred Nixon, the Platt-controlled Assembly speaker, defiantly tore up the message. When the governor learned what had happened, he immediately sent a second emergency note threatening to appear before the Assembly in person to demand its passage if it were ignored. The gambit worked. Opposition to the bill collapsed, and the Assembly approved the franchise tax bill by a comfortable margin.

The franchise tax saga continued for another six years, though as a special legislative session convened to consider a rewrite, and the affected corporations mounted multiple court challenges. In May 1905, long after Roosevelt had left Albany, the U.S. Supreme Court ruled unanimously that the law was constitutional. Corporations grudgingly paid $26 million in back taxes and interest to the State of New York.

But the tax brawl of 1899 had subverted Platt one too many times. Not only was the governor unreasonable and his views irreconcilable, the Boss believed, but he had also done purposeful damage to the party by turning off the corporate money spigot.

Roosevelt had to go.

Fifteen

Very Great Mischief

The exhilaration of battle against the Spanish in Cuba had only intensified Roosevelt's global-mindedness. After all, he had invigorated the navy for the war against Spain while serving as assistant secretary. Although the governor's office in remote Albany was hardly a war room for the nation's foreign policy, he still managed to balance the high jinks of Boss Platt and the state legislature on one figurative knee while using the other to inject himself into the McKinley administration's overseas plans. Roosevelt favored a hard line in the U.S. supervision of Cuba and the Philippines, and believed that America should move assertively to build an interoceanic canal in Central America to further its military and economic security.

The failure of the French in Panama had reawakened America's interest in a deepwater channel linking the Atlantic and the Pacific. In fact, American leaders had considered an interoceanic waterway to increase commerce and national security and shorten sea travel as far back as Benjamin Franklin and Thomas Jefferson. President James Monroe had had the strategic attributes of a canal in mind when he declared in his celebrated 1823 doctrine that the American continents were not to be colonized by Europeans, or, for that matter, anyone else.

As Latin America threw off the yolk of Spanish colonialism, worldwide interest increased in potential canal sites in Mexico, Nicaragua, and Colombia, the last of which, at the time, included the province of Panama. Surveys and explorations came and went with humdrum regularity in the mid-nineteenth century, but cost, limited technology, and an inhospitable climate prevented the turning of even one shovel of rock and soil until the French attempt.

In 1850, America and the United Kingdom had negotiated the Clayton-Bulwer Treaty to hasten the building of a canal, but also to ensure that neither country ever had exclusive control or fortifications over what would be built. As

Bishop pointed out in *The Panama Gateway*, his 1913 pioneering history of the canal, "the astonishing result was that they blocked completely for half a century every enterprise of the kind that was undertaken."[270]

In the mid-1860s, with the Civil War over, the appeal of a canal under the exclusive control of the U.S. steadily grew. By the time President Ulysses S. Grant organized a commission in 1872 to study canal possibilities once again, his secretary of state, Hamilton Fish, publicly asserted that the president was "disinclined to enter into any entanglement in participation of control over the work with other powers. He regards it as an American enterprise."[271]

By then the Panama Railway, linking the Caribbean harbor of Colón to the Pacific port of Panama City, was operating daily and earning profits for its organizers. Bishop concluded that the railroad's success demonstrated the feasibility of waterway transit through the narrow Panamanian isthmus to the exclusion of other sites. "The real pioneers of an isthmian canal were the builders of the Panama Railroad," he wrote. "They cut through pestilential jungle and morass the pathway which the canal of the future was to follow."[272] The Grant Commission findings, issued in 1876, nonetheless favored Nicaragua as the preferred canal site, and negotiations with the Nicaraguan government commenced. But before serious progress could be made, Ferdinand de Lesseps and his French engineers began digging in Panama—and the U.S. initiative in Nicaragua ground to a sudden, resentful halt.

When, in the late 1880s, the French abandoned their two-thirds-unfinished project amid bankruptcy and scandal, most canal watchers concluded that only the U.S. with its deep reservoir of public funds could finish it. Bishop repeated that the joint-control mandate of the Clayton-Bulwer Treaty blocked all subsequent American attempts to move forward. That pact, he said, "stood squarely and immovably in the way of a canal built by Americans and controlled exclusively by Americans."[273]

But with Spain routed in Cuba and the Philippines, President McKinley was willing to turn his attention to a canal. In 1898, he directed his secretary of state to approach London about a treaty to replace Clayton-Bulwer. At the time, the secretary of state was none other than the former ambassador to the United Kingdom, John Hay, the long-ago newsroom mentor of Joseph Bucklin Bishop. Recognizing that a second Boer war in South Africa had tied down the British, who wanted eagerly to free themselves from obligations in Central America, Hay quickly engaged the conciliatory Sir Julian Pauncefote, British ambassador to the U.S. Their quiet, considerate negotiations culminated in the

Hay-Pauncefote Treaty of 1900, nullifying the earlier pact. The new treaty gave the U.S. the exclusive right to create and control an isthmian canal. Further, the waterway would remain open to ships of all nations in peace and war, and was never to be blockaded. Initially, the outcome was hailed as a triumph for the McKinley administration and for John Hay personally.

Within days, however, ominous rumbles of discontent emanated from the U.S. Senate, required by the Constitution to ratify all treaties. The maverick Hay had failed to adequately consult key influential senators, notably six-term senator John Morgan of Alabama, chairman of the Committee on Oceanic Canals—known as the Morgan Committee. The former brigadier general of the old Confederate Army didn't understand why a canal—a strategic asset to be controlled by the U.S.—should be neutral in time of war. Neither did Governor Roosevelt.

Writing testily from Albany, the governor argued that the Hay-Pauncefote Treaty included a fatal error. "I do not see why we should dig the canal if we are not to fortify it, so as to ensure its being used for ourselves and against our foes in times of war."[274] His views made headlines in New York, Washington, and London. "If fortified by us, it becomes one of the most potent sources of our possible sea strength," Roosevelt argued to Hay.[275]

Understandably, the secretary of state was furious at what he considered meddling by a mere governor, even if he was a dear friend. "Et tu!" said Hay. "Cannot you leave a few things to the President and the Senate who are charged with them by the Constitution?"[276] Hay pleaded with Roosevelt no to respond immediately to his letter and to "think about it a while," but the governor shot back, condemning the treaty's "very great mischief," adding, "But oh how I wish you and the president would drop the treaty and push through a bill to build *and fortify* [emphasis added] our own canal."[277]

Persuaded by Morgan, Roosevelt, and others, the Senate amended the treaty before ratifying it. According to Hay biographer William Roscoe Thayer, Hay "watched, with alternate resentment, sarcasm, and regret" as the Senate amended the pact that he had carefully negotiated with Pauncefote. Finally, Hay had had enough. "Dear Mr. President," he wrote to McKinley, "The action of the Senate indicated views so widely divergent from mine in matters affecting, as I think, the national welfare and honor, that I fear my power to serve you . . . is at an end."[278] McKinley would not hear of it, however, responding the same day: "I return your resignation. . . . We must bear the atmosphere of the hour. It will pass away."[279]

When Britain declined to accept the amended treaty, a chastened Hay cabled Pauncefote to ask that they try again. The Senate later approved a second Hay-Pauncefote Treaty, absent the fortification restriction. "The United States was to be free to do whatever was necessary to protect the canal," David McCullough observed, "and the unwritten understanding was that this in fact authorized fortification."[280]

Delighted that the United States had won a free hand over an isthmian canal, Roosevelt later wrote of his friend Hay, "His extreme sensitiveness and his innate good breeding . . . made association with masterful but often coarse and selfish politicians peculiarly distasteful to him." Then Roosevelt added a telltale anecdote about Hay: "When, in response to a question [about] which senator he hated most, he [Hay] instantly answered, '[T]he one I have seen last.'"[281]

Sixteen

Involuntary Change

A REVOLUTION WAS TAKING PLACE AT THE *EVENING POST*. GODKIN'S HEALTH was deteriorating further. He had sailed to England to seek treatment for illness, and, although back in New York, rarely wrote editorials anymore. Godkin had made the paper an intellectual bastion to which any man of talent would be proud to belong, but he was preparing to retire with the New Year.

The *Evening Post* was losing other talent; the best people in the newsroom were going elsewhere. A dozen reporters and editors had already jumped ship, including the city editor and star police reporter Lincoln Steffens, whom historian Allan Nevins salutes as "one of the best newspapermen New York ever had."[282] Six or seven years prior, the *Evening Post* had hired the young Californian, who was curious, observant, and a skilled writer. At the time, the paper hadn't needed another reporter, but the editors agreed that Steffens could sit at a vacant desk in the newsroom so they could try him out when column inches needed filling. Steffens soon proved his ability on the rapid transit beat and, later, covering Wall Street. He eventually became one of the most successful journalists of the era, winding up as the muckraking editor of the popular magazine *McClure's*, where he attacked corruption in state politics and government with zeal.

Into this turbulence maneuvered Oswald Garrison Villard, a twenty-seven-year-old Harvard-educated liberal—if not radical—thinker, and son of the paper's owner. His father, Henry Villard, who had put Schurz and Godkin on the paper back in 1881, was a wealthy, German-born railroad and publishing magnate, and his mother, a women's suffrage advocate, the daughter of abolitionist William Lloyd Garrison, whose rallying cries Bishop would have read in his youth. The younger Villard came to the *Evening Post* via the *Philadelphia Press* in the spring of 1897, challenging Bishop as Godkin's other editorial voice for progressivism and reform. As city editor, Villard transformed the paper into a champion of the rights of blacks, upsetting the old order. His fervent anti-imperialism brought him into conflict with Theodore Roosevelt's expansionist international views.

Villard later acknowledged that "talented, younger men had chafed under the rigid conservatism of the [*Evening Post's*] new editorial management with which they had little or no personal contact." They were drawn, he said, to the rival *New York Commercial Advertiser* and "a chance to join a newspaper which was to be light, amusing, full of 'human nature' stories, and unhampered by tradition."[283]

Had Bishop survived to read Villard's 1939 memoir, he would have bristled to read the younger man's take on the *Evening Post's* treatment of T. R. "The editors were under no illusion as to Roosevelt and insisted up to the time that he became president that he had a boyish and unstable mentality. . . . The reformer in him always surrendered to the politician and to his ambition when it came to a tight place, and he never hesitated to twist the truth," [284] Villard wrote. He also contended that Roosevelt's management of the media did more to corrupt the press than anyone else's. He alleged that as president, Roosevelt "warped and twisted, consciously or unconsciously, by his fascinating personality, the judgments of the best of the reporters and correspondents, and many of the editors."[285]

Bishop would have taken special offense at Villard's charge that Roosevelt had compromised him and his fellow editors ethically, and that they had bought into his line by succumbing to his intellect and charm. T. R.'s charisma captivated Bishop, as it did so many others of the day, and Bishop deeply appreciated the many times that Roosevelt brought him in close, professionally and socially. And as we have seen, Roosevelt valued Bishop because he gave him what he needed to know, not simply what he wanted to hear.

Villard, in his memoir, went after Bishop, too, claiming that he had deliberately run down Villard's writings at the *Evening Post* in hopes of getting him out of the editors' office. "When I told Mr. [deputy editor Horace] White of Mr. Bishop's constant picking upon my writing and saying it was hopeless, he rose in his wrath and declared, 'Why, you write better today than Bishop ever did.'" Villard administered a final cut to Bishop in his recollection: "I never met any other man who had so low an opinion of women as human beings."[286]

It took more than another decade for Washington State to pass women's suffrage in 1910—the first in the nation to do so, and a lead that New York followed seven years later. But in 1899, the question of whether women should have the vote was still being debated vigorously in churches, saloons, and newspapers. Along with many people of the day, men and women alike, Godkin flatout opposed it—although he did allow the paper to say that women should have the benefit of educational and economic opportunities. It was another source of conflict between the *Evening Post* and Governor Roosevelt, who had believed in women's suffrage from the beginning, having written on the subject for his senior thesis at Harvard.

Villard's contention that Bishop had a "low opinion of women" is an unsubstantiated allegation that has demeaned Bishop's reputation unfairly for years. In his memoir, Villard failed to support the charge with evidence, but he did have an ax to grind with Bishop. Professionally, Bishop had to hew to Godkin's views on women's suffrage, but there is no record to indicate whether Bishop personally felt one way or the other about the issue, and no one who knew Bishop firsthand has ever affirmed Villard's claim. Further, there is also no evidence that Bishop was unfaithful to his wife or disrespectful to his daughter over the many years of their lives together.

But as the year, the decade, and the nineteenth century were crawling to a close, Bishop, now fifty-two, was souring. The "brilliant, young writer" of 1883 had served the *Evening Post* for sixteen years, battling Tammany Hall and advocating for reform. But it was time for him to follow Lincoln Steffens and the others to a new forum where he could control his destiny, write freely, and champion Roosevelt.

Founded as the *American Minerva* in 1793 by Connecticut-born lexicographer Noah Webster, with funds borrowed from Alexander Hamilton [who himself founded the *Evening Post* a few years later], the *Commercial Advertiser* had a noble heritage and, early on, became a prominent voice for the Federalists. When the Whig Party dissolved prior to the Civil War, the *Commercial Advertiser* became a worthy Republican organ. A succession of publishers and editors sustained it through the decades until it passed to the editorial control of city editor Henry Wright in 1897. Then the paper was struggling to maintain its reputation, along with the *Evening Post,* as an important afternoon "three-center"— albeit with a loftier tone.

"A newspaper is indeed like a woman or a politician," wrote Lincoln Steffens, now the city editor at the *Commercial Advertiser.* "When it is young, honest, and full of ideals, it is attractive, trusted, and full of the possibilities of power." But sadly, that was not the state of the paper at the time. "In 1897, it looked like a wretched old street-walker or a used-up ex-'good governor," Steffens observed. "It had a circulation of 2,500 and no influence." However, now buttressed with ex–*Evening Post* men, Steffens expressed hope. "There is a difference between a fallen human being and a painted prostitute. A newspaper can be saved—to sell again."[287]

When Bishop arrived as chief of editorial writers in the late fall of 1899, the *Commercial Advertiser* was, he said, "busy, happy, and progressively successful." It had survived an eccentric formula that Steffens had devised for the city room. It was, in the words of newspaper historian W. Joseph Campbell, "an anti-journalistic, literary model."[288] Steffens had recruited not hard-bitten reporters but young and creative writers adept at storytelling and producing essays and poetry. He proclaimed that the *Commercial Advertiser* was doing things that had never been done in journalism, an offbeat approach intended to woo thoughtful readers away from the yellow rags of Hearst and Pulitzer. Steffens's literary experiment fizzled within a year, although the paper survived.

When Edwin Godkin died in 1902, the *Evening Post* passed into the hands of Oswald Garrison Villard as publisher, and its legacy endured. "There was no other journal resembling it, and its dignity, integrity, thoughtfulness, scholarly accuracy, and pride of intellect were the reflection of Godkin's own traits," Allan Nevins observed.[289] Years later, between the wars, playwright and Roosevelt pal Owen Wister described the *Evening Post* "as a paper with a brain behind it and high independent ideals, but it had, through its incessant bitterness about evil and its too-faint praise of good, degenerated into a common scold, a paper without a country."[290]

Seventeen

An Irresistible Addition

"I DID NOT KNOW UNTIL A SHORT WHILE AGO THAT YOU WERE WITH THE *Commercial*," a surprised Governor Roosevelt wrote to Bishop on January 29, 1900. "I am anxious to see you. I have much to tell you of myself, and much that I want to hear from you."[291] Perhaps because of the unpleasant circumstances of his departure from the *Evening Post*, Bishop had told few of his influential friends that he had taken an important post at the oldest evening newspaper in New York.

"I am extremely sorry that you have found it necessary to give up the position in which you were capable of doing such good work for yourself and everybody else," wrote Secretary of State John Hay. "But there is no arguing with that Puritan conscience of yours." Hay had an optimistic conclusion. "I have no doubt that you have followed the inner light in the only way possible."[292]

Bishop had secured the high-ranking post as head of the *Commercial Advertiser*'s editorial department. From his desk at 29 Park Row, he expressed the paper's opinions on matters of the day and oversaw other editors. The Brown University alumni monthly observed at the time, "With Mr. Bishop at the head of its editorial department, the paper is assured of high ideas and a journalistic instinct ahead of the times," gushing further that "Mr. Bishop combined the qualities of conservatism and enterprise in a marked degree."[293]

Henry Wright, a former city editor at the *Evening Post*, was driving the *Advertiser*'s evolution from scrawny weakling to a dignified, readable journal. He wanted to attract the city's urbane readers who disliked the blaring headlines and lurid detail of the rival one-centers.

Troubled by Villard's persistent criticism at the *Evening Post*, Roosevelt wanted to earn the *Commercial Advertiser*'s loyalty. He understood that its editorials, with Bishop now at the helm, would drive public opinion and influence city and state leaders. Within days of his request for a tête-à-tête, Roosevelt sat down for a Sunday chat with Wright and Bishop in New York.

No record of their conversation survives, but it is clear from Roosevelt's follow-up note to Bishop that it was a satisfying get-together. "You can't imagine what a pleasure and what a real help it was to meet you two at breakfast the other day."[294]

It is also evident from Bishop's reply the following day that he and Wright had offered their support to the governor in his struggle with Boss Platt. "We wish to help you in the most effective way possible," Bishop pledged. "You must tell us how to do so. I have a private telephone if you wish to talk with me. If necessary, Wright is willing to come out squarely against Platt."[295]

Warning that his words must be kept "strictly confidential," Roosevelt shared with Bishop in a next-day letter his strategy for managing relations with the party boss. "Only by being extremely good-natured and scrupulously courteous and truthful and fair, and by convincing him that I was dealing squarely, and that where I differed from him it was not to build up a machine for myself but to serve what I believed to be the interests of the state, have I been able to get on with him."[296]

It was a wise strategy. Roosevelt's relationship with Platt would be rigorously tested in the months ahead, as national party leaders planned their June nominating convention and as President McKinley prepared to stand for reelection in the fall. Vice President Garret Hobart, long in failing health, had died the previous November, and the party's search for a running mate for the president began earnestly. On February 19, Roosevelt summoned Bishop, this time to an after-hours meeting on Madison Avenue. "I too have much to say to you," he wrote.[297]

Henry Cabot Lodge, U.S. senator from Massachusetts, had secured Roosevelt's appointment as assistant secretary of the navy in 1897. Now Cabot was determined to see his friend nominated as the Republican vice presidential candidate on the McKinley ticket. Like T. R., Lodge was a Harvard and Porcellian man. Born and raised on Boston's Beacon Hill and from an old-line Massachusetts family, Lodge began his life in politics modestly in the Massachusetts House of Representatives. He continued through the U.S. House and peaked in the U.S. Senate, beginning in 1893. Lodge shared T. R.'s expansionist bent, favoring the Spanish War in Cuba and the need for a strong navy. As early as the summer of 1899, when Roosevelt was still settling into the governor's mansion in Albany, Lodge was promoting him to the party for vice president. While T. R. pleaded that he wanted a job "with more work in it," Lodge argued that it was an ideal platform for a future presidential bid.

Boss Platt and his cronies among the state franchise owners also wanted Roosevelt to run on the ticket. Their intentions were less altruistic than Lodge's, however. They wanted T. R. out of New York so they could replace him with a machine man and their executives could resume unfettered control of policy and patronage.

"It is the purpose of Platt and [Republican state party chairman Benjamin] Odell to have you nominated for the vice presidency," Bishop alerted Roosevelt in an April 10 letter, explaining that his intelligence was "the universal conviction of the Republicans in New York City." Bishop and Wright believed that the governor could "end this trick by a flat-footed announcement that you will not accept."[298] Roosevelt had known of the scheme for a while, but Bishop's alarm triggered action.

Nicholas Murray Butler, a prominent New York educator and Roosevelt intimate, asked Bishop to shortcut Platt's ploy. He urged him to demand in print that Platt and Odell come out flatly for Roosevelt's re-nomination as governor. "Somebody has to lead aggressively, and you are the person to do that," Butler prompted.[299]

Bishop took Butler's assignment to heart since he himself strongly opposed the idea of a Vice President Roosevelt. Bishop believed, perhaps with a fair share of self-interest, that Roosevelt's usefulness lay within New York borders. On April 10, he laid out his case in a lengthy editorial. "The well-nigh universal belief among political authorities [is] . . . that he will be nominated [for vice president] in spite of himself and will be compelled to stand." Turning his gaze toward Washington, Bishop argued that if Roosevelt were re-nominated and reelected governor, the Republican national ticket would benefit. "If they wish to make it [New York] a doubtful state, they can do so by allowing him to be 'sidetracked' into the vice presidency."[300]

"The question," he continued, "is as to which of the two uses that his party managers wish to make of his popularity is the more advantageous to the party. That his first duty is to this state, no man can question. That he will be of far more public service as governor than as vice president is equally undeniable." Then Bishop called on Platt and Odell—though not by name—to declare their demand that Roosevelt be re-nominated for governor.

The determined editor also sent letters to influential national Republicans, urging them to stymie Roosevelt's nomination Secretary of State John Hay, hearing little talk of a Roosevelt candidacy in Washington, cautioned Bishop that he was "unduly alarmed." "There is no instance on record of an election of a vice president by violence," Hay wrote back.[301] Attorney and party wise man Elihu Root, who later served Roosevelt as secretary of war and secretary of state, also believed that the governorship was the best place for him. "I think Roosevelt would be wretchedly unhappy" as vice president, he told Bishop. "He is essentially a man of action and impulse, and the vice presidency is no place for such a man."[302]

Governor Roosevelt laid out his reaction to all this in a "strictly private" note to Bishop. "There is no question but that your information is correct," he wrote. Absolving Platt of any underlying responsibility for the development, he explained that "the dangerous element, as far as I am concerned, comes from the corporations. . . . They have at last come to thoroughly understand that I cannot be used . . . and I will never yield to the demagogues. . . . They would like to get me out of politics for good."

Roosevelt also shared his counterstrategy: "Now about my making another declaration declining the vice presidency, there is much to be said. I may make myself ridiculous if I announce too often that I won't take it. Then I have a horror of saying what I may not be able to do. . . . If I were actually nominated and I were unable to stem the convention's desire to nominate me, it might be impossible to refuse." Roosevelt closed the note to his friend, "I need not say how heartily I thank you, old fellow, for your interest in me."[303]

Bishop responded the next day. "I know that in this paper, I have more influence than I could exert anywhere else in your behalf—a fact that gives me such genuine joy—that I am more than reconciled to my change. Keep me informed at all points that we may work to the best advantage." Then Bishop extended a personal invitation to the governor to come to New York City to visit him and Wright. "I could lodge you at my house. . . . No one needs to know you were here"—although he admitted that "[m]y small boy would need to be strongly belted to keep him from bursting word of it."[304]

The *Commercial Advertiser* intended to have the last word in the governor versus vice president discussion when, on April 18, its editorial headline declared ROOSEVELT FOR GOVERNOR AGAIN. Reporting that "utterances and manifestations" at that week's Republican state convention had virtually re-nominated Roosevelt, Bishop wishfully—and inaccurately—predicted "all danger of his being 'sidetracked' has passed and that the state will have the inestimable benefit of his services for two years longer."[305]

Six weeks ahead of the national convention, Roosevelt remained unmoved by the building tide for his vice presidential candidacy among state delegations. His backers cared little about the political tug-of-war in New York; they understood foremost that the reformer and war hero would make an irresistible addition to the national ticket, and they wanted to beat the presumed repeat Democratic nominee, William Jennings Bryan.

Writing from Albany on April 30 to his sister Barnie, Roosevelt said, "Cabot feels that I have a career. The dear old goose actually regards me as a presidential possibility of the future, which always makes me thoroughly exasperated, because sooner or later it will have the effect of making other people think I so regard myself and that therefore, I am a ridiculous personage." The *Commercial Advertiser*'s prediction was temporarily holding, and Roosevelt intended to go where he thought he could do the most good. "The final and conclusive consideration is that I do not want the vice presidency and that I would love to be governor again because of the work there is in it."[306]

But in May his stance began to shift. He traveled to Washington to take the pulse of party luminaries, including President McKinley. The president stayed resolutely neutral on a running mate, but Roosevelt's face was said to flush in anger when he confirmed that the Republican National Committee chairman, Senator Mark Hanna of Ohio—for years the McKinley kingmaker—would fight his nomination out of personal loathing. "If the convention wants me, I shall accept," Roosevelt was said to declare in defiance of Hanna's hard line.

Soon after returning to Albany, Roosevelt wrote a letter to Bishop that illuminates the nature of their evolving camaraderie "I have been intensively amused at Washington at the effect produced by the rumor of our intimacy," he said. "Not only Senator Platt but the President alluded to it, and one of our other friends disconcerted me by remarking in the presence of diverse members of the organization that he understood that I always consulted Platt and always followed your advice."[307]

By the time Roosevelt arrived at the Philadelphia convention on June 15 the whole city was buzzing about him. One state delegation after another—Kansas, Massachusetts, Pennsylvania, California—caucused to endorse his candidacy. Political maneuvering ensued as Lodge worked the other delegations for Roosevelt while Hanna tried to stem the popular tide. It was Platt collaborator and former senator Matthew Quay of Pennsylvania who ultimately strong-armed Hanna into concession. Quay threatened to propose a popular convention rules change that would have reduced the voting strength of

Note. This letter as delayed on account of stenographer being
held up on account of wreck on Central Road.

Dated at Oyster Bay, May 15th, 1900.

J. B. Bishop. Esq.,

Editor, Commercial Advertiser,

#29 Park Row, N.Y. City.

My dear Bishop:----

I am awfully sorry you cant breakfast with
me. I have telegraphed you to come up to #4 W. 57th St. at
half past four tomorrow Wednesday. That is the best chance I
have to see you. There is much I want to tell you. I have been
intensely amused at Washington at the effect produced of the
rumor of our intimacy. Not only Senator Platt but the President
alluded to it, and one of our other friends rather disconcerted
me by remarking in the presence of divers members of the Organization that he understood that I always consulted Platt and
always followed your advice. This was apropos of the Charter
Commission. I hastily justified myself by parading Dewitt as
a proof that I had disregarded your advice on occasions. By
the way, I was very favorably impressed with Dewitt at Albany and
I believe he is going to do good work. I find that there has
been a good deal of bitterness in the Machine over the Charter
Commission. What the source is I do not know and I shall probably never find out. Evidently some one has wanted either to
procure or to prevent legislation and is greatly irritated at
finding that the Commission cannot be touched in any way.

Faithfully yours,

Theodore Roosevelt

Governor Roosevelt informs Bishop that President McKinley and other high officials
in Washington are aware of the importance of their friendship, reporting to Bishop the
observation of one: "I always consulted [Party Boss] Platt and always followed your
advice." *Theodore Roosevelt Papers, Manuscript Division, Library of Congress*

southern state delegations loyal to Hanna. After stewing about the brazen tactic, the national chairman concluded that he was boxed in. He agreed to lift his opposition to Roosevelt.

In his autobiography, Senator Platt tells his own version of how the Roosevelt nomination came to be. Summoning Hanna to his suite at the convention hotel, the two met privately. Platt remembered, "At first, Senator Hanna obdurately opposed my efforts to convince him of the party necessity of nominating Mr. Roosevelt; but finally, I won him over to my idea and he left my room promising to issue that night a statement that in his judgment, Mr. Roosevelt should be the candidate of the convention. This promise he faithfully kept, and from that moment, the nomination was assured."[308]

Platt claimed that Roosevelt then came to see him "in a state of rare excitement, even for him," supposedly telling Platt, "I shall go to the New York caucus and tell the delegates that I shall, if nominated for vice president, arise in the convention and decline." Roosevelt then added, "I can serve you, Senator Platt, far better as governor than vice president."[309]

"But you cannot be re-nominated for governor," Platt allegedly replied, "and you *are* going to be nominated for vice president." Pointing to Chairman Odell, Platt announced, "Your successor is in this room." The Boss recounted that at this turn of events Roosevelt "showed his teeth, paced up and down the room and chafed as a horse does under a tight rein and a curbed bit."[310]

Whatever the nature of the choreography, the other delegates loudly chanted, "We want Teddy" as Roosevelt strode into the convention hall to take his seat with the New York delegation. When the roll call had concluded, all 926 delegates had supported McKinley for reelection, and 925 had voted for Roosevelt as vice president. T. R. artfully had abstained from endorsing himself.

Secretary of State Hay was among the first to congratulate the nominee formally. "Nothing can keep you from doing good work wherever you are—or from getting lots of fun out of it," he wrote. "We Washingtonians, of course, have our own little point of view. You can't lose us; and we shall be uncommonly glad to see you here again."[311] A week or so later, Roosevelt swallowed hard and reached out to Hanna, offering to campaign for the ticket whenever and wherever he was needed. "I am as strong as a bull moose, and you can use me to the limit."[312]

Hanna and his campaign operatives accepted Roosevelt's offer with glee. McKinley's idea of a campaign was to stand regally on his front porch in

Canton, Ohio, and receive throngs of admirers and well-wishers. Someone else had to hit the rails and ask for votes, which Roosevelt duly did. By Election Day, he had traveled more than 21,000 miles into twenty-four states, stumping on the campaign theme of "Four More Years of the Full Dinner Pail." The nation's economy was surging in the fall of 1900, and voters glowed with reflected pride in the nation's victory in the Spanish War—and Roosevelt's role in it.

During the general election campaign, Democrats Bryan and his running mate, former vice president Adlai Stevenson, reprised the "free silver" theme of the previous presidential contest and accused McKinley-Roosevelt of replacing the cruel Spanish tyranny in Cuba with an equally brutal American occupation of the island and the Philippines. But outside the "solid South," their claims did not much count with voters, who were enjoying personal prosperity in the surging economy.

Bishop, for his part, assured Roosevelt a month out from the election that, "New York is safe by at least a 100,000 plurality."[313] Indeed, the final Republican margin in New York was closer to 150,000 votes. Although Bryan captured New York City, all of the Empire State's 36 Electoral College votes went to McKinley-Roosevelt, who glided nationally to a comfortable 52 percent to 46 percent popular vote and a triumphant 292–155 electoral vote victory.

Buoyed by his victory and the prospect of returning to the national stage, Roosevelt still insisted he was not a political lifer. At the time of his nomination in June, he had confided to Bishop that he longed to resume the study and practice of law, which he had abandoned at Columbia back in 1882. A few weeks after his election as vice president, Roosevelt wrote to another friend, "I do not expect to go any further in politics. Heaven knows that there is no reason to expect that a man of so many, and so loudly, and not always wisely-expressed convictions on so many different subjects should go so far."[314]

The vice president–elect reached out to Bishop within days of his win, suggesting a meal. "I will lunch with you with immense pleasure," Bishop responded. "Then I can say some of the joy and pride I feel in your success."[315]

At the time, presidential inaugurations followed elections by four months. Roosevelt used some of that time to wrap up his term as governor and to help Edith and the six children prepare for yet another family move. He also salivated at the prospect of a six-week hunting trip out West. As he left Albany behind on December 31, 1900, he declared, "I think I have been the best governor of my time."[316]

On March 4, 1901, Theodore Roosevelt, just forty-one years old, removed his top hat and stood behind McKinley during the presidential oath-taking on the east front of the Capitol. Then T. R. moved forward and swore to uphold the Constitution of the United States as vice president, "so help me God." Few in the animated crowd of thousands of well-wishers in Washington that late winter day could have imagined how horrifically divine providence would intervene in the lives of McKinley and Roosevelt before year's end.

Eighteen

A Handkerchief and a Telegram

"Blessed Ted," vice president–elect Roosevelt wrote his thirteen-year-old son from Keystone Ranch in Colorado in mid-January 1901, between the election and inauguration. "This time . . . the dogs caught him, and a great fight followed." T. R. had been hunting cougar in the rugged hills of the Rockies, and he wanted Ted to feel the thrill of the kill. "They could have killed him by themselves but he bit or clawed four of them, and for fear he might kill one, I ran in and stabbed him behind the shoulder, thrusting the knife you loaned me right into his heart. I have always wished to kill a cougar as I did this one, with dogs and the knife."[317]

His softer side shone through a second letter a week later, this one to his daughter, Ethel, age nine. "You would be much amused with the animals around the ranch. . . . One of the dogs has just had a litter of puppies; you would love them, with their little wrinkled noses and squeaky voices."[318] Roosevelt was continuing his established ritual. Whenever he traveled, no matter how consuming his obligations or harried his schedule, he reserved time to handwrite loving notes to his family. He described special events, knowing the children would smile, or wonder, or gasp. Often, he augmented his words with quirky line sketches of people and creatures he encountered.

Roosevelt had no idea at this time that he would serve little more than six months as vice president.

The start of his term in the spring of 1901 featured the usual frenzy of Washington receptions and official meetings, and a mere five days presiding over the Senate—the vice president's sole constitutional duty. Because President McKinley and Senator Hanna showed little inclination to include him in their strategy deliberations, and because of Congress's extraordinarily brief session, Roosevelt had little to occupy his time. Opting to return to Sagamore Hill, he boarded a train for New York. As the coach rumbled along, he resolved to

President William McKinley and Theodore Roosevelt (ca. 1896–1900). Roosevelt's image was substituted for that of Vice President Garret Hobart in an earlier McKinley photograph, an early example of photo manipulation.

Theodore Roosevelt Collection, Harvard College Library (Roosevelt R570.P69a-0C3)

overcome the enforced idleness by resuming the study of law at the knee of Chief Justice Melville Fuller when he returned to Washington in the fall.

"I am enjoying the perfect ease of my life at present," the vice president wrote his friend Judge William Howard Taft, who was heading up a presidential commission to organize a civilian government in the American-occupied Philippines. "I am just living out in the country, doing nothing but riding and rowing with Mrs. Roosevelt, and walking and playing with the children." Roosevelt further confessed that he was spending his days "chopping trees in the afternoon and reading books by a wood fire in the evening."[319] A few weeks later, alerting Taft that he was thinking of the future, Roosevelt declared, "I should like to be president, and I feel that I could do the work well."[320]

A year older than Roosevelt, Will Taft had risen high and fast from the roots of a political Ohio family. Following Yale and Cincinnati Law School, he won appointment as an Ohio Superior Court judge at the age of thirty. Three years later, Taft became solicitor general of the United States, and within a year of that he rose to a federal appeals court judgeship. McKinley had tasked him not only with directing the U.S. administration of a far-off Pacific outpost, but also with suppressing the intensifying Filipino war of independence.

"My good friend, Bishop of the *Commercial Advertiser*, is a particularly staunch adherent of yours," Roosevelt told Taft.[321] Indeed, Bishop and Taft had been communicating regularly since at least the fall of 1900. "The work is intensely interesting," Taft confided to the editor, "and has enough promise of success in it to enable one to keep cheerful."[322]

Bishop was intensely curious about the presence of the U.S. in the Philippines, and Taft understood the benefits of regularly supplying him with inside information. In return, Bishop wrote editorials enthusiastically supporting U.S. control there and spurning the arguments of anti-imperialists. When, in April 1901, the *Commercial Advertiser* applauded Taft's reported appointment as governor general of the Philippines, Taft responded to Bishop with a thirteen-page, typewritten letter.

"I dined with Roosevelt a few nights ago," Bishop wrote, "and showed him the letter. He is full of strenuous enthusiasm for you and said after reading the letter, 'By George, I wouldn't ask any higher privilege than to be allowed to nominate Taft for president at the next convention. What a glorious candidate and president he would make.'"[323] "I agreed heartily," Bishop said, "and we drank to the prospect then and there. This is not taffy, my dear judge."

Oppressive heat bore down on the throngs in Buffalo that Friday in early September 1901. Many of the women—and some men—visiting the Pan-American Exposition carried handkerchiefs to wipe the perspiration from their brows. The display halls were stuffy, without a whisper of a breeze. At the ornate Temple of Music, President McKinley was greeting well-wishers in a long reception line, brushing off the security concerns of his aides. Ordinarily, the army servicemen who guarded the president would have asked that handkerchiefs be tucked away as guests approached the president, lest they be used to conceal something that could harm him. But on this day, September 6, security officials had relaxed the rules in consideration of the unusual heat.

That morning, the president's secretary, George Cortelyou, recommended that McKinley skip the reception. The president demurred, asking, "Why should I? No one would wish to hurt me."[324] In fact, someone did.

Leon Frank Czolgosz, a twenty-eight-year-old out-of-work factory hand from Detroit, was nervously approaching the president. An anarchist who viewed government as unnecessary, Czolgosz had come to Buffalo expressly to "do his duty" and kill the president. As the organ strains of Schumann's dreamy "Traumerei" echoed off the temple walls, Czolgosz reached the head of the reception line, his hand "bandaged" with a white handkerchief. The dressing suddenly exploded in gunfire as McKinley reached for it. "Onlookers heard two sharp popping sounds, like small firecrackers. . . . One bullet had struck [McKinley's] sternum a glancing blow, causing only a superficial wound, but the other had penetrated his abdomen, a potentially fatal injury."[325] The president was wobbly but still standing as guards led the gunman away. "Don't let them hurt him," he pleaded.[326]

Roosevelt was spending the first weekend of September in the cooler Vermont air, inspecting marble quarries and meeting with the Vermont Fish and Game League at Lake Champlain. When a phone call delivered the terrible news of the attempted assassination, Roosevelt hurried by train to Buffalo to see the president and to comfort Ida McKinley. At first, the prognosis was good; doctors attending him at the home of John Milburn, the exposition's president, told Roosevelt that McKinley would make a full recovery in time. The *Commercial Advertiser* ran the headline RECOVERY OF PRESIDENT MORE PROB-ABLE: SUFFERER PASSED A GOOD NIGHT AND IS RESTING WELL. MRS. MCKINLEY GOES DRIVING.[327]

Reflecting the doctors' optimism, Roosevelt wrote to Senator Lodge. "Long before you receive this letter I believe the last particle of danger will have vanished; nor do I anticipate even a long convalescence."[328] Fully reassured, Roosevelt left Buffalo to join Edith and the children, who were enjoying a vacation at an Adirondack wilderness camp. As usual, T. R. relished the broad skies and open air of such places, instructing the children in how best to track animals and observe birds. On Friday the 13th, he climbed Mount Marcy, at 5,343 feet, the highest point in New York State.

But in Buffalo, McKinley had taken a grave turn. The second bullet, unseen by an X-ray machine that had been delivered to the scene but not used, had infected his organs, and doctors could only administer oxygen and make the president comfortable. As hope for his recovery ebbed, officials decided to alert Roosevelt.

Amid driving rain and wind, unaware of the world-changing events unfolding in Buffalo, Roosevelt descended Mount Marcy to join his family at the Tahawus Club at a lower elevation on Avalanche Lake. Within hours, mounted messengers and out-of-breath runners delivered a series of telegrams, each more ominous than the one before. The last—THE PRESIDENT APPEARS TO BE DYING, AND MEMBERS OF THE CABINET IN BUFFALO THINK YOU SHOULD LOSE NO TIME IN COMING—compelled him to order horses and a wagon for a torturous, thirty-five-mile, middle-of-the-night descent to the railhead in North Creek. Edmund Morris painted the frenzied scene:

> *He sat alone on the passenger seat, shrouded against splashes of mud in a borrowed raincoat several sizes too big. His favorite hat, a broad-brimmed slouch pulled well over his ears, kept some of the drizzle off his spectacles— not that he could see anything beyond the buckboard's tossing circle of lamplight . . . he had spoken hardly a word to the lanky youth in front of him. From time to time, he muttered to himself.*[329]

Arriving at North Creek as dawn was about to break, an aide somberly approached Roosevelt and handed him yet another telegram: THE PRESIDENT DIED AT TWO-FIFTEEN THIS MORNING. It was from John Hay, secretary of state, who had been monitoring events in Buffalo from his Washington, D.C., home, within a window's view of the White House. McKinley had lingered for a week, eventually succumbing to infection and gangrene. He died murmuring to his doctors the words of "Nearer My God to Thee."

Weary and damp, his bones aching from the race down the mountain, the new twenty-sixth president of the United States boarded a special train consisting of an engine and one parlor car and dropped into his seat. The *Commercial Advertiser*'s correspondent predicted correctly: "It is expected that all records for quick runs on the Delaware and Hudson will be broken by the special train."[330] Roosevelt's secretary, William Loeb Jr., observed that for once T. R. was without words. As the great locomotive cleared the tiny station and gathered speed, his mind roiled with anxiety, dread, and not a little anticipation. Of the moment, Roosevelt later confided to Owen Wister, "I can't know if I have the ability but I do know that I have the will to carry out the task that has befallen me."[331]

No photographs exist of the September 14, 1901, emergency presidential inauguration in Buffalo, but journalists and McKinley cabinet members who were present detailed the momentous scene. Attired in a borrowed suit and a silk top hat, standing resolutely in the small library of his friend Ansley Wilcox's home, Roosevelt declared, "And in this hour of terrible national bereavement, I wish to state that it shall be my aim to continue absolutely unbroken the policy of President McKinley for the peace, the prosperity and the honor of the country." Then he swore the constitutional oath administered by federal judge John Hazel and led those assembled in a prolonged moment of silence. The brief inaugural address, Bishop wrote in the *Commercial Advertiser,* was "not a word too many, not a word too few."[332]

The next day, as a memorial service took place for the late president in Buffalo, John Hay wrote heartfelt words of encouragement to the new president: "With your youth, your ability, your health and strength, the courage God has given you to do right, there are no bounds to the good you can accomplish for your country and the name you will leave in its annals."[333]

In an editorial, "The Real Roosevelt," Bishop welcomed the new president to office with a radiant tribute: "Nobody who has followed Theodore Roosevelt's public career or who has had the privilege of personal acquaintance with him has any doubt about his ability to fill with honor to himself and usefulness to the country the high office upon which he has entered."[334]

On the grim train ride from Buffalo to Washington, where McKinley was to lie in state, President Theodore Roosevelt thought sorrowfully about his predecessor, whose body he was escorting, and about grieving Ida McKinley and her future. Edith and the children would have to adapt to life in the White House much sooner than he had expected.

As the farms and villages of central New York whisked by, Roosevelt received aides and visitors who scurried in and out of his private carriage with urgent matters for his attention. There was the pressing economic threat of combinations, those calculated alliances of giant businesses bent on maximizing profits and minimizing wages. In the Pennsylvania coalfields, exploited miners were threatening a violent strike over the absence of union representation. Abroad, tensions between Russia and Japan were mounting. And then there was the proposed Central American shipping canal. John Hay had completed work on the treaty that gave America a free hand to build and fortify the waterway, but Congress still had not decided where to locate it. Nicaragua continued to be the favored venue, but there were reports that the French were preparing to offer the U.S. their unfinished trench in Panama, together with construction equipment and buildings, at a fire-sale price.

Roosevelt called in Loeb and began to dictate: "En route. Personal and Private. My dear Bishop, I shall soon want you to come to see me at the White House, for there is much concerning which I must talk with you."[335]

```
                                                    ( ... )

                        En Route, September 16, 1901.
    Personal and Private.



    My dear Bishop:
            I shall soon want you to come to see me at the
    White House, for there is much concerning which I must talk
    with you.
                    Faithfully yours,




    J. B. Bishop, Esq.,
            Editor The Commercial Advertiser,
                New York City.
```

Two days after McKinley's death thrust Roosevelt into the presidency, T. R. urgently summoned Bishop to Washington. The letter is unsigned perhaps because of the urgency of unfolding events. *Theodore Roosevelt Papers, Manuscript Division, Library of Congress*

PART III

BOLDNESS AND COURAGE

Nineteen

Adventures in the Presidency

McKinley was but freshly in his grave when President Roosevelt strode to his office on the second floor of the executive mansion. "The gift of the gods to Theodore Roosevelt was joy, joy in life," Lincoln Steffens wrote. "But the greatest joy in T. R.'s life was his succession to the presidency."[336]

By late morning on Friday, September 20, 1901, Roosevelt had assembled McKinley's cabinet, asked them to stay on, and repeated his intention to honor the late president's memory by advancing his policies. By afternoon, T. R. had surrounded himself with news reporters who would be known in later decades as the White House press corps. It was an early indication of the priority the new president was going to place on a good relationship with journalists. Those present recalled that T. R. firmly set down the rules: Get your facts straight on what I do, and use gentlemanly discretion in what you write. Anyone who fails to do so or deliberately misquotes me will earn my enmity. He will be exiled to the Ananias Club. In case your ancient history fails you, the club was named for an early Christian who was said to have dropped dead for lying to God.[337] Any questions?

Roosevelt's idea of a model newspaperman was Bishop. In T. R.'s mind, Bishop's facts were accurate and usually according to the Roosevelt gospel. Furthermore, his editorials were thoughtful, well-reasoned, and persuasive. Perhaps that is why Bishop was granted the privilege of meeting with the president on his first formal day in office, well after other newspapermen had departed. "He was alone in the house when I arrived, for his family had not yet come, and there was no other guest present," Bishop recalled years later.[338] "We had a long and intimate conversation. He talked freely of his policies and purposes as president."[339]

Addressing the president with a familiarity that he felt he had earned, Bishop said, "Roosevelt, no man has ever entered upon the office more absolutely free of all obligations to anyone. You owe your possession of this office to no one." Bishop continued, "On the contrary, you have acceded to it in spite of the persistent efforts of your most zealous enemies who were bent on preventing you from ever reaching it." Bishop branched to the political. "You enter upon your duties with the certainty of holding the office for seven years!"

Roosevelt replied at once, with great energy, "I don't know anything about seven years. But this I do know. I am going to be president for three years, and I am going to do my utmost to give the country a good president during that period."

"Now mind you," Roosevelt continued, "I have no intention of doing with the Republican Party what Grover Cleveland did with the Democrats. I intend to work *with* [emphasis added] my party and to make it strong by making it worthy of popular support." Bishop listened intently. "I will not abandon a single one of the principles that formed the basis of my public career. No matter how powerful the influences might be, I will not yield a hair's breath."[340]

"Roosevelt, you recognize, I'm sure, that the combined influences against you as president are far more powerful than you have yet experienced."

"I'm perfectly well aware of that, my dear Bishop. I have no fear of ultimate victory since the people will be on my side." Anticipating the influential role that newspapers and magazines would play in a Roosevelt administration, the president concluded, "I will always let the people know what I am trying to accomplish."[341]

Bishop later recorded that on this eventful day, Roosevelt was "deeply impressed" with the great responsibilities that had been placed upon him. And there was soon evidence that he addressed those obligations with a blithe outlook. In a letter three days later to Senator Lodge, T. R. wrote, "It is a dreadful thing to come into the presidency in this way; but it would be a far worse thing to be morbid about it. Here is the task, and I have got to do it to the best of my ability, and that is all there is about it."[342]

As Bishop descended the marble steps of the North Portico, he was sure of Roosevelt's resolve to succeed in the presidency; however, he was apprehensive about whether the sweeping demands of the office would add distance and, worse, irrelevance to their friendship. Would the president continue to summon him regularly for counsel? Would he see further benefit in sharing confidences? Would Bishop's editorial opinions in far-off New York still matter inside the heady Washington orbit inhabited by the administration and Congress? Lit by shimmering gas lamps, the editor crossed Pennsylvania Avenue and hurried through Lafayette Park toward John Hay's residence, his mind turning.

And now begins a curious tale. Within days, Bishop was on the phone to some of his wealthier acquaintances, intent on raising investment capital. He wanted to buy an interest in a Washington, D.C., newspaper and install himself there as editor—or at least as editor of editorials. "I should like nothing better than to work shoulder to shoulder with you," he told Roosevelt. "Here [in New York] I am at arm's length, and the opportunity is not so large."[343]

Despite years of increasingly responsible newspaper work, Bishop's salaries had not brought him independent wealth. He could not hope to match the living standards of the wealthy and powerful men with whom he associated. There were family obligations, too. Hartwell, their elder son, aspired to law school, and Farnham wanted to attend Harvard in the next few years.

Bishop explained his idea in an exchange of letters to the president and, apparently, to John Hay. Regrettably for history, the letters were deliberately destroyed by request of the senders and receivers, lest word leak to the competitive Washington newspaper community. To comprehend the intrigue, we have to supplement the few available facts with some assumptions from oblique references in other letters that do survive. Bishop wanted to buy into the *Washington Post*. Launched in 1887, the paper had gone through a succession of owners and, at the time, lay in the hands of a former Democratic congressman and banking committee chairman, Beriah Wilkins of Ohio.

"It seems to me that your plan is one calculated to do more good than anything else I can imagine in connection with newspaper work," Roosevelt wrote to Bishop during his third week in office. "If it should succeed, it would strengthen my hands beyond measure to have such a morning paper under the direction of a man of your type." The president confirmed that he had destroyed Bishop's incoming letter. Then he added, "I have not the slightest idea whether Hay could do anything or not. As soon as he returns, I shall speak to him about it."[344]

Five days later, Bishop informed the president that Hay was quite sure Wilkins would not sell. But in a missing letter Hay apparently proposed a more realistic alternative, most likely the purchase of another newspaper. "I wonder if it would be possible to do what he suggests?" Bishop later asked Roosevelt. "The capital I could command for the other project might not be available for this." Nonetheless, Bishop believed that "great good might result from a really honest, able paper there because senators and congressmen read a local paper more than any other save their home papers."[345]

It all came to naught within two weeks. "My dear Roosevelt," Bishop wrote. "I have dismissed that newspaper project for the present—at least." Clearly dejected, he rationalized, 'Of course New York is the best place for certain purposes. My only desire is to be where I can be of most service to you."

Based on the strength of their friendship, Bishop was willing to take great financial risk and either separate himself from his family in New York or relocate them in order to be of service to Roosevelt in the capital city. The president, unexpectedly elevated to the office, made time in the opening days of his administration to engage in Bishop's venture, other demands notwithstanding. In time, Roosevelt saw to it that Bishop made it to Washington, albeit not behind an editor's desk.

The advantage of a New York base allowed Bishop to keep Roosevelt informed of what the city's other influential newspapers were saying about him. Each day, Bishop scrutinized the news columns and editorial pages of the *Journal, Sun, Times,* and *World,* and often included clippings from them in his letters. Both men maintained an intense interest in the opinions of Bishops former longtime employer, the *Evening Post*. Since taking over, Oswald Villard had persisted in criticizing Roosevelt harshly. "What a lucky chap you are," Bishop said, "the Garrisons are still against you!" He admitted, however, that "I am not vindictive but I am a 'good hater,' and I hope and believe you are. If you ever forgive that outfit, I should never forgive you. That is the only ground I can see upon which we could possibly part company."[346]

As Bishop was writing about the *Evening Post,* President and Mrs. Roosevelt were recalling the prior evening's White House dinner with Booker T. Washington, the prominent Negro leader and head of the Tuskegee Institute in Alabama. It was the first time a black person—one born into slavery—had been served at the president's table. Roosevelt thought little of the precedent; he simply relished having a conversation about Southern politics with a reputable, well-informed person.

In the fall of 1901, Booker T. Washington was unquestionably the most high-profile black man in America. He had written and spoken widely about the plight of blacks in the South. He was no civil rights firebrand, to be sure, but a man who believed that blacks would gain a full role in society by demonstrating that they were responsible, self-sufficient citizens. The key to advancement, in his mind, was education. To that end, he was leading the all-black Tuskegee Normal and Industrial Institute, where students trained to teach farming and the trades.

T. R.'s mother, Mittie, hailed from a slave-owning Georgia family. The red clay soil, along with the segregationist culture, was a part of him, but the

Booker T. Washington (ca. 1895) was a pioneering educator, leader in the black community, and associate of Theodore Roosevelt.

Library of Congress Prints and Photographs Division

president, like Booker T. Washington, held an enlightened view: The lowliness of Negroes in society was transitory. Roosevelt was not convinced that blacks who lacked education and job skills should have the right to vote, but he acknowledged that equality among the races would be realized in time, after an inevitable and prolonged struggle. Roosevelt certainly had no idea of the intensity of the storm he was about to unleash.

When newsmen reported on the White House dinner and its guest, many in the South exploded with outrage. The *Richmond Times* condemned social mingling of the races in the "people's house." In Birmingham, the *Enterprise* declared that Roosevelt had humiliated the South and disgraced the nation. It demanded that a former state governor, recently appointed by Roosevelt to the federal judiciary, "owes a duty to the South . . . to promptly resign and hurl the appointment back into the very teeth of the white man who would invite a nigger to eat with his family."[347] The *Scimitar* in Memphis said Roosevelt had inflamed the anger of the Southern people and excited their disgust by inviting "a nigger to dine with him at the White House." Elsewhere on the editorial pages of the Old Confederacy, the terms "darkey" and "coon" appeared. Senator Benjamin Tillman of South Carolina predicted that Roosevelt's blunder "[would] necessitate our killing of a thousand niggers in the South before they learn[ed] their place again."[348]

The venom that his alleged indiscretion had produced caught the president off guard. For solace, he turned to public opinion in the North, to editorial pages such as those of the *Commercial Advertiser*. "Mr. Washington is entitled on his intellectual merits and on the services he is performing for the advancement of his race to be a guest at the president's table," Bishop wrote. "No southern hothead can deny that." Further down his column, Bishop declared, "If there are people in the South who think this sort of thing will move the President from his position or in the slightest degree influence his action, they have a very rudimentary knowledge of Theodore Roosevelt."[349]

On page one of the same day's paper, the *Commercial Advertiser*'s Washington correspondent reported that Roosevelt "thinks he has a right to decide for himself who shall sit at his table." The paper reminded its readers that when Roosevelt was governor, he sheltered in the Albany mansion a black singer who, following a performance at the state capital, had been denied lodging in the city's hotels. Not only that, the correspondent reported, but the governor had also invited him to have breakfast with his family in the morning.

In an unusual handwritten note to Bishop a few days later, Roosevelt wrote, "Thanks for what you said on the Booker T. Washington matter I really felt melancholy for the South at the way the southerners behaved in the matter. Do come to Washington again soon."[350]

The Christmas holidays of 1901 afforded an opportunity for the president and Bishop to contemplate the coming New Year. "Can't you dine with me on the

October 21, 1901.

My dear Bishop:

All right. I am immensely amused by the Anti's.

In great haste,

Faithfully yours,

Theodore Roosevelt

Thanks for what you said on the Booker T. Washington matter; I really felt melancholy for the South at the way the southerners behaved in the matter. Do come to Washington...

Mr. J. B. Bishop,
The Commercial Advertiser,
New York, N. Y.

In a handwritten postscript, President Roosevelt thanks Bishop for his editorial support in the midst of the fallout after Booker T. Washington's social visit to the White House. "I really felt melancholy for the South at the way the southerners behaved in the matter," T. R. observes. *Theodore Roosevelt Papers, Manuscript Division, Library of Congress*

28th?" Roosevelt asked. "I shall probably be alone. I will get three or four senators or members of the Cabinet to dine with you." Then, he offered a more social invitation: "If Mrs. Bishop is with you, won't both of you dine with us on Sunday evening, the 29th, when Mrs. Roosevelt will be here too? I am very anxious to see you."[351]

In all likelihood, the conversation around the White House dinner table on December 28 concerned the unfinished business of siting an interoceanic canal in Central America. Organized by President McKinley two years earlier to study alternatives, a canal commission had recently recommended Nicaragua as the preferred location for an American dig. The country was stable politically

Personal.

December 21, 1901.

My dear Bishop:

Can't you dine with me Saturday, the 28th? I shall
probably be alone. I will get three or four Senators or
members of the Cabinet to dine with you. Then if Mrs.
Bishop is with you, won't both of you dine with us on
Sunday evening, the 29th, when Mrs. Roosevelt will be
here too?

I am very anxious to see you.

Faithfully yours,

Mr. J. B. Bishop,
    Office, Commercial Advertiser,
        New York, N. Y.

In an unsigned 1901 letter, President Roosevelt invites Bishop to join him at the White
House for a post-Christmas strategy meeting and, later, dinner with their wives.

Theodore Roosevelt Papers, Manuscript Division, Library of Congress and free of the sad history of the French failure in nearby Panama. A two-year engineering survey by the commission, headed by Rear Admiral John Walker, had shown the topography of Nicaragua to be more hospitable than that of Panama. It had less-formidable mountains, miles of easily traversed lakes, and an abundant natural supply of water from a navigable river. The price tag was also $60 million less than what it was likely to cost the U.S. in Panama. Besides, Nicaragua was the clear choice of old John Tyler Morgan, chairman of the Senate Committee on Interoceanic Canals.

Yet behind the scenes, the Panama lobby was working incessantly to call attention to the commission's minority report that had chosen Panama as the preferred site. Prior to 1894, the half-dug French ditches and abandoned equipment had scarred the Panamanian landscape. But since then, the French had resumed blasting and excavating under the umbrella of a new entity, the Compagnie Nouvelle du Canal de Panama. No longer would de Lesseps's folly of a sea-level canal be attempted; the waterway would now have multiple locks and man-made lakes. But despite the renewed enthusiasm of French engineers, the Compagnie Nouvelle had attracted few investors and even less public support. In the last days of 1901, the French faced a clear decision: give up the effort in Panama again, or persuade America to purchase its assets, valued at $109 million.

The French watched in horror as the U.S. House of Representatives, acting on the Walker Commission's recommendation, voted 308 to 2 in early January 1902 to authorize a Nicaraguan canal; Morgan excitedly prepared the Senate to assent.

Then came a sudden change. Urgent word from Paris reached Washington that the price tag for the French assets in Panama had dropped steeply—to $40 million. That caught the attention of the president. David McCullough recounts what happened next:

> But no sooner had the House acted than Roosevelt called the members of the Walker Commission to the White House, one by one, for private consultation . . . A meeting of the full commission followed, a closed, secret meeting in the President's office during which Walker and the others were told to get together and issue a supplementary report. Roosevelt wanted the French offer to be accepted. The conclusion of the commission, he said, was to be unanimous.[352]

And so it was, four days later. Through Roosevelt's intervention, Panama had trumped Nicaragua as host nation to a canal. In the months that followed, the president, the Panama lobby, and Senator Mark Hanna's convincing rhetoric outmaneuvered the Morgan Committee chairman en route to a 42 to 34 Senate endorsement of Panama.

In the end, Roosevelt and Congress had been persuaded not only by the French discount, but also by the weight of the comparative evidence: Panama meant a shorter dig by 135 miles; transit time was a third of what it would take in Nicaragua; and, when built, a Panamanian canal would be considerably more economical to operate.

On June 28, 1902, Roosevelt signed into law the bill that would, in Bishop's words,

authorize the president to acquire for and in behalf of the United States, at a cost not exceeding $40 million, all the rights, privileges, franchises, concessions and property on the Isthmus of Panama owned by the new Panama Canal company; to acquire from the Republic of Colombia, on such terms as he might deem reasonable, control of a strip of land, not less than six miles in width between the two oceans, in which to construct and operate a canal.[553]

All that remained was to negotiate a treaty with Colombia. It was, after all, Colombia's land.

Since the collapse of the improbable campaign to transfer his typewriter to Washington, D.C., Bishop had remained occupied on Roosevelt's behalf. In early February, he joined an august roster of dinner guests at Sagamore Hill. The president, William Howard Taft, Senator Hanna, Secretary of War Elihu Root, Senator Lodge, and others sat down to discuss urgent matters of state. As the mansion's fireplaces outdueled the fierce winter winds off Long Island Sound, the presidential brain trust was no doubt thrashing out a strategy to achieve Roosevelt's grand ambition in Central America. It is also likely that, if he hadn't done so already, the president was developing an inkling that Bishop could play a consequential role in the canal drama. It would be essential to maintain political and public support for the undertaking, and who better than a loyal, erudite, and persuasive journalist to make the case?

TELEGRAM. The White House. Washington. September 2, 1902.

TO: J. B. BISHOP. PERSONAL.

THE PRESIDENT WOULD LIKE TO HAVE YOU COME OUT TO OYSTER BAY, THURSDAY, SEPTEMBER FOURTH, FOR DINNER AND TO SPEND THE NIGHT. IT IS IMPORTANT THAT YOU COME IF POSSIBLE.

SIGNED

GEORGE B. CORTELYOU, SECRETARY TO THE PRESIDENT[354]

That dinner never took place. The next day in Pittsfield, Massachusetts, a collision with an errant trolley wrecked the open carriage carrying Roosevelt, Cortelyou, and Massachusetts governor Winthrop Crane on a campaign swing. The trolley's steel wheels crushed the president's bodyguard, Bill Craig, to death. The impact threw the president to the pavement, causing lacerations to his face though no serious injuries. But onlookers saw T. R. clutching his left shin in obvious pain.

TELEGRAM. To second section, Train No. 2, Altoona, Pa. En route to Washington, September 24, 1902.

PRESIDENT ROOSEVELT:

THANK GOD ALL IS WELL . . . TAKE NO CHANCES, I IMPLORE.

J. B. BISHOP[355]

It was not the trolley accident that compelled Bishop's wire from New York. In the midst of another tour, Roosevelt underwent emergency surgery in Indianapolis for a bulging tumor on the leg he had injured in Pittsfield three weeks earlier. Reclining on a stretcher, his left leg elevated, the president was loaded aboard a train and hustled back to Edith's care. "It is an unspeakable pleasure to think of you safely back in Washington," Bishop wrote. "If you can possibly do so, I think it would be wise not to travel anymore for the present. I hear this hope expressed on all sides."[356]

"I am entirely well," Roosevelt replied the next day, "but I suppose it will be a week or ten days before I can get out. At present, I have to keep my leg up all the time because (in the strictest confidence) there has been danger of bone trouble which, if it got fairly started, would lay me up for some months. We took the thing just in time."[357]

In a personal note to Bishop just four days later, Cortelyou informed him the convalescing president wanted to see him immediately. "There are new developments in the coal strike about which he would like to talk to you."[358]

Twenty

Risk and Attainment

WHETHER IN A CROWDED CITY OR IN THE COUNTRYSIDE, HARD COAL WAS essential to winter survival at the turn of the twentieth century. Firm, shiny anthracite produced more heat and less smoke than the softer bituminous coal. The precious mineral came exclusively from hardscrabble mines in eastern Pennsylvania controlled by an oligarchy of wealthy mining companies, railroads, and bankers. When 100,000 miners went on strike in spring 1902, the nation watched with concern. What if the bitter confrontation lingered into fall and winter and coal ran out?

But conditions in Schuylkill County, Pennsylvania, were desperate. A third of the striking miners had fled to the Midwest to mine soft coal, and another 10,000 had returned to their native Eastern and Southern Europe, leaving the rest to fend for themselves without pay envelopes. Often, out of anger and despair, violence exploded against coal company property and the non-union men who continued to work the mines. There were random shootings, stabbings, and other brutal attacks. Middle-of-the-night arson was common.

John Mitchell, an Irish immigrant and experienced miner, led the United Mine Workers in the strike. He pressed coal company operators for higher wages, shorter hours, and union recognition. Speaking for the companies, George Baer, president of the Reading Railroad, replied that the "rights and interests of the laboring man will be protected and cared-for—not by the labor agitators but by the Christian men to whom God, in His infinite wisdom, has given the control of property interests of the country." The arrogance of Baer's posture infuriated the miners, but they wisely exploited it to build public support for the strike.

As the walkout dragged through the summer, positions on both sides hardened. When arson and killings in coal country escalated, President Roosevelt grew increasingly disturbed and frustrated. Attorney General Philander Knox told him pointedly that he had no authority to intervene unless the governor of Pennsylvania determined that the situation was out of hand and that federal assistance was needed to ensure public safety. "There is literally nothing, so far as I have been yet able to find out, which the national government has any power to do in the matter," Roosevelt complained to Senator Lodge. "I am at my wits end how to proceed."[359]

As Roosevelt mulled over his shortage of options, he considered what he termed the "Jackson-Lincoln theory" of the presidency. As he explained in his autobiography, "Occasionally, great national crises arise which call for immediate and vigorous executive action, and that in such cases, it is the duty of the President to act upon the theory that he is the steward of the people ... that he has the legal right to do whatever the needs of the people demand, unless the Constitution or the laws explicitly forbid him to do it."[360]

It was in this spirit that Roosevelt acted. By telegram, he summoned both sides to a summit in Washington on October 3 to discuss "a matter of vital concern to the whole nation." The White House—as it was now officially being called under T. R.'s watch—was being remodeled to do away with an out-of-date Victorian look in favor of Federalist Revival decor, so the temporary presidential quarters in a brick townhouse on Lafayette Park received a delegation of the mine operators and Mitchell and his men. It was a risky endeavor. What if the meeting produced only bluster and rancor? Would the coal men and the union bosses walk out, humiliating the president?

Confined to a wheelchair, his aching leg raised awkwardly as a consequence of a second operation, the president addressed the feuding parties around his conference table. He said that he would not take sides, except to represent the public interest. He wanted the mines open and coal to be brought to the surface without delay. The operators, he later wrote, reacted with insolence and "used language that was insulting to the miners and offensive to me."[361] But to Roosevelt's relief, Mitchell took the high road, proposing a commission of arbitration and a willingness to abide by its resolution—if the operators would do so as well.

When the parties reconvened in the afternoon, the operators again railed against the destruction and death in the coal hills they alleged were perpetrated by striking miners. Was arbitration as suggested by the union acceptable to the operators? Roosevelt asked. No, they replied. The summit adjourned in disappointment and despair.

Hours later there began a remarkable exchange between the crisis-bound president and the editorials editor of the *Commercial Advertiser*. It was a stream of encouragement and frustration, confrontation and candor that demonstrated the intensity and strength of their friendship.

"I hope you will not fail to see tonight's *Commercial*," Bishop wired the dejected president October 4, the day after the big meeting. No doubt Bishop's words brought Roosevelt little consolation. "The President's efforts to end the coal strike have failed because neither party to the contest was able to rise to the high ground of patriotism," the editorial loftily began. Bishop positioned his paper firmly in support of the operators' main alarm. "Until the supremacy of law and order over riot and anarchy is established, all other questions must be set aside."[362] Unsure of how the president would react, Bishop wired him again. "Do write me a confidential word for personal information."[363]

After reading Bishop's telegram, Roosevelt hardly paused before sending what Bishop had requested: a candid, off-the-record message. It was laced with hesitation and doubt.

The attitude of the operators was such at the meeting as to make it hopeless to expect anything, and I certainly shall not communicate with them again. Mitchell shone so in comparison with them as to make me have a very uncomfortable feeling that they might be far more to blame relative to the miners than I had supposed . . . I thought Mitchell's proposition eminently fair. I shall now try, although without much hope of success, to get him to have the miners go back to work anyhow on the understanding that I shall appoint a commission of inquiry who will report in full upon all conditions, and that I shall do whatever I may be able to do to secure motion along the line of such condition.[364]

The president subsequently assured Bishop that he too had violence at the top of his mind. "After the operators left the other day, I explained in the most friendly way to Mitchell and his companions that I most earnestly hoped they would do everything in their power to put a stop to violence ... Mitchell assured me that he had done and would continue to do everything possible to prevent all disorder."[365]

The same day in a handwritten note, Bishop cautioned, "I am very anxious about this strike question and your relations to it. I have seen and talked with many persons, and I find a very uneasy feeling lest you may incline toward the strikers. . . . There is but one opinion among intelligent and conservative men, and that is that law and order must be preserved at any cost."[366]

On October 6, Bishop felt compelled to assure the president that "there is no difference of opinion between us in the matter."[367] Taking the next critical step, Roosevelt told Mitchell that the miners must go back to work as a condition of the arbitration commission.

As the Pennsylvania National Guard descended en masse into Schuylkill County to confront the abiding violence, Mitchell told the president that his men would not return to work—that they had already met the operators more than halfway. The same day, Roosevelt sought to turn Bishop's preoccupation with violence back onto him. "As a practical matter, if I should now send troops to Pennsylvania, the first result would be a violent altercation with the Pennsylvania authorities and a possible collision between the regulars and the militia."[368]

In print, Bishop was pressing the issue: "Public sentiment is growing hourly, more keenly solicitous for a speedy settlement and a consequent resumption of coal production."[369]

"If I followed my inclination," Bishop told Roosevelt on October 11, as temperatures, though not tempers, began to cool, "I should come on to Washington tonight. But it is impossible for me to do so."[370] Instead, he drafted an editorial that argued for intervention by federal troops. He buttressed his view with a lengthy quote from John Markle, the head of a large coal company. "As soon as 'the powers to be' put into the anthracite coal fields sufficient troops to protect the men desiring to work and to protect their families day and night, there will be a gradual resumption of work, and the anthracite coal market will be relieved."[371]

More certain than ever that he could not intervene, the deeply annoyed president confronted Bishop two days later. "Do you think you are fully alive to the gross blindness of the operators? They fail absolutely to understand that they have any duty toward the public. Most emphatically, I shall not compromise with lawlessness." Citing conflicting reports on the degree of bloodshed, Roosevelt continued to make the case for arbitration. "What has happened so far in no way justifies a refusal to have some dispassionate body settle the respective rights and wrongs of the two parties." He closed his letter with an open invitation. "Come here at any time. You know that I will always be more than glad to see you."[372]

The president's letter had hardly arrived in New York when Bishop shot back. "I *am* fully alive to the 'gross blindness of the operators.'" He admitted, however, that "they are the hardest men to stand with that I have ever felt it my duty to uphold but I cannot, try as I will, see that their conduct has anything to do with the issue as it stands today." Bishop softened his tone, however. "I am sure that if I were in your place, I should be moved as deeply as you are by the human interest side of this question . . . but I cannot get away from the conviction that my duty lies in fighting strictly for what I consider to be the main issue." Then, responding to the invitation: "I am most anxious to come on to see you but it is simply impossible so long as this crisis continues."[373] Bishop needed to keep his distance, and he knew better than to risk falling under Roosevelt's intense powers of persuasion.

The breakthrough came in the unlikely person of financier and railroad magnate J. Pierpont Morgan. Acting as a middleman, recruited secretly by Secretary of War Root, Morgan brought word to the president that the operators would agree to Roosevelt's arbitration panel only if they could dictate the categories of individuals who would serve, and as long as labor was not officially recognized with a representative on the five-man commission. As soon as the tentative understanding was announced, Bishop shot off a wire to the White House: "Glory Hallelujah! You come out with all the honors."[374]

Wisely, Roosevelt was not so sure. In a personal note back to Bishop, the president admitted, "I wish they had given me a free hand in appointing the commission, both because I feel there will be difficulty about getting the miners to accept what they will feel is a packed commission, and because I think it is vital that on such a commission there should be representation for both sides."[375]

Bishop nonetheless headlined his October 14 editorial PEACE WITH HONOR. He outlined that the operators' concession provided "for the immediate resumption of coal production, for the protection of individual rights of all the mine workers, union and non-union, and refers for final determination all questions in dispute to a tribunal so constituted that it will command the confidence of all fair-minded persons."[376] He made not one mention of "violence."

In fact, the coal strike did not end until Mitchell and the union got their coveted seat at the table, and it was Roosevelt who came up with an ingenious scheme to enable it. Edgar Clark, chief of the Railway Conductors Union, took his place on the panel, acknowledged by both sides not as a labor delegate but as "a man of prominence, an eminent sociologist"—a membership category the operators themselves had proposed.

Bishop couldn't wait to pat the president's back again in another wire. "Again hallelujah! Do read what I said last night in elucidation of your success.

It's God's truth."[377] What Bishop had printed was mostly Roosevelt boosterism. "From first to last, the moving spirit in the matter has been President Roosevelt . . . He was neither on the side of the operators nor on the side of the miners; he was on the side of the public, and was working solely for the public safety and welfare."[378]

"My dear Bishop," Roosevelt responded on October 16. "I am deeply touched by the editorial . . . I can almost guarantee entire justice and wisdom from such a commission."[379] Their exchange of letters and telegrams regarding the strike ended on October 18 when the president confided to Bishop, "Now I am being very much over-praised by everybody, and although I suppose I like it, it makes me feel uncomfortable too . . . It really seems to me that any man of average courage and common sense who felt as deeply as I did about the terrible calamity impending over our people would have done just what I did. But it is awfully nice of you to think as well of me."[380]

The coal strike ended after 163 difficult days. The arbitration commission went swiftly to work, allocating an entire week to an inspection of the mines. Then they sat through three months of exhaustive hearings, taking testimony from more than 500 witnesses. After more than 10,000 pages of testimony, the panel came to conclusions seen by most fair-minded people as "right down the middle." Social conditions in the mines were found to be good. The miners' allegation that earnings were below "an American standard of living" were partially justified. The workers demanded a 20 percent raise in pay; most received 10 percent. They wanted an eight-hour workday instead of one lasting ten hours, and the commission split the difference at nine. Recognition of the United Mine Workers as voice of the miners? No.[381] As Roosevelt had expected, both operators and miners agreed to the commission's findings without hesitation, and peace returned to the coalfields.

For John Mitchell, who had begun his career digging hard coal from murky pits, the outcome was a huge moral victory. The union, he claimed, had achieved the operators' de facto recognition, if not their respect. Moreover, because of President Roosevelt's determination to take great political risk, he had achieved a historic precedent: There was and always would be a third-party role for the federal government in resolving major national labor disputes. The public interest, in the end, had been served.

In one of his many Roosevelt retrospectives, this one reviewing the president's first year in office for the *International Quarterly*, Bishop credited Roosevelt with being "the most powerful leader that any party has had since Lincoln," and predicted that "if the nominating convention had been held this year, he would have been named for reelection without a dissenting voice."[382]

"My dear Bishop," T. R. replied, "[s]uch an article as . . . yours makes me feel humble and grateful. I thank you very deeply for it, old fellow. I do not deserve it in the least, but I shall do my best not to fall so far short of what you have written that you will have cause to regret that you wrote it."[383]

Twenty-One

Puppets and Jackrabbits

IT WAS THE MOST CONTENTIOUS CHAPTER OF THEODORE ROOSEVELT'S CAREER, and questions abounded. Did he and his foreign policy team enable a national revolution in the Colombian province of Panama in late 1903? Did he engage in gunboat diplomacy to establish a receptive government in a new nation so he could negotiate a favorable interoceanic canal treaty? Or, as Joseph Bucklin Bishop contended, did the Roosevelt administration merely "take all necessary precautions to preserve order, prevent bloodshed, and fulfill its treaty obligations"?[384]

The anti-imperialists (or "anti's") believed T. R.'s hardheaded, go-through-them approach exemplified his colonialist intent. T. R. supporters maintained that the president directed a measured, treaty-based response to events unfolding in Central and South America. Long afterward, Roosevelt pled his case: "I did not lift a finger to incite the revolutionists . . . I simply ceased to stamp out the different revolutionary fuses that were already burning . . . I had no alternative, consistent with the full performance of my duty to my own people, and to the nations of mankind."[385] Secretary of State John Hay, who stood in the eye of the storm, contended, "It is hard for me to understand how anyone can criticize our action in Panama . . . I had no hesitation as to the proper course to take, and have had no doubt of the propriety of it since."[386]

Following Congress's decision in the spring of 1902 to site the canal in Panama, it fell to John Hay to negotiate an acceptable treaty with Colombia. It was the "most thankless and exasperating episode in a long career," David McCullough observed.[387] Hay found Bogotá's diplomats dull-witted, inexperienced, and in no hurry to conclude a pact. As Roosevelt tapped his foot impatiently in the White House, Colombia slowed negotiations, demanding sovereignty in the future Canal Zone, and insisting on a share of the $40 million that the U.S. had promised to pay to the Compagnie Nouvelle.

An irritated Hay finally told the Colombian chargé d'affaires, Tomás Herrán, on January 12 that if the foot-dragging did not end, Roosevelt would open treaty talks with Nicaragua. Within hours, the Hay-Herrán Treaty was signed. The U.S. won control for a hundred years of a six-mile-wide strip of land between the city limits of Colón, on the Atlantic side of the isthmus, and Panama City on the Pacific, wherein the canal would be built. Colombia wrested a concession of $10 million in gold bullion, a $250,000 annual stipend, and a vague acknowledgment of sovereignty in the zone. The U.S. Senate ratified the sweetheart deal within weeks by a 73-to-5 vote. T. R. declared himself "delighted!" All that remained was the concurrence of the Colombian Senate.

As the months dragged on, anti-U.S. sentiment in Bogotá intensified. At the behest of Colombian strongman José Marroquín, Colombian senators demanded crippling treaty amendments and $5 million more in cash—destined, no doubt, for their pockets. Hay's response was unequivocal and nonnegotiable: Take an up or down vote on the treaty now. On August 12, the Colombian Senate unanimously rejected the treaty.

To Roosevelt, Colombia's rejection of the treaty amounted to being held hostage by "puppets" and "jackrabbits." He considered pursuing the alternative canal site in Nicaragua, but in the 1846 Treaty of New Granada, the U.S. had guaranteed the neutrality of the Panamanian territory in return for a pledge of "free transit" at that time and in the event of a future canal. As he studied the implications of the old agreement, the president heard from his emissaries and others that revolution was brewing in Panama.

The most significant person to bring news of insurrection to the White House was a diminutive French engineer and Compagnie Nouvelle lobbyist, Philippe Bunau-Varilla, who co-owned the respected Parisian newspaper Le Matin. Bunau-Varilla secured a meeting with the president through Hay. When the visitor boldly asked Roosevelt whether the U.S. would support Panama's secession from Colombia, the president demurred. Avoiding a direct answer, Roosevelt intimated that the U.S. would support Panama in its decisive hour. Bunau-Varilla knew that Roosevelt would have to make a show of force off the Panamanian coast.

In fact, a homegrown junta was plotting to overthrow Colombian rule. Led by Manuel Amador Guerrero, an elderly and well-respected physician, and a small band of prominent supporters, the separatists determined that the hour of Panama's freedom had arrived in the fall of 1903. Egged on and financed in large part by Bunau-Varilla, the junta recruited dissident troops and procured arms. The Frenchman asked only that when the new nation of Panama dispatched an envoy to Washington to conclude a canal treaty, that he be tasked with the mission.

As the uprising gathered strength, the White House ordered the *Nashville* to steam at top speed from waters off Cuba to Limón Bay and the port of Colón. The message was unmistakable. At the same time, the Colombian transport ship *Cartagena* was powering to the same Panamanian waters, laden with hundreds of armed troops. Roosevelt's secret orders to the *Nashville*'s commander were unmistakable: Preserve the unrestricted movement of the Panama Railroad across the isthmus and, if necessary, preclude the landing of any "hostile" forces.

But *Nashville* Commander John Hubbard had not yet received his orders when Colombian forces disembarked from the *Cartagena* into Colón. They marched to the railhead, intent on linking up with the Colombian garrison in Panama City. The American rail superintendent, Colonel James Shaler, refused them transport, however, pleading a shortage of passenger cars. In a quiet alliance with rebels, he demanded instead that the detachment's officers split up from their men and proceed to Panama City while he arranged for more rolling stock. The Colombian forces did not realize that Shaler was separating them from their leaders, thereby rendering them useless in putting down the rebellion.

At dusk on Tuesday, November 3, crowds of anxious *simpatizantes* gathered in Panama City's historic Cathedral Plaza to celebrate the triumph of the birth of their nation. Amador Guerrero's troops had arrested the compliant Panamanian governor, jailed the *Cartagena*'s officers, and bought off the Colombian garrison. The American vice consul in Panama cabled Hay: UPRISING OCCURRED TONIGHT AT SIX; NO BLOODSHED . . . GOVERNMENT WILL BE ORGANIZED TONIGHT . . . ORDER PREVAILS SO FAR.

And order did prevail—that is, except for the Colombian warship *Bogotá* halfheartedly hurling a few shells toward Cathedral Square before steaming away, desperately short of coal. A Chinese merchant and a donkey were the only casualties of the assault.

In Colón, the *Nashville* had discharged a small contingent of marines to ensure that the railroad remained "neutral." Because both sides proceeded cautiously, not a shot was fired on land in Colón. In the absence of clear direction from their leaders, the Colombian troops took safe passage home on a British mail steamer, enriched with $8,000 in gold and cases of warm champagne.

As promised, Philippe Bunau-Varilla, the cunning midwife of the revolution, became the Panamanian government agent in Washington. Within three days, the Roosevelt administration officially recognized the new Republic of Panama.

The U.S. further ensured the survival of the infant republic when it stationed a flotilla of warships, large and small, within clear sight of Colón and Panama City. As David McCullough wrote, "[W]ithout the military presence of the United States—had there been no American gunboats standing off shore at Colón and Panama City—the Republic of Panama probably would not have lasted a week."[388]

In his memoir, Roosevelt allocated multiple pages to a justification of his actions in Panama.

> *No one connected with the American Government had any part in preparing, inciting or encouraging the revolution. . . . no one connected with the Government had any previous knowledge concerning the revolution, except such as was accessible to any person who read the newspapers and kept abreast of current questions and current affairs. Every consideration of international morality and expediency, of duty to the Panama people, and of satisfaction of our own national interests, bade us to take immediate action .*
> *. . To have acted otherwise than I did would have been, on my part, betrayal of the interests of the United States.*[389]

Looking back at events on the isthmus a few years after he had left the White House, Roosevelt took a decidedly stronger view of the episode: In a speech delivered in Berkeley, California in 1911 he declared, "The Panama Canal would not have been started if I had not taken hold of it. . . I took the Isthmus, started the canal, and then left Congress not to debate the canal but to debate me."[390]

On November 4, the *Commercial Advertiser*'s correspondent in Panama City informed his readers that, "The cause of the revolution may be briefly summed up as the result of the action of the Congress of Colombia at Bogotá in rejecting the Hay-Herrán Canal Treaty."[391] On the editorial page, the paper allowed that "sufficient information is not yet at hand to justify much comment," but nonetheless voiced early backing for the treaty obligation espoused by Roosevelt and Hay. The next day, it dismissed as "absurd" the contention that the U.S. had fomented the revolution.

Bishop turned to a spirited defense of Roosevelt in a November 6 editorial. "Statesmen who deserve the name do not turn their backs upon opportunities which give them precisely what they have long desired to attain," he wrote. "Instead, they grasp these opportunities and use them boldly."[392]

Democrats in Congress, anti-imperialists, and their editorial backers criticized the president in the days following the revolution. Bishop countered by disdainfully skewering the agenda of the anti's and declaring, "[The idea that] our government, directly or indirectly, instigated the revolution is a preposterous assertion."[393] By November 10, Bishop was ridiculing the "unseemly exhibition of hysterics" of anti-Roosevelt publications, notably his former longtime employer, the *Evening Post,* which he tagged as "the most violent patient." On the 12th: "The whole country is in a broad grin over this comic opera performance carried forward with such inimitable seriousness by the dear old 'anti's' who cannot in the least understand what all the laughter is about."[394]

As was his routine, Roosevelt pored over the newspapers. "Of all the editorials you have written, I think I like best the one on 'Statesmanship,'" the president wrote to Bishop. "Whatever may be the actual facts I like to try to believe that the lines with which you head the editorial are deserved."[395] Bishop closed his case against the "dazed critics of President Roosevelt's Panama coup" on November 18 by asserting that it was backed by the "virtually unanimous and enthusiastic sentiment of the American people."

Not three weeks later, Roosevelt laid before the U.S. Senate a signed treaty providing for the building of a canal across the Isthmus of Panama. In his third annual message to Congress—a forerunner to the contemporary State of the Union address—Roosevelt wrote to the legislators: "We have shown the utmost forbearance in exacting our own rights." He revisited the 1846 treaty with New Granada and used it again as the rationale for American intervention in Panama. "The government of the United States would have been guilty of folly and weakness, amounting in their sum to a crime against the Nation, had it acted otherwise than it did when the revolution of November 3 last took place in Panama," he said. "The course of events has shown that this canal cannot be built by private enterprise, or by any other nation than our own; therefore it must be built by the United States."[396]

Despite the grave nature of unfolding events, Roosevelt still found time to write charmingly to his children, this time to Kermit:

To-night while I was preparing to dictate a message to Congress concern-
ing the boiling cauldron on the Isthmus of Panama, which has now begun
to bubble over, up came one of the ushers with a telegram from you and Ted
about the football match. Instantly I bolted into the next room to read it
aloud to Mother and sister, and we all cheered in unison when it came to
the Rah! Rah! Rah! part of it. It was a great score. I wish I could have seen
the game.[97]

The treaty that Hay and Bunau-Varilla had concluded provided a guarantee for the future independence of Panama but ceded to the U.S. a strip of land ten miles wide between Colón and Panama City where men and machines would dig the canal. In addition to "maintaining order" in the Canal Zone, the U.S. would enjoy, in perpetuity, "all the rights, power and authority which it would possess, were it the sovereign of the territory." Compagnie Nouvelle's assets, including the Panama Railway, passed to the U.S., as did a grant of free immigration of people and supplies needed for the construction and operation of the canal. Further, the U.S. had the right to use military force and build fortifications "for the protection of the transit." For its part, Panama received the $10 million pledged earlier to Colombia and an annual payment of $250,000, to begin in 1912.

Professor Fernando Aparicio of the University of Panama argued in a 2011 interview with the author that a mix of forces led to revolution in Panama: the U.S. interest in building a canal, the French impatience to sell their failing investment, and the Panamanian people's historical inclination to become a nation. "But without the U.S.," he argued, "Panamanian insurgents would not have been able to defeat Colombia."[98] It was a stunning coup both for America and for Roosevelt.

This time, there was no barrier to ratification. The new government of Panama endorsed the treaty unanimously and without change. Once the U.S. Senate endorsed it—after intense blowback from the anti's—the stage was set for what Roosevelt called the greatest achievement of his presidency. Bishop, watching from New York, wondered whether the events of recent weeks signaled an opportunity for him to move closer to Roosevelt's side.

Twenty-Two

The Hawkeye Conspiracy

THE BREATHTAKING MARCH OF EVENTS LEADING TO THE CONSTRUCTION OF THE Panama Canal did, in fact, mark the decline of Joseph Bucklin Bishop's career as a New York editorial writer. At the height of the machinations, between the fall of 1903 and early 1904, a sundry cast of individuals swung into Bishop's orbit: an Iowa newspaper baron taking on the fourth estate in New York City, a sitting governor, a Civil War general, two members of the president's cabinet, and Theodore Roosevelt himself. Several of the personalities bored into Bishop's dark side and took him to places of anger, revenge, and vulnerability that he rarely showed.

The *Commercial Advertiser* had seen its circulation increase fivefold, to 12,000, but there it stalled, its popularity resting mainly with the city's thoughtful readers. Working-class readers and the great wave of immigrants now learning English increasingly bought the bold headlines and lurid tales of the yellow penny papers. As America's oldest-surviving evening newspaper, the *Commercial Advertiser* was ripe for takeover and makeover, a casualty of the city's fierce newspaper warfare.

On a west wind from Iowa, Samuel Strauss descended on Manhattan. Once a successful dry goods manufacturer, he later co-owned the *Des Moines Leader* and merged it with the city's *Register* newspaper before selling to the Cowles family. Now in New York, he planned to take charge of another city daily, the *Globe,* and to consolidate it with the *Commercial Advertiser.* Bishop was not part of Strauss's plans.

A moon-faced character with oversized glasses and a departing hairline, Strauss gave Bishop his notice in October. The longtime editor was incensed. "There is something more behind this business than appears on the surface," Bishop alleged in a letter to Roosevelt in the days when the president was dealing with revolution in Panama. Strauss's move, Bishop claimed, was backed by Roosevelt's Treasury secretary Leslie Shaw, a recent governor of Iowa, and

Albert Cummins, the current governor of the Hawkeye State. "Shaw thinks he is a promising candidate for the presidency . . . in 1904," Bishop wrote. He expressed some reservations about the veracity of his allegation but nonetheless warned Roosevelt, who of course had the 1904 election in mind, "I think you should know of it so that you may go to the bottom of it—at once."[399]

Bishop's handwritten letters to Roosevelt at the time refer namelessly to Strauss as "the Jew." Not once did he pen or type the new publisher's name, unable to bring himself even to acknowledge the man's authority. Bishop's reference to Strauss in such a way is the only surviving instance of such an unexpected and troubling mind-set in a record of more than 600 letters; yet it is a jarring occurrence that reminds us uncomfortably of some prevailing attitudes of the time.

Bishop refused to accept Strauss's notice. "I have my fighting blood up, and somebody is going to get injured before this thing is settled," he fumed to T. R.[400]

Roosevelt tried to calm him the next day. "Do not give a second thought to the allegation about Shaw and the presidency."[401]

Bishop sought reprieve by going over Strauss's head to Thomas Hamlin Hubbard, part-owner of the *Globe* and a Roosevelt friend. Hubbard had been a Civil War brigadier general whose physician father, John, was a fondly remembered governor of Maine. Following the war, General Hubbard had practiced law in New York and invested successfully in railroads and financial institutions. Bishop believed that his intervention, with a nod from Roosevelt, could save him.

On October 29, 1903, Bishop told T. R. that he had had a long talk with General Hubbard, whom he knew from various social clubs in New York. Their conversation had followed an exchange of letters in which Hubbard confessed that he had not known what Strauss was up to, and, once he did, had ordered Bishop's dismissal notice withdrawn. "I am complete master of the situation," Bishop now crowed to Roosevelt.[402] Yet events had humbled him. "I never knew what friends I had till this blow fell upon me," he said. "Hay was magnificent in every way. Yesterday, when I told a few friends about the matter, I was so overcome with their instant proffers of sympathy and aid of every kind, that I was forced to hurry home to keep control of myself."[403]

T. R. responded knowingly, "Nothing could have pleased me more than your letter . . . With love to your wife, and may the Unseen Power be with you always."[404]

Bishop would not, however, let go of the Shaw allegation, telling the president, "I think it pretty hard that a member of your Cabinet should vouch for a man whose first act on my paper was to seek by lying—to injure your best friend and to destroy the newspaper most devoted and most serviceable to you. The Jew is a boundless liar and a dastardly enemy of yours." His tirade concluded, Bishop then closed his letter softly: "All is well my dear, dear friend. Kiss Mrs. Roosevelt for me."[405]

Four days later, on the eve of the revolt in Panama, Roosevelt reassured Bishop:

> *I have seen Secretary Shaw, and the result is exactly as I had anticipated. The Secretary did not know of your relations with me; and, more than that, he did not know that you were on the* Commercial Advertiser. *Strauss asked him for an introduction to General Hubbard. Strauss being so prominent a figure in the editorial world of Iowa, Shaw felt that he could not well refuse the introduction. . . . Now, Shaw has expressed great surprise and regret that there should have been any move against any friend of mine.*[406]

Once the isthmus was securely in hand and it looked as though the U.S. at last would build the canal, Roosevelt dashed off a quick note to Bishop in New York. "Naturally I am selfishly interested in having you in the biggest editorial position that you can be put in. Nobody but you can write editorials containing just exactly what I should like to have said."[407] That evening on his editorial page, Bishop gratified the president further by denouncing as "preposterous" his opponents' claims that the U.S. had instigated the Panamanian revolution.

The *Commercial Advertiser* soon morphed into the *Globe and Commercial Advertiser*. Both Strauss and Bishop survived the flap, although their working relationship in the months that followed undoubtedly remained contentious. Shaw stayed as Roosevelt's influential secretary of the Treasury through the spring of 1907 and was a failed candidate for the Republican nomination for president in 1908, once T. R. was out of the running.

General Hubbard moved swiftly in the aftermath of the Bishop incident to make big money in Panama, the new U.S. ally in Central America. He asked a return favor of Bishop. Would he, by chance, intervene with the administration to have his International Banking Corporation appointed as the U.S. fiscal agent in Panama? Hubbard argued that his institution could certainly serve as the medium when the U.S. paid out $40 million to the Compagnie Nouvelle

Personal

November 5, 1903.

Dear Bishop:

Naturally I am selfishly interested in having you in the biggest editorial position that you can be put in! Nobody but you can write editorials containing just exactly what I should like to have said.

Always yours,

Theodore Roosevelt

Mr. J. B. Bishop,
The Commercial Advertiser,
167 Broadway,
New York.

President Roosevelt praises Bishop's knack for supportive editorials.

Theodore Roosevelt Papers, Manuscript Division. Library of Congress

and the $10 million to Panama as part of the canal treaty. And, Hubbard added, it could competently receive and disperse payments for labor and materials once canal construction got under way. The bank, after all, had successfully collected the $25 million Boxer indemnity from China. "All this seems to me both reasonable and proper," Bishop wrote Roosevelt, "and likely to be of service to both the government and to Americans on the Isthmus."[408]

The President was inclined to help, as he said, if he could properly do what Hubbard desired. But he needed to keep the arrangement at arm's length. "Would there be any object in my communicating with him through *you?*" [emphasis added] Roosevelt inquired of Bishop. "Would it serve a useful purpose?"[409]

"Not only useful but vitally important to deal through me," Bishop wired back the same day.[410] The editor wanted to prove to Hubbard that he was capable of repaying the job-saving favor in a large way. The following day, Bishop made completely clear his need to take full credit for whatever success Hubbard might have, in case the president had any doubt. "If, when you decide, as I hope, in favor of the request, you will let me know in advance or will in some way let H. know that I had some weight in getting this decision?" he asked. "You will help me greatly."[411]

"Will you tell General Hubbard that I shall take the matter up at once with Secretary Shaw," Roosevelt replied to Bishop. "I believe what he desires can be done and that I shall notify him through you as soon as we can come to a decision."[412]

Hubbard knew that Roosevelt, Shaw, and Bishop were pushing to get his bank selected for the assignment. But as Congress realized what a financial bonanza was at stake, the general from Maine and his allies were deftly out-maneuvered in the Senate by the "general manager of the nation," Republican Nelson Aldrich of Rhode Island, acting on behalf of the Rockefeller family—into which his daughter, Abby, had married—and their National City Bank. In May 1904, Aldrich stripped from pending legislation Shaw's provision favoring Hubbard's bank. It did not go unnoted by most observers that National City Bank became the fiscal agent of the new nation of Panama.

IMPORTANT ANNOUNCEMENT barked the editorial headline in the *Commercial Advertiser*'s January 29, 1904, edition. It heralded two "important departures." Referring to itself in the third person, the paper revealed, "Its price will be reduced to one cent so as to bring it within reach of all," and "An alternative name, the *Globe*, has been adopted and will be used in association with the old. Hereafter, the title of the paper will be the *Globe and Commercial Advertiser*." It is hard to imagine that Joseph Bucklin Bishop wrote such a prosaic notice for the editorial page, its matter-of-fact tone bearing no sign of his usual rhetorical style.

The paper's announcement went on to say: "The *Commercial Advertiser* pro-poses now to make accessible to everyone a thoroughly comprehensive newspa-per, which, enterprising and fearless as the so-called yellow press is wanton and reckless . . . relies on intelligence and brightness rather than mere frivolity to win and hold the attention of its readers."[413] As future *Globe* publisher Jason Rogers recalled, "New York woke up Monday morning, February 1, 1904, to find that its oldest and one of its most conservative, high-priced newspapers had gone to one cent. It was going to be a bigger and better newspaper for one cent than it had been previously for two cents; and 100,000 of them bought it."[414]

Twenty-Three

Poised for a Sweep

THERE WAS LITTLE DOUBT THAT THEODORE ROOSEVELT WOULD RUN FOR the presidency in 1904—and win. He wanted to demonstrate to doubters that he was more than an accidental president. Taft, still overseeing the American presence in the Philippines, took himself out of consideration early, in a ten-page letter to Bishop, knowing that Bishop would forward his sentiments to Roosevelt. "The suggestion that I should become a candidate for any place on the presidential ticket is as absurd as anything possibly could be," Taft wrote. "I am first, last and all the time for Roosevelt." Expressing distaste for what it would take: "I have not the slightest taste for political life or for a political campaign, the horrors of which are like a nightmare to me," said the man who would eventually succeed T. R. in the White House.[415]

The only threat to Roosevelt's nomination was Senator Mark Hanna, the Republican National Committee chairman and darling of conservatives. But Hanna, in fragile health and with declining influence in the party since McKinley's death, was a halfhearted alternative; he died of typhoid fever in February 1904, four months before the convention. His last letter, pencil-scrawled to Roosevelt from his deathbed, thanked the president for a visit to his Washington hotel. "You touched a tender spot, old man, when you called to inquire after me this A.M. I may be worse before I can be better but all the same, such 'drops' of kindness are good for a fellow."[416]

Roosevelt did have cause to worry, though, about a serious fracture within his party in New York, where the largest number of electoral votes was at stake. Two old adversaries, Senator Thomas Platt and Governor Benjamin Odell, were clashing over patronage. The furious Platt was threatening to send a split delegation to the national convention in June. Odell was said to be loyal to Roosevelt, but T. R.'s old nemesis, the Boss, still carried grudges from Roosevelt's days as a reform governor. In March 1903, Bishop reported a conversation to the president during which a concerned third party had urged Roosevelt's intervention in the split. "If you took sides with Odell openly, he would make sure of a solid delegation for you next year, but that unless you did so, Platt . . . would secure ten or more delegates who would go to the convention determined to knife you."[417] Roosevelt opted to stay out the fracas for now, instead making final plans for a two-month tour of the West.

The president departed the White House April 1, 1903 for eight grueling weeks, scheduled to travel 14,000 miles through twenty-five states in his private sleeper, augmented by a retinue of dignitaries, staff, and press. It was an exacting journey to be sure, but one that Roosevelt believed was crucial to cementing support in Western states. The tour was billed as official, not a campaign swing, but Roosevelt understood that if he secured the nomination in 1904, tradition precluded overt campaigning by an incumbent nominee. This trip was his best opportunity to reconnect with the people of the West, the farmers, ranchers, and cowboys with whom he felt a deep kinship. He planned to give as many as 200 speeches along the route, focusing on his accomplishments and future plans. Moreover, he yearned to explore the glorious mountain and desert wilderness of the far West and stake out a personal presence in California and the Pacific Northwest.

Before leaving, T. R. put Bishop in charge of organizing the New York reelection campaign along with the dynamic Nicholas Butler, now president of Columbia University. Bishop helped direct campaign strategy and, of course, proclaimed the gospel according to T. R. from the editorial pages of the *Globe*. He assured the candidate: "It is not unlikely that this paper, with a circulation four times what it was, may be of great service in the campaign. If I can mold that, I shall have nothing more to desire."[418]

Bishop told the touring president early in June that he was pleased Roosevelt was nearing home, safe and well. "If the results of your trip are to be judged by the political situation, they could not be better. Nobody any longer even questions your nomination, and I find nobody who thinks there is any doubt of your election."[419]

It was Bishop's custom to take off the month of July each year and to settle, with Harriet, in comfortable waterside surroundings. Often he retired to Falmouth on the southwestern leg of Cape Cod, but this year he chose Montowese House in Branford, Connecticut, on Long Island Sound. The location was not happenstance. "I could, of course get from there to Oyster Bay, at any time in case you wish to see me," he informed Roosevelt.[420] The record reveals that Roosevelt did not summon Bishop to Sagamore Hill that July.

Although of modest financial means, Bishop usually pampered himself in vacation luxury and hobnobbed with those who knew how to strut their wealth. Located on Branford's picturesque Indian Neck, Montowese House—known affectionately as the Queen of the Sound—offered Joseph and Harriet the chance to mingle with the influential and illustrious and to revel in lush accommodations. Bishop usually ignored available sport and exercise opportunities, preferring instead to invest his idle hours in reading nonfiction or working on an active manuscript. At Montowese House, he worked on *Issues of a New Epoch*, a laudatory treatise of Roosevelt's management of the coal strike, the Panama Canal, and the administration of the Philippines and Cuba, as well as a new book, *Our Political Drama: Campaigns, Conventions and Candidates.*

A year out from the election, the president intervened in the Platt–Odell feud—for the sake of the party and his own future. He summoned the opponents to Washington for a meeting but neglected to inform his New York campaign co-manager of the outcome. Bishop was annoyed. "If you are so disposed, I should really like to know the outcome of your talks," he snappishly wrote. "There is great uneasiness and uncertainty among Republicans here about what really occurred at the White House between you and Platt and Odell."[421]

"There was certain to be some tall lying about that conference," the president replied. "The facts are perfectly simple. Odell and Platt agreed to work together to avoid a split; that Platt should be leader but that Odell should be, as he was formerly, Platt's lieutenant and executive arm, who should have the management of the details."[422]

Bishop doubted the deal. "Taken by and large, I think the pair would take first and second prizes in a baby show. They seem now, for the moment at least, to have come to their senses, but the Lord only knows how long they will stay there."[423]

By tradition, direction of the national campaign—and all-important fundraising—fell to the chairman of the national committee. To succeed Hanna, Roosevelt chose his former chief of staff, George Cortelyou, a man of princely bearing and impeccable reputation who had served Cleveland and McKinley well, and, as we saw, was with McKinley in Buffalo on the day of the shooting. Cortelyou had won Roosevelt's admiration when he reorganized White House operations and indulged reporters, for the first time, with working quarters inside the White House. Most recently, Cortelyou had served with distinction as the nation's first secretary of commerce and labor, a post that offered him daily contact with the nation's chieftains of finance and industry.

By the time summer crept up on Chicago, where the Republican National Convention convened on June 21, 1904, Roosevelt was poised for a sweep. State delegations had been meeting dutifully to choose more than half the delegates whom the president would need for nomination. Roosevelt did not attend the convention; there was no reason. He had firm control over the party platform and had editing privileges over the speeches from men he had selected to orate. When necessary, he could manage events via a telephone hotline that linked a convention war room to the White House. Only the ghost of Senator Hanna, his oversized mourning portrait hanging gloomily over the speaker's rostrum in the Coliseum, spoiled the ebullience of the Roosevelt nomination.

The platform faithfully extolled the party's philosophy and Roosevelt's accomplishments: an economic policy that had restored prosperity, continuation of protective tariffs, control of a canal in Panama, Cuban independence from Spain, and the interests of the people over corporations and unions.

Since occupying the White House in the fall of 1901, Roosevelt had served without a vice president, there being no provision in the Constitution at the time to fill a vacancy. By the middle of 1904, it was not surprising that he demonstrated scant interest in choosing one for his full term. Ultimately he settled on Charles Fairbanks, a conservative-minded senator from Indiana. That he was a former Associated Press reporter who had covered Horace Greeley's eccentric 1872 presidential campaign was a plus. To Fairbanks, after all, would fall the obligation to stump coast to coast for the ticket while the president quietly orchestrated the campaign symphony from within the walls of the White House.

"Tomorrow, the National Convention meets," the president wrote to Kermit on June 21, "and barring a cataclysm I shall be nominated. There is a great deal of sullen grumbling, but it has taken more the form of resentment against what they think is my dictation as to details than against me personally. They don't dare to oppose me for the nomination," he observed, "and I suppose it is hardly likely the attempt will be made to stampede the convention for anyone."[424]

Inside the cavernous, domed hall, more than 1,000 delegates, many of whom had found accomplishment and wealth in the circumstances of the Industrial Age, assembled in their proper dark suits and starched white collars. On the hot and crowded floor, few banners flew or signs bobbed. In fact, there was hardly any hoopla. The only Roosevelt presence was a series of small, formal portraits hung in silent tribute to him on the support columns that encircled the interior of the hall. There were no challenges to the sitting president from the floor. It was a scripted show. When the formal roll call of the states concluded, Roosevelt and Fairbanks received all 994 of the adoring delegates' votes. The president's operatives had succeeded in stifling every whiff of dissent.

"How the election will turn out, no one can tell," the president told Kermit. "Of course, I hope to be elected but I realize to the full how very lucky I have been, not only to be President but to have been able to accomplish so much while President, and whatever may be the outcome I am not only content but sincerely thankful for all the good fortune I have had."[425]

From New York, Bishop reiterated to the nominee that the *Globe* would have "more influence in the campaign—a hundred times over than the old *Commercial Advertiser* was able to exercise . . . It gives me unspeakable pleasure to think that I can be of really valuable service in the campaign."[42]

Just two weeks later, Democrats gathered in St. Louis in a convention that produced considerably more excitement. William Jennings Bryan, the populist and celebrated "Great Commoner," declined a third opportunity to stand for his party. The choice this time was between the party's anointed man, Alton Parker, chief judge of the New York State Court of Appeals, and the publisher and now congressman, William Randolph Hearst. Bryan threw in with the insurgent Hearst, believing Parker a weak choice and a tool of Wall Street. The weeks leading up to the convention had seen divisive delegate contests in Illinois and other key states, but by the time delegates convened in Exposition and Music Hall, party leaders had maneuvered to ensure that Parker would be nominated on the first ballot.

As the final vote neared, however, he was nine votes short of the necessary two-thirds. Convention managers approached 2 "soft" Hearst supporters and induced them to swing behind Parker. In the end, it was 679 delegates for Parker, and just 181 for Hearst. The next president of the United States would be a New Yorker one way or the other. For a running mate, Democrats chose West Virginia millionaire and rail magnate Senator Henry Davis, at eighty-one, the oldest major party candidate ever nominated for national office.

On the same day that the Democrats opened their convention in St. Louis, Roosevelt had assembled his friends and campaign brain trust at Sagamore Hill. In the family dining room, where open windows admitted the refreshing breeze off Long Island Sound, the dinner table was set for nineteen. Cortelyou, the party chairman, sat at the president's elbow. Elihu Root, who had by now resigned as secretary of war, kept a lawful eye on the planning talk; Gifford Pinchot, the eminent conservationist, contributed substantively to the discussion, as did Roosevelt's political pal from Massachusetts, former governor Crane. Seated near Miss Eleanor Roosevelt, the president's niece and future first lady, were the New York campaign co-captains, Nicholas Butler and Joseph Bucklin Bishop.

There was talk of Root's candidacy for New York governor since the incumbent Republican, Odell, was not running, and it was common belief that a strong Republican state ticket would propel Roosevelt to triumph over Parker. In case the contest between the two New Yorkers was to be close, Roosevelt wanted no baggage on the lower ticket. Bishop boosted Root, writing soon thereafter that "Root must run whether he wants to or not, and I have assumed in today's paper that he is to be the candidate."[427] But Root's genuine reluctance to stand for election and his expressed "loathing and distaste" for state politics took him resolutely to the sidelines. As for the top-of-the-ticket race, "Everything looks very favorable here," Bishop wrote the president. "I do not find anybody who does not consider your election virtually assured. That is particularly the opinion among Wall Street men."[428]

Returning to New York from his annual New England vacation on July 30, Bishop informed Roosevelt, "My book is out, and I have a copy for you." With numerous illustrations and caricatures, *Our Political Drama* replayed tales of candidates, conventions, and campaigns of the past. The author described his work modestly as "merely the personal and dramatic side of certain events in our political history: a compilation, however imperfect." The *New York Times* was a bit more enthusiastic, praising it as "easy reading and, in points, informing." The reviewer had special praise for the illustrations. "The most interesting portion of the whole book is that which deals with the history of American political caricature from Jackson's time when, by Mr. Bishop's account, caricature first began to be used to any extent."[429]

Meanwhile, Bishop ground out daily editorial opinions for *Globe* readers and reassured President Roosevelt that the voters of New York were lining up behind him. "Everything looks so bright that it almost scares me," he said. "Nothing except some extraordinary 'break' or turn of fortune can defeat you, and there are no signs of either."[430]

Although eager to meet with voters, Roosevelt grudgingly yielded to tradition and declined to tour during the fall campaign. He passed much of the midsummer doldrums at Sagamore Hill, taking Edith boating on the placid sound and frolicking with the children in spirited lawn games. To be sure that his friend would win by a respectable margin in New York, Bishop did some opposition research. Villard's *Evening Post* had endorsed Judge Parker, and Bishop was hell-bent on exposing the paper's inconsistency, if not its hypocrisy. After some research, he alerted the president: "I have today found in the columns of the *Evening Post* some expressions of opinion, beginning in 1892 and coming down through 1897 to 1903, about Parker and his qualifications which are simply destructive of the position they now take." Bishop passed along his findings to campaign higher-ups while winking to Roosevelt with a wry aside: "All these are very strong. I can speak without partiality because I wrote most of them myself."[431]

A week later, Bishop joined senior campaign strategists at another Sagamore Hill roundtable. In addition to Cortelyou and Root, Senator Lodge attended to help plan the vice presidential nominee's fall campaign stops. (Fairbanks would stump energetically for the ticket in thirty-three of the forty-five states.) To stock the campaign war chest, Roosevelt turned to Cortelyou and Republican National Committee treasurer Cornelius Bliss. Notwithstanding predictions of a runaway win, his money men raised $2.2 million for the campaign, the equivalent of $52.7 million in 2010. Most of the funds came from bankers, financiers, and industrial magnates—the very people whom Cortelyou had overseen at the Commerce and Labor Department. To avoid any hint of impropriety, the straitlaced party chairman adamantly insisted on a high wall between campaign contributors and expected favors in the next administration. He demanded of Bliss an environment "unhampered by a single promise of any kind."

As a warm, early fall settled over New York, Senator Platt and Governor Odell were recruiting New York voters for Roosevelt as promised, yet they had drawn swords over who would run for governor. Platt favored former lieutenant governor Timothy Woodruff; Odell had selected the sitting lieutenant governor, Frank Higgins, to succeed him. Acrimonious delegate battles had occurred throughout the state during the summer, but by the time conventioneers convened in Saratoga on September 14, Platt sensed defeat and instructed Woodruff to withdraw—in favor of the lethargic but well-liked Higgins.

The outcome of the state convention worried Roosevelt, who feared that Higgins would drag down the ticket. Surrendering the mother lode of thirty-nine national electoral votes to Parker was simply unthinkable to Roosevelt; it could cost him the presidency in his own right if something were not done. The president intervened with rail magnate E. H. Harriman and one or two other

Republican millionaires of his acquaintance. It was not long before significant sums flowed into the state committee lockbox to bolster Higgins and his lackluster campaign.

Roosevelt mapped out the playbook for the national election campaign in a 12,000-word letter formally accepting the Republican nomination. He was running on his record. The basis of the prevailing economic prosperity—a world away now from the Panic of 1893—lay in the protective tariffs that kept cheap foreign goods out of the American market. The gold standard underpinned the nation's long-term financial stability. The Panama Canal was about to link the oceans and ensure the U.S. a role as a world power. And there was an effective, federal "big stick" to oversee domestic labor-management relations in the wake of the coal strike settlement.

Because Alton Parker's platform positions varied only somewhat from Roosevelt's—with the notable exception of his opposition to vigorous antitrust prosecutions—general election voters had to focus on the personalities and likability of the candidates. Parker's dour, lawyer-like style was hardened by his old-fashioned campaign strategy of staying put in his hometown, sleepy Esopus, New York, greeting delegation after delegation of traditional Democratic stalwarts. Though confined to the White House by tradition, Roosevelt remained visible to the public as president, ensuring that a dutiful press corps covered his every act. "On the whole, this has been an easy campaign for me," he admitted to his son Kermit. "I am content to stand or fall on the record I have made in these three years, and the bulk of the voters will oppose or support me on that record, and will be only secondarily influenced by what is done during the campaign proper."[432]

"Parker simply makes no impression here," Bishop reported from New York City a month out from the election. "Scarcely a person of any consequence calls upon him during his frequent visits. . . . He seems to me weaker in the estimation of the public, including a very large proportion of his own party today, than he has been at any time since his speech of acceptance."[433] That may have been due, in part, to the Democrats' feeble fund-raising efforts. By Election Day, they had raised a paltry $500,000 ($12 million in 2010), less than a quarter of what Republicans had collected. And 50 percent of the Democrats' half-million had come from just one donor, Tammany Hall enthusiast Thomas Fortune Ryan, a tobacco and transport magnate with an apt middle name.

On October 14, Bishop presented Roosevelt with evidence that he would win New York, as would Frank Higgins. "Odell showed us yesterday the results of his systematic canvass by election districts of the state," he revealed. "They give you a plurality of 96,000 in the state. Odell has perfect faith in this. He estimated that Higgins will run 80,000 behind you and be elected by 16,000." Bishop massaged his old friend's ego. "Instead of having to pull you through with a popular man on the state ticket—as was the talk early in the campaign—you are the only hope . . . of the state ticket."[434]

Although Roosevelt enjoyed the endorsements in New York of the *Globe* and the *Sun,* Joseph Pulitzer's *World* roused the campaign early in October with a frenzied front-page assault on the Republicans' alleged campaign coziness with the very trusts that the administration had been busting. Following an earlier report in the *New York Times,* Pulitzer asked the president ten specific questions regarding the money that corporations had contributed to the campaign, and whether George Cortelyou had pressured them in return for promises of future protection. Cortelyou quietly defended his honor, but Democrats pounced, believing they had an effective political opening against the administration. In time, Parker echoed the widening chorus of questioners in an eleventh-hour string of appearances in the New York area. "The attack on Cortelyou which the *Times* made and which the *World* echoed has fallen flat, so far as I can judge," Bishop reassured the president. Nonetheless, he promised Roosevelt that he would prepare rebuttal points for the Republican National Committee "to send out to the press of the country."[435]

Roosevelt felt that he could not remain silent any longer in the face of the partisan attacks on the integrity of his campaign and administration. Less than a week from Election Day, he issued a blistering statement condemning his opponents' charges as "monstrous" and a "wicked falsehood." He later explained to Kermit, "Parker's attacks became so atrocious that I determined—against the counsel of my advisers—to hit; and, as I never believe in hitting soft, I hit him in a way he will remember . . . Things look rather favorable for us."[436]

On Election Day, the president took a special train to Oyster Bay to vote, and he returned immediately to the White House to await the outcome. Steeling himself to accept the result "as a man ought to, whichever way it went," he kept his normal routine, dressing for a 7:30 dinner with Edith and the children, and Mrs. George Cortelyou, their guest. But by the time the first course was served, Roosevelt knew from early returns that his election was assured. Son Archie, his chest plastered with Roosevelt campaign buttons and badges, shuttled between the White House telegraph office and the family dining room, carrying encouraging reports. The president read each note aloud with a knowing, toothy smile.

Dee-lighted!, he crowed over the din of the table. Soon, cabinet members began arriving to join what would be a joyous celebration. To Kermit the president later wrote, "It was a great comfort to feel, all during the last days, when affairs looked doubtful, that no matter how things came out, the really important thing was the lovely life with Mother and you children." He concluded, "Compared to this home life, everything else was of very small importance from the standpoint of happiness."[437]

The next morning, an ebullient Bishop confessed to Roosevelt, "I have been literally drunk with joy since seven o'clock last night. I need not say to you that the result is more than I dared dream of."[438] Indeed, Roosevelt had won by the largest popular margin of victory in presidential history to date: 56 percent to 36 percent, and 336 to 140 in the Electoral College. Parker had won only the eleven states of the former Confederacy and the border states of Kentucky and Maryland, where anti-Roosevelt and anti-black sentiment seethed.

Roosevelt swept the remaining states including New York. His home state margin of 176,000 votes nearly doubled Odell's earlier projection and greatly eclipsed his private hope. It was more than enough to secure the prize of New York's 39 electoral votes and compel a Republican majority of more than 100 in the U.S. House of Representatives. For all the hand-wringing, Frank Higgins was easily elected governor of New York, by a margin of more than 80,000 votes.

Nearly overlooked in the excitement of the evening was a brief statement Roosevelt issued to reporters before he retired for the night. "On the fourth of March next I shall have served three and a half years, and this three and a half years constitute my first term. The wise custom which limits the President to two terms regards the substance and not the form. Under no circumstances will I be a candidate for or accept another nomination." Roosevelt had intentionally preempted himself, abruptly walking away from his entitlement by law and tradition: a second full term. The unexpected declaration stole some of the thrill from the family's Election Night revelry and effectively rendered Theodore Roosevelt a lame duck.

Bishop, however, saw it in another light:

I think your statement . . . about another term was as nearly perfect as anything human could be. . . . It showed the whole country that in the presence of the most overwhelming vote of confidence that the country has even given a

President, you were able to keep your head and to say what few men in that position would have been able to say. . . . Nothing that you have ever done has been so complete an answer to your critics as this.[439]

Roosevelt's spare words, spoken at the end of an intense day, hung heavy in the political air for four long years. He was true to his word in 1908, bowing to his friend Taft. But four years later, Roosevelt critics in both parties would pull his proclamation down from the ether and gleefully toss it back in o his face.

Twenty-Four

Most Extraordinary Things

"WHEN CAN I SEE YOU?" THE JUBILANT PRESIDENT ASKED BISHOP AS THE POST-election celebration slipped into a second day at the White House. "Can you come here to spend tomorrow night?"[440]

Bishop required little coaxing. He cabled Roosevelt the same day: "I will come with the greatest pleasure tomorrow night."[441]

When he called at the White House, weary off the late train from New York, Bishop discovered another arriving guest: John Morley, the liberal, erudite man of letters, yet to be raised to peerage as the first Viscount Morley of Blackburn. Like Roosevelt, Morley was an observer of men and affairs of state, and he had recently written a biography of Cromwell. Bishop anticipated much highbrow discourse.

In actuality, the ensuing dialogue left Morley, a "cold, deliberate, slow-speaking and formal Englishman," dumbfounded, according to Bishop's later recollection. As Roosevelt enthused about ancient history, classical literature, and the sundry character of men, Morley was nearly speechless. When the president eventually excused himself to attend to matters of state, Bishop was left to guide the awestruck Briton on a tour of the mansion's ceremonial rooms. Putting his bony hand on Bishop's shoulder as they toured the spacious East Room, Morley said in a rich, baronial tone, "My dear fellow, do you know the two most extraordinary things I have seen in your country? Niagara Falls and the president of the United States—both great wonders of nature!"[442]

In the days following his election, Roosevelt was earning plaudits world-wide. Of his landslide election, Roosevelt reflected that he owed his achievement not to political operatives or campaign financiers but to "Abraham Lincoln's plain people—to the folk who worked hard on the farm, in shops or on the railroads or who owned little stores, little businesses which they managed themselves."[443] On returning to England, Morley was said to remark about Roosevelt to a friend: "He is not an American, you know. He *is* America."[444]

Over the course of Roosevelt's full term, Bishop visited the White House and Sagamore Hill many times, socially and on business, always to engage the president in strategic discussion of politics and the press and, lately, a role for himself in the Roosevelt administration. An invitation to spend Christmas Eve with T. R., Edith, and the children arrived subsequently. Regrettably, particulars of the evening went unrecorded, but during the evening Bishop worked up the courage to ask Taft, now secretary of war, if he could share his family's Christmas Day celebrations in Washington. He did not want to return to New York. "I know it is the holiday season," he said to Taft, "and it is quite likely that you have a full house. If this is the case, you will not hesitate to say so, of course."[445]

"Mrs. Taft and I will be delighted to have you stay with us," Taft replied.[446] Again, there is no record of what the men discussed when they presumably retired to the judge's study after Christmas dinner. More than likely, Bishop was sounding out Taft for a position in the administration. As secretary of war, Taft was supervising preparations for the imminent construction of the Panama Canal, among countless other military projects. Two days later, Bishop departed the household with warm memories and an autographed photo of the secretary—but without a cherished personal item. "Did your coachman tell you that I left my umbrella in your house?" Bishop wrote Taft after returning to New York. "It has a bamboo handle, and you will easily distinguish it, I think. If you will send it by express, I shall gladly defray the expense."[447] The distinctive umbrella was apparently an essential element of Bishop's rainy-day dress, an item his Yankee frugality would not allow him to replace.

Bishop was, after thirty-five years of newspaper work, tired of scolding rascally New York politicians. With Roosevelt guaranteed four more years in office, he knew that he must relocate to Washington—the fulcrum of the action—if he wanted to advance. As it happened, the nation's capital was the location of the Isthmian Canal Commission's headquarters.

Letters reveal that Bishop and Roosevelt had discussed canal-related opportunities as far back as June 1902 when site alternatives in the Colombian isthmus and in Nicaragua were being weighed. In August 1903, he reminded Roosevelt that the president had authority over staffing the commission, enclosing an editorial entitled, "Panama—The Route." In it, Bishop listed the criteria for appointment to the commission and noted the president's power to fix the compensation of commissioners and "other personnel." Roosevelt acknowledged that, yes, he had that authority, but underlined to Bishop that he did not have license to "appoint extra ones to the Commission." Their discussions had continued off and on through the subsequent months without resolution.

On Inauguration Day, March 4, 1905, Theodore Roosevelt rode in an open landau from the White House to the east front of the Capitol, tipping his black silk topper to cheering celebrants and waving to his escorts, a mounted contingent of Rough Riders. A surviving black-and-white film shows Chief Justice Melville Fuller administering the oath of office, with the Supreme Court's chief clerk holding the Bible during the oath-taking.

Bishop stayed in New York to write about the inauguration, unwilling to compete with tens of thousands of others for Roosevelt's attention. "There is no pleasure in seeing you when the great American people get after you," Bishop admitted, "for then we simply become so many atoms in the great mass."[448] He telegraphed his congratulations, of course, and Roosevelt responded warmly: "No one has a greater right to feel proud over the Inauguration than you have."[449]

Once the U.S. had paid the requisite $40 million to the Compagnie Nouvelle and $10 million to Panama, Roosevelt enthusiastically ordered those in charge to "make the dirt fly." The mountains and jungles of the isthmus were fearsome topographical hurdles but, as Bishop observed, "The most formidable obstacle that confronted the U.S. Government . . . was the evil reputation of the Isthmus as a place of disease and death." It was, he said, "a veritable pest hole of the earth into which no dweller of the temperate zone could enter without peril to his health and life."[450]

There were still fresh memories of the thousands of laborers and technicians who had met horrific deaths from yellow fever and malaria during the mid-century construction of the Panama Railroad and, later, the French failure. Notwithstanding his impatience to get the project moving, T. R. understood that the health and hygiene of men should take precedence over construction; thus, he directed his new Isthmian Canal Commission to recruit the best medical experts they could find to make Panama hospitable for the big dig. He told his point man, Taft, to make "every possible effort" to protect Americans from the dangers of tropical diseases.

The seven-man commission, appointed by Roosevelt and chaired once again by Admiral John Walker, oversaw the canal work and brought their experience as engineers and builders to the task. As project administrator and chief engineer, the commission chose John Findlay Wallace, a veteran railroad builder, and most recently the general manager of the Illinois Central. He had the princely salary of $25,000 a year [nearly $600,000 in 2010] and reported directly to Taft.

From headquarters in Panama City, Wallace immediately sought to refurbish abandoned machinery and to recruit workers who could resume excavation at the cuts begun by the French. But from the start, his requests for new equipment and tools were met by a wall of bureaucratic red tape. Ever watchful of occasions for graft, commissioners pored over every purchase order in detail, second-guessing many of Wallace's requisitions. In his 1913 canal retrospective, Bishop criticized the Walker Commission as ineffective virtually from the start. Most commissioners were unsuited by temperament and age to get along with others or to defer to staff's judgment when it was prudent to do so. "The result was constant friction, no common policy of action and no general comprehension of the magnitude of the work."[451]

Despite an accomplished railroad career, Wallace proved unsuited to the gargantuan task at hand. Where aggressive leadership was required, he brought passivity. Where political skills were demanded, he often seemed clueless. Bishop identified Wallace as "the worst sufferer from the inefficiency of the commission." Inadequate equipment and a demoralized workforce that lacked adequate housing, food, and cooling ice slowed the work.

Beyond ineptitude, Wallace was said to be terrified of the jungle diseases ravaging his associates and the laborers. Brushing off Roosevelt's demand that yellow fever and malaria be overcome at the outset, the commission focused its attention on excavation, ignoring repeated requests for resources from its sanitation chief, Army Colonel William Gorgas.

Roosevelt had selected Dr. Gorgas, an expert on tropical diseases, to rid the isthmus of yellow fever, as he and others had done earlier during the U.S. occupation of Cuba. Gorgas and other researchers had identified the common household mosquito as the transmitter of the infection. Their eradication strategy in Panama was to rid the cities of standing water, where the mosquitoes bred, and to layer outlying swamps with oil to suffocate the larvae. Only when the death toll continued to mount and commissioners finally relented could Gorgas dispatch teams of health workers to fumigate homes and shops, and place secure covers on outdoor rain barrels and pots. This time, the workers wisely removed the bowls of water earlier placed under hospital bed legs.

Malaria, Gorgas determined, was carried to its victims by larger, brown mosquitoes that had previously bitten infected persons. He believed the key to successful eradication of the disease was to disperse victims from population centers when possible and to isolate others under mosquito-resistant nets while they recovered. Within a year and a half, the wisdom and persistence of Dr. Gorgas and his team prevailed, and both the number and severity of cases of tropical death diminished.

But reports of administrative dysfunction and subsequent critical editorials in the U.S. press troubled Roosevelt. Negotiations to settle the Russo-Japanese War and John Hay's alarmingly poor health preoccupied T. R., so he dispatched Taft on a fact-finding mission to Panama. Arriving in November 1904, the jocular, 300-pound emissary paid a courtesy call on President Amador Guerrero and undertook other diplomatic niceties. But he spent most of his visit behind closed doors with Walker and Wallace. Wallace had purchased new, ninety-five-ton, American-built Bucyrus steam shovels for use in the mountainous Culebra Cut, which was good news. But Taft soon corroborated the infighting between commission and staff and the low productivity and morale of workers, both American and the West Indian recruits. He returned to Washington with a clear message for the president. It was going badly on the isthmus. The commission was responsible, and it had to go.

Roosevelt acted decisively. He asked Congress in January 1905 for authority to reduce the seven-man commission to a workable three-man panel. When Congress balked, Roosevelt demanded that the current commissioners resign. They did as requested, and he appointed a new board headed by Theodore Perry Shonts, a railroad executive from Iowa and respected attorney. By executive order, Roosevelt established a three-member executive committee within the commission. Made up of Shonts, Wallace (bearing a fresh vote of confidence), and a new Canal Zone governor, the executive committee was instructed to pick up the pace immediately.

There was measurable progress in the wake of the reorganization, but within six months Wallace departed for consultations in Washington as rumors circulated that he wanted out. An angry Taft confronted him in New York amid reports that the chief engineer was job-hunting in the private sector. Wallace conceded as much but offered to stay if he were made commission chairman and given a large raise. Taft was incensed. He accused Wallace of deserting his duty and asked for his resignation on the spot.

In his later history of the canal project, Bishop sidestepped the Taft-Wallace confrontation, gingerly allowing only that, "All the papers on the case are on file

... They have no place in the present narrative."[452] In fact, when the meeting transcript was later released and Roosevelt accepted Wallace's resignation, the incident generated widespread debate in Congress and negative commentary in the press. Editorials questioned if the administration was capable of executing the nation's "destiny" in Panama and whether Roosevelt was paying enough attention to events there. The U.S. had already spent more than $100 million, yet conditions in Panama were in serious disarray. Theodore Roosevelt had an unexpected challenge before him—and a major public relations crisis.

As the president wrestled with the situation in Panama, Bishop stepped up his campaign to secure a salaried position at his side. In a May 14, 1905, hand-written note, Bishop recalled that it had been three months since he and the president had last met and suggested a breakfast meeting in New York, jesting, "It really seems to me that you are taking a great risk in running the govern-ment without my help."[453] Bishop received an invitation to the White House a week later. "I am coming on next Friday, the 26th, to spend the night with the President to give him the benefit of my advice," Bishop informed Taft. "I shall hope to find you sufficiently free on Saturday to enable me to perform the same useful function with yourself."[454]

He did not get to see Taft, but he laid out the outcome of his talk with the president in a candid letter to the secretary on White House stationery.

> He [Roosevelt] spoke freely of his desire to find some position for me in the public service that I could afford to accept. . . . He said he had talked the sub-ject over with you and that you and he were in cordial agreement in regard to my abilities and deserts. . . . He went over the matter of the secretaryship of the Panama Canal Commission . . . and told me of his talks with you and Mr. Shonts and Mr. Wallace about the possibility . . . of getting me on it as a kind of administrative head of a Washington bureau of publicity, or something of that sort of position that would enable me to be the historian of the canal, among other things.[455]

Bishop stressed that, whatever the post, it had to carry a first-rate salary. "I am a pauper and cannot, in justice to my family, aggravate my 'pauperness.'" Trying to raise himself up, the editor stressed: "I do not beg for it as a reward for any services that I may have done . . . I would like to work shoulder to shoulder with Roosevelt and Taft."[456]

As May slipped into June, Bishop explored other avenues of relocation to the capital. He asked Roosevelt about joining the Interstate Commerce Commission, but the president quashed the notion, saying that the current ICC secretary "knows his business and has been of real help to me." Bishop also resurrected his pipe dream of buying the *Washington Post,* but Roosevelt dashed his hope, advising that "there is not the slightest chance of the *Post* being sold at all."[457]

On June 14, Bishop had second thoughts, and he expressed remorse about pestering the president for a job. "I am deeply touched by your interest in the matter and somewhat appalled to think that I should have called your attention to it at a time when you were engaged in such world-wide matters as the restoration of peace." He applauded Roosevelt's mediation between the Russians and the Japanese: "Your success . . . is really wonderful and is the most remarkable tribute yet paid to the position which you hold in the world today."[458]

Then on July 1, 1905, John Hay died.

In the days before succumbing at his retreat on Lake Sunapee, New Hampshire, Hay told of a dream in which he went to see the president at the White House, but the president was not Roosevelt. It was Lincoln. "I was not in the least surprised at Lincoln's presence in the White House," Hay recalled of his reverie. "But the whole impression of the dream was of overpowering melancholy."[459] He died in the middle of the night after sudden difficulty breathing, attributed by doctors to a blood clot.

Roosevelt's official proclamation characterized the death of his secretary of state as "a national bereavement" and "a serious loss to all mankind," but it was in his letters to friends that the president opened his heart. "Our memories of him shall be green as long as you and I live," he confided to Lodge. To George von Lengerke Meyer, ambassador to Russia, Roosevelt observed, "No more loyal, lovable and upright man ever existed, and as a public man, he stood literally alone." Roosevelt recalled that on the eve of his recent inauguration, Hay had sent him a ring containing strands of hair from the head of Lincoln, along with a request: "Please wear it tomorrow; you are one of the men who most thoroughly understand and appreciate Lincoln."[460]

In mourning the loss of his friend, Bishop reflected back thirty-five years to when Hay bought him that $20 train ticket so that he could visit his brother in California and regain his emotional footing. Describing Hay's death as an "awful shock" to him, Bishop wrote Roosevelt, "I do not like to coddle grief but his death hangs over me constantly—in spite of all efforts to shake it off—as a punishing sadness."[461]

Hay's near-to-last diary entry served as a poetic and affirming self-tribute:

I have lived to be old, something I never expected in my youth. I have had many blessings, domestic happiness being the greatest of all. I have lived my life. I have had success beyond all the dreams of my boyhood. My name is printed in the journals of the world without descriptive qualification which may, I suppose, be called fame . . . I know death is the common lot, and what is universal ought not be deemed a misfortune; and yet—instead of confronting it with dignity and philosophy—I cling instinctively to life, as eagerly as if I had not had my chance at happiness and gained nearly all the great prizes.[462]

A gray cloud of odorous cigar smoke encircled the big man wherever he was—at his orderly desk in Panama City or in the muddy trenches with his men and machines. John "Big Smoke" Stevens, successor to Wallace as chief engineer, loomed large on the scene. Rugged and good-looking, he brought instant energy and calm resolve to the task. Raised in rural Maine, Stevens escaped his bleak surroundings at twenty and headed west to find opportunity. He taught himself the fundamentals of civil engineering and caught on with railroads in the upper Midwest. In time, he rose to chief engineer and general manager of the Great Northern Railway, and later became vice president of the Rock Island Railroad.

Lured to Panama in July 1905 at Roosevelt's insistence, Stevens arrived with the reputation as the best construction engineer in the country. He understood from the start, Bishop observed, that the canal was fundamentally a railroad job. Only in this case, it involved how best to transport tons of excavated rock and earth far distances and open up a vast path for water. Stevens therefore stopped much of the digging and turned his attention to the Panama Railroad, preparing the infrastructure for its mission. With a first-class railroad, Stevens reasoned, not only would construction spoils be hauled away efficiently, but more men and supplies could be brought in to finish the job.

Working with the sanction of Chairman Shonts in Washington, Stevens overhauled the project budget, adding millions for improved housing and docks, and, importantly, sewers and waterworks for Panama City and Colón. He was laying the infrastructure for a decade of digging. Bishop detailed Stevens's accomplishments from mid-1905 through 1906:

[T]he harmful activities of malarial mosquitoes had been greatly restricted; adequate quarters, comfortably furnished, had been provided for all employees; a system for the abundant supply of pure food at moderate prices, brought from the U.S., had been established and was working well; an ample supply of pure water had been secured for all cities, towns, villages and camps; the Panama Railroad had been double-tracked and furnished with new and heavier rails . . . New wharves at the terminals at the Atlantic and Pacific, with modern unloading machinery, had been built, and the harbors about them dredged.[463]

For U.S. tradesmen and the thousands of unskilled workers steaming in to Panama from the West Indies, Stevens built not only camp housing but also recreational clubhouses to lift morale. The ten-cents-an-hour wage offered to common laborers was humble by U.S. standards but alluring to the poor of the Caribbean. By working ten or twelve hours a day, six days a week, a man could send a comparative fortune home, or afford to send for his wife. The racism of the era found expression in worker assignments to gold and silver "rolls" instead of the more barefaced castes of black and white. At the work week's end, whites lined up for payment in gold coins; blacks received silver Panamanian balboas.

All progress aside, Stevens still did not know whether he would build a sea-level canal or a lock-and-lake type. The debate had been ongoing since the time of de Lesseps and remained unresolved until the summer of 1905, when Theodore Roosevelt created a panel of international engineers to make a conclusive recommendation. They rendered—predictably perhaps—a split decision, eight to five, in favor of a sea-level waterway. But their report conceded that digging to sea level would cost two and a half times as much as building ship locks and damming the Chagres River, and it would take more than a decade longer to finish.

Knowing that Roosevelt would not suffer such a costly and expensive delay, Taft, Shonts, and Stevens threw in with the minority and endorsed the lock canal. The canal commission agreed; so did Roosevelt and, eventually, Congress. Now, Stevens declared, the hour had come to build a dam near the Atlantic end of the isthmus, flood the jungle to create Gatun Lake, and create an endless source of hydroelectric power for the locks. To buttress Stevens, the commission recruited the army's top construction engineer, Major George Washington Goethals, a non-railroad man, who soon emerged as the pivotal figure in the history of the undertaking.

A modest display ad in a pamphlet, "Cape Cod and All the Pilgrim Lands," boasted immodestly about the pristine setting of the Vineyard Sound House—G. W. Giddings, proprietor—on upscale Falmouth Heights. It had an unobstructed view of the sound and Martha's Vineyard, delightful sea breezes, fine bathing, boating, and fishing, while shaded by oaks and pines. Bishop, in the midst of his ritual July getaway at Vineyard Sound House, was roused from his leisure by a note from T. R.: "My dear Bishop. Will you come out here Saturday, August 5th and spend Sunday and stay until Monday morning?" Roosevelt provided precise travel instructions. "Take the 4:43 train from Long Island City. There is much that I have to talk over with you."[464]

Roosevelt was despondent over the death of John Hay, but relieved that he, at last, could remove the duties of secretary of state from his desk and pass them to someone else. Roosevelt had thought first of Taft to succeed Hay, then of Elihu Root. Ultimately he realized that by selecting Root he could have both men in his Cabinet.

By the time Roosevelt and Bishop convened in early August, their talk surely had turned to Panama and a role for the president's favorite publicist to reverse the negativity that had followed in John Wallace's wake. At that point, "Big Smoke" Stevens had barely set his boots in the damp Panama soil, and who knew how he would fare? Bishop had been making the case that Shonts and Stevens needed a skilled newspaperman at the commission—someone like himself—to persuade the public that a turnaround was at hand and that Congress should loosen the purse strings.

Roosevelt understood that by appointing Bishop as secretary—in effect, the day-to-day administrator—of the Isthmian Canal Commission in Washington, not only would he have a trusted ally at his side, but he would also put a merciful end to the editor's pleadings for a role in the administration.

In two weeks, Bishop wrote T. R.: "I thank you with all my heart, both for saying what you did to Mr. Shonts and for letting me know that you said it."[465] In addition to serving as secretary, Bishop was to act as official historian of the canal, an ideal perch from which to spin the whole, big bold story in Roosevelt's favor.

On August 26, Bishop emerged from a Washington appointment with Shonts with an offer to be commission secretary at a more-than-comfortable annual salary of $10,000 ($239,000 in 2010). "I accepted it," he informed Roosevelt. "I am to begin work as soon as I can retire properly from my present position." That he was about to earn twice what congressmen and senators made probably did not strike him as an issue at the time, but it would pose a major problem on Capitol Hill in the months ahead.

In his thank-you letter to the president, Bishop accurately predicted that his critics—and those who envied his closeness to Roosevelt—would cause difficulties. "Doubtless, some of my 'dearest friends' will be unable to restrain themselves from nasty remarks of a characteristic kind, but these will not trouble me," he said. Bishop closed a seven-page handwritten letter with effusive appreciation: "My gratitude to you is beyond all hope of expression . . . good God, what a joy it will be to work with you and Taft and Shonts. What a relief from slavery! May God bless you for your generous faith and championship. The determination of my life henceforth will be to show myself worthy of your trust."[466]

From Sagamore Hill, Roosevelt responded that he was "pleased as Punch," but he advised Bishop to do some damage control with Boss Platt, who still represented New York in the Senate. "Have you got any friend who could go to Senator Platt and soften his heart toward you?" Roosevelt asked. "Unless this is done, I suppose he will try to make some trouble."[467]

Bishop quickly went to work, seeking out George Wickersham, an eminent Wall Street attorney. Wickersham "went immediately to the senator's son and, after arguing with him for an hour, persuaded him to write a very strong letter to his father recommending him to let bygones be bygones and to make no disturbance," Bishop told Roosevelt. "Wickersham is confident, as is the son, that this will remove all danger of an explosion and will prevent any annoyance in the Senate."[468]

"You are a trump, and I am awfully obliged to you," Roosevelt replied.[469]

A few weeks later, commission chairman Shonts signed a neatly typed memo:

Joseph Bucklin Bishop of New York is hereby appointed Executive Secretary of the Isthmian Canal Commission, with headquarters in Washington, D.C., at a salary of $10,000 per annum. [He] will have charge of the publicity and literary branch of its work. He will prepare the various statements which the Chairman, or the Commission as a body, may desire to make public, and will furnish all proper information to the press and public. He will also be the official historian of the Canal, preserving and compiling the authentic and authoritative record of its construction.[470]

For the moment, everyone was content.

Twenty-Five

The Ten Thousand Dollar Beauty

IT WOULD BE CALLED HIS "CROWDED YEAR." PERHAPS AT NO OTHER TIME THAN in 1905 was T. R.'s energy higher, his occupation more intense, and his achievements more noteworthy. From Panama to Algeciras, from Santo Domingo to Washington, D.C., Roosevelt's influence spread broadly and absolutely, for the welfare of the nation and mankind as a whole.

As Bishop saw it, the crowning achievement of the year was Roosevelt's leadership in ending the war between Russia and Japan. "I have had to run everything myself," the president told Lodge, "without any intermediaries."[471] At the time, John Hay was ailing; Elihu Root had left the cabinet; and Taft was in the Philippines.

Roosevelt recalled that he "grew most strongly to believe that a further continuation of the struggle would be a very bad thing for Japan, and even worse thing for Russia."[472] And so he set out to bring the warring parties together to make peace. At the time, Russia and Japan had restless naval forces and covetous imperial ambitions over Manchuria and Korea. England, France, and Germany hung cagily in the background, working to influence the outcome in their favor. The winner of the war, all parties knew, would tip the balance of power in East Asia for decades.

With great diplomatic dexterity, Roosevelt persuaded Russian and Japanese envoys to meet in the summer of 1905, first on a U.S. war vessel in Oyster Bay Harbor and later in Portsmouth, New Hampshire. "It may be said with truth that he was himself the conference," Bishop observed, "for he was its guiding and controlling force."[473] By September 5, the warring nations had signed a peace treaty whereupon. Bishop recalled, "the whole world broke into a joyous paean of praise for Roosevelt." Czar Nicholas II thanked him "for your personal energetic efforts." From Tokyo, the Mikado sent grateful appreciation "for the distinguished part you have taken in the establishment of peace."

Roosevelt was "very much pleased" with the outcome of the process but told his brother-in-law, Douglas Robinson, "my personal feelings in the matter have seemed to be of very, very small account compared to the great need of trying to do something which, it seemed to me, the interests of the whole world demanded to be done."[474] For his effort, Theodore Roosevelt received the Nobel Prize for Peace in 1906. He cherished the medal for the rest of his life and donated the $45,000 in prize money to European relief efforts during World War I.

That same year, Roosevelt, ever the ardent conservationist, also fortified the U.S. Bureau of Forestry. With the prodding of his friend Gifford Pinchot, the president demanded scientific management of the nation's timberlands. Protecting most trees and harvesting only selected ones, Roosevelt reasoned, would prevent soil erosion, averting runoff, flooding, and water pollution. "A nation that destroys its soils destroys itself," he proclaimed. "Forests are the lungs of our land, purifying the air and giving fresh strength to our people."[475]

Roosevelt's appreciation of nature had its start in his Manhattan bedroom where, as nine-year-old Teedie, he had collected species from the natural world, dissecting and preserving, skinning and mounting displays for his collection. Family journeys took him to Egypt and Syria where he used a shotgun to bring down specimens. Then at Harvard, he made a serious, although abbreviated, study of natural history. As a young man he helped to found the legendary Boone and Crockett Club to promote hunting, the preservation of game animals and their habitats, and the safeguarding of extraordinary landscapes in Yellowstone National Park. And of course in the Badlands he took alarm at the imminent extinction of the bison, believing, "It is also vandalism to wantonly destroy or permit the destruction of what is beautiful in nature, whether it be a cliff or forest, or a species of mammal or bird."[476]

As governor of New York and now as president, Roosevelt established a bold executive record of conservation and environmental protection that formed, in large part, the rationale for his enshrinement on Mount Rushmore. From the start, he refused to allow timber men and recalcitrant legislators to get in his way. By the time he departed the presidency, he could reflect on an astonishing record of preservationist accomplishment: 51 federal bird reservations, 4 national game preserves, 150 national forests, 5 national parks, and 18 national monuments including the Grand Canyon, "a natural wonder which is, in kind, unparalleled throughout the rest of the world."[477] In all, he protected some 230 million acres of public land for the generations that followed and those that will yet ensue.

Bishop, a city man for decades now, expressed little interest in natural history and conservation, but he nonetheless acknowledged Roosevelt's record. "His services in that field, which began with his Presidency and continued without a break to its end, were exceeded in lasting public benefit by none others of his career," he wrote.[478] Historian Douglas Brinkley explained the Roosevelt method succinctly: "With the power of the bully pulpit, Roosevelt—repeatedly befuddling both market hunters and insatiable developers—issued 'I So Declare It' orders over and over again."[479]

But toward the end of the year Roosevelt had to deal with a thorny political problem on the domestic front.

Primed with a generous salary and a lifelong craving for comfort, Bishop ensured that his tenure in Washington, D.C., would not classify as hardship duty. He rented rooms at the Highlands at the southwest corner of Connecticut Avenue and California Street in the northwest section of the capital. Just three years old, it was one of the finest luxury apartment buildings in the city, its hilltop view rated the best of all the city's residences. Eight stories tall, it boasted Beaux Arts style and a richly detailed facade. Bishop could take meals leisurely in the lavish octagonal dining room. When he had visitors, he greeted them in an elegant lobby of marble wainscoting and gilded arches. The building hummed with amenities: electric elevators, apartment telephones linked to a main switchboard, and the only basement automobile garage in Washington.

It is unclear whether Harriet accompanied her husband to the nation's capital. In all likelihood, she remained in New York City with Alice, venturing to Washington for special occasions but content to remain in New York to welcome Joseph back on his weekend commutes.

The newly named executive secretary of the Isthmian Canal Commission passed his working hours comfortably in the *Evening Star* building on Eleventh Street and Pennsylvania Avenue—between the White House and the Capitol. It was one of Washington's grandest commercial structures of the time. In contrast to the canal engineers and laborers who were toiling in the Panamanian tropics, the canal's administrative overseers sat high above the urban landscape, safely removed from the noise of the streetcars below and the irritating backfire of the newfangled horseless carriages.

As Roosevelt and Bishop had anticipated, Bishop's appointment drew immediate cries of cronyism and ridicule of his role as an overpaid government press agent. Boss Platt may have been mollified for the moment, but opposition Democrats in Congress seized the opportunity to wound Roosevelt politically by attacking his friend. Bishop was willing to step aside to spare the president the trouble but Roosevelt resisted. "Now don't talk nonsense, old friend," he wrote. "The only thing that could make me regret your accepting your new position would be if it changed our relations in any way."[480] Roosevelt further signaled his backing by inviting Joseph and Harriet to a White House dinner with Mrs. Roosevelt in the company of the secretary of war and Mrs. Taft, the newly elected postmaster general and Mrs. Cortelyou, and retired Civil War general Grenville Dodge.

On October 30, the commission moved to protect Bishop by upgrading his title and adding to his responsibilities. He was to be known hereafter as secretary of the commission. To the duties of publicity chief and historian were added those of keeper of the commission's minutes and records, delegated authority to requisition supplies for the Washington office, and the approval of payment vouchers. The commission clearly was striving to justify Bishop's salary, which far exceeded the pay earned by envious representatives and senators.

The spending of government money on the canal, including salaries and wages, required the consent of Congress, of course, and Democratic appropriators sought to leverage the approval process to make the president and his men squirm. "Dear Sir," wrote Democratic representative John Fitzgerald of New York to commission chairman Shonts on December 6, "Please send me at your earliest convenience the following information." He then listed six specific items, all related to Bishop's compensation, duties, prior responsibilities, and the sources of money used to pay his salary to date.[481] As Shonts read the letter, he realized that a game of political hardball had begun.

Shonts replied factually two days later in a hand-delivered letter, calming House waters for the moment. But the real tempest was brewing on the north side of the Capitol. There, the Senate Appropriations Committee was meeting to decide whether to approve $16.5 million in supplemental funding for the canal. Secretary Taft and Chairman Shonts, attired in their finest, sat at the witness table to ask for 1,100 steel flatcars, 120 steam locomotives, and $878,000 worth of lumber and cement, among other items. They also needed $4.9 million to pay workers on the gold and silver rolls and $128,000 for "salaries of commissioners and employees of the Washington office."

Theodore Roosevelt in Rough Rider uniform leads a charge of laborers toward the Panama Canal. From a *Puck* centerfold, November 14, 1906. *Library of Congress Prints and Photographs Division*

Committee chairman William Allison of Iowa and other senators quizzed the point men, Senator Benjamin Tillman, a confrontational Democrat from South Carolina, sat restlessly on the dais, fussing over a lengthy list of questions. Hotheaded and blatantly racist, Tillman had been sparring with Roosevelt over regulation of the railroads. Tillman's legacy as governor of South Carolina lay in his open and antagonistic disenfranchisement of blacks and the enactment of Jim Crow laws. In the Senate, his colleagues had censured "Pitchfork Ben" three years earlier for assaulting his South Carolina Senate colleague.

Staring down Taft with his one good eye, Tillman opened his attack on Bishop and, by association, the president: "I notice that the secretary of the Commission gets $10,000.... I cannot see why the mere keeping of the records of the work of the Commission requires so much skill and so much brains."

Taft sidestepped the provocation and answered coolly that the commission simply wanted an experienced journalist at hand to answer unwarranted criticism of the canal work. "Both on the Isthmus and here, [it] has gotten to such a point that it seemed necessary for the Commission to protect itself in some way."

"Is it the duty of this Commission to run a political campaign to defend itself?" Tillman asked.

"No, sir, but it is the duty of the Commission to correct impressions that are circulated maliciously for the purpose of interfering with its work." Then Taft dropped the other shoe. "This same gentleman [Bishop] who was employed as secretary was offered $12,000 a year to become an editorial writer for the purpose of *defeating* the project of the canal."

As surprised senators reflected on this first-ever allegation of organized political opposition to the canal, Tillman spoke up. "We had better get Mr. Bishop here ... and probe this matter a little deeper."

While a messenger fetched an unsuspecting Bishop from the *Evening Star* building, Shonts defended his aide: "No man has worked harder than he has since he has been with the Commission ... I think that he was instrumental to a remarkable degree in stating the facts as to conditions on the Isthmus and rectifying errors that were published everywhere during last summer."

Senator John Daniel, a Virginia Democrat: "Do you think his services are worth this sum of $10,000 a year to the government?"

Shonts: "I do indeed ... We feel that this work is probably the most important work now going on, and that the time will come when a truthful history of the progress of the work will be a very useful addition to our literature."

Then Republicans joined the questioning, adding a worrisome bipartisan cast to the proceedings.

Senator Eugene Hale from Maine: "Do you not think, Mr. Shonts ... that this feature of the secretary, either of a commission or of a department or of any branch of the government, taking upon himself the charge of manufacturing public sentiment through the press, is an innovation?"

Shonts: "It was not to manufacture public sentiment, Mr. Senator; it was simply to state the facts through some organized department."

Senator Hale: "Do you know of it being done in any other work?"

Shonts: "This is my first experience with public work; but we have done it in every other line of work that I have been connected with. We have tried to state the facts to the people so that they would not misunderstand our position."

The committee's unanticipated preoccupation with Bishop persisted, forcing Taft to read into the hearing record Bishop's revised job description, adopted earlier by the commission. It was dawning on Taft and Shonts that despite their best efforts, Roosevelt's commitment of title and salary to his New York friend was not going to fly with this committee. Worse, the entire $16.5 million budget request for men and materials in Panama now hung in the balance. Bishop had to save his own skin and, in the Senate committee, at least, try to salvage the money for the president's pet project.

Bishop never relished the spotlight, especially one that glared unflatteringly on him. He savored any opportunity to be seen socially with the titans of business and government, but he preferred to secret himself behind an anonymous typewriter or bring his influence to bear in small, private discussions. Whether that characteristic drew from the Yankee Puritan roots mentioned by John Hay or some insecurity of personality did not really matter at the time. What counted during the greatest political challenge of his life was his self-interest, along with his unbending loyalty to Theodore Roosevelt. He had the president's unquestioned backing and, largely because of that, Taft's loyalty as well.

As he approached Capitol Hill, summoned by senators determined to humiliate him, Bishop resolved to stand his ground, defend his appointment, and above all, to shield the president. At that moment, he may well have recalled Roosevelt's words to him: "You must be on your guard. Your personal relations with me are well known, and politicians and others who are always on the watch for hints about my purposes and plans will take note of anything you may say in that direction. You will have to be very discreet when they are about. As for me, I am so perpetually indiscreet that nobody pays the slightest attention to me."[482]

In his opening statement before the Appropriations Committee, Bishop explained his duties, as Taft and Shonts had done before him. He described the routine of an Isthmian Canal Commission press agent without defining himself as such: "Seeing the newspaper representatives who come in to inquire [about] any matter whatsoever . . . Sometimes I prepare a little statement and send it around to them. That is for their convenience more than for ours." As the canal's nascent historian: "I am keeping track of everything with a view toward [writing a history] for the government." [483] He disclosed that he had a clerk, a stenographer, and a helper known as a "type-writer," all recruited from the commission's office staff.

One senator after another probed the facets of Bishop's life as a New York newspaper editor, his current compensation, and his role as minutes-keeper of the commission. The record shows that he answered calmly, factually, and respectfully throughout. As the hearing sputtered on matter-of-factly, senators were adroitly building the record for the action they would take. Then, according to the Senate committee transcript, "Pitchfork Ben" Tillman resurrected the matter of the canal opponents and their attempt to recruit Bishop as their advocate.

Tillman: "Do you know who they are?"

Bishop: "I know some of them."

"Would you mind giving their names?"

"Yes, I would, because they tried to hire me to take charge of their bureau before I came here."

Disgruntled at Bishop's refusal to be forthcoming, Tillman persisted in his questioning. Bishop was guarded in his responses: Bishop: "I was called upon and assured that this combination of hostile interests, including the Nicaraguan route, the Darien route, the Tehuantepec route, and, so far as I could make out—although I would not want to charge that—certain railway interests had made this combination. Money was no object to them. They would pay me any salary I wished if I would take charge of a publication bureau to put out arguments against [the canal]." Bishop said the group wanted to create enough confusion and doubt about the Panama route that Congress would not fund it.

Senator Daniel: "A man who would make such a proposition is an enemy to his country. . . . What was the name of that gentleman?"

Bishop: "I must decline to state."

"On what grounds?"

"The man was recommended to me—came with a very strong letter of introduction from a man whom I would not wish to bring into this thing at all . . . The canal commission knew nothing whatever about it."

Tillman demanded any relevant correspondence sent to Bishop. He threatened to have the alleged adversaries hauled before Congress. Senators also wanted to know whether the opposition threat had prompted Bishop's hiring.

Bishop: "Not [in] the slightest . . . It was perfectly voluntary on their part. . . . After the offer was made, the salary named and I had accepted, I told the story."[484]

But the lawmakers continued to grill Bishop, delaying their consideration of critical funding for canal manpower, equipment, and supplies. When the hearing ended, senators came to no conclusion about Bishop; neither did they expressly support the president's will. They simply asked Bishop to send them some of the negative canal project press clips that had prompted his hiring. Then, anticlimactically, they closed the hearing.

Bishop left the room, pleased that he had defended his appointment with deftness and honor. Pitchfork Ben had produced no smoking gun, but the key question of Bishop's salary remained on the table. In a follow-up letter to Roosevelt, Bishop vented his indignation: "I think Tillman overdid the business, as usual, yesterday; he certainly did not hurt me by classing me with you in his blackguardism. It is incredible that decent men, in the Senate and out, should follow the lead of such a creature as Tillman."[485]

The newspapers predictably covered the story on the front page, above the fold. After all, one of their brethren had been on the hot seat. The Democratic-disposed *New York Herald*, on orders from publisher James Gordon Bennett Jr. to "roast Bishop,"[485] headlined its report TILLMAN MAKES A TARGET OF BISHOP. Its lead paragraph repeated the South Carolina senator's derogatory depiction of him as "Secretary Taft's ten thousand dollar beauty." The paper reported Senator Hale's view that having a government press agent was "a most unfortunate innovation," and revealed that Democrat Charles Culberson of Texas had proposed an amendment to forbid any money in the canal-funding bill to be used for the "support of a literary bureau or the payment of a press agent under any guise."[487]

Facing the prospect of no supplementary funding for the canal and in light of building bipartisan opposition to Bishop's appointment, Roosevelt concluded that he had to retreat—for the moment. Meeting at the White House with Hale, the president agreed to remove Bishop's salary from the bill if the Senate would approve the funds to build the canal. BISHOP SACRIFICED BY THE PRESIDENT, announced the *Herald* headline; THROWS OVER THE "TEN THOUSAND DOLLAR BEAUTY" TO PLACATE THE SENATE.

Not until the eleventh paragraph of its story did the *Herald* report that, in the midst of the dust up on Capitol Hill, Bishop was proving his value to the commission. In an interview with reporters in Washington, he refuted an assertion by Tillman and others that 300 black women from the Caribbean island of Martinique were being imported into Panama "for immoral purposes." Not true, Bishop asserted. The women were the wives of laborers, who had sent for them after demonstrating that they were capable of supporting a family in Panama.

On the Senate floor on December 16, Hale announced his deal with Roosevelt, adding that Republican senators had agreed with Democrats that subsidizing press agents with government money should be abandoned. That the press agent in question was a friend of the president's, and that Congress had had no say in filling a plum assignment, was not spoken of but certainly lay in the back of senators' minds.

Roosevelt was loath to abandon his old friend and was willing to spend the political capital required to rescue him, along with the hefty government salary he had promised. The *New York Times* scooped its rivals when it reported on December 18 that T. R. was consulting Senate leaders on a plan to get around their opposition and save Bishop's skin. HOW TO PLACE BISHOP, ROOSEVELT'S PROBLEM, headlined the *Times* story that revealed Roosevelt's scheme to appoint Bishop to a vacant seat *on* the commission. The paper's correspondent explained the scheme: "Mr. Bishop could be appointed to the vacancy, and that would give him $7,500 a year. If then, the anomalous situation was created by the commission of having one of its members act as its Secretary for an additional salary of $2,500 a year, Mr. Bishop could continue to give advice to the President and draw his $10,000 a year." The paper wisely foresaw that "trouble might be experienced in this."[488] Nonetheless, the next day, a determined Roosevelt sent the Senate an austere notice that read: "I nominate Mr. Joseph Bucklin Bishop for appointment as a member of the Isthmian Canal Commission."

Bishop battled for the size of his paychecks for years, through the end of the Roosevelt administration in March 1909 and into Taft's term. After being nominated as commissioner by Roosevelt, Bishop eagerly occupied the seat, absent Senate confirmation and in defiance of congressional opposition. He contended that his was a recess appointment—as were those of the other commissioners—and that none of the seven required immediate Senate approval. With concrete support of the other commissions over time, he continued to draw his salary while the skirmish between Congress and the White House dragged on. For all concerned, and fortunately for Bishop, the clash grew old and less important over time.

By the spring of 1907, Taft placed Bishop in charge of the commission's Washington office "by direction of the President." From Panama, John Stevens, Shonts's successor as commission chairman, immediately ordered Bishop to "make a thorough examination of office administration and take any steps that may be practicable to effect reduction of expenses without impairing efficiency."[489] Bishop was given the green light to cut the commission's administrative budget and find some savings to offset his salary, no doubt in part to assuage members of Congress.

Roosevelt had achieved his goal: to place inside the beating heart of the Isthmian Canal Commission a trusted, loyal friend who would see to it that his vision was realized. More prominent individuals would bear the titles of chief engineer or chairman and shoulder important official responsibilities, but the president turned to Bishop for the remainder of his term for regular counsel and the inside story on the events in the Canal Zone.

Bishop recalled that he was under "a virtually continuous assault by the politicians who had been stirred to wrath" by his appointment. He told of the time he was set up by a *New York Herald* writer who was part of a get-together of news correspondents in his office. The conversation turned into a frank and "far from complimentary" exchange of anecdotes about members of Congress. "I interposed soon after this talk began," Bishop remembered, "saying that they were in a government office and that I, as a government official, ought not to allow it to go on. They pooh-poohed the idea, saying that we were all newspaper men."[490]

A few days later, the *Herald* man reported the off-the-record meeting in an article headlined, "The Kind of Man Bishop Is." He quoted Bishop as having relayed some of the derogatory stories. "I started at once for the Executive Office," Bishop said. "White and trembling, I asked him [the president] if he had seen the article. Seizing the paper by one corner, Roosevelt swung it into the air, flung it to the floor and exclaimed, 'Well, by George, all the fault I have to find with you is that you pay the slightest attention to anything that appears in the *New York Herald!*'"[491]

Twenty-Six

To See for Himself

As THE AGING STEAMER MOVED AWAY FROM PORT INTO NEW YORK HARBOR, Bishop gazed back wistfully at the metropolis, apprehensive about his first journey abroad. He was not in control, and that worried him. Accompanied by Chief Engineer Stevens and other members of the Isthmian Canal Commission, he was heading for Panama on official business. It was June 28, 1906, the cusp of Bishop's traditional summer vacation. This year, instead of luxuriating in New England, he was going to the tropical rain forests of Central America for meetings and inspection tours of the canal route on the Panama Railroad.

As the ship headed south on its six-day journey, Bishop retreated to his cabin to rest before dinner with the ICC delegation. One of the commissioners now, he had escaped Washington and the uncertainty of confirmation by a balky Congress—for the moment.

Just nine days earlier his eloquence had stirred a sea of bearded and necktied men seated in an orderly fashion in hard chairs before him at the Brown University Alumni Association.

> *Let us erect not merely a library building but a* great *[emphasis original] library building. Let us build a temple of the genius, beauty and power of learning that will be an inspiration to ambitious youth in the generations that are yet to come. Let us inscribe above its portal the name of John Hay, a profound scholar who was a sagacious statesman and great diplomatist— because he employed the knowledge from books, for the glory of his country and the uplifting of humanity.*[492]

By invitation, Bishop had gone to College Hill on Providence's leafy East Side to memorialize his late friend, "the shy, dreamy, poetic youth" of undergraduate days who had risen to become secretary of state. Steel magnate Andrew Carnegie—the second-richest man in America, a philanthropist, and aficionado of libraries—had endowed the building, designed in English Renaissance style, to house the university's main book collection for, as it turned out, the next half-century. Despite the controversy over his canal appointment, Bishop's fellow alumni welcomed him respectfully, one by one shaking his hand vigorously in hearty recognition of his achievements. One of their own was an intimate of one of the most charismatic presidents the country had ever seen.

But as the ship steamed out to sea, the stink of flaming coal below, Bishop's future depended not only on President Roosevelt but also on Stevens's ability to effectively carve a trench between the oceans.

Bishop had never been one for natural science. As he settled into comfortable guest quarters on Ancon Hill in Panama City and began exploring the area, he would have seen the ever-present toucans with their giant, multicolored bills. The birds had compact bodies sporting black feathers and white, yellow, and scarlet necks and breasts. They gathered in treetops, eagerly gobbling fruit, insects, and small lizards. As they ate, they threw back their heads, allowing the food to roll the full length of their beaks before swallowing.

In the sodden forests surrounding the emerging canal, Bishop would have gazed in amazement at the long parades of leafcutter ants under foot. In a relentless march, they hauled cuttings many times their size and weight. At destination nests, yet more ants ground the leaves into fungus gardens to feed their larvae.

And he would have spotted the Christ lizards, extraordinary creatures that could run on water when threatened. At the water's edge they suddenly sprinted on their hind legs, upright, forelegs at their sides, darting for thirty feet or more on the water's surface. The lizards' oversized, webbed feet pontooned for fractions of a second at blinding speed as they strove mightily to avoid sinking below the surface, where they would have been devoured by other creatures. It was an apt metaphor.

Canal excavation continued on "the line," principally at the Culebra Cut. It was a herculean effort to carve a path through a mountain range north of Panama City. The Cut, Bishop explained, was "the chief point of attack . . . the most formidable obstacle to be fought and overcome." Because of steep vertical cliffs, landslides were common and calamitous to the men and machines at work there. "No one could say when the sun went down at night what the condition of the Cut would be when the sun rose the next morning. The work of months or years might be blotted out by an avalanche of earth or the toppling over of small mountains of rock."[493] At 100 million cubic yards of spoil, the Culebra Cut, when complete, represented fully one-quarter of all the digging done on the isthmus.

Acknowledging the arduous dimensions of the task, Stevens and Shonts persuaded Taft and Roosevelt to further consolidate decision-making at the ICC. By executive order, the three-man Executive Canal Commission dissolved, with sole authority invested in the hands of its chairman. As chief engineer, Stevens would become a member of the commission as well.

When he returned to Washington in early August, Bishop learned that Roosevelt had decided to go to Panama to inspect the project for himself. It was a historic decision. Never before had an American president left the country while in office. The dates of the presidential visit were uncertain that summer, given the demands of other business and the looming congressional elections, but Roosevelt expressed a headstrong desire to visit during the rainy season so he could experience conditions at their worst. At the behest of President Amador Guerrero, Bishop pressed the vacationing Taft for a scheduling decision. The Panamanian president was eager to finalize arrangements for the entertainment at the presidential receptions he was planning. On October 31, Bishop finally received Roosevelt's November travel dates and the go-ahead to sail again for the isthmus. He was expected to travel in advance of the president's visit and, in addition to other duties, arrange favorable press coverage of it.

As President and Mrs. Roosevelt pulled up to the Washington Navy Yard in a carriage, a blast of trumpets offered a proper salute. A front-page story in the *Washington Herald* reported that the ship's band performed the National Anthem as Roosevelt's traveling party boarded the *Mayflower,* a yacht that sailed into the Potomac to the USS *Louisiana,* waiting at Piney Point, Maryland.

The Roosevelts traveled in comfort and security during their six-day journey, through the Windward Passage between Cuba and Haiti. The 16,000-ton *Louisiana,* the navy's largest battleship, had been outfitted with a presidential suite of rooms and modern wireless devices to enable ship-to-shore communication along the route.

Roosevelt took advantage of the extended confinement and turned to his cherished pastime of letter-writing. "Blessed Archie," he began a note to his son. "We have had three days of perfect weather while this great battleship and her two convoys, *Tennessee* and *Washington,* have steamed steadily on column, ahead southward through calm seas until now we are in the tropics. . . . I was much amused at the names of the seven-inch guns . . . one called Tedd and the other, The Big Stick."[494] Then to Kermit: "It is a beautiful sight, these three, great, war vessels steaming southward in close column, and almost as beautiful at night when we see not only the lights but the loom, through the darkness, of the ships astern . . . it seems a strange thing of my now being President, going to visit the work of the Panama Canal which I have made possible."[495]

On the isthmus, Shonts, Stevens, and Bishop, along with men from Panama's new government, were fine-tuning the calendar for the president's three-day visit. Roosevelt would stay at the Tivoli Hotel in Ancon, incomplete except for a wing that was hurriedly finished and equipped. Streets in Colón and Panama City were hosed down to make a clean impression. Work gangs at key spots along the excavation route were alerted to expect a presidential inspection. There would be ceremonial train rides, receptions, and dinners, all befitting a state visit.

On November 14, the *Louisiana* emerged above the hazy horizon into Limón Bay—a day early! Understanding that his premature arrival would throw the carefully planned schedule into chaos, Roosevelt remained on board through the night as the ship's captain ordered the anchor dropped. As David McCullough relates:

At 7:30 the next morning, the appointed hour, as the official welcoming party stood at the end of the pier, all eyes searching for signs of life on the big ship, an amazing figure called, "Good morning"—from shore. [emphasis original]. He advanced into their midst. He was wearing a white suit and a seaman's sou'wester, the brim of which reached his shoulders. The pince-nez glistened with fine rain drops. He had been rowed ashore two hours earlier, he explained, and had been having a grand time 'exploring' the waterfront.[496]

Roosevelt's time in Panama consisted of inspections, official meetings, staged events, and a few spontaneous diversions from script. He triumphantly rode the Panama Railroad from Colón to Panama City, acknowledging worshipful crowds along the way. A legion of reporters, adeptly assembled and managed by Bishop, dutifully noted the enthusiastic waves and salutes of the people, many of them children, awestruck by the man in white. It was an extraordinary public relations feat, and T. R. took full advantage of every minute to glow in the spotlight.

Joseph Bucklin Bishop (in white with umbrella and coat on arm)
follows Theodore and Edith Roosevelt as they leave a mess hall in
La Boca, Panama, November 15, 1906.

Theodore Roosevelt Collection, Harvard College Library (Roosevelt 560.52 1906-0367)

Beyond a genuine desire to scrutinize the people and the work underway, Roosevelt wanted to refute the canal's critics and shore up support back home for the risky and costly project. The president knew that Congress was reading every line of every dispatch, and he wanted the message to be unfailingly upbeat. With commissioners striving mightily to keep up, and Bishop acknowledging that "the zeal and tireless energy of the President put to a severe strain the physical strength of more than one of his companions,"[497] Roosevelt inspected mess halls and the living quarters of gold- and silver-roll workers. With Dr. Gorgas, he broke away from his escorts to talk with patients in the hospital at Ancon. On the steps of the great cathedral in the square, wearing a dark

Joseph Bucklin Bishop, at left, and John F. Stevens, right, flank a seated Theodore Roosevelt during a pause on their Panama Canal inspections.

Robert Karrer—Isthmian Collectors Club

waistcoat in the steamy heat, and amid ubiquitous red, white, and blue bunting, Roosevelt proudly received the official welcome of the Amador government. The American commander in chief declared that Panama and the U.S. were joint trustees for all the world.

In the best-recorded moments of the trip, Roosevelt trod the busy Culebra work line in the pouring rain, glad-handing the sodden men with words of encouragement. On his way there, near the site of the Pedro Miguel locks, the rain-drenched president spotted a couple of Bucyrus steam shovels at work. The irresistible photo op presented itself. Roosevelt climbed aboard one of the ninety-five-ton monsters, sat next to the startled operator, and commenced his questioning: What is *this*? What does *this* do? *How* does it work? For what seemed like a half-hour the president scrutinized the noisy shovel, grabbing the controls as reporters scrawled and photographers shot. The image of T. R., in mud-stained white suit and hat—taking part in the excavation itself—traveled around the world. It required neither caption nor explanation. In that extraordinary symbolic instant, Theodore Roosevelt *was* the Panama Canal.

In other images of the trip that survive—many on hand-tinted color postcards—T. R. is posing with Edith, Stevens, and Bishop on the porch of a caboose, having a decidedly "bully" time. Or he is sitting under the awning of the rail sidecar with his official party, gesturing to the people frantically pursuing him along the rails. There's Bishop too, sullen as always, but nonetheless pleased with the coverage of the scene. Later, T. R. is on Stevens's veranda, posing regally in a chair, surrounded by a squadron of weary aides.

Bishop recalled the closing hours of Roosevelt's visit: "On the eve of his departure from the Isthmus, the entire canal force was assembled in a great building covering the largest wharf of the Canal Commission at Cristóbal, at the Atlantic entrance to the canal, in a mass reception to him."[498] The president thanked the men for their tireless work, adding that to only a few in each generation is an opportunity given to change the world. "I shall see if it is not possible to provide for some little memorial, some mark, some badge, which will always distinguish the man who, for a certain space of time, has done his work well."[499]

It was the genesis of what came to be known as the Roosevelt Medal. It would be the size of a silver dollar, bearing the portrait of the president and an aerial view of a ship sailing through the completed Culebra Cut. The motto, "The Land Divided, the World United," would be inscribed above the scene. Beginning in September 1909, more than 6,000 medals were engraved and delivered to Americans who had worked on the canal or the Panama Railroad for two years or more. The medals themselves were cast from copper, bronze, and other metals salvaged from locomotives and machinery abandoned by the French. "The bestowal of them contributed materially to the patriotic pride in the work," Bishop wrote, "which was so universal in the canal force, and which was the chief cause of its remarkable efficiency."[500]

From the deck of the *Louisiana*, leaving Panama en route home via Puerto Rico, Roosevelt recalled his adventure in a letter to Kermit. It was "most successful as well as most interesting . . . Now we have taken hold of the job . . . I haven't a doubt that it will take a little longer and cost a little more than men now appreciate, but I believe that the work is being done with a very high degree of both efficiency and honesty." Of his hours in the Culebra Cut:

There, the huge steam shovels are hard at it, scooping large masses of rock and gravel and dirt previously loosened by the drillers and dynamite blasters, loading it on trains which take it away to some dump, either in the jungle or where the dams are to be built. They are eating steadily into the mountain,

More than 6,000 Roosevelt Medals were given to Americans who worked on the canal or the Panama Railroad for two years or more. Bishop treasured his, pictured here, for the rest of his life.

Enita and Miriam Bishop collection

cutting it down and down . . . With intense energy the men and machines do their task, the white men supervising matters and handling the machines, while the tens of thousands of black men do the rough manual labor where it is not worthwhile to have machines do it. It is an epic feat and one of immense significance . . . Mother did not do the roughest work, and had time to see more of the really picturesque and beautiful side of the life, and really enjoyed herself. . . . I tramped everywhere through the mud.[501]

Roosevelt understood that his visit would have greater impact if he wrote about it in detail, so a week before Christmas 1906—no doubt with Bishop's assistance—he sent Congress a thirty-page account, complete with voluminous statistical appendices. He attached page after page of vivid black-and-white photographs of men and machines vigorously at work. "It was received with some consternation by the Senate," Bishop recalled, "being regarded as that 'truly awful thing,' an 'innovation.'" But, he added, "The august members recovered sufficiently from their alarm a few days later to order the printing of 10,000 copies for distribution by themselves to their constituents."[502]

Roosevelt's report concluded:

> *Of the success of the enterprise I am well convinced as one can be of any enterprise that is human . . . The work is now going on with a vigor and efficiency pleasant to witness . . . It is impossible to avoid some mistakes in building a giant canal through jungle-covered mountains and swamps while, at the same time, [sanitizing] tropic cities and providing for the feeding and general care of some 20,000 to 30,000 workers . . . Those best informed believe that the work will be completed in about eight years.*

T. R. further observed "the extraordinary absence of mosquitoes," and noted that "the West India [*sic*] laborers are fairly, but only fairly, satisfactory," and that "wages were not really as high as they should be." In a straitlaced aside, he added, "There seemed to me to be too many saloons in the Zone; but the new license law which goes into effect January 1st next will probably close four-fifths of them."[503]

Bishop, who had been working hard to refute "a well-nigh continuous fusillade of bitter and obviously malicious criticism" of the canal work from some of Roosevelt's critics in the press, concluded that the president's special message "turned back the flood of slander on the slanderers themselves and drove them and all imitators out of business." He credited the president's own bare-knuckle attack on his press critics in the report: "I feel for them the heartiest contempt and indignation; because, in a spirit of wanton dishonesty and malice, they are trying to interfere with and hamper the execution of the greatest work of the kind ever attempted . . . one of the giant feats of the ages."

Bishop returned from Panama after the presidential visit in late November. Having seen the need, he placed great value on the organization of leisure-time clubhouses in Panama initiated by the Young Men's Christian Association, founded a half-century earlier in response to unhealthy conditions in large cities and along railroad-construction sites. With Roosevelt's endorsement, the YMCA had staked a high-visibility presence for itself on the isthmus. By the end of 1907, ICC work crews had erected four clubhouses for the YMCA to operate. White men on the gold roll could use them anytime—as could white women for a few hours a week. For an annual membership of ten dollars, an engineer or surveyor could kick back in the evening, play pool, exercise in the gymnasium, or find solitude to write a letter home. *Collier's Weekly* magazine reasoned, "It is a simple matter of business for the government. If the men are properly taken care of they will do better work and stick to their work longer."[504]

Roosevelt and Bishop shared a passion for books—T. R. at times reading several a day, often in Greek or Latin—and so the assignment fell naturally to Bishop to stock the clubhouse libraries. From Washington he solicited recommendations, collected volumes, and saw to it that they arrived safely. Some of the larger libraries, he was told, required 600 books or more.

Gertrude Beeks, a reformer with the progressive National Civic Federation, helped Bishop collect some of the books on his list. "I find by inquiring of some of the labor men who have been to the Isthmus, as well as some who have not, that they would greatly appreciate having in each clubhouse a Century Dictionary and a set of encyclopedias, in accordance with your plan," she wrote. "They would also be pleased to have technical books and light fiction, as you suggested."[505] John Cook, the YMCA's general secretary, offered an appreciative nod to Bishop's initiative: "This is a perfectly splendid contribution to the work there, and I am glad to know that it is in your hands."[506]

In addition to books, Bishop was assembling progress reports and statistics to help Taft refute opponents' charges that the American excavation was falling behind the French results of the 1880s. "The largest total excavation made since American occupation was for April 1907 when 879,527 cubic yards were taken from the Culebra Cut," he reported. "It will thus be seen that was three times the largest amount ever removed by the French. It should be borne in mind that the French excavation was from the surface merely, and consequently comparatively easy work even in the Culebra Division, while at present nearly all the work in Culebra is from the rock."[507]

And then, in the months that followed, Bishop's life changed forever.

The shakeup began on a sweltering Wednesday. On January 30, 1907, at Culebra, John Stevens, his head wreathed in rings of Cuban blue smoke, began a six-page, handwritten letter to the president:

> Sir:
>
> *I believe in being frank and above board . . . I never sought this position . . . I allowed arguments as to what was called duty to override my own feelings and, as I still firmly believe, my better judgment . . . The idea of being*

constantly before the public, whether in favorable or unfavorable light, is extremely distasteful to me . . . My home is broken up. I am and must be separated from my family during the greater part of the time.

Since his appointment, Stevens had had a respectful relationship with the president. He recalled that Roosevelt had advised him to communicate "man to man, with entire freedom on any and all matters." And so Stevens owned up: "To me the canal is only a big ditch, and its great utility when completed, has never been so apparent to me . . . Neither the possible glory, nor any financial recompense allowable, seems at all commensurate . . . I am not anxious to continue in the service. . . . My desire is to rest and then to re-enter the railway service . . . May I ask your calm and dispassionate consideration of this matter?"

The words flowing from Stevens's pen were astonishingly outspoken, evidence perhaps that his judgment was as worn as his body and spirit. He was suffering from insomnia at the time and distressed at the deteriorating health of his wife back home. In less than two years he had straightened out the mess he had inherited from Wallace, halted premature excavation of the waterway, redirected the project's focus to the preparatory organization of men and materials, and whipped the vital Panama Railroad into an efficient transport system. Now his frustrations drove him to criticism of Roosevelt's policies, his management of the Commission, and, worse, regulation of the railroads that he, Stevens, esteemed: "The present tendency appears to be to hamper transportation lines with unjust criticisms and unjustifiable laws."[508]

When he read the letter, Roosevelt was said to be taken aback by both its content and its tone. He interpreted it as a resignation and told Taft that Stevens would have to leave at once.

Within a month, Roosevelt announced that he had placed the project in the hands of the army under the command of Lieutenant Colonel Goethals, both chief engineer and ICC chairman, effective April 1. Theodore Shonts had stepped down as chairman early in March to go into the rapid transit business in New York. To his credit, Goethals recognized the work of his predecessor: "Mr. Stevens has perfected such an organization . . . that there is nothing left for us to do but just have the organization continue in the good work it has done and is doing . . . Mr. Stevens has done an amount of work for which he will never get any credit, or if he gets any, will not get enough."[509]

The turbulence at the top of the commission troubled Bishop, who wondered whether he would survive it. Although he enjoyed Roosevelt's loyalty, certain of the president's adversaries in Congress—and a few friends—continued to harp on Bishop's presence in Washington and, of course, that inflated salary. Now that Taft stood in line to succeed Roosevelt after the 1908 election, could the commission secretary be sure of his allegiance? Roosevelt would stand by him, but would Taft? Or would the candidate presumptive deem Bishop an expendable political liability?

Taft assembled his brain trust in Washington during the June 22–23 weekend under an order from Roosevelt to slash needless expenses in Panama and ensure that everything was "clean as a hound's tooth" as the campaign season approached. By Sunday evening, the secretary of war had concluded that the commission's Washington office must close, except for procurement responsibilities, and that most of the remaining personnel be reassigned to the isthmus—well outside of the gaze of congressional critics. Bishop was politically untouchable as commission secretary, though still a visible reminder of how the president had circumvented the Senate. Taft made the case to the president that Bishop's public relations skills would best serve the administration—present and next—in Panama. After all, hadn't Bishop skillfully helped to orchestrate Roosevelt's visit and produce friendly press coverage?

Bishop received the news Sunday evening, according to a well-informed and probably leaked report in the *New York World*. But he had talked Taft into granting him a five-day reprieve. Bishop was working on a scheme, he said, to "rid you both of the burden of my official existence." He hoped to acquire the struggling *Washington Herald* with the help of the president's and Taft's friends and "make [it] a useful agent for the cause." He didn't want to go to Panama, but he had no investment capital for such an acquisition. He contended that he did have the expertise to manage the editorial side of the paper and write persuasively—especially of Republican candidates and their policies.

Mindful that July was approaching, Bishop asked Taft for two months' vacation with pay, promising to use the time to school his successor thoroughly and discreetly. "Believe me, there is much information which I alone possess that is valuable to you and without which you will be embarrassed in many ways," he warned.[50]

Whether Taft interpreted Bishop's line as a threat, he was having none of the idea. "I don't think the *Herald* project is practicable," he responded four days later, "because I don't think that the President has any money, and I don't think I could secure any for the purpose." They wanted him out of Washington without embarrassment. Taft suggested that Bishop:

> *go down on the Isthmus and try it for three or four months, and see how you like it. If, by that time, you conclude that you cannot stand it and want to come up, we can give you a leave of absence so that you can come back and make the arrangements which you now have in mind to make. The truth is that you will relieve yourself and the President and everyone else of embarrassment by going to the Isthmus. That of itself will end the criticism, and I beg of you on your own behalf to take that course.*[511]

Bishop was out of options. "I accept your decision without reluctance," he informed Taft two days later, "and shall go to the Isthmus, not sadly but cheerfully." He pledged to do his utmost for the commission and for Taft and Roosevelt. But he insisted that the public announcement of his reassignment be handled just right. "I should be glad were you to say to the pressmen . . . that you did not deliver an ultimatum to me to 'go or resign,' and that I did not appeal to the president to save me."[512]

Taft agreed to the story line, saying, "I am delighted you have reached the conclusion that you have."[513] The president, who had lain low during the confrontation, said he was "extremely pleased" that Bishop had decided to go to Panama. "I think it was wise from every standpoint," he concluded.[514]

Four days prior to sailing for Panama, Bishop penned a good-bye letter to T. R. from the banks of Vineyard Sound. Ordered into exile, he nonetheless remained true to the president while swatting at the man who was forcing him out of the country. The "automotive tourists" and capitalists with whom he and Harriet had spoken on Cape Cod had predicted, he said, that Roosevelt would run again for president in 1908 because the people would demand it. "Taft? I don't know how it is in other parts of the country, but in New England there is no sentiment whatever for him . . . With their hearts full of you, they simply will not think of anyone else." As he brought the letter to a close, Bishop turned sentimental. "The hardest part of it is that it takes me far from personal contact with you, for in that I have found my highest enjoyment . . . In the meantime don't forget me, and ask Mrs. Roosevelt not to do so also."[515]

The president wanted to give Bishop "final instructions" in person, and so he invited Harriet and Him to Sagamore Hill on the eve of their departure for Panama. "Come here for the night ... [take] the 4:10 train from the city."[516]

Bishop joined the president, Secretary of State Root, and the German ambassador, Baron Speck von Sternberg, and half a dozen others around the dinner table. "We talked much of Panama," Bishop reported to Taft the next day. "I told him, as I told you, that I shall go there determined to do everything in my power to help the Commission and be useful to the government."[517] Roosevelt's parting message was his desire for confidential reports on how Colonel Goethals was getting on, the obstacles he faced, and the remedies he required. Bishop was to be the president's eyes and ears on the isthmus.

On the sweltering afternoon of August 1, 1907, Joseph Bucklin Bishop boarded the chartered South African steamer *Dunnottar Castle* in New York harbor to start a new and unplanned chapter in his life at the age of sixty, wary and uncertain. He took some comfort in the promise, as a condition of going, of a house to be built for him on Ancon Hill in Panama City, as well as a horse and carriage for his convenience. As he ascended the ship's passageway, outfitted smartly in tropical whites, he escorted Harriet, his son Farnham, and daughter Alice, who had dutifully consented to accompany him for a month's stay.

A friend reported later, "He kept to himself all the way down, and but few on board knew who he was."[518]

Twenty-Seven

Blunder and Triumph

EN ROUTE HOME FROM PANAMA IN NOVEMBER 1906, THE *LOUISIANA* HAD hardly docked in Puerto Rico when President Roosevelt sternly cabled Secretary Taft: "Discharge is not to be suspended. The offense was most heinous, and the punishment I inflicted was imposed after due deliberation."[519] The Brownsville Incident, as it came to be known, was perhaps T. R.'s greatest blunder and the worst failure of judgment in his presidency.

It began in Brownsville, Texas, near midnight on August 13, 1906. Some twenty to thirty black soldiers shot up the town, according to the mayor and townspeople. As Bishop later put it, the soldiers "scaled the walls of the fort and went through the town, shooting whomsoever they saw, moving and firing into houses wherever they saw lights." The story went that they "came very near to killing several women and children."[520]

The infantrymen were blamed for murdering a bartender and wounding a policeman and a reporter before returning to base at Fort Brown. The incident capped a simmering period of bigotry and discrimination against the newly arrived troops by Brownsville citizens. It included a dubious claim, published in the local newspaper, that a white woman had been assaulted by a black man in an army uniform.

Fort Brown commanders—white, it should be noted—defended their charges, arguing that the soldiers could not have committed the violence because they were in their barracks at the time. But locals produced evidence of spent shells from army rifles and numerous "eyewitness" accounts.

When the men were later ordered to single out the guilty in their ranks, they refused—even when warned that entire companies of men would be discharged for insubordination. Despite what Bishop called a "full investigation of the facts" by the army, there was no hearing or trial, and the infantrymen were denied the right to face their accusers. On the basis of the military probe and their supposed conspiracy of silence, Roosevelt ordered all 167 men dishonorably discharged. As a result, the soldiers could no longer serve in the armed forces or in civil service, and they lost whatever pension entitlements they had earned.

Booker T. Washington protested, but Roosevelt rebuffed him "I have been amazed and indignant at the attitude of the Negroes and of the shortsighted sentimentalists as to my action," Roosevelt wrote in his defense. "All of the men . . . instantly banded together to shield the criminals. In other words, they took action that cannot be tolerated in any soldiers, black or white."[521] Sensing a partisan opportunity to split Roosevelt from his Northern supporters, a Senate committee conducted another investigation of the episode, but after much political jockeying it reaffirmed Roosevelt's decision.

Doubts about the incident and Roosevelt's hasty decision persisted for decades. John Weaver made a compelling case for the soldiers' innocence in his 1970 book, *The Brownsville Raid*. Two years later, the army undertook a fresh investigation and concluded that the accused had been framed in a conspiracy bred by an atmosphere of racial hate. President Richard Nixon subsequently signed papers reversing Roosevelt's order. Dorsie Williams, the sole survivor among the discharged, received a meager $25,000 in compensation.

"Roosevelt had not stopped long enough to listen to all points of view and to assess critically what had happened in Texas," observed Roosevelt historian Keith Simon. "Much of this points to gaps in his own experience with the realities of racism, as well as personal experience with the Army brass and their culture." Simon elaborated:

> *While T. R. was the son of a slave-holding Southern mother and was aware of racism in an abstract sense, like his father he was a confirmed Northerner and unionist . . . who failed to understand the psychology of a Southern racist mob. Likewise, while Roosevelt had been exposed to war firsthand, it was as an amateur. He had no experience as a professional military officer in the Army. He had no professional Army cultural or organizational background. He did not understand the willingness of the War Department to cover its tracks and protect its own.*[522]

When asked by his friend, Owen Wister, "Why didn't you order a court of enquiry for the commissioned officers?" T. R. responded: "Because I listened to the War Department, and I shouldn't [have]." After a pause, he added: "Of course, I can't know all about everything."

"And so," Wister countered, "the best you can do is to stop, look and listen—and then jump."

"Yes," Roosevelt concluded, "and then jump. And hope I've jumped right."[523]

The president's preoccupation with the Brownsville Incident and with progress on the Panama Canal did not, however, obscure a string of remarkable legislative achievements around the same time. By the end of 1906, Roosevelt and Republican majorities in Congress racked up considerable reformist successes in conservation, public health, and regulation of the railroads—a winning combination of domestic Big Stick and Square Deal.

The Antiquities Act granted him and future presidents the power to protect national monuments. With that authority, he moved swiftly to safeguard Devil's Tower in Wyoming and, later, Muir Woods in California and Arizona's Grand Canyon. The Pure Food and Drug Act of 1906 effectively ended patent-medicine scams by requiring physician-authorized prescriptions for certain drugs, and it gave the federal government authority to inspect food and medicines. Slaughterhouses and meat-packing plants—so gruesomely exposed by Upton Sinclair in *The Jungle*, and in other books—were required to meet tough sanitary standards under the Meat Inspection Act, which authorized the Department of Agriculture to examine meat animals before and after their demise. The Hepburn Act required the Interstate Commerce Commission to regulate rail-shipping rates, extending federal oversight of questionable business practices.

Writing in 1919, the year of Roosevelt's death, his friend William Roscoe Thayer pointed out the significance of these legislative accomplishments: "These things are no longer in the field of debate. They are accepted just as the railroad and the telegraph are accepted. But each in its time was a novelty, a reform, and to secure its acceptance by the American people and its sanction in the statute book, required the zeal, the energy, the courage of one man—Theodore Roosevelt."[524]

The president was determined—now that he had brokered peace between Russia and Japan and received the Nobel Prize for his efforts—that America should exhibit its place on the international stage. And so, "precisely as I took Panama, without consulting the Cabinet,"[525] he launched a "grand pageant of American sea power"—the worldwide voyage of the Great White Fleet. Sixteen battleships of the Atlantic Fleet, adorned with red, white, and blue banners on their bows, set out from Hampton Roads, Virginia, on December 16, 1907, to demonstrate American might to the world. In port after port, on continent after continent, enthusiastic crowds cheered the American ships and sailors. When the fleet returned fourteen months later, after circumnavigating the globe, everyone acknowledged that Roosevelt had staged an astounding, worldwide diplomatic and public relations feat. He called it "the most important service that I rendered to peace."[526]

The president also found time and energy in 1906 to host a lavish White House wedding for his daughter Alice and Ohio congressman Nicholas Longworth.

With the earliest ship's mail that followed his arrival in Panama, Bishop rushed the first of a string of illuminating letters to Roosevelt. Taken together, they form an insightful view of the early Goethals era on the isthmus as well as testimony of Bishop's emerging role as an influential figure in Panama. From his desk in Ancon's posh Hotel Tivoli, Bishop wrote of the cordial reception he had received from the ICC chairman and his colleagues. "It was all that I could desire," he reported. Goethals "told me to select a site for a house in which to live on Ancon Hill, to pick the kind of house I desired, and he said he would give orders to have all other site work set aside in order to build it as soon as possible." Goethals also furnished a "victoria"—a light, four-wheeled carriage with a calash top—"and fine horses for my exclusive use," Bishop verified. "Mrs. Bishop rides in it daily with inexpressible pleasure."[527]

The commission secretary took office space in the canal headquarters building nearing completion in Ancon, adjacent to his anticipated house lot. Roosevelt surely chuckled smugly as he worked through Bishop's thirteen-page, handwritten letter. He must have thought how adroitly he had converted Bishop from a significant political liability in Washington to a dutiful emissary in Panama, and how he had ensured Bishop's continued loyalty with a few family luxuries. Bishop would not disappoint.

Colonel Goethals, Bishop's junior by eleven years, took command of canal operations in Panama during the spring of 1907. Born in Brooklyn, New York, to Flemish immigrants, Goethals was commissioned a second lieutenant in the Army Corps of Engineers upon his graduation in 1880, second in his class, from West Point. Achievements in a series of river and bridge assignments led him to his first project command along the Tennessee River near Florence, Alabama, in 1891. There he built the Riverton Lock at Colbert Shoals, incorporating a revolutionary twenty-six-foot lift design over the objections of his superiors in Washington. That feat caught Roosevelt's attention, as did Goethals's starring

In 1907, the U.S. built this house in Ancon, Panama, for Joseph Bucklin Bishop and his family, as a condition of his leaving Washington, D.C. *Anita and Miriam Bishop collection*

role as chief of engineers for the U.S. Volunteers during the Spanish-American War. The successful lift design also inspired the success of future high-lift locks in Panama. "He proved to be the man of all others to do the job," Roosevelt asserted.[528]

Goethals's authority exuded, in part, from his assertive physical presence. A center part sharply divided a thatch of snow-white hair. His dark, deep-set eyes marked a stern, brown-skinned face. Goethals favored the high-collared, tropical white suit at all times. Not once in the seven years of his command on the isthmus did he don his brass-covered army uniform. There was no need; everyone knew who was in charge.

Bishop's first impressions of Panama in August 1907 were "most favorable," he reported to the president. "From one end of the line to another there was perceptible activity, energy and enthusiasm . . . [I] was astonished at the progress that had been made since you were

George Washington Goethals, "Genius of the Panama Canal," about 1915, after leaving Panama.

Library of Congress Prints and Photographs Division

here." At Gatun, where a giant dam was being built to tame the Chagres River, "little less than a miracle has been wrought," and in the Culebra Cut, "conditions were no less surprising." On and on Bishop enthused about what he saw. Worker complaints about the quality of the food "have virtually ceased," he claimed, "and the new recreation buildings are a great success."[529]

Within a few days his apprehensiveness about his overseas assignment had vanished. "It is the best thing that I have ever done, and the work is the proudest and most honorable of my life," he admitted. It was to him "the most eminently American enterprise ever, and the way in which it is going forward stirs my blood like the sound of a trumpet." Bishop's newfound outlook came as the consequence of his immediate acceptance by Goethals. Bishop shared with Roosevelt an important talk he had had: "After a long and frank conversation

Within days of arriving in Panama in 1907, Bishop began informing Roosevelt of canal construction progress and his own circumstances.

Theodore Roosevelt Papers, Manuscript Division, Library of Congress

205

with the Colonel, he said at the close, 'I am sure that your presence here will be of great value to me—far greater than you think.'"[530]

But what most excited Bishop—beyond the creature comforts he enjoyed—were his official duties. Goethals assigned him to serve as point man with workers who had job-related grievances and directed him to resolve conflicts on his own whenever he could. Unlike his predecessors, this chairman and chief engineer wanted to keep an open door, but the volume of complaints and suggestions was proving burdensome and a drain on his time. So Bishop, whose patience and judgment Taft and Roosevelt had touted, served as his first line of contact for the English-speaking workers who felt aggrieved by short pay, dangerous working conditions, or discord with a co-worker. "I hear both sides separately, then assemble them together and hold a regular court," Bishop told Roosevelt. "The result thus far has been, almost invariably, an agreement before leaving the room."[531]

Colonel Goethals did act as a kind of court of appeals, to hear a man's petition if he could not get satisfaction from Bishop or another set of gatekeepers who spoke other languages. Each Sunday morning Goethals roosted behind his desk and listened to the woes of the disgruntled men who had lined up in his waiting room. One time he agreed to a man's request for transfer to another construction division because its baseball team needed a pitcher. "He was a combination of father confessor and Day of Judgment,"[532] Bishop wryly observed.

At a later time, Goethals turned the table on Bishop. Author Frederic Jennings Haskin told of an indignant engineer's wife who informed

Colonel Goethals that Joseph Bucklin Bishop, Secretary of the Commission, gets bread from the hospital bakery and wants to know why she cannot. "I will look into the matter for you," says the chief engineer, and a note of this complaint is made. Later the telephone bell rings, and Mr. Bishop is asked if he gets bread at the hospital bakery. He replies in the affirmative, explaining that about three years ago he had breakfast with Colonel Gorgas who arranged for him to buy his bread there instead of at the commissary, this bread being more to his liking. "Can't any other employee of the Canal Commission get bread under the same terms?" queries the chief engineer. "I will see, sir," responds the Secretary of the Commission. "If they cannot," answers the chief engineer, "you must have your bread stopped at once." And it was stopped.[533]

Joseph Bucklin Bishop at his desk in Panama (ca. 1910)

Anita and Miriam Bishop collection

Of long-term significance, though, Bishop had won Goethals's approval for a free newspaper to be published regularly by the commission and directed at the canal workforce. "In it should be furnished exact information about all business of the canal work," Bishop explained, "the amount of excavation, the record made daily by each steam shovel, the condition of the work on dams and locks, health reports and actions of the Commission." And yes, he wisely added, it should report the "doings of the various baseball and other organizations . . . everything of interest to employees." As editor, he planned to pattern the publication along the lines of the *Bulletin du Canal Interocéanique* published by the French from Paris in the 1880s. "I would send it to every member of Congress and [the] Senate, to the Washington correspondents and to the leading newspapers of the country."[534]

From his decades of newspaper experience, Bishop understood how a credible communications tool could positively influence attitudes and opinions and overcome rumors and suspicions bred by an information vacuum. Early in his isthmus tenure, he correctly foresaw that the newspaper's "effect among the men would be most beneficial, for they would be stimulated to fresh energy and rivalry by knowing what their fellows are doing all along the line."[535]

After two additional weeks of discreet surveillance, Bishop assured Roosevelt that Goethals was piloting "the most perfect and smoothly running machine I have ever seen . . . Matters on the Isthmus are in better condition than they have ever been since the American occupation began."[536] Roosevelt cleverly recast the situation and couched it in terms of praise and usefulness a few weeks later: "I think Colonel Goethals was most wise to have you come to the Isthmus, for now you can put everything before me at length . . . It is of real help to me thus to have it."[537]

Goethals knew, of course, that Bishop had a back channel to the White House and used his friendship with Roosevelt to his advantage—and the canal's. Early on the president hoisted a trial balloon through the commission secretary, bypassing the commissioners and Taft, who was out of the country. Goethals had determined that the commission was cumbersome and ineffective and should be abolished. He said so to Bishop, who, the same day, floated the proposition to Roosevelt. What Goethals desired was not a structure of diffuse authority but a spare, decision-making core made up of himself, Bishop, and a few key engineering aides. Roosevelt agreed to the new arrangement in principle, believing it would accelerate progress. "Whether we get the change in law or not," the president replied to Bishop, Goethals "shall really have all the powers . . . Of course, the wise thing for him to do is, as far as possible, act first and then have his acts confirmed by the Commission."[538]

By the end of August, Bishop informed T. R. that "Goethals had taken me to his bosom" and named him executive officer of the now-advisory-only commission. "You and I must carry this thing on together," he quoted Goethals as saying.[539]

The Bishop family—Joseph, Harriet, Alice, and Farnham—had spent about a month in Panama when it was decided that all but Joseph would return temporarily to the States. Harriet and Alice would close the Washington apartment, now confident that the isthmus would be their long-term home. Farnham, twenty-one, would conclude his studies at Harvard and enter law school there. Known kiddingly to his friends as "Panama Bishop," Farnham was short, stocky, intensely nervous, and quick and incisive in speech, according to a later college profile. Like his father, his receding hairline appeared early in life.

Around this time, Farnham penned a youthful observation of the "state socialism" he had experienced on the isthmus. Its chief usefulness today is its description of the family's life there.

> *Our family lives in a house designed by an official architect, built by state labor on public land and completely furnished by a paternal government from the concrete piles it stands on to the ventilator on the roof. My mother orders tomorrow's groceries by calling up the commissary on the free public telephone and pays for them, not with money—for none would be accepted—but with coupons from one of the booklets issued by the state to its servants. The Secretary of the Isthmian Canal Commission sits in his office in the Administration Building, editing the official newspaper, answering a thousand questions and attending to as many complaints as we cannot anticipate, for his duty is to see that 40,000 employees, of more than 40 different nationalities, get fair treatment and efficient service. It would be a much harder task to discover a form of government that would be assuredly benevolent as well as despotic for the republic at large, instead of for a colony or a city . . . And though I am not a socialist with a big "S," I venture to prophesy that when we have made our home governments as lean and efficient as those of Governor [of Panama] Magoon and Colonel Goethals, socialism will succeed where capitalism has failed, as at Panama today.*[540]

Like a prideful father, Joseph Bucklin Bishop enclosed the first edition of the *Canal Record* with his September 3, 1907, letter to Roosevelt. Presented in three neatly ruled columns over eight pages, the nine-by-twelve-inch paper announced its purpose as "[t]he publication of accurate information, based upon official records, concerning all branches of the work of the canal construction." It was, of course, much more than that. It was dry and fact-filled to be sure, but the *Canal Record* functioned primarily as Roosevelt and Goethals' promotional house organ—certified proof that the improbable canal with its dams, lakes, and locks was indeed emerging from the torrid jungles of Panama.

The type and page rules were all set by hand. Printing took place on antique equipment inherited from the French in a small room on the first floor of the old commission headquarters at Cathedral Square in Panama City. It would be published weekly, Bishop, its editor, promised, and "issued free of charge, one copy each, to all employees of the Commission whose names are on the Gold Roll. Extra copies can be obtained from the newsstands of the Panama Railway for five cents each."[541]

In addition to regular progress reports, the newspaper promised readers information on "the social life of the Zone, its amusements, sports and other activities as is thought to be of general interest." Letters to the editor would be welcome, Bishop noted, "subject only to the restriction that such communication must be couched in respectful language and must be signed in each instance with the name and address of the writer."[542] Accuracy was "almost a fetish with Joseph Bucklin Bishop," wrote W. S. Haskins soon after the editor's death many years later. "Nothing would make him rave more than an error in *The Canal Record,* no matter how trivial it might seem to others."[543]

Both immediately and over the next seven years of canal construction, the newspaper provided a significant boost to morale. "What *The Canal Record* did for the men on the Isthmus was very much what *Stars and Stripes* did for the A.E.F. in France," wrote Farnham Bishop in 1930. "It showed every man what the other fellows were doing all along the line. It stimulated the growing feeling of team play and solidarity . . . It helped remove the long-established conviction in the public mind that nothing good could come out of Panama."[544]

Bishop and an assistant smartly published the excavation results of the work divisions and sections along the line, contrasting them with each other to generate competition for "best week on the Isthmus." Workmen and their supervisors rushed to read the *Canal Record* on publication day to see who had done the most that week. The winners arranged celebrations in the clubhouses and enjoyed drinks in the saloons.

The first edition's news was statistic-laden for the most part but otherwise chatty and upbeat, like a small-town weekly. There were no photos at first, and certainly no bad news. Examples:

- The work on the locks and dams has taken such shape that it is now possible to see something of their form.

- The libraries . . . for the four new recreation buildings have arrived and will be placed in the reading areas as soon as proper provision for their care can be made . . . Membership in the clubhouses is now more than 1,600, and applications are being filed each day. All classes of white men were largely represented.

- The death rate in July 1907 was about half what it was a year earlier.

- All Kentuckians have organized a [baseball] team and accepted the challenge of the Georgia men.

- The commissary prices are: chickens, 65 cents each; beef soup. 7 cents a pound; pineapples, 10 cents each.

In his 1928 retrospective, W. S. Haskins drew a rare and revealing portrait of the *Canal Record* editor at work:

> *Mr. Bishop was usually in the office promptly in the workday morning. He would look over his mail—and he always had a large personal correspondence—dictate replies to such letters as required an answer and knock off for the forenoon. In the afternoon, he would put in some time on his book, generally quitting about 4 o'clock. He also had a habit of sitting quietly in his chair for long periods of time, apparently thinking . . . [He] could be seen shortly after 4 o'clock every pleasant afternoon, in company with his daughter, riding along the Sabanas Road.*[545]

All success aside, the *Canal Record* wasn't Bishop's inspiration; in fact, he awarded his boss with much of the birthright, as any loyal soldier would do: "Colonel Goethals had perceived that there was no means by which intelligence about canal work was carried from one division to another. The resulting ignorance about the progress of the work as a whole was a distinct obstacle to that general interest which was necessary for the development of esprit de corps."[546]

Julie Green, who methodically chronicled the construction years in *The Canal Builders,* credits Gertrude Beeks—the early corporate welfare activist for the National Civic Federation of Chicago, who had helped Bishop stock the clubhouse libraries—with the idea for a weekly journal. The NCF had a notable record of progressive reform, of improving working conditions and relations between employees and employers nationwide. By 1906, it had expanded its mission beyond the private sector to the world of government and inserted itself into the highly visible U.S. project on the isthmus. Taft had asked Beeks—"a dignified sort of woman, a handsome gray-eyed figure dressed in the fine businesswoman's fashions of the day," according to Green—to go to Panama to report on working conditions there. Her assignment, Taft advised Goethals, was not to disparage or second-guess but to evaluate conditions objectively and suggest improvements where needed.

Beeks's report, produced after three weeks of inquiry, told of touring the line, interviewing workers, and inspecting clubhouses and dormitories. Her findings were insightful, bold, and controversial. "She noticed many little but essential things," noted the *New York Times*, which "would have escaped the eyes of a dozen investigating committees of men . . . She found that a great deal of improvement had been made within the last two years in the matter of taking care of the employees; she found a great deal still to complain about."[547] Beeks criticized insufficient and crowded housing; the prevalence of bedbugs, cockroaches, and fleas; the absence of hot-water showers; and monotonous food.

Beyond the assessment of everyday conditions, she thought it vital to improve general communications. Beeks proposed a weekly bulletin, "which might be called the 'Canal Zone News.'" Through it, "employees could be informed, for instance, of the loss of a ship containing vegetables which had just occurred, or the sinking of a shipload of lumber." Beeks also urged coverage of "rulings or changes which have been made with reference to mess houses or the assignment of quarters, commissaries or the employment of labor . . . This paper could be supplied with Associated Press dispatches, affording the employee, eager for news from home, something more to relieve the dreadful monotony of that life." She also concluded that it "should be distributed free of charge because it is important to be read by all."[548]

In a letter dated September 9, 1907, Bishop informed Roosevelt that he had been assigned responsibility for compiling the commissioners' comments on Beeks's report and that it was undergoing careful examination. Bishop found much fault in her criticisms. "She really asks to have a workingman's Heaven established in the Isthmus," he sniffed. "Many of her criticisms are just but most of her suggestions are so absurd, even silly, that they are likely to act as a counter-foil to her criticisms."[549]

He did not offer an opinion on her call for a local newsletter, but on the very day the first edition of the *Canal Record* was circulating widely in the Canal Zone. Readers had snapped up more than 2,000 copies of what Roosevelt characterized as an "excellent and interesting paper."

Twenty-Eight

A Big, Generous, High-Minded Fellow

As fall began to chill the blistering Washington summer, Roosevelt was thinking ahead to his annual message to Congress at the end of the year. He planned to use the speech to call for continued funding of canal construction and to boast of his accomplishments there. "Now won't you, as soon as you can, send me a not-too-long draft of what you would like me to say?" T. R. asked Bishop on September 11, 1907.[550]

By the middle of October, the secretary's draft was in the president's hands. He urged Roosevelt to decide whether or not the canal should be built by private-sector contractors. "I have summed up very briefly the fundamental reasons why a change to contract should not be made now" Bishop advised, "so, too, in regard to the question of type"[551]—meaning a lock versus sea-level canal.

"I shall put in my message what you have sent me with the approval of the Colonel," T. R. replied. "You told me exactly what I wanted to know."[552]

In his seventh annual message to Congress, delivered to the Capitol by courier on December 3, Roosevelt declared that canal work was proceeding "in a highly satisfactory manner." He announced that steam shovels and dredges had achieved record excavation totals month after month—a truly extraordinary record, especially in view of the heavy rainfall. Work on the Gatun locks and dam was going so well that masonry work could begin within fifteen months. Echoing Bishop and Goethals, Roosevelt declared, "It is the unanimous opinion of the present Commission that the work can be done better, more cheaply and more quickly by the government than by private contractors." And, he added, Goethals and his team "are firmly convinced that the 85-feet-level lock canal which they are constructing is the best that could be desired . . . I concur in this belief."[553]

Notwithstanding the president's rosy report, congressional appropriators went to the isthmus to see for themselves. Bishop escorted one delegation up and down the line and reported to Roosevelt, "They all return not only pleased but most enthusiastic about what they have seen and learned. They will give us all the money we desire." The congressional inspection tours, while politically necessary, disrupted Goethals's team and were at times unruly. The chief engineer had to relocate himself from Culebra headquarters to the Tivoli Hotel in Ancon to be on call at any hour in the event of a congressional summons. Goethals despised this part of the job; he was, above all else, an engineer.

Of one visiting delegation, Bishop observed, "They were a mixed lot. Some of them were courteous, intelligent gentlemen, some were amusing ignoramuses and some took unsavory advantage of their immunity from arrest." One zone policeman, he remembered, labeled the visiting congressmen The Savages.[554]

Life for Americans on the isthmus was taking on a homespun flavor as more stateside institutions and customs worked their way onto the social scene there. "Christmas 1907 will be remembered on the Zone as the merriest since American occupation," the *Canal Record* proclaimed to readers. "At Cristóbal on Christmas Eve, the Union Church, the women's club, the day school and the Y.M.C.A. joined together in giving an old-fashioned Christmas party in the Commission clubhouse. Santa was there in all his glory and gave presents to the children from a genuine Christmas tree brought from the States." Candy, nuts, and orangeade were served in the reading room to an estimated crowd of 500, and the Canal Zone Band furnished the music. "It was a Christmas Eve long to be remembered."[555]

As New Year 1908 dawned—a presidential election year in the U.S.—Bishop resolved to fortify his relationship with Taft. Roosevelt had affirmed his opposition to a second full term, and the secretary of war was emerging as the likely Republican nominee for president. "We have just taken possession of our new house on Ancon Hill," Bishop wrote Taft. "You put me in a field of usefulness that is immeasurably wider than I had in D.C. It arouses my engines and enthusiasm, and I am as happy in my work as I am proud to be connected with so stupendous a job."[556]

Taft replied with a reticence—perhaps even false modesty—that foreshadowed his upcoming campaign style. "With respect to the Presidency, I have no false hopes," he wrote. "If the nomination comes to me I shall be surprised, and so too if the result in the election is favorable. Somehow or other, I can't dream of myself being President."[557]

Bishop chided him lightly: "You are going to be President whether you can dream of yourself as such or not. To a man up a coconut tree at this distance, there is not the slightest doubt about it."[558]

But many influential party leaders and many Republican-leaning newspapers urged Roosevelt to reconsider and seek another four years. They knew that his accomplishments and popularity would guarantee an easy victory over whomever the Democrats selected. Writing to progressive theologian Reverend Dr. Lyman Abbott that spring, T. R. admitted, "There has never been a moment when I could not have had the Republican nomination with practical unanimity by simply raising a finger."[559] But Roosevelt wanted to honor the spirit of the two-term precedent rather than the letter. He told Republican congressman Charles Washburn of Massachusetts, "I have never for a moment altered my views as to the wisdom of my declaration after the election of 1904. It is time for someone else to stand his trick at the wheel."[560]

Roosevelt's steadfastness was not a ruse to generate a stampede for his candidacy. Bishop by now was sure that Roosevelt would not change his mind, and saw repeated evidence of the president's opposition to another term. "Taft was his [Roosevelt's] choice for his successor," Bishop wrote unequivocally.

Maybe so, but T. R. biographer Edmund Morris claims that Roosevelt's personal first choice was "wise and honest" Elihu Root, John Hay's successor as secretary of state. But, Morris noted, the realistic politician in T. R. understood that Root was probably not electable, given his background as a corporate lawyer and the current popular support for aggressive government regulation of business.[561] Roosevelt thought Taft better suited to be chief justice of the Supreme Court.

The president demonstrated his noncandidacy by organizing for Taft, someone he felt was a true progressive and whose policies would build upon his own legacy. T. R. wrote and phoned delegates rumored to be supporting him and urged them to get behind the secretary of war. His message to them likely followed his written assertion to Dr. Abbott: "Taft is the best fitted at this time to be President and to carry on the work upon which we have entered during the past six years."[562]

Weighing in at more than 300 pounds, Taft did not relish the thought of the campaign—his first ever. He may not have demonstrated a passion for the White House, but others close to him did—especially his wife, Nellie, and half-brother, Charley, a former newspaper publisher and now member of Congress. Morris characterizes Taft as "not a fighter, either open or covert. Lacking aggression, all he wanted was to be loved."[563]

What Taft did long for was the Supreme Court, which he saw as the pinnacle of his judicial career. Roosevelt had offered him an appointment to the

President Roosevelt endorses "Crown Prince" William
Howard Taft as his successor in an August 1, 1906, *Puck*
cover by Udo K. Keppler.

Library of Congress Prints and Photographs Division

court twice during the early years of his administration, but Taft had turned
him down both times so that he could fulfill his obligations in the Philippines,
where he had served as colonial governor. By the spring of 1908 there was no
opening on the bench.

In 1908, for the first time, some Republican convention delegates were
chosen by party rank and file and not handpicked by their leaders. In a head-
to-head primary in February, Ohio activists selected Taft over Governor Joseph
Foraker. The California branch of the party went for Taft as well, but Wisconsin
and Pennsylvania picked favorite sons. By the time the Republican convention

convened at the Chicago Coliseum on June 10, Taft supporters—including Roosevelt—had dispatched the few challengers to the secretary of war's candidacy. All that remained was for T. R. and the presiding chairman, Senator Lodge, to douse any lingering support for the incumbent president that might flare up on the convention floor or in the back rooms.

The next day Bishop sailed for the States, bent on enjoying two months of paid leave and perhaps taking a low-profile role in the convention's outcome. Fresh off the steamer in New York, he caught a train to Washington where, at 11:00 a.m. on the 15th, T. R. received him at the White House. It was the day of convention balloting for the presidential nomination, and Roosevelt was exchanging telegrams with party managers in Chicago, trying to put out fires ignited by his die-hard enthusiasts. As Bishop put it,

> *Several private telegrams came to him from personal friends in Chicago, saying that unless he made a fresh and most emphatic declaration that he would not accept a nomination, the convention would name him in spite of all efforts to the contrary. He was much disturbed by these messages and asked me if I thought he should make a further declaration, getting from his secretary, Mr. Loeb, copies of letters and telegrams that he had already sent to Senator Lodge and others defining his position. I read these carefully and found them so emphatic and unequivocal that I advised him to say nothing further, expressing the opinion that if he were to repeatedly follow one denial after another he would make himself ridiculous, for no fresh denial could be couched in more emphatic and conclusive language than he had already used. He accepted this view.*

The telegrams kept arriving as Bishop joined T. R., Mrs. Roosevelt, and the children for lunch on the south portico.

Taft was running on a platform that largely celebrated Roosevelt's accomplishments and pledged continued progressive reform at home and assertiveness overseas. As the convention balloting neared, a giant portrait of Theodore Roosevelt suddenly appeared above the podium, emerging from the shadows. The convention exploded, and the pandemonium induced Senator Lodge to begin calling the roll of the states. "So deafening was the noise that not till the name of Massachusetts was reached on the alphabetical list, were the reporters able to record the vote," Bishop wrote.[564] Once Wyoming had cast its vote, however, Taft had been anointed by nearly 72 percent of the delegates. No other candidate exceeded 7 percent. As Taft's running mate, the convention chose New York congressman James Sherman.

Roosevelt—despite all his efforts to the contrary—still garnered three votes. When word of Taft's official nomination reached the White House, Roosevelt was greatly relieved. Within two weeks, Taft resigned as secretary of war, and T. R. began to plan the schedule for a safari in Africa.

At the start of Bishop's July retreat to Cape Cod, Roosevelt wrote from Sagamore Hill, "Will Mrs. Bishop and you come here for the night of Friday, July 31st, taking the 4:10 train from the city? I shall have Luke Wright"—a Tennessee attorney, erstwhile governor of the Philippines, and T. R.'s choice as new secretary of war—"to meet you."[565]

Joseph and Harriet accepted the invitation and joined the president and Mrs. Roosevelt, along with Gifford Pinchot, chief of the Forest Service, for a leisurely summer dinner. No doubt their conversation centered on strategies for the fall election campaign. Earlier that month—and for the last time—Democrats had called on William Jennings Bryan to be their candidate. It was to be a skirmish between one progressive and another.

Labor Day officially signaled the start of the Taft-Bryan contest, but it soon proved to be a lackluster affair. The candidates agreed on the protective tariff, the need to corral big business, and the importance of completing the Panama Canal. Taft had asked T. R. not to campaign for him, so the president sat impatiently on the sidelines, writing letter after letter to his would-be successor.

You should put yourself prominently and emphatically into this campaign . . . It seems absurd but I am convinced that the prominence that has been given to your golf playing has not been wise . . . The American people regard the campaign as a very serious business, and we want to be very careful that your opponents do not get the chance to misrepresent you as not taking it with sufficient seriousness.[566]

Then, six days later:

Hit them hard, old man! . . . Let the audience see you smile always, because I feel that your nature shines out so transparently when you do smile—you big, generous, high-minded fellow. The trouble is that you would always

rather fight for a pri__ple or for a friend than for yourself. Now hi_ at them;
challenge Bryan on __s record. Ask that you be judged by your record, and
dare Bryan to stand __n his.[567]

Roosevelt intensely disliked Taft's opponent. "Of course, I do not dare in
public to express my real opinion of Bryan," he wrote California environmental-
ist William Kent. "He is a kindly man and well-meaning in a weak way . . . But
he is the cheapest faki__we have ever had proposed for President."[568]

The election turned on which candidate would better continue Roosevelt's
progressive policies. Taft claimed the mantle, as of course did Bryan. But the
Democrat's campaign altered when Bryan called for a government takeover of
railroads, an idea that roused predictable cries of socialism from conservatives
and engendered skepticism among moderates. Bryan also failed to pinpoint an
issue that awakened any kind of overwhelming anti-Taft sentiment.

Taft scored an impressive win on November 3, collecting nearly 52 percent
of the popular vote against 43 percent for Bryan. Bryan won the South, his
home state of Nebraska, and two others. But Taft prevailed from New England
to the Pacific Northwest. It was the worst of Bryan's three presidential losses.
When the cheering subsided, President-elect and Mrs. Taft retreated to Hot
Springs, Virginia, where Taft thanked Roosevelt. "You have always been the
chief agent in working out the present status of affairs, and my selection and
election are chiefly your work."[569]

From Ancon in the Canal Zone, Bishop also took to his typewriter, writing
to Taft: "It is an unspeakable pleasure to know that the government and the White
House are to be in the hands of such worthy successors for the next eight years.
It is simply glorious"[570] Taft replied with characteristic nonchalance. "Thank you
for writing me. . . . I have been playing golf and much enjoying t."[571] Bishop also
wrote to Roosevelt, congratulating him on "a wonderful campaign and a glorious victory—and you did it all with your little hatchet. I have been sitting here
2,000 miles away, for three months watching your proceedings with delight and
admiration, and fairly itching to take a hand myself. Talk about 'ginger'! What
you injected into the campaign was cayenne pepper . . . It is high time you went
to Africa."[572]

PART IV

AFTERMATH

Twenty-Nine

Beasts in the Wilderness

THE 1908-09 NEW YEAR'S EVE DECORATIONS AT THE TIVOLI HOTEL IN ANCON had barely come down when maids were ordered to spruce up and polish the guest rooms and the main ballroom. A delegation from the House Committee on Interstate and Foreign Commerce was arriving in Panama to hold a field hearing into questions about the integrity of the Gatun Dam and the locks now under construction.

Stateside papers had alleged that the locks rested on "clay material—slippery and treacherous," rather than on bedrock. Further, an anonymous engineer had told the *Washington Post* that the dam was "a great mistake" because the adjoining earth banks were vulnerable to the surging Chagres River and would not hold back swells of water during the worst of the rainy season. Bishop, at Colonel Goethals's direction, had lined up expert witnesses to refute the allegations, and would also stand as a witness himself.

"The walls of the Pacific-end locks at Miraflores and Pedro Miguel will rest upon rock," testified army major Chester Harding as the hearing opened on January 6 in a meeting room packed with officials and spectators. "Hard, compact and durable blue sandstone" would afford a surefire foundation, he insisted. As for the locks in the center section of the canal, a "pebbles and cement mix" to which they were being fastened would guarantee even greater durability than sandstone.

What about claims that the dam would fail to hold back 170 square miles of a newly formed Gatun Lake, committee members asked.

"Absurd," said Goethals's expert. They were "not worthy of any sleeplessness."

The Culebra Cut progress report, delivered by Major David Gaillard, was upbeat about the present and realistic about the future. Workers in the Central Division already had excavated 31 million cubic yards of spoil, he said, but 54 million cubic yards remained. Another four to five years were needed to finish the job. Major Gaillard assured the committee that the main threat from landslides at the Cut had passed.[573]

The congressmen were learning what they had hoped to hear—that significant progress was continuing under a capable team. Given their admiration for Goethals and the credibility of his aides, the committee accepted the testimony with few expressions of skepticism or doubt.

When Bishop took the witness stand at 9:00 a. m. the next day, questioning turned to whether men in the trenches had witnessed any shortcomings in workmanship on locks and dams and also the status of worker complaints. As manager of grievances, Bishop sidestepped the question of workmanship and reported that the number of complaints had dropped dramatically. "There is a great deal more contentment now than there was.... Within the last six months or more, there has scarcely been a complaint."

And the YMCA clubhouses?

"They are absolutely necessary to the contentment of the force and consequently to its efficiency" Bishop asserted. "The only complaints we have is [sic] that there are not more of the clubhouses, and I think there should be more."

And what about the *Canal Record?*

Because the paper regularly published a scorecard of excavations by division, "a healthy rivalry has been aroused which has increased the efficiency of the men." As an unintended bonus, "the *Canal Record* has encouraged the growth of the Women's Club Movement which has done a great deal for the contentment of families on the Isthmus."[574]

The congenial atmosphere that enveloped the field hearing was almost entirely absent later in the year when the House Appropriations Committee ensconced itself at the Tivoli to probe the canal project's books. In all likelihood, Democratic representative John Fitzgerald of New York had made the journey primarily to confront Bishop. The Brooklyn-born attorney had, since 1905, been the leading House critic of Bishop's salary. Now Fitzgerald grilled Bishop about the costs of producing the *Canal Record*.

The editor testified that on average 12,000 copies of the paper were printed each week, with about 20 percent going to Congress and libraries nationwide. Fitzgerald cared less about circulation figures than a document showing a 50 percent increase in the production cost of the newspaper. Bishop explained that costs had indeed grown because of the paper's expanded content and his need for an assistant, two clerks, and a messenger to meet deadlines. They were required, he said, to go onto the line to compile excavation data, arrange it in tables, and prepare other detailed reports for publication. "I have to have men who are capable of going to an engineer and talking to him intelligently," Bishop argued.

"Every newspaperman must have intelligence," Fitzgerald shot back.

But Bishop quieted Fitzgerald when he revealed that the government was not paying him anything extra to edit the *Canal Record*. His salary was for handling complaints for Colonel Goethals and conducting the official duties of being commission secretary.[575]

Although the hearing record shows that Bishop maintained composure under questioning, he was surely seething beneath. Earlier in the year, Fitzgerald had inserted a provision in the 1910 Canal Budget Act that cut Bishop's $10,000 pay in half, effective July 1, 1909. After it became law, Goethals asked the comptroller of the currency for a formal opinion on the reduction. "Congress intended to limit the salary or compensation of the Secretary to $5,000," ruled Comptroller R. J. Tracewell.[576] It was a decisive stroke against Bishop. With Roosevelt now unable to directly influence the outcome of the dispute, Bishop had to slash his family's living expenses and learn to live on a budget. It would not be easy, as it turned out. His annual expenses exceeded his diminished salary by $1,000. "It is a damned outrage," Bishop complained.[577]

"Few things were more infamous than the cutting down of your salary," Roosevelt wrote Bishop a year later. "If Taft, who was then coming in as President, had fought for you in even a slight degree, I think we would have saved your salary; but by the time the [1908] election took place, he had lost all interest in the things in which I personally believe."[578]

Taft's inauguration occurred against a backdrop of dreadful Washington weather. Snow and ice had besieged the capital, forcing the swearing-in ceremonies inside the historic old Senate chamber. But the president and the president-elect dutifully made their ceremonial carriage ride from the White House to the Capitol, bundled deep under blankets, their silk top hats failing miserably against the blizzard's fury. Inside, Taft took the oath and gave his inaugural speech. He pledged to continue work on the canal and to "stand behind the men who are doing faithful, hard work to bring about the early completion of this, the greatest constructive enterprise of modern times."[579] Roosevelt listened to his rotund friend's remarks, but his restless mind no doubt leapt ahead to the moment he would flee Washington and embark on his long-planned African safari.

Not yet fifty-one, Theodore Roosevelt had a full life yet to be lived, he believed. As Taft spoke Roosevelt would have reflected on his own time in office and acknowledged that he had changed America—and the globe. During those seven and a half years, he had forged a national conservationist ethic, tamed the greed of business combinations, settled a menacing national strike, and instituted wide-ranging social reforms. Abroad, he had paraded the muscled-up navy to a cheering world, carved through the Panamanian jungle, brokered peace between Russia and Japan, and freed Cuba and the Philippines from the Spanish crown. And he had won the Nobel Peace Prize. Through it all, from the horror of the telegram announcing McKinley's sudden death to the blizzard whirling over his successor's inauguration, Roosevelt had earned universal admiration and fame. He boldly walked away from the apex of American political life to return to the arms of his large, loving family. As he would often acknowledge, he had done it all while having himself a "bully" time.

As spring approached, Roosevelt considered the array of jobs before him. He refused all but two, accepting only $25,000 from New York publisher Charles Scribner's Sons for a running narrative of his African voyage for *Scribner's Monthly* magazine and double that sum for a book contract. He also agreed to become a special contributing editor of *The Outlook,* a popular and cautiously progressive current affairs magazine, whose editor had backed him regularly during the presidency. Ahead lay "going to Africa for a good hunt" with his nineteen-year-old son, Kermit. T. R. was eager to exit public scrutiny and leave the stage to Taft. He knew himself well enough, too: If he stayed, journalists would endlessly press him for commentary on the new administration's doings, and he would undoubtedly end up second-guessing the Taft program publicly.

What lay immediately ahead, though, was more than a routine hunting trip—it was a grandiose scientific expedition organized and underwritten mostly by the Smithsonian Institution. For two and a half years, Smithsonian agents and Roosevelt had been "making plans, assembling ... naturalists, selecting camp equipment, guns and ammunition and conferring with big game hunters."[580] In all, a team of 250 guides and porters would spend $100,000 and nearly a year in Africa. T. R. supplemented the Smithsonian's $50,000 investment with $25,000 of his own, and the same amount from financier Andrew Carnegie. In 2010 , the adventure would have cost $2.4 million.

The safari launched from Mombasa in British East Africa (now Kenya), extended into the Belgian Congo (now the Democratic Republic of the Congo), and followed the Nile to Khartoum in present-day Sudan. Led by experienced guides and scientists, members of the expedition killed or trapped thousands of creatures—from insects to elephants—including 512 big-game animals. Specimens and salted skins were shipped to the Smithsonian in Washington or to the American Museum of Natural History, co-founded by "Greatheart" Roosevelt, in New York City.

In his book *African Game Trails*, Roosevelt recalled hunting a lion on the Kapiti Plains in British East Africa:

> *Right in front of me, thirty yards off, there appeared from behind the bushes, which had first screened him from my eyes, the tawny, galloping form of a big mane-less lion. Crack! The Winchester spoke; and as the soft-nosed bullet ploughed forward through his flank, the lion swerved so that I missed him with the second shot; but my third bullet went through the spine and forward into his chest. Down he came, sixty yards off, his hind quarters dragging, his head up; his ears back, his jaws open and lips drawn up in a prodigious snarl, as he endeavored to face us. His back was broken but of this, at the moment, we could not be sure, and if it had merely been grazed, he might have recovered and then, even though dying, his charge might have done mischief. So Kermit, Sir Alfred [Pease] and I fired, almost together, into his chest. His head sank, and he died.*[581]

New York's famed taxidermist Carl Akeley, who penned the introduction to *African Game Trails*, addressed why Theodore Roosevelt—pioneering conservationist—had decided to engage in a brutal adventure that brought cruelty and death to many living creatures. "Those who are unfamiliar with hunting conditions have asked if he did not slaughter many animals unnecessarily for the pleasure of it," Akeley wrote. Roosevelt "actually killed only those specimens that his scientists considered desirable for the Smithsonian or that his safari required for food. The detailed descriptions are not an indication of blood lust or joy in killing; rather they signify a keen interest in the technique of hunting." In all, T. R. bagged nine lions, eight elephants, seven hippopotamuses, and one crocodile—among dozens of other smaller creatures—during the safari.

But no matter how deep into Africa he went or how desperately Taft tried to dominate the news back home, Roosevelt did not recede from people's lips or their political consciousness. Henry Cabot Lodge attempted to gauge the ex-president's future interest in politics. Roosevelt responded steadfastly from Juja

Farm in central British East Africa: "I shall not discuss with any human being anything so absurd as the question as to whether I shall ever return to political life in any shape or form ... The chances are infinitesimal ... My destiny at present is to shoot rhino and lions and, I hope, ultimately elephants."[582]

Five months later, as Christmas Day approached, the homesick Roosevelt wrote to his daughter Ethel from Kampala in what is now Uganda: "I am enjoying it all, but I think Kermit regards me as a little soft because I am so eagerly looking forward to the end when I shall see daily pretty Mother, my own sweetheart, and the very nicest of all nice daughters—you blessed girlie."[583] It wasn't long before the Roosevelt men rendezvoused with Edith in Khartoum, from which starting point they undertook an extraordinary tour of European capitals. It was a grand tour that cemented T. R.'s international reputation as "The Most Famous Man in the World."

When Theodore and Kermit reunited with Edith and Ethel at the Khartoum rail terminal on March 14, 1910, the scene was filled with excited hugs, kisses, and not a few happy tears. Edith was delighted to find her husband in fine physical condition. T. R. could not stop chattering about his exploits. Three days later, they were off by train and steamer to Cairo, and then on to the European circuit.

Roosevelt recalled details of the European tour in a 25,000-word letter to his dear friend, British statesman and author Sir George Otto Trevelyan. Notwithstanding his wish that the letter be kept confidential until after their deaths, Bishop sought and won Trevelyan's permission to reprint the entire letter in volume two of *Theodore Roosevelt and His Time*, following T. R.'s death. Some notable excerpts:

Naples: "I was received in a way that really embarrassed me ... When I went to the opera in the evening, the performance was interrupted for ten minutes while they cheered me ... This was a foretaste of what I experienced all through Europe, except in Germany."

Rome: "The Eternal City offers the very sharpest contrasts between the extremes of radical, modern progress, social, political and religious, and the extremes of opposition to all such progress. At the time of my visit, the Vatican represented the last."

Paris: "Frenchmen, thank goodness, do understand a liking for the things in life that are most interesting and, through official deputations, accompanied me round to the three or four museums or picture galleries which I insisted on visiting."

Oslo: "In the end I too succumbed and romped with him [Prince Olaf]—as I used to romp with my own children when they were small. Outside of his father and mother, we were the only persons who had ever really played with him in a fashion which he considered adequate, and he loudly bewailed our departure."

Copenhagen: "Through some mistake our trunks did not come on the same train with us. . . . The Crown Prince wished to know whether she [Mrs. Roosevelt] would mind coming [to dinner and a reception] in our traveling clothes . . . She said 'certainly not,' and came at once and evidently never thought the matter of it."

Berlin: "The Germans did not like me and did not like my country . . . Germany has an arrogance of a very strong power. I said to the Emperor that it seemed to me that a war between England and Germany would be an unspeakable calamity. He answered eagerly that he quite agreed with me, that such a war he regarded as unthinkable."[584]

As the Roosevelts prepared to conclude their tour in England, King Edward VII suddenly died. Taft cabled Roosevelt, asking that he represent the U.S. at the funeral of the monarch, whom Roosevelt had come to know well through regular correspondence. T. R. respectfully donned mourning dress and marched solemnly in a procession through London with one of the largest gatherings of European royalty ever seen. Enormous crowds lined the streets from Buckingham Palace to Westminster to behold what few, if any, realized was the end of the monarchal era.

As the steamer approached New York harbor in June 1910, a vast naval parade of watercraft, noisy artillery salutes, and thousands of well-wishers at the dock greeted the Roosevelts. "A truly royal welcome," Bishop wrote later. "Nothing approaching it had ever been given a private citizen coming back to his native land after a brief absence abroad." Bishop regretted that he could not be dockside to welcome home his friend, but he planned to sail from Cristóbal two days later to that same harbor on his six-week annual summer leave.

Those who heard or read Roosevelt's remarks upon arrival may have suspected a foretelling message between the lines. "I am ready and eager to do my part, so far as I am able," he said, "in helping solve problems which must be solved if we of this, the greatest democratic Republic upon which the sun has ever shone, are to see its destinies rise to the high level of our hopes and its opportunities."[585] Some observers wondered why President Taft had not come to greet his predecessor on that joyous spring day.

The Roosevelts eagerly made their way to Sagamore Hill and plunged into a succession of reunion dinners with their closest friends. How fascinating it must have been to sip consommé as Roosevelt spun tales of slaying game on the African grasslands and reveling in dazzling splendor with the crowned heads of Europe. Henry Cabot Lodge joined Nicholas and Alice Longworth at the Roosevelts' table on June 18. Bishop and Gifford Pinchot came three days later, and Bishop returned with Harriet again on the 23rd.

Pinchot's presence had great political significance. Taft had fired the top Forest Service conservationist for claiming that Taft's interior secretary was in league with big timber interests. "I cannot believe it," Roosevelt had written from the hunt when he learned the news. "It makes me very uneasy."[586] The Pinchot dismissal and its implications for an activist federal conservation policy formed the first grave fissure between Roosevelt and Taft. It would not be the last.

Between the Roosevelts' return and the looming midterm elections, a curious exchange took place between the old friends. T. R. asked Bishop to address him as "colonel," a carryover from Rough Rider days. (In that era a president did not retain his political form of address after leaving office.)

"Dear T. R.," Bishop's reply began. "I am thus addressing you because I do not consider the title of Colonel as at-all adequate, and I am shy about a more familiar form."[587]

"Surely one of my closest friends can address me in the same way that all my old friends that are really close to me do now," Roosevelt replied.[588]

Whether by that Roosevelt intimated that he would allow himself to be called "Theodore" was not clear. In time, Bishop relented and addressed his friend, "Dear Colonel."

The 1910 midterm elections spelled disaster for Republicans. Pro-Taft conservatives and Roosevelt-leaning progressives were sharply divided over conservationism. Also in the mix were tariff and trade policy, antitrust actions, and public review of judicial decisions. Taft failed to bridge his party's internal differences, and the Democrats swept to power in the House. Savvy Washington observers noted that in New Jersey, Woodrow Wilson, a Democrat and former president of Princeton University, took the governor's mansion on a platform stressing independence from machine politics.

Joseph Bucklin Bishop treasured this signed picture from his friend Theodore Roosevelt. *Anita and Miriam Bishop collection*

On *The Outlook* letterhead, dated November 21, 1910, Roosevelt dictated one of the most revealing letters of the many hundreds he had sent to Bishop over the fifteen years they had known each other. For the first time ever in their correspondence, T. R. addressed him as "Dear Joe." Whether the letter itself was a legacy statement or a wide-open expression of his state of mind, T. R. afforded Bishop a rare look inside the turmoil he was experiencing.

I told the exact truth as I saw it. I praised Taft for every action of his as to which I could conscientiously praise him. Where I could not praise him or disapprove of what he had done, I kept silent. I was opposed by the lunatic insurgents of all grades, receiving very lukewarm support I am sorry to say from such men . . . who were not contented with anything short of denunciation of Taft, and who have no conception of the difference in difficulty in tearing down and building up. On the other hand, the reactionaries, the representatives of the special interests and all those whom they control, literally went insane in their opposition.

Ironically Republican losses in New York had given him mild comfort:

[I]t prevents my having to face the very unpleasant task of deciding whether or not to accept the nomination in 1912 . . . Of course, the decision seems easy enough, on the one hand, to the well-meaning conservative person who regards Taft as a satisfactory President, and does not understand that any man sees to object to him, and who feels that any reluctance to urge his renomination by me must be due to personal ambition on my part. On the other hand, the decision seems perfectly easy to the progressives who hate Taft so bitterly that they firmly believe every honest man must share their convictions, and only that an unworthy fear on my part, or a still more unworthy desire to truckle to ultra-conservatism, prevents my coming out openly against Taft.

Roosevelt seemed to be trying to talk himself out of the inevitable:

As things are now, I feel convinced that it will not become my duty to accept. They have no business to expect me to take command of ship simply because the ship is sinking. Were I nominated under present conditions, it would mean that I should be broken down by a burden for which I was not, in any way, responsible . . . As I feel now, I would refuse the nomination if it were offered me.[39]

Roosevelt added the last sentence by hand to the rest of the typed letter. Was his turmoil driven by frustration over recent losses or genuine indecision? Whichever the case, the letter drew no immediate response from Bishop, who was dealing with his own troubles far away in Panama, for once out of touch with the shifting political winds back home.

Thirty

A Stance at Armageddon

Isolated in Panama, Bishop stood on the margins of the approaching 1912 presidential campaign, cheering for Roosevelt from a distance. Not once in the many letters that he exchanged with T. R. between 1909 and 1912 did Bishop retreat from absolute loyalty. A less steadfast man might have. Taft had been a close acquaintance, an ally, even a confidant at times during his tenure as secretary of war. Now president, he was in charge of the canal. But for Bishop there was never a doubt as to where his allegiance lay. Nevertheless, he was no fool, and he made sure to support Roosevelt's impending candidacy and disparage Taft only confidentially in handwritten letters never typed or seen by others.

During that period, Roosevelt and Bishop's correspondence often drifted from the political and grew increasingly personal or, as they phrased it at the time, intimate. Harriet Bishop, always welcomed warmly at Roosevelt's dinner table, whether at the White House or Sagamore Hill, had succeeded in charming the old lion in ways perhaps that Bishop himself, the unwavering old Yankee, could not. "Indeed, Mrs. Bishop is a trump if ever there was one," Roosevelt wrote, "and she has no stauncher admirer than I am."[590] Bishop hardly ever wrote of his wife's role in his life, but he acknowledged then to Roosevelt, "Mrs. Bishop is proud and happy that you should remember her so kindly. Between ourselves, she is an uncommon, fine woman, and it affords me no end of joy that you have perceived it."[591]

She wasn't the only wife the two men discussed, though. At the height of Roosevelt's vacillation about the 1912 race, Bishop indulged in a bit of gossip about Nellie Taft's alleged pastimes. The wife of a Washington official had told him that "Mrs. Taft had bridge parties in the White House at which the stakes insisted upon by her were so high that it was ruin for all visitors who played. Mrs. T's invitations for bridge caused a positive panic, since no one was willing to take the risk of winning from the President's wife. Can this be true?" Bishop

George W. Goethals leads President Taft on an inspection of the Panama Canal in 1910.

Library of Congress Prints and Photographs Division

wondered. "Can it be possible that any wife of a President would permit gambling in the White House? I refuse to believe it."

Another time, Bishop had a good chuckle with Roosevelt at Taft's expense. He quoted a missive to Colonel Goethals, delivered by a new American minister to Panama. "I, William Howard Taft, wish to go to the Isthmus this year because the canal is my present enterprise. Twenty-five years from now, history will record that the building of the canal was the great work of my administration, and I want to keep in close touch with it."

"It is to laugh!" exclaimed Bishop to Roosevelt. "We had a notion here that one T. R. had made the canal possible . . . It is so characteristic."[592]

But as the canal secretary approached his fourth year of duty in the tropics, homesickness crept into his letters. He expressed a longing for the northern spring and thanked Roosevelt for "feeling for us in our deprivation. . . . We are all very well but somewhat worn with the heat which has been quite unusual for several weeks."[593]

By July 1911, the completion of the canal was predicted for 1914, and Bishop was making future plans. "I have accepted an offer from Scribner's to write several articles for publication next year," he wrote to T. R. They would be "advance chapters of my book on the canal which they are to publish later."[594]

As the summer wore on, and in recognition of their increasing familiarity, Roosevelt further let down his guard in a note to Bishop. "Please go back to the days before the war and call me Theodore hereafter!"[595] Apparently, T. R. felt that even "colonel" was too straitlaced a form of address for his friend to use.

Roosevelt and Bishop—aside from their chatty exchanges—also engaged in an important correspondence that today sheds light on the former president's thinking about whether to take on Taft and reclaim the White House. In mid-summer 1910, ahead of the fall midterm elections, Roosevelt had embarked on a taxing three-week tour of sixteen western states for *The Outlook*. "The western tour was one long ovation," historian James Chace observed. "He spoke in town squares and at picnics, in ballparks and at statehouses."[596] At one stop, on August 31 in Osawatomie, Kansas, Roosevelt presented his audience with distinctly radical ideas for a Republican of the time. His call for a "new nationalism" for America defined much of what would become his 1912 campaign platform. But as he challenged the crowds with far-reaching ideas, he was alienating the conservative wing of the party.

"Labor is the superior of capital," Roosevelt bellowed to a rapt audience of 30,000 gathered to memorialize the abolitionist John Brown, adding that it "deserves the higher consideration." He argued for the right of workers to organize, the eight-hour workday and workmen's compensation law. Taking added aim at big business, Roosevelt emphasized his support for a graduated income tax, paid mostly by the wealthy; regulation of child labor; direct primary elections; and, of course, for bold conservationism. On the plains of the Midwest in the searing summer heat, he was carving his new niche on the political spectrum, leaning to the liberal left and creating a deep philosophical chasm among traditional Republicans.

Writing less than a month later, after he had read newspaper reports of the speech, Bishop sensed that Roosevelt had signaled his decision to run. "You have never been called upon or have undertaken a more useful and necessary task for your country than you are engaged in now," Bishop told him. "That you will carry it to success I have not a shadow of doubt. . . . The aroused conscience of a great nation is a force that nothing can resist."[597]

By January 1911, T. R.'s frustration with the Taft administration was palpable. "I really do not trust myself to put on paper—even to you—some of the things I so deeply feel about your treatment and about certain acts of the administration," he wrote to Bishop.[598]

In October, Taft brought an antitrust suit against U.S. Steel without giving T. R. the courtesy of advance notice. During his presidency, the great trust-buster had approved U.S. Steel's controversial purchase of the Tennessee Coal and Iron Company. Taft's suit alleged that the decision gave the green light to monopoly and clearly condemned Roosevelt's earlier approval. The former president struck back in the pages of *The Outlook*, defending his action and arguing in favor of a regulatory strategy by the federal government, rather than legal challenges, to confront unfair business practices.

After reading *The Outlook* piece, Bishop congratulated T. R. on a "thorough-going Roosevelt document" and observed, "Of course, it cuts you loose irrefutably from the Taft Administration—but you have been getting away steadily for a year or more. . . . Taft is doomed and must take himself out of the way."[599]

As 1911 came to an uncertain close, Roosevelt settled on a strategy.

As for the nomination, I should regard it from my personal standpoint no little short of calamity. I not merely do not want it, but if I honorably can, I desire to avoid it. On the other hand, I certainly will not put myself in a position which would make it necessary for me to shirk a plain duty if it came unmistakably as a plain duty . . . At any rate, as far as I am concerned, my anxieties are in this order: first, not to be nominated if it can honorably be avoided; and second, if nominated, to have it made perfectly clear that it is in response to a genuine popular demand and because the public wishes me to serve them for their purpose, and not to gratify any ambition of mine.[600]

Two weeks later, Roosevelt vented to Bishop about the man he had anointed to succeed him. "Taft is utterly hopeless. I think he would be beaten if nominated, but in any event it would be a misfortune to have him in the presidential chair for another term, for he has shown himself to be an entirely unfit President, and he merely discredits the Republican Party . . . I want to see the presidency handled along the lines that the job of digging the Panama Canal has been handled."[601]

Roosevelt's decision to run finally gelled on February 10, 1912, when seven Republican governors wrote to convey their encouragement and endorsement. Buoyed by their promises of assistance, he traveled to Ohio—Taft country—to address the state's constitutional convention. There he repeated much of his extraordinary Osawatomie message. Then, he went further out on the radical limb, urging the recall of judicial decisions in instances when the people thought they were wrong. "Our aim," he asserted, "must be the moralization of the individual, of the government, of the people as a whole." As James Chace put it, "T. R.'s proposal reflected his view that a comprehensive program of reform could not be passed unless the nation's courts were first curbed."[602]

Influential Republicans swelled with outrage at the thought of citizens second-guessing court rulings; many in the rank and file believed that Roosevelt was advocating the popular recall of routine judicial rulings, a situation that could, they thought, produce chaos. For Elihu Root and Henry Cabot Lodge, the recall proposal was the deal-breaker. They sided with Taft. In fact, Roosevelt intended that judicial recall should be used only in cases of constitutional rulings, but his words were vague, and it was too late to take them back.

Heading home through Cleveland, an energized Roosevelt told a reporter while waiting at the rail station, "My hat is in the ring. The fight is on, and I am stripped to the buff."[603]

On the isthmus, in the torrid heat and perpetual downpours, work persisted on dams and locks and in the massive mountain gash at Culebra. Major David Gaillard had taken charge of the Cut—the most demanding phase of the entire project—and he responded with Goethals-like determination. Each day, under his gaze, up to 6,000 laborers dug and drilled into the forbidding rock, planted dynamite, and blasted massive chunks of earth skyward like rockets. As many as 160 trains a day hauled away tons of debris along the tracks of the Panama Railroad. At Gatun, on the Atlantic side, the main dam that would birth a giant lake and irrigate the future necklace of canal locks was materializing under the fulsome oversight of its engineers. Smaller dams were taking shape, too—to the south of the Cut at Miraflores and at Pedro Miguel.

To Goethals, mastermind and chief engineer, it was both a mundane and thrilling undertaking. Bishop quoted him as saying that the task "was not at all big but only a mass of irritating details . . . grinding out the details from day to day, enabling the big thing to take final shape."[604] But, Farnham Bishop wrote in his chapters of a reverential biography of Goethals after Joseph's death, the chief "knew that he was changing the whole map of the world; a change that promised to be far more permanent and profound than any brought about by a mere conqueror."[605]

By 1911, when the Senate Interstate Commerce Committee came to Ancon to hold its oversight hearing, the severest critics of the project fell silent.

Colonel George Goetnals poses with other members of the Isthmian Canal Commission at Culebra, Panama, August 25, 1910. Joseph Bucklin is second from left.

Anita and Miriam Bishop collection

To visiting dignitaries, the achievements spoke for themselves and were corroborated back home in the filings of on-site journalists. Bishop continued to assert—this time in testimony before Senator Moses Clapp of Minnesota and his panel—that his *Canal Record* also had a "very salutatory effect in stopping miscellaneous and malicious information about the work." Its weekly circulation had crested at more than 14,000, he reported. When asked by another senator whether the paper should discontinue once the canal was finished, Bishop responded emphatically "Yes, sir!"[606] Bishop knew he would leave Panama upon the canal's completion, and he did not see any need for the publication to continue without him. In fact, the *Canal Record* persisted long after the canal opened to ship traffic in 1914, and for more than 10 years after Bishop's death. However, it gradually devolved into a boilerplate digest of dreary statistical transits and cargo loadings, finally ceasing publication on the eve of World War II.

"It was a fight that had to be made," Roosevelt admitted to Bishop in mid-March 1912. "There was no alternative to my having to make it." But Roosevelt was not sure that he could beat Taft for the nomination and overcome the power of the party bosses and the money they controlled. "Do not get the idea into your head that I am going to win in this fight," he warned.[607]

Taft stood by the status quo and rejected Roosevelt's New Nationalism, as first expressed in Osawatomie as "some new principle, not definitely formulated." Speaking to the New York Republican Club, he labeled Roosevelt and his followers "extremists" and "political emotionalists or neurotics."

"This was nothing less than a direct assault upon Roosevelt," Bishop observed. "It removed from his mind the last lingering doubt as to the irreconcilable difference on matters of principle which existed between himself and Mr. Taft."[608]

T. R. had decided to skirt the party machinery and appeal directly to voters in the thirteen states that had direct primaries. If he succeeded, he could claim the mantle of popular support for his candidacy. In contrast, Taft's approach to securing the nomination depended on machinations in smoke-filled rooms where elected leaders, patronage chiefs, and other party rulers made private deals and handpicked loyal delegates.

Roosevelt raised campaign funds through a few friendly Republican "angels" and put together an organization determined to get him onto the ballots in the primary states. That strategy demanded, however, that he take his message over the heads of local politicians and campaign vigorously in those states. So, in the spring of 1912, Roosevelt embarked on a grueling campaign swing. From state to state, Roosevelt's appeal was predictably bold and stirring. Speaking at Carnegie Hall in March, he said, "We need leaders of inspired idealism, leaders to whom are granted great visions, who dream greatly and strive to make their dreams come true; who can kindle the people from the fire of their own burning souls."[609] Taft—relying on party organizers to deliver votes in the primaries—spoke dryly as usual, seemingly out of duty rather than passion.

As the weather warmed, farmers planted, and players trained for the coming baseball season, Roosevelt swept to victory in the Pennsylvania primary and then won the popular vote in the key states of California, Illinois, and Maryland. He even overturned Taft in Ohio. To his credit, Taft showed strength in delegate-rich New York—including 70 percent of the vote in New York City—and in Michigan and Massachusetts. In the Bay State, Lodge organized what proved to be a narrow defeat of Roosevelt.

At the end of the direct primary season, Roosevelt claimed a huge popular-vote margin over Taft, as well as "Fighting Bob" La Follette, a radically progressive senator from Wisconsin, also in the race. But in states with party conventions, Taft had the lead heading into the national convention.

It was hot and humid in Chicago when Roosevelt's steam train pulled into the LaSalle Street Station for the national convention. "The sight of Theodore Roosevelt waving his romantic soldier's hat drove the crowd into a frenzy," Chace wrote. "They followed him down the street, three brass bands playing, shouted at him from office windows, stood on windowsills and the tops of automobiles, and ran beside his car until he reached the Congress Hotel."[610]

On Roosevelt's train, everyone worried that Taft forces in control of the Republican National Committee had already awarded a disproportionate number of contested delegate seats to the president—whether he deserved them or not. Their goal, of course, was to ensure that when the roll of states was called, Taft would be the nominee. With Elihu Root planted in the convention chair, the results were predictable. As voting progressed, chants of "Steamroller!" arose, mingling with cigar smoke among the rafters. In the end, with 344 Roosevelt delegates sitting on their hands in protest, Taft secured an ill-won nomination, with 561 delegates to just 107 for Roosevelt, and a handful for La Follette. To Bishop, Republican leaders "had deliberately chosen defeat for their party."[611]

Assembling his disgruntled followers in the nearby Auditorium Theater soon afterward, Roosevelt declared that he would undertake a third-party run under a progressive banner—what became known as the Bull Moose Party. The name was coined after the time T. R. had declared to an inquiring reporter, "I'm as fit as a bull moose."

> To-night we come together to protest against a crime which strikes straight at the heart of every principle of political decency and honesty, a crime which represents treason to the people, and the usurpation of the sovereignty of the people by irresponsible political bosses, inspired by the sinister influences of moneyed privilege . . . We stand at Armageddon, and we battle for the Lord.[612]

Roosevelt's speech drew riotous applause and cheers.

A few weeks later at a hurriedly organized convention at the same Chicago venue where Taft had been nominated, Roosevelt unanimously received the

Progressive Party nomination. His charge was to take on Taft and the recent Democratic nominee, New Jersey Governor Woodrow Wilson. The Progressive Party platform echoed much of what Roosevelt had espoused in the primary run: pro-labor reform, women's suffrage, and national conservation. Though it was a spirited general election campaign, Bishop later observed that the result "was virtually certain from the outset, for with two Republican candidates in the field, the success of the Democratic candidate was reasonably well-assured."[613]

In Bishop's mind, even though Wilson was "flabby, mentally and morally,"[614] he had nonetheless legitimately secured his party's nomination after forty-six contentious ballots and the decisive intervention of William Jennings Bryan. In Wilson's short time in Trenton, he had compiled an impressive record of progressive success on state issues. He only had to take an equally forward-looking approach to a national audience and make the case to voters that, unlike Roosevelt, he could win.

Although Roosevelt and his running mate, Governor Hiram Johnson of California, whistle-stopped fervently through more than thirty states, Bishop believed that his old friend had little hope of winning. "He was not making the fight for personal success, but in the defense of the principles for which he stood."[615] Taft's campaign activity, by contrast, consisted of a handful of important speeches but no national tour.

"Lynch him! Lynch him!" cried the frenzied crowd outside of the Pfister Hotel in Milwaukee on October 14, 1912. Someone had shot Theodore Roosevelt.

"Don't hurt him! Bring him here. I want to look at him," ordered the wounded candidate as he stood in his open-air touring car. The assailant was John Flammang Schrank, a half-crazed, Bavarian-born saloonkeeper who had been stalking Roosevelt for weeks. Investigators later learned that Schrank thought he had been "advised" by the ghost of William McKinley to avenge his death by slaying his successor—someone who dared run for a third term.

The bullet, fired from just a few feet away, punctured Roosevelt in the right side of the chest, but, in his suit pocket, his steel spectacle case and the thick manuscript of the speech he was about to give deflected the bullet from piercing any major organs. Despite pleas from authorities, T. R. refused immediate medical treatment, insisting instead that he be driven to the site of the scheduled speech. "It may be the last I shall deliver," he asserted, "but I am going to deliver this one."[616] Roosevelt knew that he had been hit, but he believed the wound was nothing serious because, he explained, he had not spit up any blood.

Arriving at his venue Roosevelt told the audience, "I don't know whether you fully understand but I have just been shot; but it takes more than that to kill a bull moose."[617] For ninety incredible minutes thereafter he read from the pages of his lifesaving speech, his voice often a hoarse whisper as blood soaked his shirt. In his later biography of Roosevelt, Bishop quoted a doctor who examined Roosevelt: "He is one of the most powerful men I have ever seen laid out on an operating table. The bullet lodged in the massive muscle of the chest instead of penetrating the lung."[618]

Of the attempt on his life, Roosevelt later philosophized, "It is a trade risk which every prominent man ought to accept as a matter of course."[619] He survived the shooting well enough to resume campaigning before Election Day, still carrying the bullet inside of him because, doctors said, it was safer to leave it where it was than risk removing it. Roosevelt took the bullet with him to his grave.

John Schrank was confined to a state mental institution, where he died of natural causes thirty-one years later.

When the votes were tallied in November, Wilson swept to an easy 42 percent popular-vote victory, winning forty states and becoming the only Democrat in the White House between Grover Cleveland and Franklin Roosevelt. The physically indestructible Bull Moose won a string of northern-tier states and California, collecting a respectable 27 percent of the vote, while the incumbent president earned just 23 percent, topping out only in Vermont and Utah. The Electoral College tally was a blowout for Wilson, 435 to Roosevelt's 88 and Taft's 8. Taft remains the only incumbent president ever to come in third in a general election.

But for Taft, the loss surpassed the presidency. His long friendship with Roosevelt had come to a sad, bitter end, he felt. Henry Pringle, Taft's biographer, recounted a telling moment in Boston during the heated primary campaign. Taft had retired to his private railroad car when a reporter from the *New York World* approached. Louis Siebold remembered the president seated with his head buried in his hands, murmuring, "Roosevelt was my closest friend." Taft wept.[620]

Without its founder, the Progressive Party could not sustain itself, and gradually faded away. But its nominee had made history with the most successful third-party presidential run ever.

Thirty-One

Beginnings and Endings

W<small>OODROW</small> W<small>ILSON</small> <small>STRODE BRISKLY AND WITH SELF-ASSURANCE THE FEW</small> steps from the White House to the Old Executive Office Building next door. It was the beginning of the best publicity stunt of the decade. Exquisitely turned out and decidedly professorial, the new president was symbolically opening the Panama Canal. On October 10, 1913, a continent away, Colonel Goethals, his engineers, and thousands of spectators were waiting impatiently on a bluff over-looking the Culebra Cut.

At 2:01 p.m., Wilson pushed the button that relayed an electrical pulse by telegraph, overland and underwater, from cable station to cable station, until it reached its target in Panama and exploded forty tons of dynamite. The Gamboa Dike erupted, admitting the waters of Gatun Lake into the Culebra Cut. Months earlier, another section of the Cut had been blocked by a landslide known as the Cucaracha Slide. It took months to clear away the fallen earth and rock. Nonetheless, everyone on the bluff that memorable October day applauded with enthusiasm as the earth settled and the Cut rapidly filled with onrushing water.

In fact, the canal opened in sections. Dry excavation elsewhere had been completed a month earlier, and water first flowed into the Gatun Locks at about the same time. Joseph Bucklin Bishop remembered that scene:

> *Special trains were run, and the canal men and their families turned out by the thousands to line the lock walls and watch the muddy fountains spurt up out of the round openings in the dusty floors of the lock chamber. With the water came hundreds of big bullfrogs, washed down through the sluices from the lake above. [They] swam round and round in comic bewilderment as the water line rose higher and higher. When the water in the lowest lock was even with the surface of the sea-level canal outside, the mighty guard gates and sea gates split apart and wheeled slowly back through the swirling waters into their niches in the walls.*[621]

High above, Colonel Goethals strode back and forth on the lock wall as the tug *Gatun* inched its way from the lake into the lock. Its passage was effortless.

With most of its work now finished, the Isthmian Canal Commission embarked on a concluding task: the organized dismissal of the workforce. At its peak, it had exceeded 55,000 workers. Now, Goethals believed that only 5,000 would be needed to operate the canal. The discharged laborers, engineers, and their families crowded onto vessels bound for the West Indies, America, and Europe—some gleefully, others reluctantly. Across the isthmus, old work buildings and dormitories fell under the crush of bulldozers, and people fled some of the former camp towns as flood waters approached.

Early in 1914, about the time Goethals accepted Wilson's appointment as the first governor of the Panama Canal Zone—at a one-third salary cut—an old crane boat made an exploratory crossing of the canal. The honor fell, appropriately, to a relic of the French era, the *Alexandre La Valley*. But it wasn't until August of that year that the first oceangoing vessel, the *Cristóbal*, negotiated the remnants of the Cucaracha Slide and passed from ocean to ocean. "For years, this voyage had been looked forward-to as a great event in the history of the world," Bishop wrote. "But when it came to pass, it received scant notice."[622] The world's eyes had turned away from the isthmus toward Europe, where the gales of a world war had begun to gust.

Before hostilities erupted, however, the nations of the world laid extensive plans to commemorate the waterway's opening on New Year's Day, 1915, with the passage of an armada of ships through the canal. The fleet was to launch at Hampton Roads, Virginia, traverse the isthmus, and dock at San Francisco to inaugurate the Panama-Pacific International Exhibition, a world's fair organized to mark the completion of the canal. When plans were scrubbed because of the war, officials made do with an anticlimactic, ceremonial sail of the steamship *Ancon* on August 15, 1914. With war news on the front pages and everyone's lips, few paid attention.

Even fewer realized that the canal was opening to commerce six months ahead of schedule. Officially the U.S. spent $352 million on the canal—below final estimates. Astonishingly, one of the greatest excavation and construction projects of modern history finished early, under budget, and absent major scandal. More than 5,000 people had lost their lives to accident and disease since the U.S. took charge, but most observers rightly saw it as a matchless achievement, a singular moment in world history. To some, the accomplishment remains unmatched even now.

T. R. observed, perhaps with hyperbole: "There is not an action of the American government, in connection with foreign affairs, from the day when the Constitution was adopted down to the present time, so important as the action taken by this government in connection with the acquisition and building of the Panama Canal."[623]

Bishop did not attend the concluding events in Panama. He did not witness the fruition of his work. With the abolition of the commission in January and a nudge out the door from the Wilson administration, he had sailed from the isthmus for the last time in July. His departure, not unlike his arrival, was turbulent.

The commission's employment contracts were terminated as of March 31, 1914, but Bishop, at Goethals's direction, stayed on as a "special secretary" in the Executive Office of the Panama Canal at his same $5,000 annual salary, beginning April 1. He had hoped to serve on a task force planning the grand international sail-through. In May, Major Frank Boggs, the Army Corps's Washington chief, arrived on the isthmus with word that Secretary of War Lindley Garrison, a friend of President Wilson, "didn't think Bishop should be considered" for the planning commission. Bishop was, after all, a man of another time, another party, and another president.

To recompense Bishop for his dedication, Goethals instituted a last rescue plan. On July 2, he signed papers directing Bishop to sail for New York and then to Washington, D.C., "to confer with Major Boggs on the Panama-Pacific exhibition." Bishop's tenure would conclude after he had submitted a report on this vague assignment. Goethals saw to it that Major Boggs covered his faithful aide's salary and expenses and that his travel was "official and necessary to the public service."[624]

Bishop's final task was less about his stated mission than about ensuring a dignified exit for the commission's indispensable "press agent." Goethals recognized that Bishop, a skilled molder of positive news coverage and a midwife of productivity and morale, had a transforming influence on political and public opinion affecting the canal. Montana representative Frank Mondell, at congressional hearings in Culebra in 1913, agreed, and saluted Bishop from the dais: "You have conducted your work with wonderful personal modesty, with remarkable thoroughness and with a view to giving the world the information they asked for, without any effort in any way to puff up the organization."[625]

As the SS *Alliança* steamed out of Cristóbal for New York on July 3, Bishop looked back over Limón Bay at the receding isthmus. Now sixty-seven, he was planning the last act of his eventful life—as an author in New York City. His friendship with Roosevelt remained as strong as ever. It would, in fact, intensify over the next few years and rise to the pinnacle of its significance. But now, as he retreated to his cabin ahead of six hot and tedious days at sea, ever the stern and steadfast Yankee, he refused to dwell sentimentally on his years in Panama. War in Europe was brewing, and as always, he had his mind on national politics, the start of the 1916 presidential campaign, and Roosevelt's unspecified intentions.

Bishop also pondered the recent loss of his elder son, Hartwell, who had died suddenly on June 4, 1913, a few weeks short of his thirty-third birthday. A Harvard alumnus and a civil engineer with United Railways Company, Hartwell had traveled to Boston from his home in San Francisco with his wife, Catherine Weiner, whom he had wed just seventeen months earlier. He suffered an abscess of the brain and had contracted fatal meningitis.

In 1913, Joseph, Harriet, and Alice had sailed from the isthmus for New York the day before Hartwell died. Bishop's official travel record documented the trip as "annual leave," but the family no doubt had heard of Hartwell's illness and was trying to rush to his bedside. Not once in the hundreds of Bishop's surviving letters in the Library of Congress—to Roosevelt and others—did he mention Hartwell. Farnham, his younger son, a writer, sometime playwright, and lecturer, made frequent appearances in letters, but was usually nameless, mentioned only as "my son." It is as if Hartwell, by his absence from the letters, had never existed.

Farnham was clearly his favorite, and the young man emulated his father in return. Also a Harvard alum, Farnham flunked out of Harvard Law School but earned a master's degree in 1910. His dissertation, *Our Socialist State in Panama*, delivered at commencement, benefited of course from the summers he had spent with his parents there. Roosevelt, who was in the audience "listened attentively, and warmly shook Bishop's hand as [he] came down from the platform of Sanders Theater."[26] By the time Bishop was sailing home for the last time, in 1914, Farnham had written an all-inclusive book, *Panama: Past, Present, and Future*, and a handful of in-depth magazine pieces on the canal. He was becoming, to his father's delight, an authoritative voice on the subject.

As Joseph steamed toward New York on the *Allianca*, he took satisfaction in knowing that his own book, *The Panama Gateway*, a comprehensive history of the canal, was winning favorable reviews. At 421 pages, with dramatic photos and detailed appendices, it instantly became the definitive work on the subject. The *New York Herald* thought it had "unusual value" and that it "may well be remembered because of the accurate information it conveys." The *New York Times* agreed, recommending it as a "valuable chronicle" and a "permanent and absolutely reliable record" of the canal's construction.[627] Roosevelt wrote to the author after reading it: "I wish to congratulate you with all my heart. I am genuinely impressed by it."[628]

Following his 1912 election loss, Roosevelt, too, sought refuge in the written word. *The Outlook* editor Lawrence Abbott wanted to serialize T. R.'s life story in the magazine. But Roosevelt cared less about boosting *The Outlook*'s circulation than about chronicling a life committed to public policy reform and connecting with voters. Historian Kathleen Dalton also points out that "[b]y describing the slow but sincere development of his progressive views, he hoped to prove to his public that he was not a power-hungry fake."[629]

When Scribner's published Roosevelt's *An Autobiography* in 1913, Bishop told his old friend that he was "charmed" after reading the first installment. "It is in perfect form, tone and taste."[630] Roosevelt pronounced himself "greatly pleased" with Bishop's assessment, adding, "I especially value it because I have absolute confidence in your taste."[631]

A few months before the publication of *An Autobiography,* Roosevelt had returned to New York from a harrowing expedition in the Brazilian wilderness. He had lost fifty pounds and nearly died from malaria, fever, and infection. He had been planning the journey for years, as far back as the White House days. It was, he said, his last chance to be a boy. He mapped out a speaking tour through South America, supplemented by a jungle expedition to collect bird and animal specimens for the American Museum of Natural History. Kermit grudgingly agreed to accompany his father at the quiet insistence of Edith, who was concerned with the strain it would place on her husband's health.

The crowds were large and adoring during the fall of 1913 as Roosevelt expounded on his progressive views during six weeks of speaking in Brazil, Argentina, Uruguay, and Chile. At first, though, he was unsure of the trip's value, telling his friend, British MP Arthur Lee, "As I speak in English, and nobody will understand it, the trip seems really pointless."[632] But he warmed to the idea when Edith decided to go along for part of it.

Once he had fulfilled his speech-making obligations and Edith had departed for New York, Roosevelt and his party at last turned their attention to the quest for natural specimens. They roamed the center of South America on land and water. Of the journey up the Paraguay River in Brazil Roosevelt remembered, "The river was like glass. In the white moonlight, the palms on the edge of the bank stood mirrored in the still water. We sat forward and as we rounded the curve the long silver reaches of the great stream stretched ahead of us, and the ghostly outlines of hills rose in the distance. Here and there prairie fires burned, and the red glow warred with the moon's brilliance."[63]

In Rio de Janeiro, Lauro Müller, the Brazilian foreign minister, buttonholed Roosevelt with the proposal of a daring addition to the expedition. By following the planned land route deep into the country's interior, Müller said, the party would encounter the Rio da Dúvido—the River of Doubt, an uncharted watercourse in need of official exploration by a courageous team. Ever the adventurer, T. R. welcomed the challenge. He also understood that the journey would add immeasurable interest to the chronicle he had agreed to write for *The Outlook* and for his planned book, *Through the Brazilian Wilderness*.

The uncertain journey down the River of Doubt began in late February 1914, the height of the rainy season. There were about twenty in Roosevelt's party, including native porters and rowers. They had supplied themselves with canoes and dugouts, arms, medical supplies, and enough food for forty days. Roosevelt had welcomed the challenge, but he had given inadequate forethought to its inherent risks and dangers. William Roscoe Thayer related the story:

> *With high hopes they put their craft into the water and moved downstream. But on the fourth day they found rapids ahead, and from that time on they were constantly obliged to land and carry their dugouts and stores round a cataract. The peril of being swept over the falls was always imminent, and as the trail which constituted their portages had to be cut through the matted forest, their labors were increased . . . Some of their canoes were smashed on the rocks; two of the natives were drowned. They watched their provisions shrink . . . Tropical insects bit them day and night and caused inflammation and even infection. Man-eating fish lived in the river, making it dangerous for the men when they tried to cool their inflamed bodies by a swim. Most of the party had malaria, and could be kept going only by large doses of quinine.*[634]

At one point, as he worked in the water to free jumbled canoes, Roosevelt accidentally cut his leg at the spot where he had injured it years before in the Massachusetts carriage accident. The wound abscessed and spawned a dangerously high fever. When he began to ramble deliriously and proved unable to walk with the rest of the expedition, they laid him in a dugout and the *camaradas* hauled him along. Kermit worried that his father would not survive; another party member, Smithsonian naturalist George Cherrie, feared, "He can't possibly live until morning." Roosevelt pleaded to be left behind, afraid of endangering the lives of his comrades. Kermit, Cherrie, and others kept watch over him to ensure that he did not intentionally overdose himself to save the others.

Just as the expedition ran out of food and was losing hope for survival, it came upon the only human being they had seen in weeks, an old man harvesting rubber. He gave them food and directed them to the Madeira River, where in late April they boarded a steamer to the Amazon River and charted a course home.

"Edith's insistence on sending Kermit to protect T. R. saved his life," concluded Kathleen Dalton. "Kermit stayed up with his father and made sure the morphine was out of reach . . . No one rose to the test with more foresight and concern for others."[635] Roosevelt's sister Corinne Robinson later observed, "Such perseverance, such persistence are really superhuman; but perhaps it is also true that the human being must eventually pay the price of what the superman achieves."[636] Indeed, Roosevelt gradually regained his health, but in Thayer's view, "he had never again the iron physique with which he had embarked the year before."[637]

In typical fashion, Roosevelt minimized the horrors of the venture and his frightful condition on emerging from the jungle. In a formal thank-you letter to the Brazilian foreign minister, he said only, "We have had a hard and somewhat dangerous but very successful trip."[638] The party charted more than 900 miles of the River of Doubt. In recognition of the expedition's achievement and in tribute to the former president, the Brazilian government later renamed the waterway Rio Teodoro.

A few weeks after Roosevelt had returned to Sagamore Hill and Bishop had taken up temporary quarters at the Hotel Wellington in New York City, Gavrilo Princip raised his revolver in Sarajevo and took deadly aim at the heir to the throne of Austria-Hungry. The deaths of Archduke Franz Ferdinand and Archduchess Sophie ignited public outrage and martial passions that had been simmering for decades. Ultimately, the assasinations triggered the "War to End all Wars" that left 15 million people dead.

Pervasive imperialism, the buildup of arms, and entwined alliances among European nations and their overseas possessions found expression in attack and invasion. A line formed between the Allies—the UK, France, and Russia—and the Central Powers dominated by Germany, Austria-Hungary, and the Ottoman Empire. In America, President Wilson mirrored the isolationist mood of the people and guardedly watched events unfurl, determined to keep the U.S. out of the line of fire. As conflict stretched into the spring of 1915 and attrition settled over the trenches, a German U-boat torpedoed the Cunard liner RMS *Lusitania* eleven miles off the coast of Ireland. It sank in just eighteen minutes, leading to the loss of 1,198 lives, 128 of them American men, women, and children. That incident brought Roosevelt loudly into the debate over American intervention.

Originally T. R. had sided with Wilson's neutrality policy, but, when he learned of atrocities committed on Belgian civilians by the Kaiser's troops, he broke with the president's stance. The war, Roosevelt now saw clearly, had become one of German aggression. He criticized Wilson intensely for meekly promoting universal peace and proposing useless arbitration treaties And with Bishop egging him on in a series of bellicose letters, T. R. declared the attack on the *Lusitania* "an act of piracy," demanding that Wilson end trade with Germany and initiate universal military training in the U.S. in anticipation of intervention.

"What an awful mess Wilson has got us into," Bishop wrote Roosevelt on May 12.[639]

"I can't express sufficiently my scorn and contempt for Wilson and [Secretary of State William Jennings] Bryan," Roosevelt shot back two days later.[640]

In August, T. R. traveled to a Plattsburg, New York, training camp to speak with men enrolled in a voluntary officers' readiness program. Their number included, by no small coincidence, his sons Ted, Archie, and Quentin. There he berated Wilson for a war policy he considered pro-German. Bishop considered Wilson's war strategy "slush" and "spineless," and urged Roosevelt to "keep on with your violent and excessively strong language."[641] That advice contradicted the counsel of many of T. R.'s other advisors who urged him to cool the rhetoric. Bishop persisted nonetheless, telling Roosevelt in October that "Wilson is afraid of you."[642]

It wasn't the first time Roosevelt and Wilson had clashed politically since the 1912 presidential contest. A year before the Great War broke out, Bryan had convinced Wilson that the U.S. should express official regret to Colombia for its intercession in the 1903 Panamanian revolution and pay a $25 million indemnity. Roosevelt was incensed. He denounced a proposed treaty as a "crime against the U.S." and an attack on its honor. Henry Cabot Lodge agreed to block the treaty from coming to a vote in the Senate and prevailed twice—in 1913, and again during Wilson's second term in 1917. It wasn't until four years later, when Republican Warren Harding occupied the White House—and Roosevelt lay in his grave—that Lodge finally relented and allowed the indemnity to be paid, minus the apology.

As hostilities raged in Europe in mid-1915, Theodore and Edith Roosevelt joined Governor Goethals at the Panama-Pacific International Exhibition in San Francisco. Four years and millions of dollars in the planning, the colossal world's fair was a major event—a "wonder of the world." Promoted by Perham Nahl's striking poster of Hercules separating the mountains to make way for a flowing waterway and ship, the exhibition celebrated man's triumph over nature.

Visitors could visit a square mile of elaborate pavilions and palaces enhanced by elegant landscaping and lighting. They stood in the sun and watched an aeroplane fly and gazed in awe at a string of Model Ts moving along an assembly line. They touched the traveling Liberty Bell and listened as Alexander Graham Bell placed the world's first transcontinental telephone call. The event also served as a showcase for San Francisco's recovery from the 1906 earthquake and the subsequent devastating fires.

Before departing Panama a year earlier, Bishop had helped plan the exhibition's Panama Canal showcase. Its centerpiece was a five-acre working model of the canal, furnished with scaled-to-size locks, dams, and lakes. Visitors rode a moving walkway, observing powered model ships and towing trains alongside the waterway. They laid their hands on full-sized excavating machines, workmen's tools, and locomotives and cars from the Panama Railway. Elsewhere in the pavilion, a display of black-and-white photographs presented stark images of the canal's construction.

"No fair had ever been more important, more financially successful, more visited, more beautiful, more encouraging of world peace," said historian Julie Greene, "or, depending on one's point of view regarding international affairs, more effective at preparing the nation for war."[543]

July 21 was designated Theodore Roosevelt Day at the exhibition, and the colonel took full advantage of the platform to recall events earlier in the century in the context of the day's interventionist debate. Speaking to a cheering crowd of 60,000, Roosevelt counseled that if the U.S. had reacted to the 1903

Panamanian revolution simply with diplomatic niceties, as Wilson was now doing with the war in Europe, the canal never would have been built. He antagonistically questioned the stance of "too proud to fight" pacifists and declared, "Men who are not ready to fight . . . are not fit to live in a free democracy."[644]

Governor Goethals—promoted by now to the rank of major general—also was honored with a day, September 7, for managing "the century's greatest single work," and declared the entire exhibition "worthy of the canal it commemorates." The nine-and-a-half-month exhibition was a huge success, both in terms of its 18 million visitors, and in putting San Francisco back on the map.

At the time, Bishop had resumed writing in New York to support himself. He told Roosevelt in November 1915 that Maxwell Perkins, an eminent editor at Scribner's, had engaged him "at a satisfactory price" to prepare a series of articles on Roosevelt's record "for use in time of need."[645] With T. R.'s cooperation Bishop dived into the task, researching old presidential papers, articles, and speeches. "Jiminy, how I am enjoying the work!" he admitted to his subject.[646] Clearly, Perkins wanted to have authoritative material prepared well ahead of Roosevelt's eventual death.

The end was drawing near.

Thirty-Two

Benedictions

BISHOP'S UNFLAGGING BOOSTERISM OF ROOSEVELT FLARED AGAIN AT THE close of 1915 when he told the colonel, "There is clearly a perceptible undercurrent of sentiment for you that I must tell you about it." The talk in the lounges and at the dining tables at New York's University Club broadly favored a Roosevelt challenge to Woodrow Wilson in 1916. The consensus, he advised, was that T. R. "should make no effort to secure delegates but trust to a spontaneous movement"[647] in his favor.

Roosevelt was having none of it. In March 1916, on concluding a Trinidad vacation with Edith, he issued a Sherman-like statement. "I do not wish the nomination." He further insisted, "I am not the least interested in the political fortunes either of myself or any other man." Roosevelt saw no chance that the Republicans would nominate him and had no interest in another third-party try by the Progressives on his behalf. What did interest him, he said, was "the triumph of the great principles for which, with all my heart and soul, I have striven and shall continue to strive."[648] That meant speaking in favor of national preparedness and against Wilson's war "weaseling."

Despite Roosevelt's expressed lack of interest, Bull Moose leaders pressured him to reconsider. Meeting in convention in Chicago on June 10, they nominated him for president. From Oyster Bay Roosevelt wired his refusal. The same day in the same city, Republicans chose Charles Evans Hughes, former governor of New York and sitting associate justice of the Supreme Court, as their nominee. Hughes, Roosevelt observed, "is an able, upright man whose instincts are right. . . . At his worst, he will be better than Wilson, and there is always the chance that he will do very well indeed."[649]

It took about two weeks for Roosevelt to declare his support for Hughes, and he urged his progressive followers to do the same. "This action marked the final dissolution of the Progressive Party," Bishop recalled. "The great bulk of its members followed Roosevelt's lead and supported Mr Hughes, thereby returning to the Republican fold."[650]

As the summer of 1916 warmed, Roosevelt continued to write and speak on behalf of the nation's preparedness. But the fifty-seven-year-old former president, now using a cane, doubted his continued relevance. "I am already an old man," he confessed to E. A. Van Valkenburg, editor of the *Philadelphia North American,* "and the chances are very small that I will ever again grow into touch with the people of this country to the degree that will make me useful as a leader."[651]

Bishop, meanwhile, embarked on his July vacation, eschewing Cape Cod for lakeside tranquility at the Mountain Lodge in the Adirondacks. There had been another, more serious development, however. Harriet had suffered a stroke the summer before. Dr. Alexander Lambert, physician to the Roosevelt and Bishop families, assured Joseph at the time that she would recover completely. "She is improving slowly," Bishop had written to T. R. a few months after the event, "but I have irrepressible misgivings."[652] Though frail, Harriet had recovered enough to travel to the Adirondacks in the summer of 1916, and their daughter Alice likely accompanied them to care for her. "Mrs. Bishop seems perceptibly stronger here," Bishop noted, "and I am sure the air and quiet are doing her much good."[653]

In the country, Bishop put the finishing touches on the manuscript of *Presidential Nominations and Elections,* a retrospective of campaigns, conventions, and inaugurations. The book gained wide popular attention because he had wisely augmented his text and tables with an amusing array of historically significant political cartoons. While relaxing with his wife on the broad veranda of the main lodge, Bishop also researched a commissioned work, *The Chronicle of One Hundred and Fifty Years,* a laudatory history of the New York State Chamber of Commerce since 1768.

Returning to New York City and the start of the fall presidential campaign, Bishop took on the role of opposition researcher. He burrowed into old files at Republican headquarters, looking for past utterances that would embarrass the incumbent. His goal was "not only to defeat Wilson but to repudiate him with such overwhelming force as to show the whole world what the American people think of him."[654] He found nothing.

As in 1908, when Taft's listless campaign required Roosevelt's intervention, Hughes's lackluster performance prompted Republican leaders to plead for assistance from the master of Sagamore Hill. Roosevelt agreed to ride the rails for the man he now quietly derided as "the bearded iceberg," but he would not allow others to control his message. Almost immediately, he urged Hughes to defy the party platform and endorse a women's suffrage amendment to the Constitution. At the time, women in twelve states could vote for president, and Hughes's advocacy energized suffrage activists—both men and women—to his campaign.

Beginning in mid-October, Roosevelt whistle-stopped for Hughes in the South and West, igniting the campaign with fresh energy and an unmistakable progressive message. Hughes echoed—albeit less stridently—Roosevelt's criticism of Wilson's neutrality and the former president's insistence on national readiness. Wilson took note of the Roosevelt-Hughes tandem, warning voters that if they supported a Republican for president, Hughes's election would mean certain dispatch of young American men to the battlefields of France.

Late in the campaign, Hughes and California governor Hiram Johnson— T. R.'s 1912 running mate—were staying in the same Long Beach hotel. For whatever reason, Hughes neglected to make a courtesy call on the governor, and Johnson interpreted the oversight as a deliberate cold shoulder. As a consequence, the governor sat on his hands in the presidential race for the remainder of the campaign.

California proved to be the pivotal state. Following the vote in November, Hughes's early lead in the East and Midwest evaporated as Wilson staged a comeback in the South and West. Nearly a million California ballots gave Wilson the win by only 3,773 votes, a 0.3 percent margin. The incumbent president, therefore, won the state's 13 electoral votes and another four years at 1600 Pennsylvania Avenue. Had Hughes carried the Golden State and had nothing else changed, he would have defeated Wilson 267–264 in the Electoral College and, some speculated, rewarded Theodore Roosevelt with an appointment as secretary of state.

Roosevelt, still thinking of himself as the center of attention, misinterpreted the election outcome in a letter to Arthur Lee, refusing to assign responsibility for Hughes's defeat to the judgment of the American people but rather to the chieftains of his own party: "The Republicans, by an overwhelming majority, nominated Hughes precisely because he did not represent my views; they thought it wise to dodge the issues I thought it vital to raise."[655]

In the weeks following the election, Roosevelt found two new platforms for his views. He agreed to write opinion pieces each month for *Metropolitan* magazine and syndicated columns for the *Kansas City Star*. Coupled with his endless speechmaking, the forums propelled the colonel into the role of "the accepted leader of the opposition to the dilatory and pacifist tendencies of the Wilson Administration." Roosevelt had become "the foremost champion of vigorous, militant and unadulterated Americanism."[656]

Five days into the New Year of 1917, Harriet was admitted to a private hospital in Queens, where she was treated for a life-threatening buildup of fluid in her lungs. Her condition deteriorated over four days, and on January 9, at age sixty-nine, she died.

Beginning with the pre-Christmas candlelight ceremony in the old Newman Church in Rumford, Rhode Island, Joseph and Harriet had enjoyed forty-four years together. They had reared three children, enjoyed the vicissitudes of life in Manhattan, and shared seven adventuresome years in Panama. As with Hartwell's death in 1913, there is no mention of Harriet's passing in all of the surviving Bishop-Roosevelt correspondence.

War-related events proceeded at an alarming pace even as Wilson advocated "peace without victory" in Europe. Before he could take his second oath of office, the president had to confront intensified aggression in Europe. The German navy had been pressing Kaiser Wilhelm II for authority to resume unrestricted submarine warfare to isolate Britain. On February 1, 1917, U-boat commanders received the go-ahead to sink merchant ships in the war zone. Within forty-eight hours, Wilson had cut off diplomatic relations with Germany. Then he announced a secret German plot to ally with Mexico and Japan against the U.S. if America were to enter the war. The country's last hope to avoid hostilities ended in March when the Germans sank seven U.S. merchant vessels.

The cherry blossom trees that Japan had given to the nation four years earlier had begun to blossom in Washington when Wilson somberly mounted the dais in the House of Representatives, clutching his notes. "There are serious, very serious choices of policy to be made, and made immediately," he intoned to the deathly still congressional assembly. "The world must be made safe for democracy."[657] Four days later, Congress declared war on Germany. At last, Roosevelt had gotten his way. American soldiers and fliers would be going to Europe to help the Allies resist the Central Powers, principally Germany. Congratulating the president on a "great state paper," Roosevelt urged that America "strike as hard, as soon, and as efficiently as possible in aggressive war with the government of Germany."[658]

But Roosevelt knew, in the spring of 1917, that the U.S. had an undersized army that required significant reinforcements in order to fight effectively. For months, as a private citizen, he had been organizing a volunteer force to supplement the regular troops. To many Roosevelt watchers, it was a predictable encore of 1898, when T. R. had formed the Rough Riders' volunteer cavalry to help liberate Cuba. Wherever the U.S. deployed troops, Roosevelt had to be part of it, it seemed. This time, he declared, so would his four sons.

"In view of the fact that Germany is now actively engaged in war with us," Roosevelt wrote Secretary of War Newton Baker, "I again earnestly ask permission to be allowed to raise a division for immediate service at the front." When Baker and the White House reacted coolly, Roosevelt requested and received a meeting with Wilson. On April 9, the president met him courteously at the White House, Roosevelt said, and "doubtless would, in his own good time, come to a decision." T. R. explained that his division would be composed of men over the age of twenty-five who would be exempt from the conscription that Congress was considering. "They would eagerly enlist to go to the front."[659]

Bishop related what followed: "Applications to enlist in his division poured in at such volume that, on May 7, 1917, Roosevelt announced that they were coming in at a rate of over 2,000 a day, and that he was confident he could offer the government the services of 250,000 men within a short time."[660] The following day, Roosevelt told a Brooklyn audience, "I ask only that I be given a chance to render a service which I know I can render, and nine out of ten of those who oppose my rendering it do so because they believe I will render it too well."[661]

Roosevelt's friends in Congress also took up the cause, adding a provision authorizing the raising of volunteer divisions to the pending draft bill. On the Senate floor, Hiram Johnson led the oratory: "What is it that is asked? It is asked only by a man who is now really in the twilight of life that he finally lay down his life for the country that has been his."[662]

When Congress presented Wilson with the conscription bill—including the license to raise volunteer forces—the president signed it, but in the next breath he announced his answer to the colonel's plea: no. Wilson would not exercise the option of supplementing regular army combat troops with volunteers—Roosevelt's or anyone else's. "It would be very agreeable for me to pay Mr. Roosevelt this compliment and the Allies the compliment of sending to their aid one of their most distinguished public men," Wilson said in a statement.

"But this is not the time or the occasion for compliment or for any action not calculated to contribute to the immediate success of the war."[663]

Roosevelt was crushed. Further, it pained him to avow that he would obey the decision of the commander in chief. Grudgingly releasing the men who had signed up with him from any further obligation, he reiterated, "Our sole aim is to help in every way the successful prosecution of the war, and we most heartily feel that no individual's personal interest should for one moment be considered save as it serves the general public interest." He denied that any political consideration or personal advantage played into his scheme. "Our undiviced purpose was to contribute effectively to the success of the war."[664]

Then Roosevelt tried to volunteer for France's and the UK's armies, but again, there were no takers. The reward of having Roosevelt and his men at the front was not worth risking the wrath of their new senior ally, the American president.

Historian Patricia O'Toole summed it up well: "Theodore Roosevelt had been declared superfluous."[665]

Bishop, now on the cusp of seventy, was too old to think of serving, but he, like so many men of the time, wanted to contribute to the war effort. Bishop found his niche in the American Society for the Relief of French War Orphans, which promised "philanthropy on the biggest scale the world has even seen." Organized in New York City in the fall of 1916 by financiers and political and religious leaders, it set out to raise $130 million or more for the children of dead French soldiers—said to number 200,000 at the time. By the spring of 1917, Bishop's name sat on the society's masthead as general manager, in charge of day-to-day administration.

Farnham Bishop, now thirty-two, was struggling to support himself by writing pulp fiction—"The Red Witch," "The Quest of Gaimar the Grim"— for *Adventure* magazine. He had joined the New York National Guard, First Armored Motor Battery. But drawn to do more and no doubt supported by his father, Farnham enlisted in the infantry in February 1918. He was assigned for training at Fort McDowell, on picturesque Angel Island in San Francisco Bay. In the summer of 1916, while serving with the National Guard, Farnham had written to Theodore Roosevelt, asking to be considered for the proposed volunteer division. "There is no way I can help you unless I raise the division," Roosevelt replied. "If I do, I shall at once take up the matter and have you assigned to it."[666] Farnham stayed stateside for the war and never saw combat.

He was honorably discharged as a second lieutenant in December 1918. But while at Fort McDowell he took advantage of a five-day furlough and slipped away to Berkeley. There he married his sweetheart, Miriam Suplee.

In the summer of 1918, with the U.S. in full-blown war mobilization and the Selective Service Act producing the first of 2.8 million men for the army, up to 10,000 doughboys a day were embarking for the battlefields of France. Their ranks included two of Roosevelt's sons, Ted and Archie.

"My dear General Pershing," T. R. addressed the newly named commander of the American Expeditionary Force, "I write to you now to request that my two sons, Theodore Roosevelt, Jr., age 27, and Archibald Roosevelt, age 23, both of Harvard, be allowed to enlist as privates under you, to go over with the first troops." He added wistfully, "If I were physically fit, instead of old, and heavy and stiff, I should myself ask to go."[667]

Thoroughly trained at Plattsburg, Ted was commissioned as a major. Assigned as a battalion commander in France, he courageously led his men into combat under a battlefield cloud of mustard gas. Promoted to lieutenant colonel and placed in charge of the 26th Infantry Regiment, he saw further hostilities and was gravely wounded in the Battle of Soissons in the summer of 1918. Ted received a Silver Star and France's Croix de Guerre. "Throughout World War I, Ted Jr. would be alternately praised and criticized as an officer who routinely and boldly moved ahead of the line in battle after battle," wrote author Edward Renehan Jr. "He was at once idolized by his men, with whom he shared all dangers, and criticized by career officers who respected Ted's bravery more than they did his judgment."[668]

Second Lieutenant Archie Roosevelt also was designated to an infantry unit. A commanding officer praised him as a "natural leader, energetic and able to bring out the best in his men." One early morning in the spring of 1918, now-captain Archie Roosevelt and his company came under heavy artillery fire, and Archie was hit in the arm and leg. Slowly recuperating in an army hospital, he was rewarded with the Croix de Guerre, and later discharged with full disability.

Unwilling to wait for America's entry into the war, Kermit signed on with the British to battle the Ottoman Turks in Mesopotamia (now Iraq). He became a self-described "warrior on wheels"—in charge of a motor battery in a machine gun corps. Despite life-threatening skirmishes in the desert, for which he was awarded the British Military Cross, Kermit was bored and eager to test himself in France. He arranged a transfer to the AEF on the Western Front and won a commission as a field artillery captain. The combat he sought never materialized, and as the war ground to an end he was transferred to Spain. Kermit recalled his wartime role in *War in the Garden of Eden*, a fine memoir of his time fighting with the British in the Middle East.

Ethel, the young men's sister, and her husband, surgeon Richard Derby, went to work in the American Hospital in Paris, taking care of wounded U.S soldiers. Derby managed the surgical ward, while Ethel helped to nurse patients back onto their feet. "I can't believe that men should do things [like this] to each other," she wrote to her mother.

In July 1918, the *New York Sun* ran an editorial congratulating twenty-year-old Quentin Roosevelt for his wartime bravery "in attacking three enemy airplanes single-handed and shooting one of them down." The Roosevelts' youngest child had trained as a pilot and hurriedly engaged in aerial warfare with German fighters over Europe. This was just after dropping out of Harvard and announcing his intention to marry Flora Payne Whitney, a great-grand-daughter of Cornelius Vanderbilt. "He was reckless to such a degree that his commanding officers had to caution him repeatedly," wrote Captain Eddie Rickenbacker, the American fighter ace, in his memoirs. "His bravery was so notorious that we all knew that he would either achieve some great spectacular success or be killed in the attempt."[669]

"I don't believe in all the United States there is any father who has quite the same right that I have to be proud of his four sons," Roosevelt wrote to Kermit in February 1918 from a New York hospital room. The colonel was still fighting the residual consequences of his expedition along the River of Doubt. "I have been [here] for nearly a fortnight and shall be for a fortnight more," he revealed. "[My] old Brazilian trouble, both the fever and the abscesses, recurred and I had to go under the knife."[670] The hearing in Roosevelt's left ear had deteriorated to nothing, and he finally admitted to friends that he was blind in one eye, the result of a boxing match in the White House years before. The *New York Times* reported on February 27 that he, nonetheless, was "in excellent spirits" and had enjoyed visits from associates—including Bishop.

Despite his severe physical limitations, Republican leaders wanted Roosevelt to retake his seat as governor of New York. He had no intention of running, but he agreed to speak at a party conference in Saratoga on July 17. As he was preparing to leave Oyster Bay, a reporter knocked on the door, delivering an unofficial report that Quentin's plane had been shot down over Germany. "How am I going to break it to her?" Roosevelt wondered aloud as he went inside to tell Edith.

Quentin Roosevelt, a World War I aviator and the president's youngest child, was shot and killed by German fighters over France on July 14, 1918.

Theodore Roosevelt Collection, Harvard College Library

From historical reports, Edith appears to have taken the news stoically, worrying principally about the fallout from Quentin's death on Theodore: "We must do everything we can do to help him. The burden must not rest entirely on his shoulders," she said.

Bishop later recalled the stoic words that the distraught father had used to address assembled journalists from the veranda. "Quentin's mother and I are very glad that he got to the front and had a chance to render some service to his country, and to show the stuff there was in him before his fate befell him."[671]

Three days later, a telegram arrived at Sagamore Hill from President Wilson. "[I] am greatly distressed that the news of your son's death is confirmed. I had hoped for other news."

Lieutenant Edward Buford, another American pilot on the same mission, gave an eyewitness account of Quentin's final minutes. He reported that while they were on an early-morning air patrol, four American fighters engaged in a free-for-all with seven enemy aircraft.

About a half a mile away, I saw one of our planes with three Boche [low-flying observation planes] on him, and he seemed to be having a pretty hard time with them, so I shook the two I was maneuvering with and tried to get over him, but before I could reach him, his machine turned over on its back and plunged down out of control. . . . Of course at the time of the fight, I did not know who the pilot was I had seen go down but as Quentin did not come back, it must have been him. His loss was one of the severest blows we have ever had in the squadron but he certainly died fighting.[672]

Quentin died in the air from two aircraft bullets to the head. Out of respect for the Roosevelt family and the bravery its young son had shown, German fliers buried Quentin in the village of Chaméry and decorated the gravesite with a simple cross and the shattered propellers of his plane.

General Pershing attempted to console the Roosevelt family a week later. "Quentin died as he had lived and served, nobly and unselfishly, in the full strength and vigor of his youth, fighting the enemy in clean combat. You may well be proud of your gift to the nation in his supreme sacrifice."[673]

"My only regret is that I have not been beside him in the fighting," Roosevelt confessed to a friend.[674]

Quentin's death was the defining moment in Roosevelt's last year of life. Although he took amusement at the talk of his "inevitable" nomination for president in 1920 and continued to hammer away at Wilson's war policy, he would never be the same. "His old exuberance had left him, never to return," wrote Edward Renehan Jr. "The boy in him had died."

Edith beheld the colonel's cheerless mood and said to Kermit, "I can see how constantly he thinks of him [Quentin], and not the merry, happy, silly recollections which I have but sad thoughts of what Quentin would have counted for in the future."[675]

In September, Roosevelt's voice turned philosophical in "The Great Adventure," a piece he prepared for *Metropolitan*. "Only those are fit to live who do not fear to die," he wrote. "And none are fit to die who have shrunk from the joy of life and the duty of life. Both life and death are part of the same Great Adventure." Bishop said of the article, "The universal verdict upon it [is that] Roosevelt struck a higher note than he had ever before reached." When Bishop later asked him about the piece, Roosevelt replied, "Ah. That was Quentin!"[675]

For much of the latter half of 1918, Roosevelt busied himself with speeches and writing that favored an aggressive war effort and undiluted patriotism. Bishop observed that he yet showed "undiminished zeal and energy" during a Western speaking tour and later, back in New York. There, Roosevelt thundered to a rapt audience of German-Americans: "We must win the peace of over-whelming victory and accept no peace but unconditional surrender."[677]

On November 11, 1918, the same day the Allies and Central Powers signed an armistice in France's Compiègne Forest that ended the fighting of the Great War, Roosevelt returned to the hospital. The first signs of inflammatory rheumatism had appeared, and the pain and swelling in his joints were intense. Doctors worried that as it worsened, he would face life in a wheelchair.

Roosevelt remained hospitalized until Christmas Day, "suffering severely during the greater part of the time," remembered Bishop. But Roosevelt maintained "complete cheerfulness and serenity of spirit."[678] From his bed and side chair, T. R. followed end-of-the-war events in the newspapers, welcomed Edith and a few close friends, and wrote a few personal letters.

"I saw him almost daily during this period," Bishop recalled. The two old friends reviewed draft chapters of *Theodore Roosevelt and His Time* and, of course, talked presidential politics. When Bishop asked Roosevelt about 1920, he candidly shared his thinking:

> *I am indifferent to the subject. I would not lift a finger to get the nomina-tion. Since Quentin's death the world seems to have shut down on me. My other boys are on the other side of the water fighting or being made ready to fight for their country. If they do not come back, what would the presidency mean to me? At best, I have only a few remaining years, and nothing could give me greater joy than to spend them with my family.*

But Roosevelt could not imagine a world in which he would not be called to serve:

> *I have been President for seven years, and I am not eager to be President again. But if the leaders of the party come to me and say that they are con-vinced that I am the man the people want, and the only man who can be elected, and that they are all for me, I don't see how I could refuse to run. If I do consent, it will be because as President I could accomplish some things that I should like to see accomplished before I die.*[679]

It was during one of their hospital room conversations that Bishop took from his briefcase a clutch of letters he had come upon. Roosevelt had written them from the White House to his children while they were at school. "When you have read them, I will tell you something I have in mind," Bishop said.

"By George," Roosevelt exclaimed after perusing a few. "These are pretty good. I had forgotten all about them."[680]

When Bishop told Roosevelt that he wanted to edit a book of T. R.'s letters to his children, the former president at first demurred but eventually warmed to the idea. He asked Edith to reclaim other letters, stored at Sagamore Hill, that he had written to the children when they were small, ones that included charming pen-and-ink sketches of animals and fictional human characters.

"The last time I saw him was on the afternoon of the day before Christmas 1918," Bishop recalled. "He was sitting in a chair and was to leave the hospital on the next morning for Oyster Bay." After thumbing through a compilation of the children's letters, Roosevelt declared to Bishop, "I would rather have that book published than anything that has ever been written about me."[681]

With Christmas Day came Theodore Roosevelt's release from the hospital, "stiff, weak and very pale," in the words of author Patricia O'Toole. Sagamore Hill was decorated with a giant evergreen tree and lights and presents for all the family. Edith reveled in the company of Alice, Ethel, and Archie, and the assembled grandchildren. T. R. chuckled about Ethel's two-year-old daughter, saying to his sister, "Little Eddie is the busiest person imaginable, and runs around exactly as if she was a small mechanical toy."

The start of 1919 found Roosevelt passing his daytime hours on a sofa at Sagamore Hill, dashing off feisty letters despite agonizing pain and a soaring temperature. One of the last he wrote scolded New York Tribune editor Ogden Reid for his description of Woodrow Wilson and his League of Nations proposal as an idealist. "He is not," Roosevelt insisted. "He is a silly doctrinaire at times and an utterly selfish and cold-blooded politician always."[682]

When James Amos, T. R.'s long-time valet, arrived at Sagamore Hill on January 4, he was shocked at the colonel's appearance. "His face bore a tired expression," Amos recalled. "There was a look of weariness in his eyes. It was perfectly plain that he had suffered deeply. And it made me sick at heart to see him so."[683]

On Sunday, January 5, following a quiet day, Roosevelt retired at about 10:30 p.m., complaining that he had "a curious feeling." Amos remembered the events that followed: "I removed his robe and had to almost lift him into bed. Mrs. Roosevelt was in and out of the room and, at about eleven o'clock, kissed him goodnight and retired . . . Just after Mrs. Roosevelt had left the room, Mr. Roosevelt said, 'James, will you please put out the light?'

"I put it out, and sat in a chair where I could see the bed," Amos recalled. "I could see him lying there on the bed, very still, and I could tell by his breathing that he was asleep. I was alone with Theodore Roosevelt as he slept in a sound and peaceful slumber from which he was never to awake."

About 4:00 a.m., the shallowness of Roosevelt's breathing woke Amos, who took alarm and ran for a nurse. "In a few moments, Mrs. Roosevelt came in," Amos wrote. "She was calm and went to her husband's side. She leaned over him and called, 'Theodore darling!' But there was no answer."[684] Theodore Roosevelt, age sixty, had died peacefully without waking, succumbing to an embolism, most likely in a coronary artery.

"He died as he would have wished-to," Bishop observed, "in the home that he loved, with his family about him, in the full possession of his faculties, in the midst of work that was nearest to his heart, and at the summit of his fame."[685]

Amid tall, bare trees and the soiled snow, Roosevelt was buried two days later on a steep slope in Young's Cemetery not far from Sagamore Hill. Hundreds of dignitaries and friends had attended the spare service in Christ Church, Oyster Bay, where not a note of music was played. Nor did anyone give a eulogy. Edith stayed home, as was the custom of the day, and quietly read funeral prayers.

In the U. S. Senate soon thereafter, Henry Cabot Lodge read a forty-five-page tribute to a hushed chamber: "Theodore Roosevelt's power and the main source of his achievement was not in the offices that he held, for those offices were only opportunities, but in the extraordinary hold which he established and retained over great bodies of men," Lodge recalled. "Roosevelt was always advancing, always struggling to make things better, to carry some much-needed reform, and help humanity to a larger chance, to a fairer condition, to a happier life."[686]

Bishop later remarked in his memoirs, "I consider it a benediction to have lived in the same country and in the same time with Theodore Roosevelt, and to have had the priceless gift of his friendship."[687]

Thirty-Three

An Admirable Self-Revelation

THEODORE ROOSEVELT'S LETTERS TO HIS CHILDREN WAS PUBLISHED SEPTEMBER 12, 1919, to wide acclaim. "It commanded a very large sale," Bishop remembered, "and called forth a great volume of letters from people who said it had completely changed their estimate of the man."[688]

The New York *Evening Sun* judged the book "an enduring monument to the man," adding "rarely in the history of the world have we had so full and luminous a portrayal of the personality of [one of] the few very great men."[689] The *Evening Post* set aside its usual criticism of Roosevelt to praise the letters, "[as] spontaneous as they are tender." They reveal, said the reviewer, "the softer side of a personality that dazzles peculiarly because of its robustness and vigor, and will prove the former President a man no less vivid in his dome tic affections than he was in his political relations."[690]

The book became a national best-seller, recorded as the third most popular on the 1920 nonfiction list. The royalties ensured Bishop's financial comfort for the rest of his life.

The story of how Bishop came to write Roosevelt's authorized biography had begun unexpectedly in the latter half of 1914. Bishop had arrived in New York from Panama, intent on jump-starting a late-in-life literary career. Meantime, Roosevelt had limped back to New York after nearly dying in the jungles of Brazil. Each man, no doubt, had mortality on his mind.

"I know what I wish you would do," Roosevelt announced to Bishop during one of their frequent get-togethers. "Write the story of my public life. You know it almost as well as I know it myself." The unexpectedness of the request certainly surprised Bishop, and at the same time his heart surely raced with anticipation. "I will turn all my official and private correspondence over to you for exclusive control," Roosevelt assured him.

"We agreed," Bishop remembered, "that as far as possible . . . the story should be told in his own letters, and this was done."[691]

The project languished for two years as each man occupied himself with work, the Great War, and family obligations. Then, two weeks before Christmas of 1916, with the reelection of Wilson consummated, the colonel wrote to his friend, Herbert Putnam, the librarian of Congress. "Mrs. Roosevelt and I have been talking over the disposition of my great mass of papers," he revealed. "They include, in immense numbers, copies of my letters and of letters to me while I was President . . . If I sent them to you, could they be catalogued and arranged, and permission given to me, or any of my representatives, to examine them at any time, with a clear understanding that no one else was to see them until after my death?"[692]

"We would receive them with the greatest satisfaction," replied Putnam, agreeing to the colonel's conditions. They made arrangements, and in January 1917 a library packer arrived at Oyster Bay to assess the collection. Most of it was stored in a bank, the packer reported, in six unusually large and heavy cases. They were in such poor condition, he said, that they would have to be repackaged before being shipped to Washington. The locked cases of papers documenting much of Roosevelt's public years arrived safely in Washington soon thereafter—but without the key to open them! "The Lord only knows where the key is," the colonel remarked in exasperation. "Break the cases open, and start to work on them!"[693]

Edith dutifully dispatched a set of keys, but it would take months before staff opened the boxes, since they had been assigned to other government agencies to help with the war effort.

Just a few months before his death, Roosevelt gave crucial direction to the matter of his papers. "Will you give my friend, J. B. Bishop, full access to my papers?" he requested of Putnam. "I will be grateful if you will help him in every way possible."[694] The librarian complied, and Bishop began the overwhelming task of sifting through stacks of letters and documents dating to Roosevelt's election to the New York Assembly in 1881.

"This was an arduous but not a difficult task to perform," Bishop recalled. "It was arduous because the material was virtually inexhaustible, but it was not difficult because of the quality of Roosevelt's letters. One of his private secretaries has estimated that during his public career, he wrote 150,000 letters."[695]

Then and since, much has been written about the extraordinary quality of the Roosevelt correspondence that formed the basis of Bishop's pioneering biography. It was Bishop who perhaps said it best:

His letters are not merely like his talk, they are his talk, frank and free. with rays of irrepressible and always-joyous humor playing about it, and with deft and sure thrusts at the foibles, vanities, perversities and weaknesses of mankind . . . His letters give us a veritable "inside history" of his time They push aside the screen that hides the wires which control great events, and we see them operating before our eyes. We see in very truth history in the making, shown and explained to us by the man who himself is making it. We get also a complete self-revelation of the man, of the motives, desires and principles which guide his life. It is this quality of self-revelation, more than any other perhaps, which makes his letters so admirable a vehicle for telling the story of his career.[695]

Roosevelt added minimally to the trove, but it was Bishop—describing himself dubiously as Roosevelt's literary executor—who noticed the gaps in the letters and dug deeper into the recesses of Sagamore Hill. He found three additional cases in late January and sent them off to Washington, prompting library officials to rejoice that the collection was now complete. Yet in late March, Bishop delivered still more. "I have found the missing papers of the Roosevelt files," he proclaimed to John Fitzpatrick, acting chief of the library's manuscripts division. "They were in the hayloft of the barn at Oyster Bay! They fill four large cases and will be sent to the library next week.'[697] Bishop's latest find covered much of Roosevelt's immediate post-presidential years, including his 1912 challenge to President Taft.

In the ensuing years, Edith and other family members added significantly to the Roosevelt papers. Alice donated her father's diaries from his days at Harvard and the Dakota ranches. In 1922, two years after *Theodore Roosevelt and His Time* appeared, Edith and Bishop discovered, in the garret of the house, letter books, scrapbooks, and other documents of T. R.'s time as governor of New York. They, too, made their way to Washington for archiving.

Bishop doggedly executed Roosevelt's wishes for the deposition of his material and contributed appreciably to what would become the Theodore Roosevelt Papers at the Library of Congress. Today, the collection represents one of the library's largest holdings, numbering about a quarter of a million documents.

As Bishop researched the holdings in 1918, he and Roosevelt collaborated to persuade Charles Scribner II, president of Charles Scribner's Sons, the New

York publishing house, to offer a contract for the biography. Scribner also committed to preview excerpts in the popular illustrated monthly *Scribner's Magazine*. Whatever hesitation the publisher had about the project dissolved in March when Bishop told the colonel, "Your letter to Scribner has done the trick. I had a long talk with him yesterday in which he accepted my plan."[698]

Bishop began work on Roosevelt's life in the spring of 1918, six months before he had full access to the letters. He chronicled a year at a time. But unlike many biographers, Bishop had access to his subject while researching and writing. "Before I begin on your career as Civil Service Commissioner, I should like very much to have a talk with you . . . as to the most desirable treatment," he told Roosevelt in mid-June.[699]

"As each year's record was written, I went over it with him and had the inestimable advantage of his suggestions and his contribution of incidents and anecdotes," Bishop told George Otto Trevelyan. "At the time of his death, I had brought the narrative down to 1905 and had secured his warm approval of both my plan and method of treatment. Since his death, I have completed the first draft of the narrative to the end of his presidency." Though he faced a solemn and exigent responsibility to portray Theodore Roosevelt authentically through his letters, Bishop was certain of his own role: "I am little more than a Boswell or a showman in preparing it for publication."[700]

Bishop's path to publication hit trouble in the month following Roosevelt's death. William Roscoe Thayer, T. R.'s Harvard classmate, friend, and the author of the acclaimed two-volume *Life and Letters of John Hay*, announced that he, too, was writing the Roosevelt story. The prospect of dueling biographies brought the Roosevelt family into the fuss and generated a face-off between two of the nation's best-known publishers. All of it could perhaps have been avoided, however. Surviving letters reveal that Bishop and Thayer had tried to meet for lunch in Cambridge, Massachusetts, in late 1914 while Thayer was writing the Hay life. But their schedules did not mesh, and the meeting never took place.

When word of Thayer's project reached Bishop's publisher in February 1919, Scribner fired off a preemptive dispatch to Thayer's publisher, Ferris Greenslet, editor in chief of Houghton Mifflin. "It did not seem to me that it would be right for both of us to make little books which would appeal to exactly the same readers," Scribner began. "I had thought that you might be very willing to concede the field to us." In case Greenslet did not get the implication, Scribner warned, "We would not well favor any publication which would, in any way, tend to divide public interest."[701]

The key to an authoritative life of the former president was, of course, possession of Roosevelt's unpublished letters, and Bishop had exclusive access to them. Scribner affirmed Bishop's right to use them, in spite of Thayer's huffing and puffing, time and again.

Said to be indignant over the situation, Thayer approached Corinne Robinson, T. R.'s younger sister, also an author. He advised her that Henry Cabot Lodge, not Bishop, would be the "fittest person" to write the definitive Roosevelt biography. In the same breath, Thayer conceded that his book would "fall short of what I should like" because he had lost sight in one eye. Playing to Corinne's instinct to safeguard her brother's legacy, Thayer repeated Lodge's observation that Bishop seemed overwhelmed. "Well he may be," Thayer added. "How a man, at 71, can begin to learn the difficult and elusive art of biography makes me wonder."[702]

Bishop's rival kept up the pressure, writing to Corinne two weeks later. "Senator Lodge tells me that she [Edith Roosevelt] alone is Theodore's literary executor and that neither the Scribners nor Mr. Bishop has a right to say what shall be quoted and what shall not from Theodore's private letters."[703] Thayer's direct appeal to Edith landed a small concession: He could, of course, quote from the letters that T. R. had sent to him—but from no others.

"It's all a mystery to me," Corinne said to Thayer, "and I feel there must be some screw loose about the whole thing."[704] She wisely refused to let them drag her into the dispute. "I am very confident that your book will express his greatness in your own incomparable fashion."[705] After speaking with Bishop, Corinne assured Thayer that Bishop "does not consider himself the final biographer by any means." In an attempt to reassure Thayer, she added, "I am sure he is approaching his part of the work with reverence and humility."[706]

In the end, Thayer completed *Theodore Roosevelt: An Intimate Biography*, without access to the cache of letters, and it appeared to warm reviews a year ahead of Bishop's book. "But for Theodore's sake, I hope for the best," Thayer confided in Corinne, "and even if his [Bishop's] official biography does not fulfill our prayerful expectations, sooner or later the right biographer will come."[707]

Under the terms of a legal document signed by Bishop, Scribner, and Edith on August 1, 1919, Bishop was granted "the privilege of selecting from the correspondence of Theodore Roosevelt such letters as he may desire to use in his work, *Theodore Roosevelt and His Time*.' Additionally, he received the "exclusive right" to them for ten years after publication. Bishop accepted an $8,000 advance (worth nearly $100,000 today) against a flat royalty of 20 percent.

Thereafter, he and the colonel's executors—Edith, Theodore Roosevelt Jr., and a cousin, George Roosevelt—would split the 20 percent royalty 50/50—10 percent going to Bishop and 10 percent to the family.[708]

As they came out of Bishop's typewriter, the early chapters of the book appeared in *Scribner's Magazine*, beginning in September 1919. There, on the cover of volume 66, number 3, was a handsome engraving of an animated T. R. in profile surrounded by the headline THEODORE ROOSEVELT—PEACEMAKER. HIS OWN LETTERS TELL THE STORY OF THE JAPANESE RUSSIAN TREATY— EDITED BY JOSEPH BUCKLIN BISHOP. The first excerpt from *Theodore Roosevelt and His Time* revealed that Japan had reached out to President Roosevelt to initiate peace talks with the Russians in 1905. The *New York Times* headlined the revelation JAPAN ASKED PEACE THROUGH ROOSEVELT, and the prepublication promotion of Bishop's book was successfully launched. "I have been following your articles in *Scribner's* with the greatest interest," Rudyard Kipling informed Bishop.[709]

As 1919 turned into 1920, Bishop rushed to complete the manuscript. By April he was reviewing page proofs. In October he declared to Fitzpatrick, "My book is out, as you know, and I feel as I imagine a woman must feel who has been safely delivered of twins."[710] The librarian of Congress hailed the accomplishment, accurately predicting that "Your work will be the foundational basis, the starting point, of every future life of Roosevelt . . . no matter the viewpoint of the future authors."[711] Once he had opened a book-sized package that had arrived from America, George Otto Trevelyan advised Bishop from England, "The size of it is perfect: two readable and beautifully printed volumes which I earnestly hope future generations may leave as they are."[712]

After reading *Theodore Roosevelt and His Time*, Brander Matthews wrote in the *New York Times*, "It seems to those of us who knew him long and loved him, almost as though we could hear him speaking, that we could smile at his vivacity and thrill with the fire of his utterance." Bishop's book, he continued, "has been carried to completion with . . . delicate discretion, with instinctive tact and a high courage which Roosevelt would be the first to recognize." Anticipating the disparagement that would inevitably follow an admiring portrait, the *Times* concluded, "The book is undoubtedly partisan—which does not prevent it from being a thoroughly good and complete biography."[713] Bishop expected that Roosevelt's best friend would be an unforgiving critic, but Henry Cabot Lodge wrote to say that he found the portrait "a very admirable piece of work."[714]

Roosevelt's papers of course underpinned the success of *Theodore Roosevelt and His Time*. In preparing the book's introduction, Bishop observed, "Many writers have sought to depict the man Roosevelt, and many others will repeat the effort, but none has and no one can depict him as he really was with that vivid clearness in which he stands self-revealed in his letters."[715] In portraying the significance of Roosevelt's own words as the key to understanding the man, Bishop encapsulated the life and the lifeblood of his subject:

All ideas of the many-sided man are disclosed: the intellectual which cov-ered all fields of human knowledge, ancient and modern; the political which shows him to have been a sagacious statesman of the first rank rather than a politician—for as a politician, he repeatedly broke the fundamental rules of the game; the executive and administrator, first of a great state, and then of a great nation whose motto was action, action and still more action and who accomplished great and supposedly impossible tasks by the driving force of his character; the diplomatist and peacemaker, a role which he played with greater success than any other man of his time; and finally, the inspiring and uplifting leader of his countrymen, the intense, vigilant, militant and uncompromising patriot, eager to serve the nation in peace or in war who, throughout his life, was first and always an American.[716]

But of all the testimonials accorded to the author, none was more compelling than Edith Roosevelt's. After reading a *Scribner's* excerpt, she wrote Bishop, "I marvel at the taste and judgment with which you have accomplished your task and can never adequately speak of my gratitude. I am so entirely content."[717] In a later note after she had finished reading the book, she appraised not only the work but the man who had achieved it: "None of Theodore's friends should cease being grateful to you for the book. I do not wish to flatter, but who else could have done it."[718]

Epilogue

In the End the Triumph

"Presidents come and go, but monuments are always with us," *Time* magazine reflected in its 2006 retrospective of Theodore Roosevelt. "Roosevelt not only remade America but he also charmed the pants off everybody while he did it."[719] Indeed.

T. R. is enshrined between Jefferson and Lincoln, in the company of Washington, on the granite face of Mount Rushmore in South Dakota. Sculptor Gutzon Borglum put him there for the ages in the 1930s because he had conserved so much of America's natural landscape.

Roosevelt confronted issues that still confound us today: the role of the U.S. as a world power, a regulator of free enterprise, a guardian of human rights, and a bulwark against the greed of big business. We remember him not principally as a partisan figure—although he was—but as a righteous and selfless public servant whose deep desire to do right and do well motivated him. In the end, his genius was the engine of his triumph, and his integrity the salve.

In 2001, President Bill Clinton awarded Theodore Roosevelt the Medal of Honor for "gallantry and intrepidity at the risk of his life, above and beyond the call of duty, in action with the enemy" at San Juan Hill in 1898. Roosevelt is the only president to receive the nation's highest honor for actions in wartime. The Medal of Honor stands together with, and in stark contrast to, his Nobel Peace Prize, both testimony to an extraordinarily diverse life.

Edith Roosevelt lived for nearly thirty years after her husband's death, traveling the world and giving to charities that clothed the poor. "Everything she did was for the happiness of others," is how she asked to be remembered on her tombstone. But in 1948, when she died at eighty-seven, there was space on the gravestone only for her name and dates, as the wife of Theodore Roosevelt. She stoically faced the premature deaths of three of her five children: Quentin in World War I aerial combat; Ted in France, a month after landing at Normandy;

and Kermit, her favorite, of a gunshot wound to the head, by his own hand, in Alaska in 1943. The hero of the River of Doubt expedition had been unable to overcome the depression and alcoholism that tortured his later life.

William Howard Taft, the man whom Roosevelt had anointed and deposed inside four turbulent years, and the secretary of war who dispatched Joseph Bucklin Bishop to Panama, finally achieved his own ambition. In 1921, he became chief justice of the United States and served with distinction until his death nine years later. Fortunately, Taft and Roosevelt reconciled during a chance meeting in Chicago a few months before the colonel's death. At Roosevelt's funeral in Oyster Bay, Taft stood silent at the gravesite, his head bent, wells of tears flooding his eyes. He characterized his old friend as "the most commanding, the most original, the most interesting and the most brilliant personality in American public life since Lincoln."[720]

With nothing further to accomplish after his monumental achievement, Major General Goethals left Panama in the fall of 1916. "The two oceans have been united," he declared. "The construction of the canal means nothing in comparison to its coming usefulness to the world and what it will bring about."[721] He directed army logistics during World War I before retiring in 1919 to consult. At his West Point funeral in January 1928, there was no eulogy except for the understated words of a church rector: "We thank Thee, dear Lord, for the splendid service rendered by this, Thy departed servant."[722] In the Canal Zone, U.S. flags flew at half-mast in solemn tribute to the great engineer and administrator.

It was remembered that Bishop stood uncovered and shivering at the West Point gravesite, stooped by his eighty years, weary after a long march up the frozen incline behind the caisson. His doctor later traced his physical decline to this midwinter tribute to his mentor and friend. Goethals never wrote a memoir; his story fell to Bishop and Farnham to tell in the acclaimed *Goethals: Genius of the Panama Canal*, published in 1930.

Roosevelt never returned to Panama to see the canal in operation. Had he stopped en route from South America in 1915, it would have impressed him: 1,258 vessels with 5.7 million tons of cargo crossing in the first year, contributing nearly $5 million in tolls. The canal's utility for world commerce and tourism grew exponentially over the years, even as resentment of the U.S. presence erupted into street violence in the 1960s and 1970s. President Jimmy Carter, with the grudging consent of the Senate following a titanic political

Joseph Bucklin Bishop traveled the world following the success of his Theodore
Roosevelt books (ca. 1924). *Anita and Miriam Bishop collection*

battle, returned the canal to Panamanian control, effective in 1999. Despite the
doomsday fears of conservative opponents, the Panamanians have administered
the canal both with ability and integrity. They are lengthening and widening the
locks for mammoth vessels currently too big to go through the canal. The new
locks are set to open in 2014, for the celebration of the canal's centennial.

Notoriety and the stream of royalties from his two popular Roosevelt books
gave Joseph Bucklin Bishop the means to travel the world in his eighth decade.
He cruised the West Indies and the Mediterranean, and he toured Egypt and
Europe. Belgium's foreign minister awarded him La Médaille du Roi Albert
for his work on behalf of the orphans of World War I. The inscription reads: IT
PLEASES THE KING TO ORDER HIM CONFERRED.

In February 1921, the former Isthmian Canal Commission secretary set out
on a sentimental return to Panama—after a seven-year absence—on assignment
for *Scribner's Magazine*. "A marvelous transformation had been wrought," he wrote
upon returning to New York. "All plans had been carried to execution, and the result
was a harmonious and perfect whole in a setting of wondrous natural beauty."[723]

Venturing back to Providence in June 1923, Bishop accepted an honorary doctorate from Brown University. "Your long career as writer and author, your sound exposition of American principles and ideals, and your wide influence throughout your life upon the thinking of our country all render such action on our part eminently fitting," said Brown President William Faunce. Then tragedy struck. In the fall of 1924, while traveling with her father in Paris, Alice Bishop died of a heart attack at age forty-eight. She would not be the last of his children to die young.

Back in New York City, secluded in his room at the University Club, Bishop began work on a memoir. Dedicated to Alice, his "cheering and helping comrade," *Notes and Anecdotes of Many Years* warmly remembered his favorite acquaintances and friends: Horace Greeley, Edwin Godkin, John Hay, and, of course, Theodore Roosevelt. In a cautious word to his readers, Bishop explained, "I am emboldened to run the risk of being adjudged a victim of the old-age infirmity of anecdotage."[724] It was the last of uncounted articles and eleven books that he would complete.

To mark his eightieth year, as he enjoyed "the vigor and buoyancy of a much younger man,"[725] Bishop set out for California. There he spent the summer of 1928 in San Rafael with Farnham—who had ventured west to accept an English-teaching assignment at San Rafael Military Academy—and Farnham's wife, Miriam.

"On the 29th [of July] we were all at lunch at the Hotel Rafael when the fire engines came," his daughter-in-law recorded in her diary. " 'Mr. Bishop had better get his things from his room,' we were told. Farnham and his father went up and brought down practically everything just in time, for the whole hotel was in blaze and burned to the ground in a short time." Miriam added, "It is believed that a boy of 18—escaped from an asylum—set the place on fire."[726] Undeterred, Bishop camped for the night in Miriam and Farnham's dining room, then set out the next day in a friend's Packard for a motor tour of Yosemite National Park, an extraordinary natural wonder saved from exploitation by President Roosevelt twenty-two years earlier.

Once back in New York, Bishop began work on *Goethals: Genius of the Panama Canal*. On December 12, he was socializing with friends in the University Club's dark-paneled sitting room, recounting tales of Goethals's childhood and early career. He had completed four chapters of the biography and was working on the fifth. Retiring for the night, he took an elevator upstairs and closed and locked the door to his room. That night, as frost crept onto

A page from daughter-in-law Miriam Bishop's diary notes Bishop's death n December 1928. *Anita and Miriam Bishop collection*

the panes of his darkened windows, Bishop took gravely ill. The next morning, when he did not come down for his usual breakfast meal, the club staff went to his room and discovered his body. The official cause of death was carditis, an inflammation of the heart muscle.

"Another epoch has ended," Miriam Bishop scribbled tearfully in her diary. "Farnham left [Thursday] night on the Overland Limited."[727]

On December 17, in the Church of the Incarnation on Madison Avenue, the congregation of mourners recited the Lord's Prayer at the direction of Reverend Horace Silver, the rector who had buried General Goethals eleven months earlier. Under his son's supervision, Bishop's remains were cremated at the Fresh Pond Crematorium in Queens and laid to rest alongside Hartwell, Harriet, and Alice at Kensico Cemetery in Valhalla, New York, in a twelve-foot-by-twelve-foot plot Joseph had bought for $216 at the time of his wife's death. The family monument rests in a garden of stones on a graceful plain, atop one of the highest knolls in the graveyard, beneath a towering maple and a broad expanse of sky.

From Bishop's will, Farnham, Miriam, and their two young sons, Joseph and Brewster, inherited furniture, six oriental rugs, framed pictures and books, and cash, securities, and insurance policies worth more than half a million dollars in today's money. At Christmas, Miriam opened a special gift. It was "a white gold wrist watch, the last present from dear Father, bought during the summer while he was visiting us."[728]

Farnham stayed in New York to finish *Goethals* in the upstairs library of the Roosevelt birthplace in Manhattan. Although he completed the manuscript in 1929, Farnham acknowledged that "history had suffered a loss" with the passing of his father. "No living man knows what he knew about Goethals and Roosevelt and the other actors, great and small, before and behind the scenes," he wrote in the book's preface.[729] The *New York Times* predicted—accurately, as it turned out—that the Bishops' portrait of Goethals would be "the last word on the subject"[730] for decades.

Weeks after finishing the biography his father had begun, Farnham contracted pneumonia, lingered for two weeks, and died in Berkeley, California, a month after his forty-fourth birthday. Incredibly, Miriam died just three days later of the same virulent infection. Six-year-old Brewster contracted it as well. Bedridden with cough, fever, and difficulty breathing, he was, according to doctors, "touch and go" for weeks before eventually recovering.

Joeseph Bucklin Bishop, his surviving son, and daughter-in-law had all died in a mournful instant. Family survivors were in shock. The care of Brewster and five-year-old Joseph Bucklin Bishop II fell to Miriam's mother, Bertha Suplee, who often recalled the time she had crossed Panama on horseback in 1884 to avoid traveling through the American West of Geronimo and the Apaches. That strength served her well, as she lived to be 103.

Carved into the walls of the grand rotunda of today's Panama Canal Administration Building in Ancon are these words of Theodore Roosevelt:

It is not the critic who counts, not the man who points out how the strong man stumbled or where the doer of deeds could have done them better. The credit belongs to the man who is actually in the arena, whose face is marred by dust and sweat and blood; who strives valiantly, who errs and comes short again and again; who knows the great enthusiasms, the great devotions, and spends himself in a worthy cause; who, at the best, knows in the end the triumph of high achievement; and who, at the worst, if he fails, at least fails while daring greatly, so that his place shall never be with those cold and timid souls who knew neither victory nor defeat.[731]

When he uttered these memorable lines, Roosevelt had the greatest of men in mind, perhaps even his own achievements. But the words, carved in marble for generations to contemplate, apply just as well to the dearest of his friends—men such as Joseph Bucklin Bishop, who continuously met the toughest of challenges, to be an endlessly loyal friend of Theodore Roosevelt.

Acknowledgments

THE GENESIS OF *THE LION AND THE JOURNALIST* TRACES BACK TO A 1962 HIGH school English class in Woonsocket, Rhode Island. There, Miss Sarah Smith encouraged my tentative sixteen-year-old self to pursue a nascent interest in the written word. Her charge to read Addison and Steele's *Selections from the Tatler and the Spectator* ignited a tiny literary flame.

About the same time, an uncle, J. Wallace Bishop, told me an absorbing tale of his grandfather's brother, Joseph, a friend of Theodore Roosevelt and a writer of note. Wallace recalled that in 1929 Farnham and Miriam Bishop and their sons, Joe Buck and Brewster, paid a memorable visit to his home in Albion, Rhode Island. Seeing my curiosity, Uncle Wallace later trudged to his attic to retrieve one after another of Joseph's books, signed to his father and grandfather, carefully stockpiled for a solemn transfer such as this. Today, those books form the foundation of my Joseph Bucklin Bishop collection.

In the spring of 2008, ensconced on Cape Cod with my wife and feline friend, Fantasia, I began reading Joseph's musty books and others about Theodore Roosevelt, with the goal of chronicling the Bishop-Roosevelt story a few years later in my retirement. My enthusiasm would not allow postponement; research and writing did not stop for thirty-one hectic months.

Like most books, *The Lion and the Journalist* is a product of many people, who, together and apart, believed in my mission and contributed worthwhile knowledge, information, and direction to the project.

The first to thank is my loving and loyal wife, Jane, to whom this work is dedicated with heartfelt affection and indebtedness. Jane stood by me without question or reservation, month after month, as I purloined precious time from her and the needs of our lives. She listened with genuine interest day after day as I read out loud naked chapters fresh from the keyboard. Her insight and critiques were unfailingly incisive and always on the mark.

It took Jane and me months to find them—in the Russian River Valley of Northern California—but Joseph Bucklin Bishop's descendants have been incalculably helpful and wholly supportive of this project. By granting unrestricted access to unpublished Bishop and Roosevelt letters, photos, and the diary of Miriam Bishop, Anita Gonzales-Reyes Bishop and her daughter, Miriam Bishop, added immeasurably to the scope and color of the story. Mexican-born Anita—the widow of Farnham Bishop's younger son, Brewster—still radiates beauty and charm at ninety. Miriam, named after Farnham's wife, is an effervescent personality and a dedicated school nurse who hopes someday to care for the poor in Panama. Their bountiful hospitality during our research visit in 2008 will always be recalled with utmost appreciation. So, too, are we grateful for quality time spent with the young San Francisco sommelier William Brewster Bishop III, Joseph's great-great-grandson.

Much credit for this book belongs to my literary manager, Alan Nevins, who recognized the potential in the manuscript when he first perused it in Boston during an improbable "speed-dating" exercise, and to his able and selfless assistant, Anthony Mattero, who patiently guided this first-time author through the publishing thicket. James Jayo, my editor, took an early manuscript and, with patience, talent, and skill, molded it into something first-rate. I'm grateful as well to the talented team at Lyons Press and Globe Pequot Press for their enthusiasm, sure-footed guidance, and, above all, their confidence in me.

Arlene Kirsch of Expressions Manuscripts and Vantage Consulting of Cape Cod is another person I can never repay. She volunteered countless hours to copyedit my original manuscript with great skill and sensitivity, and she made many suggestions that improved it immeasurably.

Libraries, of course, are essential resources for any researcher, the keepers of hidden treasures. In writing the story of the Roosevelt-Bishop friendship, the staffs of several libraries were of special assistance. Foremost is Wallace F. Dailey, curator of the Theodore Roosevelt Collection at Harvard's Houghton Library. He made available the Library of Congress's priceless trove of more than 600 letters exchanged between Theodore Roosevelt and Joseph Bucklin Bishop between 1897 and 1918. He showed me originals of many of Roosevelt's letters to Bishop and volunteered rarely seen letters between Corinne Robinson and William Roscoe Thayer that shed new light on the competition to write the seminal Roosevelt biography.

I owe special thanks to Todd and Sarah Nichols for spending dozens of hours at the Houghton Library, transferring the Bishop-Roosevelt letters from microfilm to disk. This book would not exist without their tireless commitment to that arduous task.

The saga of the "Ten Thousand Dollar Beauty" would not have come to light in such rich detail had it not been for determined research by Amy

Rowland into the archives of the *New York Evening Post* and the New York Public Library.

My gratitude goes to the staff of the Seekonk Public Library for helping to unlock the mystery of Joseph Bucklin Bishop's father, James Madison Bishop. Paul Arsenault of the Pawtucket Library in Rhode Island found and shared fascinating details of the people and places that shaped Joseph's early school years.

Eric Lindenbusch of the Sonoma County Library in California was dogged in his pursuit of the obituary of Joseph's grandson, William Brewster Bishop, a find which led us to Anita and Miriam Bishop. To Gayle Lynch and the staff of the John Hay Library at Brown University, thank you for sharing the prized letters of Hay and Bishop, and for opening the vault on the history of their college years. It was at Brown's Sciences Library that I enthusiastically paged through volume after volume of Bishop's *Canal Record,* the essential chronicle of the Panama Canal's construction era. The Providence Public Library has a worthy microfilm collection of the *Providence Journal,* which yielded rich details of Bishop's years in school.

Thank you to the staff of the Manuscripts Division of the Library of Congress in Washington, D.C., who helped our son, Joseph N. Bishop, and his then-fiancée, Katherine Francis, locate and duplicate several hundred letters between Joseph Bucklin Bishop and Secretary of War William Howard Taft during the all-important period leading up to the Panama chapters of the book. Joe's and Katherine's expert work allowed me to add the rich dimension of the Bishop-Taft relationship to the broader tale.

Joseph Schwartz of the National Archives at College Park, Maryland, gave me access to the historical records of the Isthmian Canal Commission, including Joseph Bucklin Bishop's thick and illuminating personnel file. Cynthia Cullen of the Dennis Public Library in Massachusetts is a whiz at finding rare books through Inter-Library Loan, and I am deeply in her debt.

Roosevelt scholar Keith Simon always made himself available to pass judgment on manuscript entries and contribute worthwhile guidance and perspective. Thomas Benton Bishop of Charlottesville, Virginia, the namesake descendant of Joseph's brother, sent me facts and photographs that rounded out the fascinating tale of Joseph's visit to San Francisco at the lowest point of his life.

Mark Koziol, formerly of the Cultural Resources Office at the Sagamore Hill National Historic Site in Oyster Bay, New York, helped considerably by sending copies of the revealing dinner-guest registers from Sagamore Hill and the White House. Lida Holland Churchville of the Historical Society of Washington, D.C., was wonderfully helpful in directing me to details of The Highlands, Joseph's home base during his stint in the nation's capital. Edna Anness of the East Providence Historical Society of Rhode Island (and our Cape Cod neighbor) helped us to locate Joseph's birthplace (now a private home) in Rumford, Rhode Island.

Douglas Ellis, who may be the world's foremost authority on the works of Farnham Bishop, was consistently generous with his research findings. Frank Stevens Hawks, the great grandson of John Stevens, lent valuable material and his encouragement to the project, as did General Goethals's grandson Thomas and his great-grandson, Professor A. Goethals of the University of Richmond.

Our research trip to Panama in 2008–09 was memorable and fruitful thanks to Anne Coleman-Hann of the U.S. Embassy in Panama City; Marc Quinn of the Theodore Roosevelt Medal Descendants Society; Rolando Cochez Lara and his helpful staff at the Panama Canal Administration Library in Balboa; Maria Beatríz Barletta of the communications office of the Autoridad del Canal de Panamá; Professor Fernando Aparicio of the history department at the University of Panama; Clement Austin, our expert guide to perilous Colón; and the staff and taxi operators associated with La Estancia Bed and Breakfast of Ancon.

On Cape Cod, I was supported and encouraged by Rick Sawyer, Kimberly White, and Jamie Ghetti of Grouper Design of Yarmouth Port; also, Tom Chartrand of Shoreline Digital Productions of Marstons Mills; and Kristen Hilley of Cape Cod Computer, Inc., of Harwich.

Our long search for Joseph Bucklin Bishop's final resting place would not have succeeded without the help of Reverend J. Douglas Ousley, rector of the Church of the Incarnation in New York City, and especially Judy Mitchell, our genial historian escort at Kensico Cemetery at Valhalla, New York.

Thanks as well to my new feline pal, Benjamin, who invariably schmoozed his way into my writing workspace to give me welcome breaks from the keyboard—respites that I didn't know I needed.

To all the others whose names I have failed to mention, thank you for your support and assistance. I am certain that the spirits of Theodore Roosevelt and Joseph Bucklin Bishop somehow are aware and appreciative of our team effort and shared labor of love.

Endnotes

1 Dalton, Kathleen. *Theodore Roosevelt: A Strenuous Life.* New York: Alfred A. Knopf, 2002, p. 507.

2 Manners, William. *T.R. and Will: A Friendship that Split the Republican Party.* New York: Harcourt, Brace & World, Inc., 1969.

3 *New York Times* obituary, January 6, 1919.

4 Ibid.

5 Ibid.

6 Ibid.

7 Theodore Roosevelt Association, *Life of Theodore Roosevelt,* May 31, 2008, p. 1. Available online at www.TheodoreRoosevelt.org/life/timeline.htm.

8 Ibid., p. 2.

9 Ibid., p. 3.

10 Ibid.

11 Ibid.

12 Roosevelt, Theodore. Address to the Naval War College, Newport, Rhode Island, June 2, 1897.

13 Theodore Roosevelt Association, *Life of Theodore Roosevelt,* p. 5.

14 Morris, Edmund. *The Rise of Theodore Roosevelt.* New York: Coward, McCann & Geoghegan, 1979, p. 771.

15 Bishop, Joseph Bucklin. *Notes and Anecdotes of Many Years.* New York: Charles Scribner's Sons, 1925, p. 149.

16 Bishop, *Notes and Anecdotes of Many Years,* p. 154.

17 McCullough, David. *The Path Between the Seas.* New York: Simon and Schuster Paperbacks, 1977, p. 536.

18 Bishop, *Notes and Anecdotes of Many Years,* p. 52.

19 Bishop, Joseph Bucklin. *Theodore Roosevelt and His Time,* Vol. 1. New York: Charles Scribner's Sons, 1920, p. viii.

20 Theodore Roosevelt to Joseph Bucklin Bishop, June 3, 1902.

21 Roosevelt to Bishop, November 27, 1901.

22 Erhardt, John. *Historical Seekonk, Mass. and East Providence, R.I. (1812–1900),* Vol. IV. Seekonk, MA: J. G. Erhardt, 2001.

23 Ibid.

24 Estate inventory of the late James M. Bishop. ca. 1864. Courtesy of Linda Fields.

25 Ibid.

26 Morris, *The Rise of Theodore Roosevelt,* p. 38.

27 McCullough, David. *Mornings on Horseback*. New York: Simon & Schuster Paperbacks, 2003, p. 28.

28 *Brown University Alumni Monthly*, October 1917, p. 60.

29 Bronson, Walter Cochrane, Ph.D. *History of Brown University 1764–1914*. Providence, R.I.: Brown University, 1914, p. 374.

30 *Providence Journal*, December 24, 1905, p. 18.

31 Ibid.

32 Ibid.

33 Ibid.

34 *New York Sun* obituary, December 14, 1928.

35 Morris, *The Rise of Theodore Roosevelt*, p. 91.

36 Donald, Aida D. *Lion in the White House*. Philadelphia: Basic Books, 2007, p. 34.

37 McCullough, *Mornings on Horseback*, p. 113.

38 Morris, *The Rise of Theodore Roosevelt*, p. 30.

39 Bishop, *Notes and Anecdotes of Many Years*, p. 8.

40 Ibid., p. 9.

41 Nevins, Allan. *Dictionary of American Biography*, 1931, p. 31.

42 Safire, William. *On Language ... To be Sure*, New York Times Magazine, February 5, 1995, online at www.nytimes.com/1995/02/05/magazine/on-language-to-be-sure. html?pagewanted=3&src=pm.

43 Bishop, *Notes and Anecdotes of Many Years*, pp. 21-22.

44 Ibid., p. 23.

45 Ibid., p. 50.

46 Ibid., p. 44.

47 Ibid.

48 Thayer, William Roscoe. *The Life and Letters of John Hay*. Vol. I, p. 329. Boston: Houghton Mifflin, 1915.

49 Bishop, Joseph Bucklin. *John Hay: Scholar, Statesman*. An address delivered before the Alumni Association of Brown University, Providence, Rhode Island, June 19, 1906, p. 5.

50 Bishop, *Notes and Anecdotes of Many Years*, p. 51.

51 Ibid., p. 52,

52 Ibid., pp. 66-67.

53 Axelrod, Alan and Charles Phillips. *What Every American Should Know about American History*. Avon, Mass.: Adams Media, 2008, pp. 161–62.

54 Hale, William Harlan. *Horace Greeley: Voice of the People*. New York: Collier Books, 1961.

55 Bishop, *Notes and Anecdotes of Many Years*, p. 25.

56 Hale, *Horace Greeley: Voice of the People*, p. 346.

57 Bishop, *Notes and Anecdotes of Many Years*, p. 34.

58 Cutter, William Richard (ed.). *New England Families: Genealogical and Memorial*. New York: Lewis Historical Publishing Co., 1915.

59 Bishop to John Hay, February 17, 1877.

60 Ibid.
61 Morris, *The Rise of Theodore Roosevelt*, pp. 54–56.
62 "Land Ownership in California and the Transition to a New Government." Available online at www.archives.gov/pacific/education/curriculum/4th-grade/land-ownership.html.
63 *Brown University Monthly*, April 1906.
64 Telephone discussion with the author, fall 2008.
65 Bishop to Hay, April 24, 1877
66 Bishop to Hay, April 27, 1877.
67 Ibid.
68 Bishop to Hay, November 26, 1878.
69 *New York Daily Tribune*, November 6, 1881, p. 6.
70 Bishop, *Notes and Anecdotes of Many Years*, pp. 55–56.
71 Ibid., p. 57.
72 *New York Daily Tribune*, "Our Hero," p. 6.
73 McCullough, *Mornings on Horseback*, p. 254.
74 Roosevelt, Theodore. *An Autobiography*. New York: Scribner, 1913, p. 65.
75 Ibid., p. 77.
76 McCullough, *Mornings on Horseback*, p. 266.
77 Bishop to Hay, November 26, 1878.
78 *Rice University Guide to the Frank Harrison Hill London Daily Newspapers 1870–1876*, available online at www.lib.utexas.edu.
79 Bishop, *Notes and Anecdotes of Many Years*, p. 102.
80 Ibid., p. 87.
81 Ibid., p. 100.
82 *The New York Post*, available online at www.Spartacus.schoolnet.co.uk/USAnypost.htm, p. 1.
83 Nevins, Allan. *The Evening Post: A Century of Journalism*. New York: Boni and Liveright, 1922, p. 454.
84 Ibid., p. 455.
85 Bishop, *Notes and Anecdotes of Many Years*, p. 91.
86 Ibid., p. 100.
87 Ibid., p. 102.
88 Lepore, Jill. "Rock, Paper, Scissors," *The New Yorker*, October 13, 2008.
89 McCullough, *Mornings on Horseback*, p. 318.
90 Roosevelt, *An Autobiography*, p. 94.
91 Ibid., p.96.
92 Morris, *The Rise of Theodore Roosevelt*, p. 229.
93 McCullough, *Mornings on Horseback*, p. 288.
94 Cordery, Stacy A. *Alice*. New York: Penguin Books, 2007, p. 19.
95 Bishop, Joseph Bucklin. *The Panama Gateway*. New York: Charles Scribner's Sons, 1913, pp. 71-3.

96 "Construction of the First Transcontinental Railroad," Panama Canal Railway Company, available online at www.panarail.com/en/history/index.htm.

97 Bishop, *The Panama Gateway*, p. 84.

98 Ibid., p. 65.

99 Ibid., p. 68.

100 Ibid., p. 76.

101 Ibid., p. 78.

102 Ibid., p. 84.

103 Ibid., p. 91.

104 Ibid., p. 92.

105 Ibid., p. 85.

106 Ibid., p. 90.

107 McCullough, *The Path Between the Seas*, pp. 234–35.

108 Bishop, *The Panama Gateway* p. 63.

109 McCullough, *Mornings on Horseback*, p. 156.

110 Bishop, Joseph Buckin. *Presidential Nominations and Elections*. New York: Charles Scribner's Sons, 1916, p. 57.

111 McCullough, *Mornings on Horseback*, p. 290.

112 Ibid., p. 291.

113 Bishop, *Notes and Anecdotes of Many Years*, p.103.

114 *Official Proceedings of the Republican National Conventions 1884–1888*. Minneapolis: Charles W Johnson Publishers, 1903, p. 10.

115 *New York Tribune*, June 10, 1884, p. 1.

116 "The Presidential Elections 1860–1912: 1884 Cleveland vs. Blaine," HarpWeek, available online at www.Elections.HarpWeek.com/1884/Overview-1884-3.htm.

117 Nevins, *The Evening Post: A Century of Journalism*, p. 459.

118 Ibid., p. 461.

119 Ibid.

120 "Election of 1884," The American Presidency Project, available online at www.presidency.ucsb.edu/showelection.php?year=1884.

121 Hagedorn, Hermann. *Roosevelt in the Bad Lands*. Boston: Houghton Mifflin, 1921, p. 308.

122 Roosevelt, *An Autobiography*, pp. 94–95.

123 Gilder, Rodman. *Statue of Liberty Enlightening the World*. New York: New York Trust Co., 1943.

124 *New York Sun*, October 26, 1886.

125 *The Nation*, October 14, 1885.

126 *The Evening Post*, October 27, 1886.

127 Putnam, Carleton. *Theodore Roosevelt: The Formative Years 1858–1886*. New York: Charles Scribner's Sons, 1958, p. 210.

128 McCullough, *Mornings on Horseback*, p. 358.

129 Morris, *The Rise of Theodore Roosevelt*, p. 297.

130 Hamilton, Allan McLane. *Recollections of an Alienist, Personal and Professional.* New York: George H. Doran Co., 1916, p. 115.

131 White, Horace. *The Evening Post Hundredth Anniversary 1801–1901.* Magazine supplement to the daily edition, November 16, 1901. New York: Evening Post Publishing Co., 1901, p. 69.

132 Ibid., p. 70.

133 *New York Times,* June 3, 1886.

134 "Grover Cleveland: Mrs. Halpin and the Child," *The Health and Medical History of President Grover Cleveland,* available online at www.doctor zebra.com/prez/z_x22halpin_g.htm.

135 Ponder, Stephen. *Managing the Press: Origins of the Media Presidency 1897–1933.* New York: Palgrave, 1999, p. 3.

136 Bishop, Joseph B. "Newspaper Espionage," *Forum Magazine, [1886],* Vol. 1, pp. 529–37.

137 Nevins, *The Evening Post: A Century of Journalism,* p. 481.

138 Ibid., p. 482.

139 Bishop, *Theodore Roosevelt and His Time,* pp. 58–62.

140 *Evening Post,* May 9, 1895, p. 6.

141 Bishop, *Theodore Roosevelt and His Time,* pp. 59–60.

142 Ponder, *Managing the Press,* p. 21.

143 *Evening Post,* May 6, 1895, p. 1.

144 *New York Tribune,* April 26, 1895.

145 Bishop, *Theodore Roosevelt and His Time,* p. 59.

146 *New York Times,* May 7, 1895.

147 *New York Times,* June 4, 1895.

148 *Evening Post,* July 3, 1895, p. 3.

149 Ibid.

150 Roosevelt, *An Autobiography,* p. 133.

151 Bishop, *Theodore Roosevelt and His Time,* p. 46.

152 Ibid., p. 45.

153 Ibid., p. 47.

154 Roosevelt, *An Autobiography,* pp. 141-143.

155 Bishop, *Theodore Roosevelt and His Time,* p. 50.

156 *New York Times,* December 25, 1892.

157 Bishop, *Theodore Roosevelt and His Time,* p. 53.

158 Roosevelt, *An Autobiography,* p. 162.

159 Bishop to Hay, March 12, 1897.

160 Morris, *The Rise of Theodore Roosevelt,* p. 502.

161 Roosevelt, *An Autobiography,* p. 205.

162 Ellis, Edward Robb. *The Epic of New York City: A Narrative History.* New York: Carroll & Graf, 2005, p. 435.

163 Roosevelt, *An Autobiography,* p. 174.

164 Bishop, *Theodore Roosevelt and His Time,* p. 67.

165 Roosevelt, *An Autobiography*, p. 204.

166 Ibid., p. 206.

167 Ellis, *The Epic of New York City: A Narrative History*, p. 435.

168 Bishop, *Notes and Anecdotes of Many Years*, p. 113.

169 *New York Sun*, June 27, 1896.

170 Bishop, *Theodore Roosevelt and His Time*, p. 62.

171 Bishop, *Notes and Anecdotes of Many Years*, p. 114.

172 Morris, *The Rise of Theodore Roosevelt*, p. 543.

173 Bishop, *Theodore Roosevelt and His Time*, pp. 63–64.

174 Bishop, *Notes and Anecdotes of Many Years*, p. 115.

175 Ibid., p. 116.

176 Bishop, *Theodore Roosevelt and His Time*, p. 65.

177 Ibid., pp. 68–69.

178 Henry Cabot Lodge to Roosevelt, March 8, 1897.

179 Bishop, *Theodore Roosevelt and His Time*, p. 71.

180 Ibid., p. 72.

181 Ibid., p. 74.

182 Ibid., p. 75.

183 Roosevelt to Cecil Arthur Spring-Rice, August 11, 1897.

184 Roosevelt to Bishop, June 13, 1897.

185 Ibid., June 15, 1897.

186 Ibid., June 17, 1897.

187 Bishop, Joseph Bucklin. "Are the Bosses Stronger than the People?" *Century*, Vol. 54, Issue 3, July 1897, pp. 465–67.

188 Morris, *The Rise of Theodore Roosevelt*, p. 582.

189 Roosevelt, *An Autobiography*, p. 212.

190 Bishop, *Theodore Roosevelt and His Time*, p. 81.

191 Roosevelt to Lodge, September 15, 1897, p. 82.

192 Roosevelt to John Long, January 14, 1898. In Bishop, *Theodore Roosevelt and His Time*, p. 83.

193 Nevins, *The Evening Post: A Century of Journalism*, p. 494.

194 Ibid., p. 495.

195 Dalton, *Theodore Roosevelt: A Strenuous Life*, p. 167.

196 Roosevelt to a friend, February 16, 1898. In Bishop, *Theodore Roosevelt and His Time*, p. 85.

197 Roosevelt, *An Autobiography*, p. 213.

198 Nevins, *The Evening Post: A Century of Journalism*, p. 508.

199 Ibid., p. 511.

200 Roosevelt to Brooks Adams, March 21, 1893. In Bishop, *Theodore Roosevelt and His Time*, p. 87.

201 Cable: Roosevelt to Dewey, February 25, 1898. In Bishop, *Theodore Roosevelt and His Time*, p. 95.

202 Grondahl, Paul. *I Rose Like a Rocket*. Lincoln: University of Nebraska Press, 2007, p. 248.

203 White, *The Evening Post Hundredth Anniversary 1801–1901*, pp. 83–84.

204 Bishop, *Theodore Roosevelt and His Time*, p. 103.

205 Long to Roosevelt, May 7, 1898. In Bishop, *Theodore Roosevelt and His Time*, p. 104.

206 Roosevelt, *An Autobiography*, p. 222.

207 Dalton, *Theodore Roosevelt: A Strenuous Life*, p. 171.

208 Bishop, *Theodore Roosevelt and His Time*, pp. 103–04.

209 Roosevelt, *An Autobiography*, p. 232.

210 *Evening Post*, June 18, 1898.

211 Morris, *The Rise of Theodore Roosevelt*, p. 653.

212 Dalton, *Theodore Roosevelt: A Strenuous Life*, p. 172.

213 Roosevelt, May 6, 1898. In Bishop, Joseph Bucklin (ed.), *Theodore Roosevelt's Letters to his Children*, New York: Charles Scribner's Sons, 1919, p. 13.

214 Bishop, *Theodore Roosevelt's Letters to his Children*, p. 3.

215 Davis, Richard Harding. *Notes of a War Correspondent*. New York: Charles Scribner's Sons, 1911, pp. 46–47.

216 Roosevelt, *An Autobiography*, p. 240.

217 *Tarrytown Argus*, July 2, 1898.

218 Roosevelt, *An Autobiography*, p. 241.

219 Theodore Roosevelt to Corinne Roosevelt, June 25, 1898. In Brands, H. W. (ed.), *The Selected Letters of Theodore Roosevelt*, New York: Cooper Square Press, 2001.

220 Davis, *Notes of a War Correspondent*, pp. 63–64.

221 Ponder, *Managing the Press*, p. 9.

222 Allen, Douglas. *Frederic Remington and the Spanish-American War*. New York: Crown Publishers, 1971, p. 11.

223 Ponder, *Managing the Press*, p.135.

224 Roosevelt, *An Autobiography*, p. 247.

225 Davis, *Notes of a War Correspondent*, p. 95.

226 Roosevelt, *An Autobiography*, p. 248.

227 Morris, *The Rise of Theodore Roosevelt*, p. 687.

228 Ibid.

229 Roosevelt, *The Rough Riders*. New York: Charles Scribner's Sons, 1899, pp. 74-81.

230 Roosevelt, *An Autobiography*, p. 248.

231 Hay to Roosevelt, July 27, 1898.

232 Morison, Elting and John Blum (eds.), *The Letters of Theodore Roosevelt*. Cambridge: Harvard University Press, 1951-54, p. 861.

233 Roosevelt, *An Autobiography*, pp. 235-236.

234 "Appreciations of Richard Harding Davis." Available online at www .pinetreeweb.com/davis-appreciations.htm.

235 Roosevelt to Lodge, July 19, 1898.

236 Roosevelt, Theodore. *Rough Riders*. New York: The Review of Reviews Co., 1904, p. 219.

237 Ibid., p. 220.

238 Platt, Thomas Collier, and Louis J. Lang (ed.). *The Autobiography of Thomas Collier Platt*. New York: B.W. Dodge Co., 1910, p. 369.

239 Roosevelt, *An Autobiography*, p. 280.

240 Ibid., p. 281.

241 Nevins, *The Evening Post: A Century of Journalism*, p. 515.

242 Dalton, *Theodore Roosevelt: A Strenuous Life*, p. 179.

243 Bishop, *Theodore Roosevelt and His Time*, p. 112.

244 Roosevelt to Bishop, January 5, 1899.

245 Dalton, *Theodore Roosevelt: A Strenuous Life*, p. 181.

246 Bishop, *Theodore Roosevelt and His Time*, p. 114.

247 Ibid., p. 113.

248 Roosevelt to Bishop, January 12, 1899.

249 Roosevelt, *An Autobiography*, pp. 294–95.

250 Roosevelt to Bishop, January 12, 1899.

251 Bishop, *Theodore Roosevelt and His Time*, pp. 116–17.

252 Platt and Lang (ed.), *The Autobiography of Thomas Collier Platt*, p. 374.

253 Wister, Owen. *Roosevelt: The Story of a Friendship*. New York: The Macmillan Company, 1930, p. 70.

254 Villard, Oswald Garrison. *The Fighting Years: Memoirs of a Liberal Editor.* New York: Harcourt, Brace and Company, 1939, p. 144.

255 Roosevelt to Bishop, February 16, 1899.

256 *Evening Post*, April 13, 1899, p. 1.

257 *Evening Post*, April 14, 1899, p. 6.

258 Roosevelt to Bishop, April 14, 1899.

259 *Evening Post*, April 17, 1899, p. 6.

260 Roosevelt to Bishop, April 17, 1899.

261 Roosevelt to Bishop, April 18, 1899.

262 *Evening Post*, April 20, 1899, p. 6.

263 *Evening Post*, April 21, 1899, p. 2.

264 Roosevelt to Edward Cary April 2, 1900. In Ponder, *Managing the Press*, p. 21.

265 Roosevelt to Bishop, April 11, 1900.

266 Roosevelt to State Conservation Commission, November 28, 1899.

267 Roosevelt, *An Autobiography*, p. 308.

268 Platt and Lang (ed.), *The Autobiography of Thomas Collier Platt*, p. 375.

269 Bishop, *Theodore Roosevelt and His Time*, p. 121.

270 Bishop, *The Panama Gateway*, p. 54.

271 Hamilton Fish to S. A. Hurlbut, U.S. Minister to Colombia, September 4, 1369.

272 Bishop, *The Panama Gateway*, p. 47.

273 Ibid., p. 58.

274 Roosevelt to Capt. Mahan, February 14, 1900.

275 Roosevelt to Hay, February 18, 1900.

276 Hay to Roosevelt, February 12, 1900.

277 Roosevelt to Hay, February 13, 1900.

278 Hay to William McKinley, March 13, 1900.

279 McKinley to Hay, March 13, 1900.

280 McCullough, *The Path Between the Seas*, p. 259.

281 Roosevelt, Theodore. *The Works of Theodore Roosevelt*, Vol. XI. New York: Charles Scribner's Sons, National Edition, 1926, p. 247.

282 Nevins, *The Evening Post: A Century of Journalism*, p. 519.

283 Ibid., p. 118.

284 Villard, *The Fighting Years*, pp. 145–46.

285 Ibid., p. 151.

286 Ibid., p. 129.

287 Steffens, Lincoln. *The Autobiography of Lincoln Steffens.* New York. Harcourt, Brace & Co., 1931, p. 311.

288 Campbell, W. Joseph. *The Year that Defined American Journalism: 1897 and the Clash of Paradigms*. New York: Routledge, 2006, p. 70.

289 Nevins, *The Evening Post: A Century of Journalism*, p. 519.

290 Wister, *Roosevelt: The Story of a Friendship*, p. 70.

291 Roosevelt to Bishop, January 29, 1900.

292 Hay to Bishop, January 10, 1900.

293 *Brown University Alumni Monthly,* 1900.

294 Roosevelt to Bishop, February 14, 1900.

295 Bishop to Roosevelt, February 15, 1900.

296 Roosevelt to Bishop, February 16, 1900.

297 Roosevelt to Bishop, February 19, 1900.

298 Bishop to Roosevelt, April 10, 1900.

299 Nicholas Murray Butler to Bishop, April 10, 1900.

300 *Evening Post,* April 10, 1900.

301 Hay to Bishop, April 14, 1890.

302 Elihu Root to Bishop, April 11, 1900.

303 Roosevelt to Bishop, April 11, 1900.

304 Bishop to Roosevelt, April 12, 1900.

305 *Commercial Advertiser,* April 18, 1900.

306 Roosevelt to Anna Roosevelt Cowles, April 30, 1890. In Brands, *The Selected Letters of Theodore Roosevelt,* pp. 239–41.

307 Roosevelt to Bishop, May 15, 1900.

308 Platt and Lang (ed.), *The Autobiography of Thomas Collier Platt*, pp. 388-89.

309 Ibid., p. 389.

310 Ibid., pp. 388–90.

311 Hay to Roosevelt, June 21, 1900.

312 Roosevelt to Mark Hanna, June 27, 1900.

313 Bishop to Roosevelt, October 4, 1900.

314 Roosevelt to Edward S. Martin, November 22, 1900.

315 Bishop to Roosevelt, November 9, 1900.

316 Pringle, Henry. *Theodore Roosevelt: A Biography*. New York: Harcourt, Brace & Co., 1931, p. 214.

317 Bishop (ed.), *Theodore Roosevelt's Letters to his Children*, pp. 22–23.

318 Ibid., pp. 24–25.

319 Roosevelt to William Howard Taft, April 26, 1901. In Brands, *The Selected Letters of Theodore Roosevelt*, pp. 256–60.

320 Roosevelt to Taft, July 15, 1901.

321 Ibid.

322 Taft to Bishop, November 30, 1900.

323 Bishop to Taft, June 24, 1901.

324 Olcott, Charles S. *The Life of William McKinley*, Vol. II. Boston: Houghton Mifflin, 1916, p. 314.

325 *American History* magazine, October 2001.

326 Olcott, *The Life of William McKinley*, p. 316.

327 *Commercial Advertiser*, September 8, 1901, p. 1.

328 Roosevelt to Lodge, September 9, 1901. In Brands, *The Selected Letters of Theodore Roosevelt*, p. 267.

329 Morris, Edmund. *Theodore Rex*. New York: Random House, 2001, p. 4.

330 *Commercial Advertiser*, September 13, 1901.

331 Wister, *Roosevelt: The Story of a Friendship*, p. 86.

332 *Commercial Advertiser*, September 16, 1901, p. 6.

333 Hay to Roosevelt, September 15, 1901.

334 *Commercial Advertiser*, September 16, 1901, p. 6.

335 Roosevelt to Bishop, September 16, 1901.

336 Steffens, *The Autobiography of Lincoln Steffens*, p. 502.

337 Brands, H. W. *Traitor to his Class*. New York: Doubleday, 2008, p. 297.

338 Bishop, *Notes and Anecdotes of Many Years*, p. 119.

339 Bishop, *Theodore Roosevelt and His Time*, p. 150.

340 Ibid.

341 Ibid., pp.150–51.

342 Roosevelt to Lodge, September 23, 1901.

343 Bishop to Roosevelt, October 7, 1901.

344 Roosevelt to Bishop, October 2, 1901.

345 Bishop to Roosevelt, October 7, 1901.

346 Ibid., October 17, 1901.

347 As quoted in the *Commercial Advertiser*, October 19, 1901, p. 8.

348 Kantrowitz, Stephen David. *Ben Tillman and the Reconstruction of the White Supremacy*. Chapel Hill: University of North Carolina Press, 2000, p. 259.

349 *Commercial Advertiser*, October 19, 1901, p. 8.

350 Roosevelt to Bishop, October 21, 1901.

351 Roosevelt to Bishop, December 21, 1901.

352 McCullough, *The Path Between the Seas*, pp. 266–67.

353 Bishop, *The Panama Gateway*, pp. 115–16.

354 Theodore Roosevelt Collection, Library of Congress, Washington, D.C.

355 Bishop to Roosevelt, September 24, 1902.

356 Ibid.

357 Roosevelt to Bishop, September 25, 1902.

358 George Cortelyou to Bishop, September 29, 1902.

359 Roosevelt to Lodge, September 27, 1902.

360 Roosevelt, *An Autobiography*, p. 479.

361 Ibid., p. 481.

362 *Commercial Advertiser*, October 4, 1902, p. 10.

363 Bishop to Roosevelt, October 5, 1902.

364 Ibid.

365 Ibid.

366 Bishop to Roosevelt, October 5, 1902.

367 Bishop to Roosevelt, October 6, 1902.

368 Roosevelt to Bishop, October 9, 1902.

369 *Commercial Advertiser*, October 10, 1902.

370 Bishop to Roosevelt, October 11, 1902.

371 *Commercial Advertiser*, October 11, 1902.

372 Roosevelt to Bishop, October 13, 1902.

373 Bishop to Roosevelt, October 13, 1902.

374 Bishop telegram to Roosevelt, October 14, 1902.

375 Roosevelt to Bishop, October 14, 1902.

376 *Commercial Advertiser*. October 14, 1902.

377 Bishop telegram to Roosevelt, October 16, 1902.

378 *Commercial Advertiser*, October 15, 1902.

379 Roosevelt to Bishop, October 16, 1902.

380 Roosevelt to Bishop, October 18, 1902.

381 U.S. Department of Labor History. "The Coal Strike of 1902: Turning Point in U.S. Policy," available online at www.dol.gov/oasam/programs/history/coalstrike. htm.

382 *International Quarterly*. "The Quarterly Chronicle." December 1902–March 1903, pp. 450–62.

383 Roosevelt to Bishop, December 24, 1902.

384 Bishop, *The Panama Gateway*, pp. 136–37.

385 Roosevelt, *An Autobiography*, pp. 540–41.

386 Hay to James F. Rhodes, December 8, 1903.

387 McCullough, *The Path Between the Seas*, p. 329.

388 Ibid., p. 379.

389 Roosevelt, *An Autobiography*, pp. 537–41.

390 Roosevelt, Theodore. "Remarks," Berkeley, California, March 23, 1911.

391 *Commercial Advertiser*, November 4, 1903, p. 2.

392 *Commercial Advertiser*, November 6, 1903.

393 Ibid.

394 *Commercial Advertiser,* November 12, 1903.

395 Roosevelt to Bishop, November 19, 1903.

396 Roosevelt, Theodore. "Third Annual Message to Congress," Washington, D.C., December 7, 1903.

397 Theodore Roosevelt to Kermit Roosevelt, November 4 1903.

398 In-person interview, Balboa, Panama, January 5, 2010.

399 Bishop to Roosevelt, October 24, 1903.

400 Ibid.

401 Roosevelt to Bishop, October 25, 1903.

402 Bishop to Roosevelt, October 29, 1903.

403 Bishop to Roosevelt, February 21, 1903.

404 Roosevelt to Bishop, October 23, 1903.

405 Bishop to Roosevelt, February 21, 1903.

406 Roosevelt to Bishop, November 2, 1903.

407 Roosevelt to Bishop, November 6, 1903.

408 Bishop to Roosevelt, January 21, 1904.

409 Roosevelt to Bishop, January 17, 1904.

410 Bishop to Roosevelt, January 20, 1904.

411 Bishop to Roosevelt, January 21, 1904.

412 Roosevelt to Bishop, January 22, 1904.

413 *Commercial Advertiser,* January 29, 1904.

414 Rogers, Jason. *Newspaper Building.* New York: Harper & Brothers, 1910, p. 109.

415 William Howard Taft to Bishop, January 24, 1903.

416 Mark Hanna to Roosevelt, February 1904.

417 Bishop to Roosevelt, March 27, 1903.

418 Bishop to Roosevelt, February 25, 1904.

419 Bishop to Roosevelt, June 1, 1903.

420 Bishop to Roosevelt, June 11, 1903.

421 Bishop to Roosevelt, November 24 and November 30, 1903.

422 Roosevelt to Bishop, December 1, 1903.

423 Bishop to Roosevelt, December 3, 1903.

424 Theodore Roosevelt to Kermit Roosevelt, June 21, 1904.

425 Ibid.

426 Bishop to Roosevelt, June 24, 1904.

427 Bishop to Roosevelt, July 30, 1904.

428 Ibid.

429 *New York Times,* August 13, 1904.

430 Bishop to Roosevelt, August 12, 1904.

431 Bishop to Roosevelt, August 16, 1904.

432 Theodore Roosevelt to Kermit Roosevelt October 26, 1904.

433 Bishop to Roosevelt, October 4, 1904.

434 Bishop to Roosevelt, October 14, 1904.

435 Ibid.

436 Theodore Roosevelt to Kermit Roosevelt, November 6, 1904.

437 Theodore Roosevelt to Kermit Roosevelt, November 10, 1904.

438 Bishop to Roosevelt, November 9, 1904.

439 Ibid.

440 Roosevelt to Bishop, November 9, 1904.

441 Bishop to Roosevelt, November 9, 1904.

442 Bishop, *Notes and Anecdotes of Many Years*, pp. 122–23.

443 Roosevelt to Owen Wister, November 19, 1904. In Bishop, *Theodore Roosevelt and his Time*, p. 345.

444 Lodge to Roosevelt, September 15, 1905. In Massachusetts Historical Society: Henry Cabot Lodge Collection.

445 Bishop to Taft, December 19, 1904.

446 Taft to Bishop, December 22, 1904.

447 Bishop to Taft, December 29, 1904.

448 Bishop to Roosevelt, March 7, 1905.

449 Roosevelt to Bishop, March 6, 1905.

450 Bishop, *The Panama Gateway*, p. 143.

451 Ibid., p. 155.

452 Ibid., p. 161.

453 Bishop to Roosevelt, May 14, 1905.

454 Bishop to Taft, May 19, 1905.

455 Bishop to Taft, May 26, 1905.

456 Ibid.

457 Roosevelt to Bishop, June 8, 1905

458 Bishop to Roosevelt, June 14, 1905.

459 John Hay diary entry. June 13, 1905, as reported by William Roscoe Thayer in *The Life of John Hay*, New York: Houghton Mifflin, 1908, Vol. II, p. 405.

460 Hay to Roosevelt, March 3, 1905.

461 Bishop to Roosevelt, July 11, 1905.

462 John Hay diary entry, June 14, 1905, in *The Life of John Hay*, Vol. II, pp. 408-9.

463 Bishop, *The Panama Gateway*, pp. 163-64.

464 Roosevelt to Bishop, July 13, 1905.

465 Bishop to Roosevelt, August 21, 1905.

466 Bishop to Roosevelt, August 27, 1905.

467 Roosevelt to Bishop, August 28, 1905.

468 Roosevelt to Bishop, August 31, 1905.

469 Roosevelt to Bishop, September 1, 1905.

470 Shonts, Theodore P. Appointment Memo, September 7, 1905.

471 Roosevelt to Lodge, September 2, 1905.

472 Roosevelt, *An Autobiography*, p. 555.

473 Bishop, *Theodore Roosevelt and his Time*, p. 405.

474 Roosevelt to Douglas Robinson, August 31, 1905.

475 "Environmental Hero: Theodore Roosevelt," Environmental Defense Fund, available online at www.edf.org/article.cfm?contentid=2759.

476 "Theodore Roosevelt and Conservation," National Park Service. Available online at www.nps.gov/thro/historyculture/theodore-roosevelt-and-conservation.htm.

477 Ibid.

478 Bishop, *Theodore Roosevelt and his Time*, pp. 153–54

479 Brinkley, Douglas. *Wilderness Warrior: Theodore Roosevelt and the Crusade for America*. New York: HarperCollins, 2009, p. 20.

480 Roosevelt to Bishop, September 14, 1905.

481 John J. Fitzgerald to Theodore P. Shonts, December 6, 1905.

482 Bishop, *Notes and Anecdotes of Many Years*, pp. 124–25.

483 U.S. Senate Transcript Document No. 69, 59th Congress, First Session, *Hearing of the Committee on Appropriations*, December 12, 1905.

484 Ibid.

485 Bishop to Roosevelt, December 16, 1905.

486 Bishop, *Notes and Anecdotes of Many Years*, p. 127.

487 *New York Herald*, December 13, 1905, p. 1.

488 *New York Times*, December 18, 1905.

489 Cablegram to Bishop from John F. Stevens, March 5, 1907.

490 Bishop, *Notes and Anecdotes of Many Years*, p. 126.

491 Ibid., pp. 126-27.

492 Bishop, *John Hay: Scholar, Statesman*, p. 28.

493 Bishop, *The Panama Gateway*, pp. 193–94.

494 Theodore Roosevelt to Archie Roosevelt, November 11, 1906.

495 Theodore Roosevelt to Kermit Roosevelt, November 13, 1906.

496 McCullough, *The Path Between the Seas*, p. 494.

497 Bishop, *Theodore Roosevelt and His Time*, p. 452.

498 Ibid., p. 453.

499 Ibid.

500 Ibid., p. 454.

501 Theodore Roosevelt to Kermit Roosevelt, November 20, 1906.

502 Bishop, *The Panama Gateway*, pp. 172–73.

503 Roosevelt, Theodore. "Special Message of the President of the United States," Washington, D.C.: December 17, 1906.

504 *Collier's Weekly*, April 27, 1907.

505 Gertrude Beeks to Bishop, undated, Washington, D.C.: Manuscript Division of the Library of Congress.

506 John W. Cook to Bishop, April 30, 1907.

507 Bishop to Taft, June 1, 1907.

508 John F. Stevens to Theodore Roosevelt, January 30, 1907.

509 Bishop, Joseph Bucklin, and Farnham Bishop. *Goethals: Genius of the Panama Canal*. New York: Harper & Brothers, 1930, pp. 151-52.

510 Bishop to Taft, June 25, 1907.

511 Taft to Bishop, June 29, 1907.

512 Bishop to Taft, July 1, 1907.

513 Taft to Bishop, July 2, 1907.

514 Roosevelt to Bishop, July 12, 1907.

515 Bishop to Roosevelt, July 28, 1907.

516 Roosevelt to Bishop, July 1, 1907.

517 Bishop to Taft, August 1, 1907.

518 *The Star and Record,* Panama City, Panama, December 16, 1928.

519 Telegram from Roosevelt to Taft, November 21, 1906.

520 Bishop, *Theodore Roosevelt and his Time,* p. 27.

521 Roosevelt to Silas McBee, November 27, 1906.

522 Simon, Keith. E-mail to the author, July 26, 2010.

523 Abstracted from Morris, Edmund, *Theodore Rex,* pp.474–75.

524 Thayer, William Roscoe. *Theodore Roosevelt: An Intimate Biography.* Boston: Houghton Mifflin Company, 1919, p. xi.

525 Roosevelt, Theodore. Undated letter to Carl Schurz. In *An Autobiography,* p. 563.

526 Ibid.

527 Bishop to Roosevelt, August 13, 1907.

528 Roosevelt, *An Autobiography,* p. 543.

529 Bishop to Roosevelt, August 13, 1907.

530 Ibid.

531 Bishop to Roosevelt, August 29, 1907.

532 Bishop, *The Panama Gateway,* p. 295.

533 Haskin, Frederic Jennings. *The Panama Canal.* New York: Doubleday, Page & Co., 1913, p. 128.

534 Bishop to Roosevelt, August 13, 1907.

535 Ibid., August 13, 1907.

536 Bishop to Roosevelt, August 29, 1907.

537 Roosevelt to Bishop, September 11, 1907.

538 Roosevelt to Bishop, September 6, 1907.

539 Bishop to Roosevelt, August 29, 1907.

540 Farnham Bishop in family papers, provided by Anita and Miriam Bishop, 2008.

541 Bishop to Roosevelt, September 3, 1907.

542 *The Canal Record,* Vol. 1. No. 1, September 4, 1907.

543 Haskins, W. S. "Joseph Bucklin Bishop and his Pet: *The Canal Record,*" *Star and Herald,* December 16, 1928.

544 Bishop and Bishop, *Goethals: Genius of the Panama Canal,* pp. 187–88.

545 Haskins, "Joseph Bucklin Bishop and his Pet: *The Canal Record.*"

546 Bishop and Bishop, *Goethals: Genius of the Panama Canal,* p. 182.

547 *New York Times,* September 30, 1907.

548 Beeks, Gertrude. "Conditions of Employment at Panama," *National Civic Federation Review,* October 1907, p. 17.

549 Bishop to Roosevelt, September 9, 1907.

550 Roosevelt to Bishop, September 11, 1907.

551 Bishop to Roosevelt, October 16, 1907.

552 Roosevelt to Bishop, October 25, 1907.

553 Roosevelt, "Seventh Annual Message to Congress," Washington, D.C., December 3, 1907.

554 Bishop and Bishop, *Goethals: Genius of the Panama Canal*, pp. 230–31.

555 *The Canal Record*, Vol 1, No. 18, January 1, 1908, p. 140.

556 Bishop to Taft, January 8, 1908.

557 Taft to Bishop, January 19, 1908.

558 Bishop to Taft, February 2, 1908.

559 Roosevelt to Rev. Dr. Lyman Abbott, May 29, 1908.

560 Roosevelt to Charles Washburn, April 17, 1907.

561 Morris, *Theodore Rex*, p. 458.

562 Roosevelt to Rev. Dr. Abbott, May 29, 1908.

563 Morris, *Theodore Rex*, p. 536.

564 Bishop, *Theodore Roosevelt and His Time*, p. 90.

565 Roosevelt to Bishop, July 1, 1908.

566 Roosevelt to Taft, September 5, 1908.

567 Roosevelt to Taft, September 11, 1908.

568 Roosevelt to William Kent, September 28, 1908.

569 Taft to Roosevelt, November 7, 1908.

570 Bishop to Taft, November 8, 1908.

571 Taft to Bishop, November 18, 1908.

572 Bishop to Roosevelt, November 8, 1908.

573 U.S. House Committee on Interstate and Foreign Commerce Field Hearing Record, Ancon, Panama, January 6, 1909, pp. 93–96.

574 U.S. House Committee on Interstate and Foreign Commerce Field Hearing Record, Ancon, Panama, January 7, 1909, pp. 98–99.

575 U.S. House Committee on Appropriations Field Hearing Record, Ancon, Panama, November 1909, p. 458.

576 R. J. Tracewell to George Goethals, August 18, 1909.

577 Bishop to Roosevelt, January 2, 1911.

578 Roosevelt to Bishop, November 21, 1910.

579 Taft Inaugural Address, March 4, 1909.

580 Akeley, Carl. Foreword, *African Game Trails*, by Theodore Roosevelt. New York: Charles Scribner's Sons (National Edition), 1926, Vol. IV, p. xi.

581 Roosevelt, Theodore, *African Game Trails*, vol. IV, 1926, pp. 62–65.

582 Roosevelt to Lodge, July 26, 1909.

583 Theodore Roosevelt to Ethel Roosevelt, December 23, 1909.

584 Theodore Roosevelt to George Otto Trevelyan, October 1, 1911.

585 Theodore Roosevelt. Remarks on arrival in New York, N.Y., June 18, 1910

586 Roosevelt to Gifford Pinchot, January 17, 1910.

587 Bishop to Roosevelt, September 26, 1910.

588 Roosevelt to Bishop, October 20, 1910.

589 Roosevelt to Bishop, November 21, 1910.

590 Roosevelt to Bishop, January 4, 1909.

591 Bishop to Roosevelt, December 26, 1908.

592 Bishop to Roosevelt, September 28, 1910.

593 Ibid., April 24, 1911.

594 Bishop to Roosevelt, July 19, 1911.

595 Roosevelt to Bishop, July 21, 1911.

596 Chace, James. *1912: Wilson, Roosevelt, Taft and Debs: The Election that Changed the Country.* New York: Simon and Schuster, 2004, p. 57.

597 Bishop to Roosevelt, September 26, 1910.

598 Roosevelt to Bishop, January 17, 1911.

599 Bishop to Roosevelt, December 1, 1911.

600 Roosevelt to Bishop, December 13, 1911.

601 Roosevelt to Bishop, December 29, 1911.

602 Chace, *1912: Wilson, Roosevelt, Taft and Debs: The Election that Changed the Country,* p. 105.

603 Ibid., p. 106.

604 Bishop and Bishop, *Goethals: Genius of the Panama Canal,* p. 230.

605 Ibid., p. 241.

606 U.S. Senate Committee on Interstate Commerce, Official hearing transcript, Ancon, Panama. October 1911, p. 178.

607 Roosevelt to Bishop, March 18, 1912.

608 Bishop, *Theodore Roosevelt and His Time,* p. 317.

609 Theodore Roosevelt remarks. Carnegie Hall, New York. March 20, 1912.

610 Chace, *1912: Wilson, Roosevelt, Taft and Debs: The Election that Changed the Country,* p. 117.

611 Bishop, *Theodore Roosevelt and His Time,* p. 336.

612 Theodore Roosevelt, Remarks to separatist delegates. Chicago, Illinois, June 17, 1912.

613 Bishop, *Theodore Roosevelt and His Time,* p. 336.

614 Bishop to Roosevelt, January 24, 1912.

615 Bishop, *Theodore Roosevelt and His Time,* p. 336.

616 Ibid., p. 337.

617 Ibid., p. 338.

618 Ibid.

619 Roosevelt to Cecil Spring-Rice, December 31, 1912.

620 Pringle, Henry. *The Life and Times of William Howard Taft.* New York: Farrar and Rinehart, 1939, pp. 781–82.

621 Bishop and Bishop, *Goethals: Genius of the Panama Canal,* p. 250.

622 Ibid., p. 261.

623 Roosevelt, Theodore. Essay prepared for the American Historical Association conference, Panama-Pacific International Exhibition. July 19-23, 1915.

624 Goethals to Major Frank C. Boggs, College Park, MD: National Archives, July 2, 1914.

625 U.S. House Appropriations Committee Hearings, Culebra, Panama, November 20, 1913, p. 89.

626 *History of the Harvard Class of 1908,* p. 60.

627 "Some Canal Problems: Mr. Joseph Bishop Tells How the Great Engineering Project has been Accomplished," *New York Times,* August 31, 1913.

628 Roosevelt to Bishop, October 15, 1913.

629 Dalton, *Theodore Roosevelt: A Strenuous Life,* p. 414.

630 Bishop to Roosevelt, March 2, 1913.

631 Roosevelt to Bishop, March 20, 1913.

632 Roosevelt to Arthur Lee, MP, September 2, 1913.

633 Roosevelt, Theodore. *Through the Brazilian Wilderness: The Works of Theodore Roosevelt,* National Election, Vol. V, pp. 46–47.

634 Thayer, *Theodore Roosevelt: An Intimate Biography,* p. 392.

635 Dalton, *Theodore Roosevelt: A Strenuous Life,* pp. 436–37.

636 Robinson, Corinne Roosevelt. *My Brother: Theodore Roosevelt.* New York: Charles Scribner's Sons, 1921, p. 278.

637 Thayer, *Theodore Roosevelt: An Intimate Biography,* p. 394.

638 Roosevelt to Lauro Severiano Müller, April 30, 1914.

639 Bishop to Roosevelt, May 12, 1915.

640 Roosevelt to Bishop, May 14, 1915.

641 Bishop to Roosevelt, August 26, 1915.

642 Bishop to Theodore and Edith Roosevelt, October 19, 1915.

643 Greene, Julie. *The Canal Builders.* New York: The Penguin Press, 2009, p. 353.

644 O'Toole, Patricia. *When Trumpets Call: Theodore Roosevelt After the White House.* New York: Simon & Schuster, 2005, p. 283.

645 Bishop to Roosevelt, November 15, 1915.

646 Bishop to Roosevelt, November 26, 1915.

647 Bishop to Roosevelt, November 29, 1915.

648 Roosevelt, telegram to Henry L. Stoddard, editor of the New York *Evening Mail,* March 1916.

649 Roosevelt to British Viscount James Bryce, June 19, 1916.

650 Bishop, *Theodore Roosevelt and His Time,* pp. 412–13.

651 Roosevelt to E. A. Van Valkenburg, September 5, 1916.

652 Bishop to Roosevelt, August 26, 1915.

653 Ibid., July 13, 1916.

654 Ibid., September 19, 1916.

655 Roosevelt to Arthur H. Lee, November 10, 1916.

656 Bishop, *Theodore Roosevelt and His Time,* p. 416.

657 Woodrow Wilson, Address to a special session of Congress, April 2, 1917.

658 Statement by Theodore Roosevelt, April 2, 1917.

659 Statement by Theodore Roosevelt at the White House, April 9, 1917.

660 Bishop, *Theodore Roosevelt and His Time*, p. 424.

661 Ibid.

662 O'Toole, *When Trumpets Call: Theodore Roosevelt After the White House*, p. 312.

663 Bishop, *Theodore Roosevelt and His Time*, p. 425.

664 Ibid., p. 426.

665 O'Toole, *When Trumpets Call: Theodore Roosevelt After the White House*, p. 313.

666 Roosevelt to Farnham Bishop, July 19, 1916.

667 Roosevelt to Major General John Pershing, May 20, 1917.

668 Renehan, Edward, Jr. *The Lion's Pride: Theodore Roosevelt and His Family in Peace and War.* New York: Oxford University Press, 1998.

669 Rickenbacker, Capt. Edward. *Fighting The Flying Circus.* Philadelphia & New York: J.B. Lippincott, 1919, p. 193.

670 Theodore Roosevelt to Kermit Roosevelt, February 18, 1918.

671 Bishop, *Theodore Roosevelt and His Time*, p. 451.

672 Roosevelt, Kermit. *Quentin Roosevelt: A Sketch with Letters.* Palo Alto, CA: Martindale Press, 1921, pp. 169–71.

673 Gen. John Pershing to Theodore and Edith Roosevelt, July 27, 1918.

674 Theodore Roosevelt to Right Hon. Arthur James Balfour, July 23, 1918.

675 Morris, Sylvia Jukes. *Edith Kermit Roosevelt—Portrait of a First Lady.* New York: The Modern Library Edition, 2001, p. 428.

676 Bishop, *Theodore Roosevelt and His Time*, p. 458.

677 Roosevelt, Theodore. Remarks to the Liederkranz Society, New York City, October 15, 1918.

678 Bishop, *Theodore Roosevelt and His Time*, p. 468.

679 Ibid., pp. 468–69.

680 Bishop, *Notes and Anecdotes of Many Years*, pp. 150-51.

681 Ibid., pp. 149–50.

682 Roosevelt to Ogden Reid, January 1, 1919.

683 Amos, James. *Hero to His Valet*, New York: The John Day Co., 1927. pp. 154–55.

684 Ibid., pp. 156–57.

685 Bishop, *Theodore Roosevelt and His Time*, p. 475.

686 Lodge, Henry Cabot, Address to the United States Senate, January 1919.

687 Bishop, *Notes and Anecdotes of Many Years*, p. 155.

688 Ibid., p. 151.

689 *Evening Sun*, September 13, 1919.

690 Ibid.

691 Bishop, *Notes and Anecdotes of Many Years*, p. 146.

692 Roosevelt to Herbert Putnam, December 5, 1916.

693 Roosevelt to Herbert Putnam, January 17, 1917.

694 Ibid., September 21, 1918.

695 Bishop, *Theodore Roosevelt and His Time*, p. vii.

696 Ibid., pp. viii-ix.

697 Bishop to John C. Fitzpatrick, March 22, 1919.

698 Bishop to Roosevelt, March 25, 1918.

699 Ibid., June 13, 1918.

700 Bishop to Sir George Otto Trevelyan, April 10, 1919.

701 Charles Scribner to Ferris Greenslet, February 12, 1919.

702 Thayer to Corinne Roosevelt Robinson, February 28, 1919.

703 Ibid., March 4, 1919.

704 Corinne Roosevelt Robinson to Thayer, March 18, 1919.

705 Ibid., March 26, 1919.

706 Ibid., March 20, 1919.

707 Thayer to Corinne Roosevelt Robinson, February 28, 1919.

708 Rights of Publication Agreement dated August 1, 1919 Sagamore Hill National Historic Site Personal Paper Archives, Box 1, Folder 11

709 Rudyard Kipling to Bishop, February 9, 1920.

710 Bishop to John C. Fitzpatrick, October 16, 1920.

711 John C. Fitzpatrick to Bishop, October 18, 1920.

712 Trevelyan to Bishop, September 30, 1920.

713 *New York Times,* October 3, 1920.

714 Lodge to Bishop, January 17, 1921.

715 Bishop, *Theodore Roosevelt and His Time,* pp. viii–ix.

716 Ibid.

717 Edith Roosevelt to Bishop, July 17, 1920.

718 Ibid., November 24, 1920.

719 Lacayo, Richard. "The Making of America: Theodore Roosevelt," *Time,* June 25, 2006. Available online: www.time.com/time/magazine/article/0,9171,1207820,00.html.

720 Lewis, William Draper. *The Life of Theodore Roosevelt.* Philadelphia: The John C. Winston Co., 1919, p. xxii.

721 Goethals, General George. Remarks to the Society of the Chagres, Ancon Panama, March 6, 1915.

722 Bishop and Bishop, *Goethals: Genius of the Panama Canal,* p. 456.

723 Bishop, "The Panama Canal Today." *Scribner's Magazine,* July 1921, p. 34.

724 Bishop, *Notes and Anecdotes of Many Years,* p. 7.

725 *Oakland Tribune,* n.d., 1928, p. 4.

726 Diary of Miriam (Mrs. Farnham) Bishop, pp. 172–73.

727 Ibid., p. 180.

728 Ibid., n.p.

729 Bishop and Bishop, *Goethals: Genius of the Panama Canal,* p. xi.

730 *New York Times* Book Review, *How the Western Hemisphere Was Halved at Panama,* October 5, 1930, p. 3.

731 Roosevelt, Theodore. "Citizenship in a Republic: An Address," Paris April 23, 1910.

Bibliography

Books

Allen, Douglas. *Frederic Remington and the Spanish-American War.* New York: Crown Publishers, 1971.

Amos, James. *Hero to His Valet.* New York: The John Day Co., 1927.

Axelrod, Alan, and Charles Phillips. *What Every American Should Know about American History.* Avon, MA: Adams Media, 2008.

Bishop, Joseph Bucklin. *Notes & Anecdotes of Many Years.* New York: Charles Scribner's Sons, 1925.

————. *The Panama Gateway.* New York: Charles Scribner's Sons, 1913.

————. *Presidential Nominations and Elections.* New York: Charles Scribner's Sons, 1916.

————. *Theodore Roosevelt and His Time,* Vols. I & II. New York: Charles Scribner's Sons, 1920.

————. (ed). *Theodore Roosevelt's Letters to His Children.* New York: Charles Scribner's Sons, 1919.

Bishop, Joseph Bucklin, and Farnham Bishop. *Goethals: Genius of the Panama Canal.* New York: Harper & Brothers, 1930.

Bonfanti, Leo. *The Witchcraft Hysteria of 1692.* Wakefield, MA: Pride Publications, 1971.

Brands, H. W. (ed). *The Selected Letters of Theodore Roosevelt.* New York: Cooper Square Press, 2001.

————. *Traitor to his Class.* New York: Doubleday, 2008.

Brinkley, Douglas. *Wilderness Warrior: Theodore Roosevelt and the Crusade for America.* New York: HarperCollins, 2009.

Bronson, Walter Cochrane, PhD. *History of Brown University 1764–1914.* Providence, RI: Brown University, 1914.

Campbell, W. Joseph. *The Year that Defined American Journalism: 1897 and the Clash of Paradigms.* New York: Routledge, 2006.

Chace, James. *1912: Wilson, Roosevelt, Taft and Debs: The Election that Changed the Country.* New York: Simon and Schuster, 2004.

Cordery, Stacy A. *Alice.* New York: Penguin Books, 2007.

Cutter, William Richard (ed). *New England Families: Genealogical and Memorial.* New York: Lewis Historical Publishing Co., 1915.

Dalton, Kathleen. *Theodore Roosevelt: A Strenuous Life.* New York: Alfred A. Knopf, 2002.

Davis, Richard Harding. *Notes of a War Correspondent.* New York: Charles Scribner's Sons, 1911.

Donald, Aida D. *Lion in the White House.* Philadelphia: Basic Books, 2007

Ellis, Edward Robb. *The Epic of New York City: A Narrative History.* New York: Carroll & Graf, 2005.

Erhardt, John G. *Historical Seekonk, Mass. and East Providence, R.I. (1812–1990).* Seekonk, MA: J. G. Erhardt, 2001.

Field, Edward. *State of Rhode Island and Providence Plantations at the End of the Century: A History,* Vol. III. Boston: Mason Publishing Co., 1902.

Greene, Julie. *The Canal Builders.* New York: The Penguin Press, 2009.

Grondahl, Paul. *I Rose Like a Rocket.* Lincoln: University of Nebraska Press, 2007.

Hagedorn, Herman. *Roosevelt in the Bad Lands.* Boston: Houghton Mifflin, 1921.

Hale, William Harlan. *Horace Greeley: Voice of the People.* New York: Collier Books, 1961.

Hamilton, Allan McLane. *Recollections of an Alienist, Personal and Professional.* New York: George H. Doran Co., 1916.

Haskin, Frederic Jennings. *The Panama Canal.* New York: Doubleday, Page & Co., 1913.

Kantrowitz, Stephen David. *Ben Tillman and the Reconstruction of the White Supremacy.* Chapel Hill: University of North Carolina Press, 2000.

Lewis, William Draper, PhD. *The Life of Theodore Roosevelt.* Philadelphia: John C. Winston Co., 1919.

Manners, William. *T. R. and Will: A Friendship that Split the Republican Party.* New York: Harcourt, Brace & World, Inc., 1969.

McCullough, David. *Mornings on Horseback.* New York: Simon & Schuster, 2003
———. *The Path Between the Seas.* New York: Simon & Schuster, 1977.

Morison, Elting E., and John Blum (eds). *The Letters of Theodore Roosevelt.* Cambridge: Harvard University Press, 1951–54.

Morris, Edmund. *The Rise of Theodore Roosevelt.* New York: Coward, McCann & Geoghegan, 1979.
———. *Theodore Rex.* New York: Random House, 2001.

Morris, Sylvia Jukes. *Edith Kermit Roosevelt: Portrait of a First Lady.* New York: The Modern Library Edition, 2001.

Nevins, Allan. *The Evening Post: A Century of Journalism.* New York: Boni and Liveright, 1922.

Olcott, Charles S. *The Life of William McKinley.* Boston: Houghton Mifflin Co., 1916.

O'Toole, Patricia. *When Trumpets Call: Theodore Roosevelt After the White House.* New York: Simon & Schuster, 2005.

Platt, Thomas Collier, and Louis J. Lang (ed). *The Autobiography of Thomas Collier Platt.* New York: B. W. Dodge Co., 1910.

Ponder, Stephen. *Managing the Press: Origins of the Media Presidency 1897–1933.* New York: Palgrave, 1999.

Pringle, Henry. *The Life and Times of William Howard Taft.* New York: Farrar and Rinehart, 1939.

————. *Theodore Roosevelt: A Biography.* New York: Harcourt, Brace & Co., 1931.

Putnam, Carleton. *Theodore Roosevelt: The Formative Years 1858–1886.* New York: Charles Scribner's Sons, 1958.

Renehan, Edward, Jr. *The Lion's Pride: Theodore Roosevelt and His Family in Peace and War.* New York: Oxford University Press, 1998.

Rickenbacker, Capt. Edward. *Fighting the Flying Circus.* Philadelphia & New York: J.B. Lippincott, 1919.

Robinson, Corinne Roosevelt. *My Brother: Theodore Roosevelt.* New York: Charles Scribner's Sons, 1921.

Rogers, Jason. *Newspaper Building.* New York: Harper & Brothers, 1910.

Roosevelt, Kermit. *Quentin Roosevelt: A Sketch with Letters.* New York: Charles Scribner's Sons, 1921.

Roosevelt, Theodore. *An Autobiography.* New York: Scribner, 1913.

————. *Hunting Trips of a Ranchman.* New York: G. P. Putnam's Sons, Medora, 1885.

————. *Rough Riders.* New York: The Review of Reviews Co., 1904.

————. *The Works of Theodore Roosevelt,* Vols. I–XX. New York: Charles Scribner's Sons, National Edition, 1926.

Steffens, Lincoln. *The Autobiography of Lincoln Steffens.* New York: Harcourt, Brace & Co., 1931.

Thayer, William Roscoe. *The Life and Letters of John Hay.* Boston: Houghton Mifflin, 1915.

————. *Theodore Roosevelt: An Intimate Biography.* Boston: Houghton Mifflin Company, 1919.

Villard, Oswald Garrison. *The Fighting Years: Memoirs of a Liberal Editor.* New York: Harcourt, Brace & Co., 1939.

Wister, Owen. *Roosevelt: The Story of a Friendship.* New York: The Macmillan Co., 1930.

Manuscripts and Collections

Bishop, Joseph Bucklin. "John Hay: Scholar, Statesman." An address delivered before the Alumni Association of Brown University, Providence, Rhode Island, June 19, 1906.

————. Joseph Bucklin Bishop Papers. Houghton Library, Harvard University, MS Am 1514.

Gilder, Rodman. *Statue of Liberty Enlightening the World.* New York: New York Trust Co., 1943.

John Hay Collections, Special Collections Division, John Hay Library, Brown University, Providence, Rhode Island.

Official Proceedings of the Republican National Conventions 1884–1888. Minneapolis: Charles W. Johnson Publishers, 1903.

Rice University Guide to the Frank Harrison Hill London Daily Newspapers 1870–1876, available online at www.lib.utexas.edu.

Robinson, Corinne Roosevelt papers, Theodore Roosevelt Collection, Houghton Library, Harvard University, MA Am 1785.

Roosevelt, Theodore. "Address to the Naval War College." Newport, Rhode Island, June 2, 1897.

———. "Charter Day Address, University of California," Berkeley, : March 23, 1911.

———. "Citizenship in a Republic. An Address." Paris: April 23, 1910.

———. "Seventh Annual Message to Congress," Washington, D.C.: December 3, 1907.

———. "Special Message of the President of the United States," Washington, D.C.: December 17, 1906.

———. "Third Annual Message to Congress," Washington, D.C.: December 7, 1903.

Taft, William H. papers, Washington, D.C.: Microfilm Collection, Manuscripts Division, Library of Congress.

Thayer, William Roscoe papers, Houghton Library, Harvard University, MA Am 1081.

Theodore Roosevelt Collection, Cambridge, MA: Harvard College Library, Houghton and Widener Libraries. Available online at http://hcl.harvard.edu/libraries/houghton/collections/roosevelt.cfm.

U.S. House Committee on Appropriations Hearings, Culebra, Panama, November 20, 1913.

U.S. House Committee on Appropriations Field Hearing Record, Ancon, Panama, November 1909.

U.S. House Committee on Interstate and Foreign Commerce Field Hearing Record, Ancon, Panama, January 1909.

U.S. Senate Committee on Interstate Commerce, Official Hearing Transcript, Ancon, Panama. October 1911.

U.S. Senate Transcript Document No. 69, 59th Congress, First Session, *Hearing of the Committee on Appropriations,* December 12, 1905.

White, Horace. *The Evening Post Hundredth Anniversary: November 16, 1801–1901.* New York: Evening Post Publishing Co., 1901.

Periodicals and Newspapers

Brown University Alumni Monthly
Brown University Monthly
The Canal Record
Century Magazine
Forum Magazine
The International Quarterly
The Nation
New York Commercial Advertiser

New York Daily Tribune
New York Evening Post
New York Globe and Commercial Advertiser
New York Sun
New York Times
New York Tribune
The New Yorker
Pawtucket (RI) Times
Pawtucket (RI) Times Historical Magazine
Providence (RI) Journal
Tarrytown (NY) Argus

Websites

"Appreciations of Richard Harding Davis." Available online at www.pinetree web.com/ davis appreciations.htm

"The Coal Strike of 1902: Turning Point in U.S. Policy," U.S. Department of Labor History, available online at www.dol.gov/oasam/programs/history/coalstrike.htm

"Construction of the First Transcontinental Railroad," Panama Canal Railway Company, available at www.panarail.com/en/history/index.html

"Election of 1884," The American Presidency Project, available online at http://www. presidency.ucsb.edu/showelection.php?year=1884

"Environmental Hero: Theodore Roosevelt," Environmental Defense Fund, available online at www.edf.org/article.cfm?contentid=2759

"Grover Cleveland: Mrs. Halpin and the Child," *The Health and Medical History of President Grover Cleveland,* available online at www.doctorzebra .com/prez/z_x22halpin_g.htm

Lacayo, Richard. "The Making of America: Theodore Roosevelt," Time, June 25, 2006. Available online: www.time.com/time/magazine/article/ 0,9171,1207820,00.html

"Land Ownership in California and the Transition to a New Government," www. Archives.gov/pacific/education/curriculum/4th-grade/land-owner ship.html

"Life of Theodore Roosevelt," Theodore Roosevelt Association, May 31, 2008, p.1. Available online at www.TheodoreRoosevelt.org/life/timeline.htm

"The Presidential Elections 1860–1912: 1884 Cleveland vs. Blaine," HarpWeek, available online at www.Elections.HarpWeek.com/1884/Overview-1884-3.htm

"Theodore Roosevelt and Conservation," National Park Service. Available online at www.nps.gov/thro/historyculture/theodore-roosevelt-and-conservation.htm

www.Brown.edu

www.MayflowerFamilies.com

www.nps.gov/historyculture/theodore-roosevelt-the-rancher.htm

www.nps.gov/thro/historyculture/maltese-cross-cabin.htm

www.Spartacus.schoolnet.co.uk/USAnypost.htm

Index

Note: Abbreviations TR, JB, and NYC stand for Theodore Roosevelt, Joseph Bucklin Bishop, and New York City, respectively.

About the Author

Chip Bishop is the great-grandnephew of Joseph Bucklin Bishop. He has written for radio, television, newspapers, and trade journals. A member of the Theodore Roosevelt Association and the president and CEO of his own marketing and communications consultancy, he lives and works on Cape Cod with his wife. This is his first book.